The Scriptwriter's Handbook

William J. Van Nostran

Focal Press

Boston/Oxford/Johannesburg/Melbourne/New Delhi/Singapore

Focal Press is an imprint of Butterworth–Heinemann.

Copyright © 1996 by Butterworth–Heinemann

ℛ A member of the Reed Elsevier group

∞ Recognizing the importance of preserving what has been written, Butterworth–Heinemann prints its books on acid-free paper whenever possible.

Library of Congress Cataloging-in-Publication Data

Van Nostran, William.
      The scriptwriter's handbook : corporate and educational media writing / William J. Van Nostran.
        p. cm.
      Rev. ed. of : The nonbroadcast television writer's handbook. 1983.
      Includes bibliographical references.
      ISBN 0-240-80252-7
      1. Television authorship. 2. Video recordings. 3. Industrial television. 4. Interactive video.
5. Videoconferencing. I. Van Nostran, William. Nonbroadcast television writer's handbook.
II. Title.
PN1992.7.V36   1996
808.2'25—dc20

                   96-5084
                   CIP

British Library Cataloguing-in-Publication Data
A catalogue record for this book is available from the British Library.

The publisher offers special discounts on bulk orders of this book.
For information, please contact:
Manager of Special Sales
Butterworth–Heinemann
313 Washington Street
Newton, MA 02158–1626
Tel: 617-928-2500
Fax: 617-928-2620

For information on all Focal Press publications available, contact our World Wide Web home page at:
http://www.bh.com/bh/

10 9 8 7 6 5 4 3

Printed in the United States of America

Table of Contents

List of Figures. v

1   Introduction 1
2   Media: A Message from McLuhan 11

Introduction to Part I 29

Step 1: Assimilation. 34

3   Collecting Information for the Script 35
4   Organizing Information: Translating Research into an Action Plan. 53

Step 2: Rehearsal. 72

5   Idea Development 73

Step 3: Drafting. 119

6   Drafting the Shooting Script. 121
7   The Imaginative Eye 139
8   The Imaginative Ear 167

Step 4: Revision. 195

9   Making the Most of Feedback 197

Step 5: Editing. 209

Introduction to Part II 213

10 Wearing the Instructional Dramatist's Two Hats. .215
11 Writing Unscripted Formats 265
12 Writing for Multi-Image, Multi-Media and Videowalls 285
13 Writing for Interactive Design 303
14 Writing for Live Media. 345
15 The Business of Writing for the New Media. 365

Glossary 387
Bibliography 393
Appendix 399

About the Author 403

List of Figures

Figure 2.1   Medium: Multi-Image 16
Figure 2.2   Medium: Television. 18
Figure 2.3   Medium: Film. 20
Figure 2.4   Medium: Audiocassette. 22
Figure 2.5   Medium: Print 27

Figure I.1   Steps in the Scriptwriting Process 31

Figure 3.1   Elements of the Research Agenda. 41
Figure 3.2   Sample 42
Figure 3.3   Direct Observation 45
Figure 3.4   Goldin/Lewis Questionnaire .48

Figure 4.1   Audience Involvement Needed to Attain Objectives 61
Figure 4.2   Excerpt: Key Content Points .62

Figure 5.1   Examples of Mixed Formats .80
Figure 5.2   Structure in a Script 83
Figure 5.3   Unadvertised Structure 87
Figure 5.4   Unpredictable Structure 92
Figure 5.5   From "Sexual Harassment: Fact or Fiction". 98
Figure 5.6   Excerpt from "Sexual Harassment" 103
Figure 5.7   Concept Evaluation Matrix .106
Figure 5.8   Sample Television Treatment 110

Figure 6.1   Camera Shots 123
Figure 6.2   Sample of Split Page Format. 125
Figure 6.3   Linking Visual Elements to a Music Track. 127
Figure 6.4   Using Visual and Audio Transitions. 132
Figure 6.5   Sample of Motion Picture Format. 135
Figure 6.6   Sample Production Storyboard 136

Figure 7.1   Selected Symbols 142
Figure 7.2   Using a Visual Analogy 145
Figure 7.3   Use of Setting and Backdrop. 148
Figure 7.4   Excerpt Describing Video 151
Figure 7.5   Excerpt Showing Action. 153
Figure 7.6   Excerpt Describing Stage Business. 155
Figure 7.7   Using a Custom Transitional Device 160
Figure 7.8   Excerpt Describing Transition. 161
Figure 7.9   Sample 163

Figure 8.1   Integrating Music in the Script 177
Figure 8.2   Imaginative Approach to Audio Programs. 183
Figure 8.3   Additional Approaches to Audio Programs. 190

Figure 9.1   Twelve Revision Strategies 208

Figure 10.1   Use of Role Methods. 217
Figure 10.2   Use of Comedy 220
Figure 10.3   Use of Character Types. 223
Figure 10.4   Use of Pure Dramatization 224
Figure 10.5   Use of Character Narrating 228
Figure 10.6   Actor Playing Role of Joel Cheek 230
Figure 10.7   Use of Dramatization with Off-Camera Narration. 231
Figure 10.8   Use of Dramatization with On-Camera Narration 235
Figure 10.9   Use of Conflict 237
Figure 10.10 Character Analysis-Miss Piggy 244
Figure 10.11 Use of Caricature. 245
Figure 10.12 Scripting White-Collar Dialog 246
Figure 10.13 Scripting Blue-Collar Dialog 248
Figure 10.14 Character Sketch. 249
Figure 10.15 Character Chart. 250
Figure 10.16 Bringing an Abstract Concept to Life 253
Figure 10.17 Surprising the Audience 259
Figure 10.18 Another Word on Comedy 263

Figure 11.1   Scene from Real Life-Documentary 267
Figure 11.2   Interviewing Subjects in Workplace. 271
Figure 11.3   Content Outline for an Unscripted Program 274
Figure 11.4   Interview Sheet for Unscripted Format. 276
Figure 11.5   File Card of Interview Comments for an Unscripted Format. 280
Figure 11.6   Edit Log Sheet for an Unscripted Format 282

Figure 12.1   15-Projector Overlapping Screen Configuration. 287
Figure 12.2   Multi-Image Production Script and Storyboard. 291
Figure 12.3   Sample Multi-Image Planning Documents 297
Figure 12.4   Photo of VideoWalls 303

Figure 13.1   Interactive Video Reference Checklist. 306
Figure 13.2   Optical Videodisc Features that Aid Interactive Design. 307
Figure 13.3   Excerpt from Interactive Videodisc Program. 309
Figure 13.4   Design Overview, Storyboards and Script Excerpt from
               "Play Away, Please" 314
Figure 13.5   Design Documents for Interactive Techniques and
               Training Applications 332
Figure 13.7   Flow Chart for Technical Training Videodisc 335
Figure 13.8   Interactive Flowchart Symbols 336
Figure 13.9   Major Segments of the Design Worksheet 341

Figure 14.1   Example of Industrial Show Material .350
Figure 14.2   Sample Teleconference Launch Action Plan 358

Figure 15.1   Ratio of Creativity to Risk 376
Figure 15.2   Programming and Creativity 377

ACKNOWLEDGEMENTS

The persistence, patience and professional tenacity of my editor, Ellen Lazer, are largely responsible for this undertaking and its completion. Janet Moore at Industry Publications, Inc., have also provided guidance, professional advice, editorial and typesetter Linda Holder have also provided guidance, professional advice, editorial supervision and plain old hard work during the long journey from concept to finished product.

At the same, time, Ellen's case for a revised edition of *The Nonbroadcast Television Writer's Handbook* (the genesis of this work) was strengthened because of new insights I gained into the writing process. Hearing Lucy McCormick Calkins speak on the writing process she and others at Columbia University's Teachers College Writing Project use with children provided new perspectives and aroused my interest in adapting these concepts to teaching a more specialized type of writing to adults. Through her work I began reading Donald Murray whose influence will be seen throughout the chapters on the scriptwriting process.

David Lyman, founder and director of the Maine Photographic Workshops, provided another source of input and stimulation through his teaching of creativity and the creative process. His influence led me into a fuller study of the creative process through the readings of pioneers in cognitive psychology and creativity such as Howard Gardner and D. N. Perkins.

My own scripts and daily work have been influenced by the many producers, directors and clients who provide the feedback, insight and debate to make first drafts into better shooting scripts. These people include Jim Libby, Bill Hoppe, Barry Byrne, David Emmerling, Walter Schoenknecht, Pat O'Hara, David Peller, Steve Cartwright and many, many others. I am fortunate to work with these people and also count on them as business associates, sources of ideas and support, and, most of all, for their many acts of friendship.

I must also thank fellow writers who graciously permitted me to reproduce their works to give greater variety and scope to excerpts used as examples throughout this book.

This book also owes its completion to the support and belief of my wife, Lynne, and daughters, Kirsten and Kendra, who have taught me much about creativity in daily living and have enriched my "creative well" by deep enjoyment of shared lives.

And, as with the first book, I must acknowledge the enormous contribution of workshop and seminar participants who make me "think on my feet" and provoke the discussions which lead to greater clarity in describing media scriptwriting principles, processes and practices.

DEDICATION

In memory of my father,
who gave me passion for the arts. . .
and my grandfather,
who taught me to play baseball.

1 Introduction

The Scriptwriter's Handbook differs from *The Nonbroadcast Television Writer's Handbook,* published in 1983, in four ways:

1) It encompasses *all* audiovisual media—including new material on writing for multi-image, live events, such as teleconferences, and audiocassettes.
2) The book is organized according to a writing process that I've adapted from the current master teachers of writing.
3) The material is updated to reflect the many media trends taking place in the 1990s.
4) Since many professors adopted the first book for college-level scriptwriting courses, the book is designed to be used either in a classroom situation or as a practical guide for a working scriptwriter.

Even more than the first book, *The Scriptwriter's Handbook* is process oriented. After two introductory chapters, Chapters 3 through 10 describe a proven scriptwriting process. (A companion workbook that provides opportunities to customize this process to specific, personal scriptwriting tasks is being prepared.)

The last chapters deal with writing for specific media and more advanced writing applications such as dramatization, the creative process and the practical side of scriptwriting.

Beginning writers or those coming from print backgrounds will find a process they can adapt to develop audiovisual scripts which meet the needs of today's mushrooming media environment. Experienced media writers can adapt the process to bring their work into sharper focus.

I hope this book will also serve as a handy reference. Many readers may not need to apply material on scripting audiocassettes or multi-image slide shows until the day they receive such an assignment. Hopefully, they will then pull this book from the shelf for specific guidance.

Finally, I hope scriptwriters will find this book motivational as well as instructional. Writing is a lonely occupation. And even though audiovisual media are colla-

1

borative by nature, the scriptwriter often slugs it out in relative isolation from the many individuals who make scripts come to life through the production process. As in any kind of support group, it helps, sometimes, simply knowing you are not alone. So, enjoy. . . .

INT. BALLROOM, MARRIOTT MARQUIS HOTEL NEW YORK CITY— OCTOBER 1985—DAY

It's lunchtime at Video Expo, the exhibition and seminars that Knowledge Industry Publications, Inc. (KIPI) sponsors each fall in New York City. That year it was held at the then-new Marriott Marquis Hotel in the heart of the theater district. (I remember because the meeting rooms are named after American playwrights. I gave my *Communicating Through Characters* seminar in the Arthur Miller Room— something of a humbling experience.)

I'm sitting with Ellen Lazer, Senior Editor at KIPI. As the rolls and butter patties circle, we talk about the possibility of doing a second edition of *The Nonbroadcast Television Writer's Handbook.* Being asked to write a second edition is flattering.

(It also reminded me of the wits of the Algonquin roundtable, those writers of the Twenties and Thirties who hung out at the Algonquin Hotel. Their spiritual leader, Alexander Wolcott, came to lunch one day with his latest book. Fondling the newly minted binding at the table and feeling expansive, he intoned: "What is so rare as a Wolcott first edition?"

"A Wolcott *second* edition," came the ego-crushing retort.)

So Ellen and I discussed a second edition. We talked tentative timing. Later, there was even an exchange of letters. From a business standpoint, revising those chapters to bring them up to date was probably good to do. But deep down inside, I felt little enthusiasm for the project. The creative work on the book had been done once. Being a first book, the process had proved laborious and protracted. Going back would be covering old ground.

Over time, Ellen and I both let the matter drop. And so the book eventually went into a second printing of the good old first edition.

SLOW DISSOLVE TO. . .

INT. AUDITORIUM INTERNATIONAL FILM AND TELEVISION WORKSHOPS ROCKPORT, ME—SUMMER 1986—NIGHT

We're all crowding into Union Hall, Rockport's former Town Hall which now does duty as the main auditorium for David Lyman's summer programs in photography, film and television. This evening I'm off to see the early films of John Korty, who is teaching the Director's Master Class. I'm leading a week-long version of my corporate video writing workshop. I have a group of eleven very earnest writers.

I sit at the very back of the auditorium on one of the old, worn wooden benches built right into the walls. John Korty will be introducing his films tonight—mostly short works done early in his career. In fact, he begins with the first professional film he ever made: a cinematic treatment of a short story.

Korty says a few words about each film; then the lights dim and we watch in communal silence. As the evening goes on, one begins to get a sense of the decision-making process Korty goes through when selecting a project. For one thing, he likes doing short stories. One of the most striking and memorable screened that night was an adaptation of Updike's "The Music School." In that film, Korty eschewed dramatizing scenes for a more subtle approach. The story was read verbatim as a voice-over by the principal character. Korty then visualized each major scene in the story with strong, bold and rich imagery. As he told the group later, nothing was improvised; all the visual "fireworks" were plotted out in great detail before he shot a foot of film.

Between each film, Korty talked of making movies, of camera angles, close ups and lighting. In addition, he made one point I remember to this day. "Of course, it goes without saying, we have to know our craft," Korty said. "But in addition, we have to learn how to manage our careers. And that's sometimes as difficult as learning the craft."

Managing a Writing Career

What a telling point for writers as well as filmmakers. We, too, must hone our craft, learning how to "slap" nouns and verbs together into sentences that keep the momentum moving forward. But there is also the need to manage a writing career.

What projects do we decide to take on and why? Granted, many of us don't have the luxury of picking and choosing projects. If you are a staff writer in a corporate, medical or educational setting your projects come in as assignments. But that block of time in which you work as a staff writer for the organization, that's a finite period you're devoting to a specific writing agenda. How do you know when it's time to move on? Where does your writing take you next?

For the freelance writer, every assignment can be considered a conscious choice. While the beginning freelancer tends to take on anything and everything—for all the right reasons—at some point, the freelancer has to start "managing" his or her career, as Korty urged, with greater purpose.

Eventually, you start looking at projects in terms of how they will stretch and challenge you as a writer. You begin to distinguish between the projects that are "just another corporate job" and those that have the potential to be ground-breaking experiences for yourself as a writer or, those even more rare projects, which can be ground-breaking in the industry. So here we are, back to the fundamental question. "Why is Van Nostran writing this book?" A good question.

CUT TO:

INT. VAN NOSTRAN'S OFFICE—SPRING 1989—DAY

Let's pan around the office and look for clues to the corporate/educational/ medical video state of the art. ZOOM IN to TIGHT SHOT on file cabinet. Let's browse through my fat file of clippings to see what's been happening to the media as the 1990s approach.

Videowalls

Here's a 1987 *Videography* story on "Wall-to-Wall Video," also called video-walls. *Videography* describes wall-to-wall video this way: "A grid of monitors (sometimes as many as 48) combining to display a single video image or a mosaic of individual fragments with a different image on each screen (or the same image on all screens)." The videowall is designed for display in public areas, trade shows or exhibition halls. As the article points out, 48 video screens can be difficult to ignore, "a point marketing and sales people in electronics, fashion, and advertising have seized upon. Videowalls are soon to be ubiquitous."

Implications for the scriptwriter? The possibility of different images appearing simultaneously on different monitors or sets of monitors is much more like writing and planning a multi-image presentation with multiple screen areas than traditional TV writing. Scripting for a videowall requires a nontraditional way of thinking about the possibilities of television images.

Satellite Networks

Consider a more recent article in *Business Week's* "Information Processing" column (March 20, 1989). Called "Why Business Is Glued to the Tube," it talks about the growth of satellite networks devoted to in-house programming in companies like Federal Express, Texas Instruments and Domino's Pizza.

"Last year [1988] there were 61 satellite-based business TV networks, up from four in 1983," says *Business Week.* They also cite the trend toward independent business TV networks serving broad industry segments, such as the Automotive Satellite Network (ASTN), and other broadcasters beginning to serve the food-processing, hospital and securities industries. "Industry observers expect that by 1992 there will be 141 TV networks, a 131% increase," the article concludes.

Certainly there is room here for imaginative television writing, or so it would seem. At the conclusion of the story, the reporter cites the one major hurdle still facing business TV: "program quality. . . too many shows are just plain dull. 'How many times can you watch a lecture about some car without going crazy?' asks one auto dealer."

Back to another *Videography* clip, from 1987, entitled "Look-Up(link) in the Sky." It describes "point-to-multipoint" business TV networks from a more technical standpoint. "Each consists of a single uplink transmitting to one of the geosynchronous communications satellites orbiting the earth. The signal is picked up by receiving dishes, or downlinks, at the company's various sites, aligned to the proper satellite and tuned into the specific transponder frequency carrying the company's programming."

"So-called 'return audio,' via toll-free 800 phone numbers, is often a standard part of business TV programming, enabling people in the field to interact with teachers or top management during live broadcasts."

The growth of business, educational and medical teleconferencing applications is symbolized by a magazine that wasn't even on the scene when I wrote the first book. *Business TV* is sort of a "*TV Guide* for the corporate world." The magazine carries program and network listings for business networks and organizations like the American Hospital Association and American Law Network.

Interactive Video

Another clipping, this time from *Video Manager* (May 1987) relates to interactive video. *The Nonbroadcast Television Writer's Handbook* devoted an entire chapter to interactive video, and made the case that you didn't need videodiscs and computer hardware to make video interactive.

Although still true, interactive videodisc applications have proliferated. The computer linked to the TV screen is a fact of life. It's especially noticeable in the medical and pharmaceutical field where training is on-going and highly technical.

Video Manager also reported on technology that could give interactive video a still bigger boost, "an integrated 'Level 3' touchscreen monitor, with videodisc interface and a family of software and organizational support." The system is a powerful, user-friendly presentation tool that integrates video, audio, graphics and synthetic speech with graphic overlay capability. It comes with software packages—to help nonprogrammers design presentations without program languages.

Sounds to me like video scriptwriters may not only be *writing* interactive materials, but, using such a system, could rather easily learn to program their own material.

"Max Headroom" versus "The Wonder Years"

As we flip through the clippings, we come to *Newsweek* (April 20, 1987). The thrust of the cover story dramatically underscores how much the commercial TV scene is changing. The cover is graced with the smiling visage of Max Headroom. "Mad About Max—the Making of a Video Cult" takes a behind-the-scenes look at the Max Headroom phenomenon. (Does anyone still remember Max?)

"Max Headroom," the ABC TV series, is described as "a slashing futuristic satire of the TV industry and a cornea-zapping demonstration of the medium's technological potential." Max himself is described as "a disembodied head with a slight stutter—the result of a glitch in his software—who lives only on a TV screen but has an uncanny ability to poke his image into anything, anytime, on the airwaves. 'The deliciousness of the show,' muses executive producer Peter Wagg, 'is that a network is allowing us to show how the system works, how ratings are important, why Americans are given the same old material.' "

More than anything, Max can be seen as a symbol for the erosion of network TV dominance in an era when the home VCR has come to stand for time-shifting, commercial-zapping freedom from network tyranny. The late 1980s takeovers (ABC by Capitol Cities Entertainment and GE's buy-out of RCA, NBC's parent company) illustrate the trend that Max Headroom parodies.

Even if the show fails to survive, posits *Newsweek,* "bits and pieces of its ingenuity are virtually certain to filter into the rest of prime time."

Perhaps. With perfect 20-20 hindsight, it's easy to see that Max was merely superficial cleverness and not genuine creativity. Ironically, Max debuted the same season as a "quieter, gentler" program, "The Wonder Years." This program demonstrates anew that people like stories about other people and that imaginative storytelling can capture critics and ratings alike. People like watching people they can relate to and stories with honest emotion.

Current Projects

Before leaving the office, let's PAN to files containing current projects to see what they say about the changing nature of the media writer.

One recently completed script remains in the "open project" file. Originally, the project involved a multi-media presentation for physicians at the American Academy of Neurologists annual dinner. The show, a historical look at Dilantin, the drug of choice for epilepsy for more than fifty years, was a multi-media extravaganza featuring eighteen slide projectors, 16mm film interview footage and a laser light show.

The project's file has remained open because the client is getting more "bang for the bucks." Still slated is a video version of the presentation for use with the pharmaceutical company field sales force as well as a videowall-type treatment of the material for next year's medical conventions.

I'm currently working on scripts for an eight-city teleconference for that same client. We're considering using two video projection screens at the receiving stations to go from tape to live material in a more dramatic fashion. The taped segments of the telecast are formatted as a take-off on "Star Trek."

I'm actively involved in video publishing ventures with several clients. One, with Prudential's Audiovisual Communications Department and a Dallas-based personnel counsulting firm Karli & Associates, is a job search skills training program aimed at welfare recipients. It's the most socially significant project I have been involved in.

Another active project is significant not for its audience or distribution, but because of the content. A documentary for Bell Communications Research, the research arm of the Bell operating companies in the post-diverstiture era, the program is an update on Integrated Services Digital Networks (ISDN). These networks make digital voice and data communication services part of the public telephone network. The new configuration will have enormous impact on the kinds of information services available to the individual phone user.

ISDN will change the way writers conduct their research, write and deliver scripts, and will facilitate script conferences with such features as simultaneous voice and data text editing over the public phone lines.

CUT TO:

INT. AUDITORIUM, BELL COMMUNICATIONS RESEARCH (NAVISINK, NJ)—NIGHT

The room is packed with members of the International Television Association (ITVA), the industry trade group for corporate and educational video. It's the monthly meeting of the North Jersey ITVA chapter and high definition television (HDTV) is the big drawing card.

High Definition Television

This new system takes television a step beyond the current technology by going from a picture composed of 525 scan lines to one made up of 1125 scan lines. Once again, we see the familiar three-by-four aspect ratio giving way to something new: large-screen projection of a picture which stretches the horizontal aspect ratio.

Scenes of a football game are screened. Viewers have the sense of being right in the action. The HD Display System has all the qualities of 35mm film. In fact, scenes were previewed from a motion picture shot in Canada on HDTV. The technology permits film-style lighting and contrast ratios, yet retains the "live" look of the electronic TV picture.

More recently, HDTV has been the subject of a *Business Week* cover story and two broadcast documentaries; one on PBS's "Innovation" series, the other on ABC's "20/20."

HDTV will have enormous impact on corporate, medical and educational video. It is ideally suited for the high-impact presentation needed for sales meetings, conventions and trade shows. The media writer will be scripting for a large-screen dramatic "canvas."

CUT TO:

**INT. MURRAY AVENUE ELEMENTARY SCHOOL—
(LARCHMONT, NY)—NIGHT**

This year, parents have more than one opportunity to see their child in the spring orchestra and chorus concerts. In fact, the musicians themselves will have an opportunity to view the program. The concerts are being videotaped for local access cable. On two days in the following week, Channel 36 will feature the musical talents of the Murray Avenue Elementary School. Across the country, high school sporting events, plays and concerts are appearing on local access cable. "The hills are alive. . . ."

SPECIAL EFFX TRANSITION TO:

EXT. A SOFTBALL FIELD (LAKE MAHOPAC, NY)—DAY

It's the annual spring softball game hosted by Jim Libby and featuring a motley crew of assorted middle-aged couples on teams chosen in a "draft" conducted in a Manhattan bar. On the field, a non-player wanders about taking in the action with super intensity. No, it's not an umpire. This man shoulders a video camera.

CUT TO:

INT. A SUMMER HOME, (LAKE MAHOPAC, NY)—DAY

My wife and I have moved indoors to the living room to say "goodbye" to the weekend softball heros and heroines. A group of people is lounging on the floor in front of the 27-inch television. "Is that the Preakness?" No. Nor is it New York's beloved Mets. (Both events were on commercial TV about that time.) They *are,* however, watching a sports event—cheering and jeering a replay of the ragged soft-ball game which they all participated in just hours before. Need I say more?

SO WHY THIS BOOK?

A lot has happened since writing *The Nonbroadcast Television Writer's Handbook* in the early 1980s. The scenes described above dramatize the rapid changes taking place in the electronic media. The computer has insinuated itself into all aspects of television. (This text is generated on a cathode ray tube, using a sophisticated word processor. The IBM Selectric used to type the manuscript of the first book is now relegated to the occasional typing of address labels. The typewriter is a dinosaur in our household.)

I've also grown and, I like to think, matured as a writer and teacher of writing. I've been influenced by participation in workshops on the teaching of writing conducted by the energetic Lucy McCormick Calkins, who spearheads the workshops for teachers of writing at Columbia Teachers College.

I've also read Calkins' mentors, such as writing coach Donald Murray. The scriptwriting process in this book is strongly influenced by these master teachers.

David Lyman, founder and director of The Maine Photographic Workshops, has stimulated an on-going interest in the creative process and vagaries of the Nine Muses.

As I've grown more confident as a craftsperson, my own projects have become more complex, challenging and engaging.

As Ellen and I discovered early in the game, this is not a second edition of *The Nonbroadcast Television Writer's Handbook* but a second book, using some material from the first book. Too much had changed to simply update the first book. And nonbroadcast TV applications continue to change dramatically as the video landscape widens. Home video is now an undeniable force. It will only continue to grow.

The diversity of nonbroadcast video applications is also expanding—from video publishing to teleconferencing and interactive programming.

At the same time, the big-screen, multi-image slide show refuses to die—especially for those all-important sales meetings and new product launches. Will large-screen, high definition television display someday become the preferred medium for such applications?

And what is the future of 16mm and 35mm film? They, too, refuse to leave the scene just because video has become so entrenched. Today's script writer must be versed in all media and understand the pros and cons of various media applications. Ironically, this results from the fact that video is an all-embracing medium insinuating itself into every nook and cranny of media life.

To script a videowall production, the writer must think like a multi-image slide show writer as well as a video artist. To write material destined for video publishing, the scriptwriter must have the ability to entertain as well as inform and instruct.

Dramatic Changes

In short, the video scene has changed dramatically since the first book, primarily as a result of new and maturing technologies. Those who cut their teeth in the non-broadcast end of the business have matured as well—grown up with the medium. I think in the early days (beginning around 1972) there was a tendency toward low self-esteem among those who worked in corporate television. The work seemed to have limited exposure; programs were viewed only by small groups of employees and salespeople. Network TV was where the "big bucks" lay.

But today, much of the truly innovative work going on in television is happening in the nonbroadcast field. Yet even that term is a misnomer, a category which seems dated in its reference to broadcast television.

If there is a thesis to this book, it is that the exciting opportunities for media writers no longer lie in commercial television and film but in the new media created by corporate television, video publishing, teleconferencing, interactive video and the like. This book explores the dynamic craft of writing for these media. I hope you will find it useful.

2 Media: A Message from McLuhan

The year: 1964. Lyndon Baines Johnson becomes president in a landslide election. Jack Ruby is found quilty of killing Lee Harvey Oswald. Race riots erupt in Harlem and spread across the country. Cassius Clay slugs his way to the world heavyweight crown, "whipping" Sonny Liston.

How about the top ten network television shows from 1964?

1. "Bonanza"
2. "Bewitched"
3. "Gomer Pyle, USMC"
4. "The Andy Griffith Show"
5. "The Fugitive"
6. "The Red Skelton Hour"
7. "The Dick Van Dyke Show"
8. "The Lucy Show"
9. "Peyton Place II"
10. "Combat"

On the big screen, Kubrick's *Dr. Strangelove* hits the local theaters like an A-bomb. Gossip columns are filled with Elizabeth Taylor's divorce from Eddie Fisher and marriage to Richard Burton ten days later. On the international front, a U.S. destroyer is allegedly attacked off North Vietnam. U.S. fighters hit North Vietnamese bases in reprisal.

Against this backdrop, a Canadian media scholar, Marshall McLuhan, published a paperback version of his book *Understanding Media: The Extensions of Man.* The book instantly became required reading for sixties students engaged in the new study of mass communication and the media.

I remember having to plow through McLuhan. But much like Father Guido Sarducci's mail order diploma where the only thing you need to know about economics is the "law of supply and demand," the one McLuhanism I remember years later is his phrase "the medium is the message."

That phrase found its way into the collective consciousness of media mavens. Today, many who have never read McLuhan are fond of saying "the medium is the message." And, of course, there are those who also studiously avoid McLuhan and readily damn his touchstone phrase. "The *message* is the *message*," they intone with the conviction of Gertrude Stein on the subject of roses.

ALL MEDIA ARE DIFFERENT

In order to write for the media, it helps to have a basic appreciation of how each medium works and its strengths and weaknesses in the context of communicating a range of messages. As a prelude to this chapter, I thought it would be helpful to reread McLuhan—to see if the sixties pundit still had something to say to today's working media practioners.

I was delighted to find that much of what he wrote still stands up. One of the things that struck me in this perusal of McLuhan (if anyone can peruse such writing) is his all-inclusive reference to what he calls the *electric* media; i.e., "In the electric age we wear all mankind as our skin."[1]

So sensitive is McLuhan to this concept of the *electric* age that he uses the light bulb to drive home his contention that the effect of media is distinct from the content that they convey. He calls the electric light pure information—a medium without a message unless used to "spell out some verbal ad or name."

McLuhan is more interested in each medium's innate power to change man's environment than the content which comprises programming. He dramatizes the point by referring again to the transforming power of the electric light:

> "The electric light ended the regime of night and day, of indoors and out-of-doors. But it is when the light encounters already existing patterns of human organization that the hybrid energy is released. Cars can travel all night, ball players can play all night [and the games can be televised and picked up on cable stations] and windows can be left out of buildings. In a word, the message of the electric light is total change. It is pure information without any content to restrict its transforming and informing power."[2]

McLuhan is less interested in "programming" in its broadest sense, focusing instead on the effect a medium has as an extension of man's senses. Through his insistence that the "medium is the message," McLuhan urges us to become more sensitive to the qualities of individual media:

> ". . .the medium is the message. This is merely to say that the personal and social consequences of any medium—that is, of any extension of ourselves—result from the new scale that is introduced into our affairs by each extension of ourselves, or by any new technology."[3]

Today, the videocassette has personalized the electronic medium, giving individuals ownership of programming content. I'm in the process of building a videocassette library. The content of my library is individual and unique to me. But to McLuhan, the content of the individual library is not nearly so telling as the fact that millions of homes in America now contain videocassette libraries as well as libraries of books. Both are extensions of man.

More proof that the "medium is the message": I own two books on retriever hunting dog training, *Water Dog* and *Game Dog,* both by Richard Wolters. Yet, I still felt the need to purchase the videocassette of Richard Wolters training gun dogs. While the content of the books and tapes is identical, the *experience* of the two is quite different and that is why both reside on my bookshelf. (McLuhan would find it fitting that bookshelves must give room to these packaged videocassettes.)

THE MEDIUM IS THE MESSAGE

It is precisely because McLuhan urges us to consider media in the macro sense that he coined the phrase "the medium is the message." For the media writer, the implications are enormous. We need to become sensitized to the qualities of a medium which make it distinctly different from any other medium and, therefore, must always in some way "color" content.

Selecting a specific medium should channel the writer's thought in a certain direction—unleashing various potential visual and auditory energies. This is why we may take identical content but treat it quite differently in writing for television, compared to writing for an 18-projector multi-image show. The medium does, indeed, affect the treatment of the content and, ultimately, the content itself.

This is part of what McLuhan gets at when he talks about the impact of one medium on another:

> "What I am saying is that media as extensions of our senses institute new ratios, not only among our private senses, but among themselves, when they interact among themselves. Radio changed the form of the news story as much as it altered the film image in the talkies. TV caused drastic changes in radio programming, and in the form of the thing or documentary novel."[4]

McLuhan contends artists are always the first to seize upon the capabilities of new media. As media writers, we are generally called upon to be part artist, part communicator, part teacher, and part football coach delivering a half-time pep talk.

Early on in writing any media presentation comes a consideration of the medium itself. What are its innate qualities? Its production and communication strengths and weaknesses? McLuhan's value is that he forces us to consider the characteristics that are inherent in any medium—*regardless* of content.

"Mechanization was never so vividly fragmented or sequential as in the birth of the movies," he writes. "The movie, by sheer speeding up the mechanical, carried us from the world of sequence and connections into the world of creative configuration and structure."[5]

McLuhan's linkage of the movie to the mechanical is valid as long as movies are made the way we know them today. The motion picture is largely a mechanical medium, especially when compared to the electronic medium of television.

The mechanical nature of the motion picture is clearly demonstrated by Thomas Edison's account of the problems he encountered in developing and perfecting the motion picture. On the one hand, he faced the chemical problems associated with the film emulsion, materials and configuration. His second set of problems, as Edison himself writes, was all mechanical in nature:

> "It is almost impossible for the layman to appreciate the extreme niceties of adjustment we had to overcome. Try to realize that we were dealing always with minute fractions of seconds. For instance, allowing forty-six exposures per second, as we did at first, we had to face the fact that the film had to be stopped and started again after each exposure. Now, allowing a minimum of 1/100 part of a second for every impression that was registered, you can see that practically half of our time was already gone, and in the remainder of the time we had to move the film forward the necessary distance for the next exposures.

> "And all this had to be done with the exactness of a watch movement. If there was the slightest variation in the movement of the film, or if it slipped at any time by so much as a hair's breadth, this fact was certain to show up in the enlargements."[6]

Edison's role in the electric media goes far beyond the motion picture invention. As inventor of the light bulb, the "Wizard of Menlo Park" envisioned a world in which electricity was subdivided so *all* could benefit from his invention. And in his own writings, he describes the close link between the invention of the phonograph (his personal "baby") and the motion picture. Edison linked one to the other—foreseeing the age of the talkie. He also worked by analogy, saying that his objective with the motion picture was to do "for the eye what the phonograph did for the ear."

Were McLuhan around today, he would likely recognize interactive video as the ultimate transition from lineal connections to configurations. Interactive video is, to use McLuhan's terminology, a medium "hybrid"—a mixture of television, video-disc and computer. McLuhan is quite perceptive in seeing the powerful effects of one medium upon another. " 'As the silent film cried out for sound, so does the sound film cry out for color,' wrote Sergei Eisenstein in his *Notes of a Film Director.*"[7]

Today, media interactions are all about us. The videowall is an interaction between television and the multi-image slide show. The multi-image slide show is a linkage of the slide projector and the computer. Add 16mm motion pictures to the experience of a multi-image presentation and you have a multi-media event. Integrate a live spokesperson or actor into the content of a multi-media event and its effect upon the audience changes yet again.

McLuhan continues along these lines:

> ". . .In fact, of all the great hybrid unions that breed furious release of energy and change, there is none to surpass the meeting of literate and oral cultures. The giving to man of an eye for an ear by phonetic literacy is, socially and politically, probably the most radical explosion that can occur in any social structure."[8]

One need only consider the ill-fated interaction between the European white man and native American Indians to realize the full impact of this "explosion." This interaction will become relevant when we explore how an oral tradition can serve as role model for audiocassette writing in Chapter 8.

Content in Different Media

To understand the influence of media on message, one needs only to look at a typical scenario in business and educational video programming. How often have trainers decided that they could capture on tape the excitement of a dynamic classroom presentor by simply videotaping the class? Invariably, watching the videotape is like being shut out of the classroom; on the outside looking in. The dynamic presentation seems to take longer than it did for those engaged in the live media presentation. The videotape viewing experience is a poor substitute for the live classroom experience. The content is identical but the change in media alters the experience to a significant degree.

The Message for Media Writers

Media writers should be skilled in scripting for all media. The starting point must be an appreciation for the individual characteristics of the medium itself. Once the inherent qualities of a medium are understood and assimilated, the writer can focus on the *content* of the assignment at hand. The remainder of this book will

Figure 2.1: Medium: Multi-image

General Characteristics

Uses 35mm slide projectors in synchronization.

Most simple, basic format is a single screen, two-projector dissolve unit.

Number of projectors and screen areas can be increased for greater visual impact. Most configurations are based on multiples of three: 3 projectors, 6 projectors, 9 projectors, etc.

With more projectors, screens are often overlapped. (See Figure 12.1 in Chapter 12.)

With more projectors and larger screen formats, stereo sound effects are used in producing the audio track.

Projectors and sound track and other effects (such as special lighting) are programmed for control by multi-image computer programmers.

Special effects techniques allow still images to be programmed at a rate of speed calculated to simulate live action or animation.

Strengths

Ideal for presentations to large audiences because of the large-screen format and high-quality resolution of 35mm slides.

Typical multi-image presentation is more motivational than informational or instructional. Ideal for sales meetings or presentations requiring high impact.

Large-screen formats with use of special effects and multiple screen areas allow creators to design high-density visual imagery—lots going on simultaneously.

Stereo sound capabilities excellent for musical-visual interludes. Strong emotional appeal.

Weaknesses

The more complex the show and program, the more professional set-up and projection is required.

Shows require large rooms with high ceilings for maximum impact.

Figure 2.1: Medium: Multi-image (Cont.)

Multiple-screen shows do not easily convert to film or videotape.

As a result of the above restrictions, multi-image shows are often produced for a one-time event. Generally not the ideal medium if shelf-life is desired.

The more complex the show, the more difficult it becomes to update or change.

Special Considerations for Writer

Must know number of projectors, screen configuration and programming effects capabilities to get maximum impact.

Need to work closely with art director and multi-image programmer in developing concepts.

The novice often "over-writes" for this medium. Visuals and music generally predominate with narration secondary. Too much copy can make the presentation ponderous.

Most multi-image modules are short—in the two- to five-minute range.

Most multi-image presentations are built around a strong creative concept. Demands good conceptual skills of the creative team.

---

focus quite specifically on content—how the media writer arrives at the content of a presentation and then shapes and crafts that content for the medium of choice. But first, let's take McLuhan to heart and look at the specific characteristics of the media most often available to us. Figures 2.1–2.5 are meant to help with this assessment.

Hybrid Media

McLuhan talks about the power of two media coming together. Today, the media writer must be conversant with a variety of hybrid media—each of which creates new forms and special demands on the media writer. Following is a brief rundown of the most common media hybrids.

Interactive Video

Interactive video is a combination of television, computer and videodisc. Since the videodisc permits nearly instantaneous access to up to 54,000 frames, this com-

Figure 2.2: Medium: Television

General Characteristics

Uses an electronically created visual image. The picture consists of high-speed electrons, each producing a luminous spot on a cathode-ray tube. A complete image is composed of horizontal scan lines.

Frames/second: 30

Television is most often viewed on a cathode-ray tube screen, although use of large screen projection systems has become commonplace.

Television images can be recorded, played back and transmitted on videotape and videodisc and via broadcast, cable and satellite.

The pure electronic image (shot, recorded and played back on video equipment) has a live presence.

Electronic production techniques and digital manipulation of video images provide a wide range of special effects, computer generated graphics and animated effects.

Stereo sound is now a production option.

Strengths

Television is a motion medium.

Television and videotape have immediacy. This results from both the live-looking electronic image as well as videotape's instant playback capability.

People relate to television in a highly personal way because of years of conditioning as home viewers.

Television can be viewed in a fully lighted room.

Videocassette technology makes playback highly portable without need for special set up or skills.

Widespread home VCR ownership provides additional viewing opportunities for producers of specialized video material.

Television easily incorporates other media such as film and 35mm slides.

Figure 2.2: Medium: Television (Cont.)

Weaknesses

With typical screen size of 24 inches diagonally, size of viewing audience is limited to about 20 people.

Because of dependence on a small screen, television is often referred to as a close-up medium.

Typical single-screen format is in a fixed 3 by 4 aspect ratio.

Compared to the 35mm slide or 16mm film image, the TV picture has relatively poor resolution of detail.

Special Considerations for Writer

Since video production facilities vary widely in terms of sophistication, the video writer should have a feel for the budget and production capabilities of those who will be charged with executing the program. This will have an impact on special effects used, etc.

Since video viewing can range from a single person in front of a tiny monitor to large screen projection and videowalls, the video writer should have a good understanding of the program's ultimate viewing environment.

bination offers tremendous random access capabilities. It permits construction of video programming which is non-linear and allows the viewer to choose from several options at differing branch points.

For this reason, interactive video is extremely valuable for detailed one-on-one training (which makes use of computer-assisted instruction techniques) or for point-of-purchase displays in which the viewer selects from various product or informational segments. Interaction can be accomplished through touch-sensitive screens, keyboards or special display pads.

For the media writer, it is vital to develop an approach to subject matter which is non-linear and truly interactive. The media writer will often collaborate with other creative specialists on interactive video projects—perhaps an instructional designer and most certainly the programmer of the interactive computer software and video-disc configuration.

Figure 2.3: Medium: Film

General Characteristics

Uses a photographically created visual image.

Frames/second: 24.

Aspect ratio: wider than television.

Film is generally projected for viewing; however, film transfers excellently to video-tape. So film may often be transferred to tape for editing and/or viewing.

Strengths

Film is a motion medium.

Film production gear is still more portable and better suited to low-light documentary situations than video.

Film is a big-screen medium, allowing for a breadth and scope that goes beyond television.

Film has excellent resolution and contrast ratio; superior to videotape in this regard.

Since film is a mechanical medium, it can be shot faster or slower than 24 **FPS**. When shot slower, the projected images will appear as fast action; when shot faster than 24 FPS, the projected images appear as slowmotion footage.

Weaknesses

Because it has a photographic image, film is always "past tense."

Film requires lab processing at various stages of the production process, adding cost and time.

Film does not allow for instant playback while shooting.

Film animation is done quite differently than electronic video animation. Hand-drawn cell artwork is combined, then shot one frame at a time to create the sense of motion.

Figure 2.3: Medium: Film (Cont.)

Special Considerations for Writer

The writer needs to know whether the film is intended for projection or will be transferred to tape and viewed on a TV screen.

The writer should meet with the director to gain an appreciation of the film and lighting techniques which will be employed on production.

The Videowall

Although it uses a video input, the effect of a videowall is very much like that of a multi-projector, multi-image presentation. The media writer engaged in a video-wall presentation must, therefore, think like a multi-image writer. In order to gain maximum effectiveness from the presentation, the writer must be cognizant of the number of monitors comprising the wall, their size and overall configuration. The writer should also know the motion capabilities and other requirements for the software program feeding the videowall.

Multi-Media

Any presentation involving two or more media at the same time, a multi-media presentation typically incorporates motion picture or videotape material into the format of a multi-image presentation. In its most exotic form, the multi-media show could include laser show effects and/or integration of live talent with other media.

As in any multi-image production, the writer needs to be aware of screen configurations and projector capabilities to determine the optimum use of the combined media.

Keeping the Audio in Audiovisual

All these media are *audio*visual media—sight and sound hybrids. The use of the two senses in concert can be more compelling than either used alone. Unfortunately, audio is often the weak link in media presentations. One of the reasons for this is the mind-numbing lack of musical creativity in the production of legally cleared library music for mixing tracks.

But the case can be made (at least I'll make one) that the functional use of music, sound effects and "voice" is often ignored by media writers. This is particularly true in corporate video. Multi-image tracks, intended to create emotional appeal

Figure 2.4: Medium: Audiocassette

General Characteristics

A "one-dimensional" aural medium.

Extremely portable playback capability.

Strengths

The audiocassette's primary advantage for corporate, educational and organizational communicators is portability. Sales representatives can play audiocassettes in their car while driving in their territory.

With a Walkman^{TM}, personal cassettes can be listened to while jogging or engaging in other physical activities.

Relatively speaking, the audiocassette is inexpensive to produce.

Can be a good "one-on-one" tutorial aid, especially for some types of task training and when combined with a workbook or manual that provides the necessary visualization.

Ironically, the medium's greatest strength results from its biggest drawback: because it lacks a visual component, writing for the ear provides tremendous latitude in time and space. Vivid locations and situations can be created with a few words, sound effects and music.

Can be used effectively to communicate content involving human interaction—e.g., sales situations, interviewing techniques, employee counseling, etc.

Can also be used to present an expert on a subject or to provide a motivational platform for executives.

Weaknesses

The main drawback to audiocassettes is that they do not engage the eye. The audiocassette in a classroom environment, for example, leaves listeners free to be distracted; concentration may be difficult.

The ability to show while telling is lost with this medium, making it unsuitable for mechanical subjects or other instructional content difficult to convey through words alone. Long segments of uninterrupted narration can become tedious.

Figure 2.4: Medium: Audiocassette (Cont.)

Special Considerations for Writer

The writer must be open to the creative possibilities of the audiocassette and write imaginatively for the ear.

Role models, such as early radio dramatic writing or tales from oral cultures (such as American Indian), provide examples of how the lack of a visual component can be turned to good advantage by allowing listeners to create their own mental imagery.

(and often using copyrighted music because of the one-time, private nature of the performances) and documentary film tracks (which are more often originally scored) tend to be stronger counterparts to the picture.

Unfortunately, media writers are often guilty of becoming totally word oriented, eschewing the thoughtful use of musical directions or integrating visual and narrative elements. Media writers need to become more sensitive to the emotional pull inherent in the purposeful use of music. Part of this consists of "growing bigger ears"—becoming more sensitive to the skilled use of sound. While watching movies, for example, students of media should consciously listen to the score. They will find such delightful surprises as listening to the grating punch delivered in Mike Oldfield's soundtrack for *The Killing Fields*—the electronic musical sound that mimics the chop-chop of helicopter blades as the "choppers" descend on the crumbling American embassy. Listen to Randy Newman's wonderful work for both *Ragtime* and *The Natural.* In the former, he evokes the ragtime rhythms of Scott Joplin; in the latter, the Americana grandeur of Copland. Or check out Philip Glass's high-energy score for the film *Mishima.* We'll have more to say on this subject in Chapter 8, "The Imaginative Ear."

Film versus Tape

The remainder of this book takes on the nature of a "how-to," offering specific techniques for dealing with each phase of the media writing process. Before leaving this examination of media, however, imagine a discussion between a TV monitor and a 16mm projector on the subject of film versus tape. It might go something like this. . .

TV   Film versus tape! Film versus tape! It's all so tedious.

FILM   Because you always come out on the short end of the stick.

TV   Oh, really, now. In what way?

FILM   It happens all the time. People who really know their media recognize that film is of a higher quality.

TV   Bull. People who use that argument simply show their ignorance of the two media. The real difference is between a tape-look and a film-look. Tape has an electronic, live presence. Film is photographic and one step removed from my instantaneous live look.

FILM   Why do you persist in this delusion that there's no quality difference between the film image and the videotape look? Film has greater resolution—all the resolution fine photography is capable of. . .

TV   (Interrupting.) That's my point. You're a medium based in photography. Always have been. Always will be. I'm a pure electronic medium.

FILM   Let me finish. Because film has greater resolution and a greater contrast ratio, film lighting can be far more subtle and far more dramatic than TV lighting.

TV   A lot of that's myth.

FILM   Myth? Thought myths were about Greek gods.

TV   It's carryover from the old studio days of television when every inch of the studio had to be lit to 250 footcandles.

FILM   That flat, boring, TV lighting look. I hate it.

TV   You oughtta look more closely at how videographers, trained in film, light. They're not afraid of shadows or black holes in the picture. TV can handle that. Lighting directors from the film school have more guts when it comes to television lighting. Of course, it makes some video engineers crazy.

FILM   Fine and dandy—but what happens when that video picture gets projected? Film looks great projected—the bigger the screen the better.

TV   Just wait for high definition TV!

FILM   I'm not talkin' about some future technology. I'm talkin' about *now*. Today. If you want to produce something for the big screen—you're gonna shoot film.

TV   High definition TV will bury you.

FILM   TV—you were supposed to bury me back in the fifities when every middleclass home was tuned to "Howdy Doody" and "The Lone Ranger." I've survived just fine. What's been the backbone of the videocassette sales and rental industry? The *motion picture*—that's what.

TV   The very fact that you're so sensitive about the subject of HDTV tells me that it makes you w-o-r-r-i-e-d.

FILM   You think I'm so worried? Let's look at something else. Music videos. (Sneering.) What a misnomer.

TV   What you driving at?

FILM   I'm talkin' music videos. You watch MTV lately? O.K. So they got V.J.s. That part's video. But look at the overwhelming preponderence of music videos shot and finished on *film.*

TV   Some of those are shot on film and *finished* on tape!

FILM   Who cares? The point is—they're shot on film and when they're screened on MTV they have the film look. Yet every bozo rock star talks about their latest rock *video*. They don't even know the difference.

TV   You can really get on my nerves, you know that?

FILM   Well, people should know better.

TV   Of course, people should know better—but they don't.

FILM   I hate to tell you, but there happen to be media illiterates walking around who are *in the business* for god's sake.

TV   Speaking of being in the business—let me tell you a funny story. I was at an ITVA convention not too far back—videotaping the keynote address by Linda Ellerbee. By the way, it was also being projected simultaneously so people could see it better. Anyway, Ellerbee's telling about sitting around her apartment with friends. The debate is raging—live versus tape. There are advocates of both sides. (By the way—in film, there's no such thing as live.) Anyway, Ellerbee's kid finally pipes up and says: "Listen, it's very simple. This," she says pointing to the people in the room, "this is live. That" she says pointing to the TV set, "that's television."

FILM   So?

TV   So!

FILM   So what's the point? What's the message?

TV   The medium is the message and the message of the television medium is a happening now, live feel. And you don't get that with film. Film is always past tense. Never now.

FILM   Film still offers a certain facility when it comes to shooting in the field.

TV   With film, you're still a "slave" to the processing lab.

FILM   Film's better for large audiences. . .

TV   (Childishly.) TV can be viewed with the lights on. . .

FILM   Film offers more aesthetic potential!

TV   (After a pause.)
        Film versus tape! Film versus tape! It's all so tedious. . .

FADE TO BLACK

Figure 2.5: Medium: Print

General Characteristics

A highly personal, "one-to-one" medium. At the same time, through its ease of duplication and distribution, print represents the first mass medium.

Extremely portable.

Uses the phonetic alphabet and therefore requires a degree of literacy for full comprehension/appreciation.

Print has a permanency other media lack.

Strengths

The invention of movable type in the 15th century made print the first "mass medium."

From its inception, the alphabet and an individual's ability to interpret these phonetic symbols has translated into a personal power. The ability to read and write is perhaps the most intellectually liberating force in any culture.

McLuhan points out that "the alphabet meant power and authority. . . ." This is why nearly all judicial, military, corporate and organizational rules/regulations become committed to print.

In our computer literate world, the printed "documentation" that accompanies software is often considered an integral part of the product. Good documentation allows the computer user to master software quickly and expediently; poor printed documentation places distance between software and user.

Using modern printing technology, the printed page can also incorporate photo-graphic and graphic imagery—so the presentational and discursive symbolism of Langer can exist side by side and complement one another.

Weaknesses

Ironically, print's major drawback is the necessity for literacy on the part of both sender and receiver. Literacy exists on many levels. The ability to read and write does not guarantee facility, sophistication or versatility in the use of written language. This is why so many high school students and drop-outs remain "functional illiterates."

Figure 2.5: Medium: Print (Cont.)

Paradoxically, although written language is often used to codify and clarify rules, regulations and contractual relationships, it is still open to individual interpretation due to the subtle and detailed discursive richness of language. (The same richness which made Shakespeare a playwright for the ages accounts for the glut of litigation in America's judicial system.)

This is why corporate communicators consider delivery of a uniform, consistent message one of the strengths of a video presentation. The video medium's ability to incorporate spoken word (with appropriate interpretive inflections) and presentational images makes it less open to individual interpretation as it moves throughout an organization.

Special Considerations for Writer

Both writer's and reader's degree of literacy bear significantly on the effectiveness and shared meaning inherent in written communications.

Although the language of any communication must be geared to the audience's level of understanding, this is especially vital in print communications. Writing for an audience of 10-year-olds is quite different from writing to an audience of Ph.Ds.

Media writers must as a matter of course have facility writing for the print medium since many audiovisual media presentations are distributed with collateral print in the form of brochures, manuals, viewer notes, etc. Furthermore, many of the scriptwriter's initial "products" appear in print in the form of objectives, audience profiles, content outlines and treatments.

Footnotes

1. Marshall McLuhan, *Understanding Media: The Extensions of Man* (New York: McGraw-Hill Book Company, 1964), p. 47.
2. *Ibid.,* p. 52.
3. *Ibid.,* p. 7.
4. *Ibid.,* p. 53.
5. *Ibid.,* p. 40.
6. Thomas A. Edison, *The Diary & Sundry Observations of Thomas Alva Edison* (New York: Philosophical Library, 1948), p. 76.
7. McLuhan, p. 49.
8. *Ibid.,* p. 49.

Introduction to Part I

The Scriptwiting Process

Learning to write good media scripts is more like learning to play the violin than learning to ride a bike. Though frustrating at first, learning to ride a bike eventually comes in a joyous flash. From that moment on, bike-riding is mastered. Years may pass without any practice, but all it takes is a minute or two and one is artfully riding again.

Playing the violin is a different story. It takes several years to become good enough to play decently before friends and relatives. Constant practice and daily repetition to maintain "technique" is vital. With talent and good instruction, the young violinist may achieve a measure of virtuosity. But it generally takes constant playing, concertizing and life experience (the school of hard knocks) for one to become a consummate musician whose music seems to come straight from the heart with little or no effort.

Writing involves the same patient labor and craftsmanship to develop mastery of form and content. Reading this book will not transform you overnight into an accomplished media writer. That takes constant practice in the school of hard knocks.

The next chapters do, however, offer an approach to media writing assignments grounded in practical experience and coupled with a good deal of study and research in the teaching of writing.

"CATCHING ON"

Whatever your present stage of evolution as a writer, we are not dealing in a field of absolutes. Each new media writing project presents new problems and challenges. The learning curve for all writers consists of a series of peaks and valleys along the way to competency and craftsmanship. John Gardner put it well in his advice to aspiring novelists. . .

> "If the aspiring writer keeps on writing—writes day after day,
> month after month—and if he reads very carefully, he will begin
> to 'catch on.' Catching on is important in the arts, as in athletics.

29

Practical sciences, including the verbal engineering of commercial fiction can be taught and learned. The arts can be taught, up to a point; but except for certain matters of technique, one does not learn the arts, one simply catches on.

"If my own experience is representative, what one mainly catches on to is the value of painstaking—almost ridiculously painstaking—work."[1]

For media writers, what one mainly "catches on to" is a way of thinking and working that is *process* driven. The goal is to develop a personal writing strategy which yields consistently good results in terms of both creativity and productivity. The skillful writer internalizes the steps in the scriptwriting process, automatically asking himself or herself the appropriate question at the right time as the process unfolds.

A MEDIA WRITING PROCESS

Chapters 3 through 10 offer a systematic approach to the problems posed at various stages of the media writing process. The process involves five discrete steps:

Step 1: ASSIMILATION

Chapter 3: Collecting Information
Chapter 4: Organizing Information

Step 2: REHEARSAL

Chapter 5: Idea Development

Step 3: DRAFTING

Chapter 6: Creating the Shooting Script
Chapter 7: The Imaginative Eye
Chapter 8: The Imaginative Ear

Step 4: REVISION

Chapter 9: Making the Most of Feedback

Step 5: EDITING

These steps are illustrated in greater detail in Figure I.1.

Figure I.1: Steps in the Scriptwriting Process

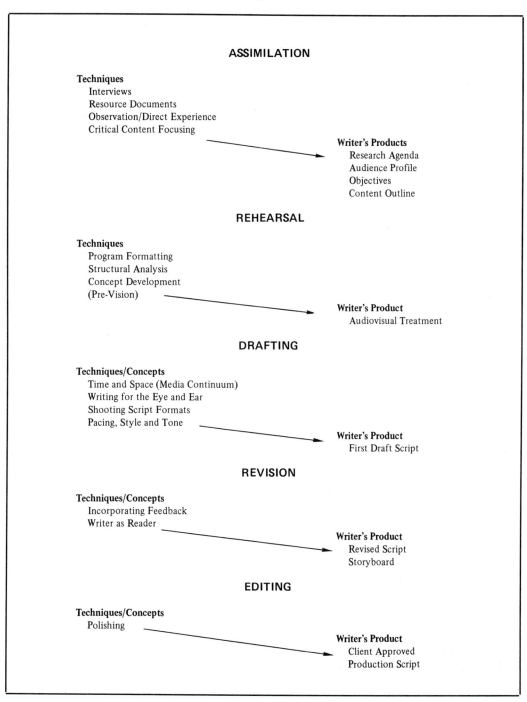

The left side of the page under each step in the process describes the techniques and activities the scriptwriter performs during that stage of the process.

The right side of the page describes the specific writing products which result at the conclusion of each phase. By the end of the Assimilation phase, for instance, the writer has produced a research agenda, an analytical audience profile, objectives, and a content outline. Rehearsal results in a creative media treatment. The Drafting phase concludes with a finished first-draft script.

The products flow from the techniques or activities the writer engages in during each step. These products are ways of communicating your decisions to others involved in the project—the client, the producer and director, the multi-image designer, the interactive videodisc programmer and the like.

These are the people who *read* your scripts. (The viewing audience will experience your work only through sights and sounds appearing on-screen in a time-based chronology.) Those who actually read your script base their production decisions on your documents. They approve expenditures of money (sometimes large expenditures of money) based on the blueprint laid out in the script.

Although many writing products result during each of these steps, the ultimate aim is the finished shooting script—a script the client has approved as meeting the needs of the audience; a script the subject matter expert deems technically accurate; a script the producer uses to develop a budget; and a script the director or multi-image producer uses to break down the production into discrete steps and assign tasks to production personnel.

THE PRODUCTION SCRIPT: A DEFINITION

At this point, let's define what we mean by a media script:

> A script is the written description of a chronological sequence
> of events, describing sounds, pictures and ideas, using media
> production terminology.

The media writer is not so much engaged in setting words down on paper (like a poet) as in describing a specific sequence of events which become the individual scenes and sequences seen and heard on screen. The television and film writer uses TV and film media terms—LONG SHOT, MEDIUM SHOT, CLOSE-UP, PAN, TILT, DOLLY and ZOOM.

The multi-image writer uses a similar syntax—MONTAGE, SPLIT SCREEN, WIPE, SOUND EFFX, and PANORAMA. (For a complete description of such terms, see the Glossary.) The best media scripts serve as useful, practical production tools.

FORM AND CONTENT

Throughout this process, the writer searches for "ways of marrying form and content," as the biographer Leon Edel writes. As Edel puts it: "A writer of lives is allowed the imagination of form but not of fact."[2]

The media scriptwriter is almost invariably in the same boat. We are allowed the imagination of form but not of fact. The facts, or content of our scripts, lie within the objectives of our clients and the technical knowledge of the subject matter experts.

We write programs aimed at specific audiences and intended to accomplish specific objectives with that audience. The media writer is often part trainer, part professional communicator, part teacher, part dramatist, part football coach and part showman.

The first phase in the media writer's process, Assimilation, is always intended to discover and delineate the *content* which must be imparted to a specific audience in a highly defined viewing environment.

FOOTNOTES

1.   John Gardner, *On Becoming a Novelist* (New York: Harper & Row, Publishers, 1983), p. 17.
2.   Leon Edel, *Writing Lives* (New York: W. W. Norton & Co., 1984), p. 13.

Step 1: Assimilation

3 Collecting Information for the Script

Research is the first part of the Assimilation process. Good scripts begin with the writer's immersion in the subject matter. Before the scriptwriter can even consider "imagination of form," the hard facts of the subject must be uncovered. The program's objectives, audience and viewing environment must be thoroughly appreciated; now is when the foundation for a good script is laid. The thoroughness and quality of the research bears on every other aspect of the scriptwriting process. Selection of a format, style, and narrative voice; the creative concept; use of music and special effects—all such decisions are driven by the writer's understanding of the topic at hand.

This is because, as Stephen Sondheim puts it. . .

> "An important principle I've always believed in is: content dictates form."[1]

Without total immersion in content, it is premature to begin scripting.

In my writing workshops, I like to introduce the Assimilation process with a short exercise. First, I ask the group to think of a time when they were personally "invested" in a piece of writing. The writing need not be a script. It could be a poem, a corporate report—even a love letter. Whatever the specific writing experience, it must have been positive; one in which the writing achieved its goal and the writer was pleased by the outcome. I then give the class a few moments to jot down all the reasons why they "connected" with this piece of writing.

Next, I ask them to think of a time when they did not connect with a piece of writing and the writing was difficult, tedious. They were unsatisfied with the result, happy only that the grim task was completed. I then give the class a few moments to jot down all the reasons why they found this writing experience a chore.

Then we discuss the responses and list them in two columns on a flip chart. Invariably, the successful writing experience is characterized by such assertions as:

> "I knew the subject matter cold."
> "I enjoyed creative freedom."

35

"I was able to express what was in my mind."
"I had the full support of the client and subject matter experts."
"The writing flowed effortlessly."
"I knew exactly what the objectives were."

Turning to the second column, typical answers include:

"The objectives were never nailed down."
"I didn't grasp all the details."
"I was trying to satisfy a committee."
"I wasn't allowed to write the material the way I wanted to."
"My boss kept trying to second-guess me."
"I didn't have access to the executives I was writing for."

If you analyze the differences in the two writing experiences, two themes emerge. First, successful writing experiences rely on the writer's mastery of the subject matter, purpose of the project and the nature of the audience. Then, the writer must be permitted reasonable creative freedom to shape the content into the form that matches the writer's inner, creative vision.

Research is more than looking up cold facts or recording the client's perception of the need for the program. Research is an active journey into the heart of a communication or training problem. Research is the writer's "indoctrination." (I write my best scripts when I believe most strongly in the communication's cause.)

The highly imaginative naturalist writer Rachel Carson describes "Assimilation" this way:

"The writer must never attempt to impose himself upon his subject. He must not try to mold it according to what his readers or editors want to read. His *initial task* is to come to know his subject intimately, to understand its every aspect, to let it fill his mind. Then, at some *turning point,* the subject takes command and the true act of creation begins. . .

"The discipline of the writer is to learn to be still and listen to what his subject has to say to him."[2]

In short, the writer must not only *research* the subject, the writer must *assimilate* the content—making it a part of his or her being. Only then can the "true act of creation begin." So let's explore research techniques, seeking to do such a thorough job that the subject "fills" the scriptwriter's mind.

THE GOALS OF RESEARCH

There are three main goals of research:

1. To determine what the media presentation will be *about*.
2. To collect and assimilate the content, making it part of one's self.
3. To determine the communication environment.

Many business, medical and educational A/V presentations involve highly technical, complex subjects. By and large, these subjects cannot be researched through publicly available material. It takes access to inside information, which must be pieced together by talking with content specialists. Furthermore, for most informational or training audiovisual presentations, research should go beyond content. It's generally equally important to develop an appreciation of your client's total communication or training environment. Insight into the audience's likely attitude toward the topic, the logistics of the viewing environment and even cultural attitudes within an organization all yield insights which become invaluable once it's time to decide on a program's form and style.

Although research is always the first step in the writing process, specific research activities vary from project to project. A field trip may be essential for one project and totally inappropriate for the next. Interviews with the target audience may generate valid input for treating some topics yet be superfluous in other instances. The research task facing an audiovisual scriptwriter can be quite substantial. And it's not uncommon to conduct research under deadline pressure. The media writer needs solid research methods—a system that yields comprehensive data, yet is also efficient and flexible.

The Core Question

For any media scripting project, the goal of all research activities is to develop an answer to one fundamental question. It goes like this:

What do you want to say, to whom, and for what purpose?

Answers to the core question fall into one of three categories of information:

1. "What do you want to say. . ." provides information relevant to the *content* of the communication.
2. "To whom. . ." focuses on the *audience* for the finished program.

3. "For what purpose. . ." gives the writer an understanding of
objectives–what the presentation intends to accomplish.

There are many ways to get answers to this question. Obviously, a comprehensive answer could become more detailed than your finished production script. Research activities often span several weeks, involving meetings with many individuals, site surveys to observe activities firsthand and, of course, a certain amount of reading. Ultimately, when client and writer agree on answers to the core question, it's time to move from researching to writing.

The Research Agenda

The research agenda offers a method of coming to grips with the complexities of each assignment. Through the research agenda, the writer formulates a specific plan of attack for gathering both the hard data and the psychological insights necessary to proceed to more conceptual work. The research agenda identifies and itemizes specific steps that will be taken to gather input on content, audience and objectives. It includes activities such as interviews, observations, readings and questionnaires (see Figure 3.1).

Getting an Overview

To formulate a research agenda, the writer needs an overview perspective on the program's proposed content, audience and objectives. Usually, this information is gained from an initial discussion with the client, possibly a subject matter expert and, sometimes, the show's producer and director. In this first meeting, you're seeking a big-picture answer to the core question: "What do you want to say, to whom, for what purpose?" Guard against bogging down in details on content, audience or objectives. Focus instead on developing a sense of the total communication/training task, the medium the client foresees using and the communication environment. For now, keep your interview technique exploratory and open-ended, encouraging the client to discuss the rationale for doing the program as well as the subject matter itself.

Probe with questions that relate to elements of the core question, beginning with "What do you want to say?" Fortunately, you'll find the client usually answers in general terms at first. For example:

> "We want to demonstrate in a short film that Goldin/Lewis is
> the best damn firm in the fiercely competitive construction
> management business."

Often, there's a temptation to jump into details right away. Resist. Ask only those follow-up questions that are essential for you to comprehend the client's statement of content. If you're called in to write a script about blood gas analyzers and you haven't the vaguest idea what blood gas analyzers are all about, now's the time to find out more. But don't press for detailed content until you get a complete description of the assignment.

Once you've got the gist of the subject matter in general, go directly to the next part of the question.

What do you want to say, *to whom.* . .

Informational or training presentations are always targeted to a specific viewing audience. The composition of that audience, their predisposition to the subject, the viewing environment—all these factors bear significantly on the writer's ultimate creative strategy. So, during this initial meeting, look for a basic description of the audience. The client may tell you. . .

> "We want to tell our story *to the corporate/institutional buyers of construction management services.* We're already well-known and established with the entrepreneurial developer."

The client has a specific target audience in mind. By viewing subject matter in the context of the intended audience, the writer learns a great deal about the nature of the research and writing assignment. Change the audience, and you face an entirely different communication environment.

> "We want to give *new employees* an overview of what it's like to work at Goldin/Lewis."

Even when the content is unchanged, the nature of the communication or training task changes radically based on the client's intended audience. When the audience consists of sales representatives, for example, the approach to subject matter will be markedly different in both content and tone than a similar subject presented to potential customers. Beware the client who wants to address multiple audiences in a single presentation. This usually results in a program that lacks focus.

Depending on the writer's familiarity with the target audience, a significant portion of the research agenda may focus on gathering insight into the audience's attitudes or level of knowledge. Interviews with representative audience members, observation of their work activities or use of research tools such as attitude surveys are techniques the writer may find helpful for some assignments. However it's accomplished, the writer must construct a valid profile of the target audience—their current understanding of the subject matter as well as their receptivity to the message.

But before getting too involved in profiling the audience, complete the overview interview by asking about the purpose, or objective, of the program. . .

What do you want to say, to whom, *for what purpose*?

The answer to this final part of the core question forms the foundation for delineating program objectives. Remember, informational and training audiovisual programs are generated by clients who expect the medium to work for them. The writer's work is ultimately measured by the success of the finished program in fulfilling the client's purpose and meeting stated objectives.

In general, the most common objectives for audiovisual presentations are to inform, to instruct, to demonstrate, to motivate. Frequently, an audiovisual communication involves multiple objectives. As with the content and the audience, the writer's task in research is to arrive at a specific understanding and agreement with the client on objectives. It starts with an overview. . .

> ". . .the construction business is subject to cyclical ups and downs. When the economy is strong, entrepreneurial developers are very active. But in a soft economy, they tend to pull back. Our goal is *to sell ourselves to corporate buyers of construction management services* to help offset the cyclical nature of the construction business. Corporate building decisions are not so vulnerable to economic cycles."

With this overview of the program's content, audience and objectives, the writer is ready to delve into specifics.

Establishing a Research Agenda

The research agenda is a list of the people the writer must interview, what the writer should observe firsthand, and written documents that will serve as reference material. A research agenda may include any or all of the components shown in Figure 3.1. We'll explore these one at a time.

CONTENT RESEARCH

Use of Interviews

Typically, interviews are conducted with content experts—individuals possessing special knowledge and insight into the "what" of a communication. Often, more

Figure 3.1: Elements of the Research Agenda

Content research— Interviews
                         Observations
                         Readings
                         Questionnaires/Surveys

Audience research— Interviews
                         Observations
                         Readings
                         Questionnaires/Surveys

Verfication of
objectives and
communication
environment—Ongoing throughout the research stage.

Definitions

Interviews—a list of the content experts or members of the target audience you must talk with to gain their knowledge or insights on the project.

Observations—those physical locations or processes you must see to gain knowledge of the visual possibilities inherent in the content.

Readings—those sources, often primary ones, that you need as reference material.

Questionnaires/Surveys—formal documents the writer prepares to elicit hard data from those involved in the project.

than one expert will be involved in providing input, and sometimes the client also serves as a subject matter expert. Whenever possible, interview those who can provide overview material first. That way, you'll develop the proper perspective for interviews with those specialists who provide details on only a single aspect of the subject. The research agenda in Figure 3.2 refers to a sales and marketing project for a major construction management firm. Notice how the writer seeks specific points of view from each interview subject.

There are several things to note about this research agenda. First, it's clear that this is the writer's initial research agenda following an overview interview with one of the principals in the construction management firm. The research agenda identifies several additional people to interview—some in person, some by telephone.

Figure 3.2: Sample

RESEARCH AGENDA

CLIENT: GOLDIN/LEWIS, INC.
PROJECT: Sales and Marketing Presentation

Personal Interviews:

Arthur Lewis	Since we have spoken previously with Roger Goldin, we'd like to meet first with Arthur, then the "supporting cast" and return to Roger for a final interview at the end.
Gene McDowell (outside legal counsel)	Since McDowell has been the firm's attorney from the beginning, he is in a unique position to comment on the firm's growth and accomplishments.
John Miller and/or Bill Robertson	Envision conducting this interview at a construction site to begin exploring visual potential and production logistics for location shooting.
Hayward Simpson (PR firm)	Given the public relations applications for the completed film, it may prove beneficial to establish a personal working relationship with Simpson.

Telephone Interviews:

William Link (architect)	Since the Plaza Building is likely to be featured in the presentation, Link might be a good architect to start with. (Should someone from Goldin/Lewis make an initial contact so our call will be expected?)
Plaza Project contact	You suggested we speak with clients. Who on the Plaza project should we consider the prime contact?
Other architects?	Without going into "overkill" at this stage, what other architects would you suggest we talk with?
Any additional clients or sub-contractors?	

Figure 3.2: Sample (Cont.)

SITE SURVEYS

Construction sites and buildings	Obviously, past accomplishments, current construction and drawing board projects are critical to the film. Initial thought should be given to which are featured. These probably should be special cases, extraordinary logistical problems, etc. What do you think is most representative of the special construction management expertise you offer clients?
Monday morning staff meeting and office tour	As Roger Goldin suggested, sitting in on a Monday morning staff meeting should provide insight into the operational side of the business, management style and what's "on the plate."

QUESTIONNAIRE

We're preparing a brief questionnaire which we'd like Roger Goldin and Arthur Lewis to complete independently. We may also ask Gene McDowell and Hayward Simpson to give use some input via the questionnaire as well.

Note that the right hand column comments on how each person will contribute to the overall perspective. The writer's research task is like piecing together a mosaic in which the complete understanding of the whole comes from investigation of individual pieces.

Notice, too, that the research agenda includes sites and locations to be visited primarily for *observation*.

Given the complexity of this research assignment—documenting a construction management firm's projects over several years and identifying the organizational and construction management techniques which distinguish the firm from its competitors—the research agenda is likely to evolve as research progresses. An interview with one individual may lead the writer to others who should also be interviewed.

Interviewing Skills

Successful interviewing involves mental preparation, concentration, listening skills and an ability to probe with follow-up questions. In preparing interview questions, try to take the audience's point of view—devil's advocate questioning can be a valuable interview technique:

What makes Goldin/Lewis better than older, more established and well-known construction management companies?

How have you maintained control during this period of rapid growth from a small office to an organization of hundreds in many different cities?

Questions like these are also open-ended, beginning with words like *how, what* or *why.* Because they require explanations, not a simple yes or no, open-ended questions are ideal for getting interview subjects talking freely and in detail.

Good interviewers are good listeners. While you will prepare a list of questions in advance, interviews invariably take on a life of their own. The ability to keep probing for complete answers or to pursue a totally unexpected line of questioning will help you get what you need from content sources.

Some interviewers take notes, others prefer audiocassette recordings. I lean toward taking notes even while recording; you never know when gremlins may invade the tape recorder. Further, if you've got only an audio recording, chances are you will have to play back the entire interview again in order to take notes. So why not work productively and listen critically just once?

Remember that you are serving as a surrogate researcher for the audience. In this vein, never feel inhibited about asking the content expert to clarify a fuzzy point. If *you* don't fully understand the subject, how can you explain it to the audience? Often, the audience would want to ask the identical question. Pursuing content from the audience's point of view is the only way to write convincingly and to make intelligent, informed recommendations about program format, structure and style.

Observations

The eye is a vital research tool of the audiovisual writer, since, eventually, you'll organize content for the eye of the audience. While there are, of course, certain abstract or conceptual topics (such as financial presentations, mathematical concepts, etc.) that require the writer to devise an entire visual framework from the mind, more frequently, you need to consider the various visual sources you must *see* to do an adequate research job. In addition to field trips, the writer should not overlook existing artwork, graphics, photographs, slides, film footage or other visuals that relate to the subject. Such materials may not be suitable for integrating into the production, but find out what does exist. Consider those materials as a way of developing your own visual fluency in the topic.

Sometimes the subject matter demands personal observation, as with the Goldin/Lewis marketing program. Writing about the firm's construction expertise

Figure 3.3: Direct Observation

Often you have to go and see your subject with your
own eyes. Photo by James G. Libby, for *The Lehrer-
McGovern Experience.* Used with permission.

takes first-hand knowledge of projects. The research agenda for Goldin/Lewis
eventually took the writer to a variety of construction sites.

Likewise, if you're writing about a manufacturing process, a new surgical technique or a new product, it's imperative to gain personal, visual knowledge of what
is involved. What does the manufacturing process look like? What's involved in the
new surgical technique? How does the new product work?

In doing this visual research, focus on the physical characteristics of the process
or machinery and how well such visual elements can be translated to the screen.
Learn to look for what is *in*visible as well as visible. If key elements of a manufacturing process are hidden from view, then you might consider animation as a means of
visualizing the process. On the other hand, if you're looking at a manufacturing

process in which the finished product is created in clearly visible stages, then watch the process with an eye toward location shooting.

Another important consideration in observation research is the correlation between real time and screen time. Real-time events often need to be condensed and compressed through editing to arrive at pacing suitable for a viewing experience. A laboratory experiment, for example, may take hours, even days, to accomplish in real time. In researching such a process the writer should focus on those discrete steps that are essential to the communication and fashion an explanation appropriate for screen time.

In some instances, local color may be an important visual element of the communication. If your subject is an orientation to a college campus, walk the campus with an eye toward potential visual input which will help convey the character of the institution.

Bear in mind that interviewing generally accompanies this observation. Be prepared to ask questions of those who live or work in the environment.

Sometimes it's necessary for you to go through what your audience is ultimately expected to experience. In preparing to write a video training package to teach job hunting skills to people on welfare, I began by sitting through a week-long class, learning the same skills from an experienced instructor. My association with the participants during breaks provided valuable insight into the nature of the audience.

A camera can prove invaluable in recording visual sources for your own reference and for pre-production planning sessions with the director. Document your observations with snapshots or instant photographs.

Readings

Your research agenda should include a list of written sources that will serve as reference material. In gathering this material, most writers prefer too much rather than too little. These references can include published documents such as annual reports, product literature, press releases, promotional copy, training manuals, technical bulletins or benefits booklets. Often, however, the most useful written sources are more informal documents: research reports, internal memos, planning and implementation schedules, field test reports, or marketing intelligence. Experience will develop the sense of inquiry needed to uncover these valuable references. Occasionally, the client or content expert plans ahead and has several pertinent documents ready and waiting for the writer. If not, ask for both formal and informal source material.

Rapport and trust must be established with the client. Sometimes you will need proprietary, confidential or otherwise sensitive information as background for understanding your assignment. When sensitive subject matter is involved, business ethics require writers to honor client requests for confidentiality.

Finally, don't overlook the library as a research source. If you're writing on a general or extremely topical subject, the library is a good place to bone up, particularly for initial interviews. I do a lot of pharmaceutical product presentations and always check out library books written for patients suffering from the disease or condition the client's drug is intended to treat.

Additionally, the audiovisual writer can often use special business or medical libraries. Corporate headquarters sometimes contain libraries or information centers with a wealth of material pertinent to their business. Don't be shy about asking librarians for help—that's their job. Trade associations generally produce reams of material and publish periodicals and books.

Questionnaires and Surveys

Questionnaires and surveys can elicit information in a more objective way than informal interviews. Not every subject will lend itself to this formal technique, but the writer should always be on the lookout for occasions when a well-designed survey will yield useful information.

In the Goldin/Lewis project, scores of people inside and outside the firm were interviewed in an attempt to identify the characteristics which made their organization stand out from the competition. We wanted to verify our hunches and also make certain we were developing a presentation for the intended audience: the *corporate* buyer of construction services. As a final step in the research process, we asked Messrs. Goldin and Lewis to complete the questionnaire in Figure 3.4.

The form continued by listing a variety of projects which might be potential subject matter for the film. Although more extensive than one would typically develop, the questionnaire proved to be a valuable tool to focus research results. In an eight–to–ten minute film or video presentation it's important to make every second count.

AUDIENCE RESEARCH

In audience research, a staff writer holds a decided edge over the freelance writer. In any environment, the staff person has greater opportunity for daily contact with the people who constitute various segments of the organizational population.

Personal knowledge of the audience is most critical when a communication is likely to meet resistance. One research objective, then, should be to determine the daily dynamics of the communication environment. When you're dealing with a negative communication environment, or when the objective of the communication involves motivation or persuasion, then firsthand knowledge of the audience, their opinions and their attitudes is extremely valuable. And because an approach that generates enthusiasm in one organization could sound paternalistic in another, the

Figure 3.4: Goldin/Lewis Questionnaire

---

1. Rank the following attributes (from "1" to "10") in order of importance to most *corporate* buyers of construction services.
   (1 = Most Important; 10 = Least Important.)

   _____ Reputation for quality
   _____ Reputation for on-time completion
   _____ Reputation for sub-contractor bidding, negotiations, agreements and cost control
   _____ On-site construction supervision expertise
   _____ Capability to provide both construction and interior finishing
   _____ Top management involvement
   _____ Organizational size and corporate resources
   _____ Experience of project managers and middle management
   _____ Creativity and problem solving
   _____ Aggressiveness, dedication & commitment
   _____ Other [Specify: _____]

2. Rank the same attributes in order of importance to most building *owner/developer buyers* of construction services.

   _____ Reputation for quality
   _____ Reputation for on-time completion
   _____ Reputation for sub-contractor bidding, negotiations, agreements and cost control
   _____ On-site construction supervision expertise
   _____ Capability to provide both construction and interior finishing
   _____ Top management involvement
   _____ Organizational size and corporate resources
   _____ Experience of project managers and middle management
   _____ Creativity and problem solving
   _____ Aggressiveness, dedication & commitment
   _____ Other [Specify: _____]

3. With the objectives of your corporate image presentation in mind, evaluate the following potential messages. Select *five* you think are most important and rank them "1" through "5" with "1" being most important:

   _____ "Goldin/Lewis has the construction management experience to solve any complex construction challenge."

Figure 3.4: Goldin/Lewis Questionnaire (Cont.)

_____ "Goldin/Lewis' top management is personally involved in every project."

_____ "The Goldin/Lewis organization consists of a core of highly motivated team members who have direct access to top management."

_____ "Goldin/Lewis people take pride in solving unique construction problems and working on buildings that make significant architectural statements."

_____ "Goldin/Lewis people take pride in developing creative solutions to the unique construction problems presented by each client's needs."

_____ "Goldin/Lewis fosters a productive, responsive Owner/Architect/Construction Management team relationship."

_____ "Although Goldin/Lewis is a young organization, the combined construction experience of principals and key project managers equals decades of practical experience in every phase of the business."

_____ "Goldin/Lewis is expanding its organizational base through a network of local construction management offices."

_____ "Goldin/Lewis is involved in significant European construction projects."

_____ "Goldin/Lewis was formed with the sole intent of managing major construction projects."

_____ "Although Goldin/Lewis' growth has been spectacular since its formation, growth has always been carefully controlled, responding to client needs for expertise, service and individual attention."

_____ "Although many projects pose special challenges, the *process* of construction management involves the application of analytical, almost scientific, problem-solving techniques. The same thought process is brought to bear on every project."

_____ Other: _____

4. Consider the following list of projects in terms of their significance in the overall presentation.

    759 Second Avenue:
    _____ Of major importance; must be included
    _____ Important
    _____ Of some importance
    _____ Not important

    If you check "Of major importance" or "Important," describe the one idea or impression the audience should receive from our description of the project:

    _____
    _____
    _____
    _____

Figure 3.4: Goldin/Lewis Questionnaire (Cont.)

Plaza Center, Philadelphia

_____ Of major importance; must be included

_____ Important

_____ Of some importance

_____ Not important

If you check "Of major importance" or "Important," describe the one idea or impression the audience should receive from our description of the project:

_____

_____

Central Bank Plaza

_____ Of major importance; must be included

_____ Important

_____ Of some importance

_____ Not important

If you check "Of major importance" or "Important," describe the one idea or impression the audience should receive from our description of the project:

_____

_____

_____

tone of the communication and your motivational appeal becomes increasingly important.

Interviewing representative audience members is one way to develop the psychological insight necessary to present content effectively. Go about the selection process in the same manner as for content interviews. Devise a research agenda indicating whom you should talk to and what unique perspective they bring to the subject. Be sure to set the proper tone for audience interviews at the outset. If you're interviewing hourly employees, for instance, bear in mind they will perceive you as a management representative. You must gain their trust and establish rapport in order to generate anything more than the most superficial responses.

For some topics, observation of the audience may be more relevant than interviewing. If the subject involves training in the operation of specific equipment, observe an operator in action and ask questions as appropriate. Also, don't abandon the devil's advocate line of questioning. Seek honesty and spontaneity in these sessions. When the subject is sensitive, abandon note taking or audio recording. You're not after content in these discussions; probe feelings, attitudes and individual perceptions. Avoid the tendency to lead the subject. A lengthy pause will often get a better response than a complex follow-up question.

Surveys or questionnaires can also be designed to go to the target audience for a program and can be a productive way to get the audience's predisposition toward the subject matter. Don't overlook the possibility of existing surveys which can augment your research. In new product development, focus groups are often employed to react to the product's concept, features and benefits. Get a copy of the final results. Many new employee benefits programs are preceded by extensive research to determine the employee's perceptions of the company and its compensation policies. That's great background for understanding the employee audience.

WHEN IS RESEARCH OVER?

In researching content and audience, keep the client's overall objective in mind. As you develop greater knowledge of the subject and the communication task, continue to analyze whether you have sufficient data to meet the client's needs. If not, either more research is required or the objective should be reassessed.

How do you know when research is over? There are several signs. First, you begin to hear the same answers over and over. When you can predict standard answers to your research questions, you've likely begun to understand the subject as thoroughly as the content experts. Another sign is when you run out of questions. During the initial phase of interviewing, answers to each question are likely to suggest new questions. When you've gone down this path to its logical conclusion, you've exhausted your questioning possibilities. Of course, if you work from a structured research agenda, you'll know research is over when you complete all the items on the research agenda—another reason to adopt the research agenda.

In many instances, you'll know research is over simply because you run out of time. William Goldman talks about the research he did for the motion picture *Butch Cassidy and the Sundance Kid*:

> "Eventually, I'd done all the research I could bear. I hoped I had a story that would prove coherent, so I sat down and wrote the first draft in 1966.
>
> "It took four weeks.
>
> "When someone asks how long it takes to write a screenplay, I'm never sure what to answer. Because I don't think it took four weeks to do *Butch*. For me, eight years is closer to the truth."[3]

Admittedly, it's rare that an informational scriptwriter would be allowed the luxury of eight years to complete the research task. Often, eight days seems like a luxury. The point is, your research should ultimately allow you to assimilate the subject matter—which is why Goldman could produce his first-draft screenplay so rapidly.

If you feel confident that you have the necessary data to achieve the client's objective with the target audience, it's a good indication your research job is complete. When you begin to hear and read the same points repeated with little new information added, you can be confident that the research effort has been thorough and comprehensive.

A Parting Shot

At seminars I teach on scriptwriting someone invariably asks: "What do you do when you come across a boring subject?" I always get on my soap box with this retort: "There's no such thing as a boring subject—there's only boring writing."

Your job as writer is to discover ways of making the subject come to life for the viewer. If you're bored by the subject, how can you possibly hope to make it interesting to others? The writer's task, as Rachel Carson advised, is "to come to know his subject intimately, to understand its every aspect, to let it fill his mind. Then at some turning point the subject takes command and the true act of creation begins. . ."[4] To achieve that degree of intimacy with the subject matter you have to approach the topic with enthusiasm and excitement over the task at hand. Good writing springs from sound research.

FOOTNOTES

1. Sheila Davis, *The Craft of Lyric Writing* (Cincinnati: Writer's Digest Books, 1985), p. 29.
2. Paul Brooks, *Rachel Carson at Work—The House of Life* (Boston: G. K. Hall & Company, 1985), pp. 1, 2.
3. William Goldman, *Adventures in the Screen Trade* (New York, New York: Warner Books, Inc., 1983), pp. 123-124.
4. Paul Brooks, *op. cit.*

Organizing Information: Translating Research into an Action Plan

4

The documents the media writer generates communicate the writer's solutions to the communication/training problems inherent in the project at key stages of its evolution. Now it's time to generate the first written products which result from the initial round of research and assimilation. These written products—not yet scripts—are ways of communicating the results of your research to others involved in the project—the client, producer, director, multi-image designer, interactive videodisc programmer, etc.

These documents go by many names: proposal, recommendations, research report or action plan. We'll use the term "action plan." Whatever you call it, the Assimilation phase of the scriptwriting process should always address these four items:

- Audience profile
- Objectives
- Content outline
- Treatment

By organizing research results into a format that sets down parameters for the project, you discover exactly where you're headed and how you plan to get there. Just as the shooting script functions as a blueprint for the production crew, the action plan serves as a blueprint for the media writer. It's easier, faster and far more efficient to generate a first draft shooting script working from a content outline and a screen treatment than from a mound of disjointed research findings, random notes and tape-recorded interviews.

More important, the action plan provides a superb checkpoint of communication between writer and client. It's an ideal method of feeding back research results and verifying your understanding of the program's audience, objectives and content. It's a way of saying to the client: "This is what I heard you and others involved in the project say you wanted. Did I hear you correctly?" Usually, the client finds areas requiring a slightly different focus—an oversight in content, a shift of emphasis here and there.

The action plan also provides an ideal format for introducing creative ideas in the form of a screen treatment. Once agreed to by the client, the action plan forms a contract between writer and client—a go-ahead to proceed as planned. Finally, the action plan allows the producer and director to respond to the writer's initial ideas. From the content outline and treatment, the director can begin to formulate the program as a production. The producer should be able to budget and schedule the production. If you're a writer working for a production company or agency, these initial documents may constitute a bid package for a client.

In short, the action plan lets client, producer, director and others involved in the production know just what the writer has learned from research and where the project is headed substantively and creatively.

This chapter focuses on writing the first three elements of the action plan: audience profile, objectives and content outline. Only after clarifying these aspects of the project should the writer pursue the conceptual and visual thinking needed to create a screen treatment. That gets into the next phase of the creative writing process: Rehearsal. First, your creative concepts must be grounded in a thorough appreciation of audience, objectives and content.

THE AUDIENCE PROFILE

Writing an insightful description of the target audience often gets overlooked in the crush of a project. After all, you may reason, doesn't the client know the target audience better than the writer? Why expend effort on feeding back what the client already knows?

Clients often want to tell the audience what *they* think the audience needs to hear. In reality, the audience's information/training needs may be quite different from the client's perception of reality. Additionally, it's important that you verify your perception of the target audience's attitude toward the viewing experience and make certain you and others on the project are in synch. An analytical audience profile is your way of letting the client know you understand and appreciate the dynamics of the communication environment.

For any communication, your audience brings a specific "mindset" or predisposition toward the subject matter. In most cases, the audience will enter the viewing experience with either a positive, negative or neutral attitude. The writer's handling of the content will vary based on the audience's initial mindset. You'd write quite differently for an audience that views the message as good news compared to one that is likely to be negative toward the communication.

Take the subject of a new product introduction aimed at an audience of manufacturer's sales representatives. On the surface, this appears to be a positive communication environment. Sales people love to sell and the challenge of a new product usually gets their juices flowing. But consider this scenario: these sales representatives consist of a combined sales force brought about by the merger of two companies. After the merger, the combined sales staff was trimmed back to a leaner, meaner group. One of the companies has recently had a rash of new products that have gone "belly-up" in the marketplace. To top it all off, there's a new vice president for sales who has been brought in from the outside. Suddenly, our seemingly positive message is frought with negative overtones.

Internal and External Audiences

In the broadest terms, your audiovisual presentation will be aimed at either an internal or external audience. Internal audiences consist of employees, staff members of hospitals or institutions, or members of professional groups. The program to introduce a new product to a national sales force, for example, typifies the internal communication. The writer's point of view focuses on what the sales force needs to know to sell the product successfully.

Introducing the same new product to potential buyers, however, becomes an external communication requiring a different perspective. External audiences are public audiences—customers, patients, government officials, financial analysts. The writer not only conveys information but portrays an image of the organization to outsiders. That image should be consistent with an organization's overall public relations posture.

Knowing whether you're writing for an internal or external audience provides an initial handle on the perspective to take in shaping the material. Then come more subtle audience considerations.

The Target Audience

For any project, the target audience may not always be a homogeneous group. A company's sales force could consist of grizzled veterans alongside eager recruits. Each may respond to identical content in different ways. A single A/V presentation cannot be all things to all people.

An analytical audience profile contains more than a two-word description, such as "sales representatives," "new employees," "security analysts" or "physicians and nurses." Those are occupational classifications, not descriptions of clearly perceived target audiences characterized by common attributes and shared motivations. Strive instead for a profile of the audience that lets the client know you appreciate the nuances of its makeup.

Take a look at this audience profile for an internal project, a video announce-ment for a new and massive national television advertising campaign to beef up sales for an over-the-counter multiple vitamin product:

> The audience is the pharmaceutical sales force. During the past 18 months, the home office has placed a priority on *physician* details. In this video program, we will be asking the sales force to build inventories at the *retail* pharmacy level. Unless properly positioned, the sales force could perceive this as a case of conflicting priorities and lack of coordinated direction.

Here, the writer pinpoints a characteristic of the audience that directly affects their attitude: the company's recent emphasis on physician details (pharmaceutical jargon for sales calls) as opposed to selling to the retail pharmacy. This descriptive audience profile tells the client that the writer appreciates the audience's unique point of view.

Media presentations are directed toward audiences who share a particular in-terest in the subject matter. In describing the target, then, seek to delineate their point of view toward the subject matter. Here is the audience profile for the large construction management firm described in Chapter 3:

> The film's content will be skewed toward the corporate/institu-tional buyer of construction management services. In general, the corporate/institutional buyer tends to be more conservative than the entrepreneurial developer/owner. The presentation, in addition to describing Goldin/Lewis capabilities and accomplish-ments, is intended to project an image that gives corporate pros-pects a sense of comfort with the organization.

Here the writer reports his or her research findings of the viewing audience's point of view toward the subject matter. This viewpoint will definitely be reflected in selection of key content points, motivational appeals and narrative style and tone.

Take a look at this next profile of an external, public audience. The client manufactures a line of high-quality home video recording tape stock and faces a highly competitive market environment.

> This videocassette presentation will be suitable for use as a retail point-of-purchase demonstration tape with the *consumer* of blank video tape stock. As a rule, consumers of blank stock tend to purchase primarily on price. They neither perceive nor understand that the quality of blank tape can have an effect on

performance—particularly in critical applications such as slow record and playback functions or during freeze framing and rapid search modes.

This audience, however, is composed of people who have made sizable investments in home video gear and may be motivated to purchase a higher-priced quality tape stock if benefits in terms of picture quality and/or machine wear can be demonstrated.

The analytical profile is far more functional to client and writer than a terse: "The audience is the consumer of blank tape stock." Through this profile, the writer tells the client he or she has a firm grip on the psychological makeup of the audience. To make an impact, the video demonstration will have to show the benefits of a high-grade, quality blank stock. Further, the writer suggests the key to motivating this audience through appeals to their investment in videocassette hardware.

In all three examples, the client is given sufficient feedback to agree with the writer's perceptions or to correct and clarify that perception. The writer may simply be parroting back what the client expressed during research interviews, but now there is a basis for consensus—on paper.

The Viewing Situation

In the above audience profile, the writer included information about the viewing situation. The program will be viewed at point-of-purchase in all the hubbub of a retail store. Playback environments and the resulting psychological effects on the audience often influence writing decisions. There's a world of difference between a message that will be seen in the structured viewing environment of a corporate conference room and one that is caught by a random, casual public audience in a retail store. The psychological world of viewers who are patients in a hospital is miles apart from that of a national sales meeting at a posh resort. Whenever the physical viewing situation has an impact on audience psychology and response, consider a reference to that viewing situation in the audience profile.

Multiple Audiences

Frequently, clients expect an audiovisual presentation to do double duty. A single program cannot, however, be all things to all viewers. So the writer should carefully consider how secondary audiences will relate to the program. For instance, suppose our client who manufactures blank tape stock has a secondary audience in mind for the presentation: the retail floor salesperson. Here's how that secondary audience might be described:

The retail salesperson, unfortunately, is ill-equipped to explain the differences in quality which characterize a higher-priced blank tape stock. Through this presentation, the retail salesperson will receive useful product knowledge on the interface between home video recorder and blank stock through exposure to the presentation to consumers.

The writer has clearly positioned the primary and secondary audiences as separate and distinct groups. The program will speak directly to the consumer, the primary audience. The secondary audience, the retail floor salesperson, will absorb the content, viewing the program "over-the-shoulder" of the target audience. At no time, however, will content be presented directly to the retail salesperson. In this way, the client is forewarned there are limitations in what can be communicated to the secondary audience. You wouldn't, for example, employ a theme such as "Remember, your profit margin is higher when you sell higher-priced tape" in a presentation for consumers!

The following audience profile solves the problem of multiple audiences another way.

There are two distinct audiences. . .

1) The Ohaus dealer representatives and inside sales personnel.
2) Prospective buyers of the GT Series precision scales.

To develop a shooting script that appeals to the needs and interests of these two distinct audiences, we will want to talk with dealers and satisfied customers as part of our research. This will provide the insights necessary to structure the message to hit on the "hot buttons" of target audience members.

We also recognize a familiar problem in your desire to address two quite distinct audiences. You will not necessarily want to say something the same way to the audience of dealer representatives as you would to your prospects. Our recommendation is that we develop two versions of the script—using the same basic on-camera action but with narration targeted to each of the two audiences. You will get two versions of the same program, but economies of scale in production planning will minimize the additional expense.

Sometimes, scripting two versions with an eye toward using common scenes or visuals allows the client to accommodate multiple needs without the expense of two entirely separate programs. The more general the content and objectives, the more potential there will be for developing "spin-off" uses for a single program.

We saw that the target audience for the construction management firm's film was the corporate/institutional buyer of construction management services. Since the program was designed to showcase the firm's construction management expertise in general, spin-off applications for the finished program came readily to mind. For example:

Spin-off Audiences

The message on corporate philosophy, style and accomplishments will be equally meaningful to the following secondary audiences:

Owners/developers
Financial analysts
Architects/contractors and other industry "insiders"
Potential new hires

Whenever there is more than one target audience, analyze whether their points of view are sufficiently diverse to affect what content can or cannot be presented to both. Then you can either identify a primary audience (the single group the content will be pitched at) and describe how the secondary audience will relate to the content or suggest different treatments of the same content to accommodate the needs of distinct viewing audiences.

OBJECTIVES: STATEMENTS OF EXPECTATION

Stating program objectives is about as important a piece of writing as you can do on a project. Objectives express what everyone with a stake in the project expects the final product to accomplish. Presentations that satisfy stated objectives fulfill the client's expectations for the project. No matter how spectacular or innovative the production, if a program fails to deliver on objectives, it must be deemed a "turkey."

When the client approves a writer's list of objectives, two things occur simultaneously. Most important, goals and expectations are established. At the same time, the client limits the scope and range of the work. In this light, objectives are as significant for what they do not state as for what they do.

Think about the typical preview screening of a finished videotape, film or slide show. Invariably, the client invites a number of cronies to sit in. Typically, these newcomers had no involvement in the creative process. At the conclusion of the screening, there's a pregnant pause. Eventually, the client says simply, "That was very good. I think that's just what we need." The ice is broken. More insightful comments surface.

Inevitably, one crony ventures this opinion: "You know, I thought it was fine as far as it went. But you really didn't get into the responsibility of plant engineering to provide input to R&D engineering. How come?"

For the writer's sake, the answer to that question had best be: "We considered that point early on but determined that wasn't one of our objectives because. . . ."

Once objectives are agreed to on paper, they remain operative throughout the production. The writer will script to them, and the producer and director should create the viewing experience with identical objectives in mind. Since objectives define expectations for the program, they form the foundation for the client's ultimate evaluation of the finished product.

For these reasons, the media writer must develop skill at expressing the intent of each communication through a precise, realistic description of what the program can achieve. If objectives raise unrealistic expectations, it always comes back to haunt the writer. Let's look at what is involved in formulating and writing objectives.

Simply put, an objective describes a change that a presentation is intended to effect in its viewers. Change can be as internal and subtle as a heightened awareness resulting from exposure to new information. Or, the change may go further, seeking to influence the audience's attitudes, beliefs or level of motivation. Most dramatically, a program may actually attempt to change overt, observable actions—people's behavior. These three generic objectives can be called informational, motivational and behavioral. If you plot the audience involvement necessary to attain these three generic types, as in Figure 4.1, there is a definite movement from a rather passive, uninvolved audience to one which must become actively involved, learning new skills or concepts. And, as we'll discuss, the degree of audience involvement directly affects the ease with which the results of a program can be measured.

Informational Objectives

Programs designed to meet informational objectives ask the audience only to view the presentation. The audience is not expected to *act* on information presented. The corporate television news program typifies the communication with informational objectives. Following are two examples of written informational objectives:

> To demonstrate that Acme Industries is a key supplier of
> material handling equipment, capable of delivering a wide range
> of products and systems to solve diverse industrial problems.

Figure 4.1: Audience Involvement Needed to Attain Objectives

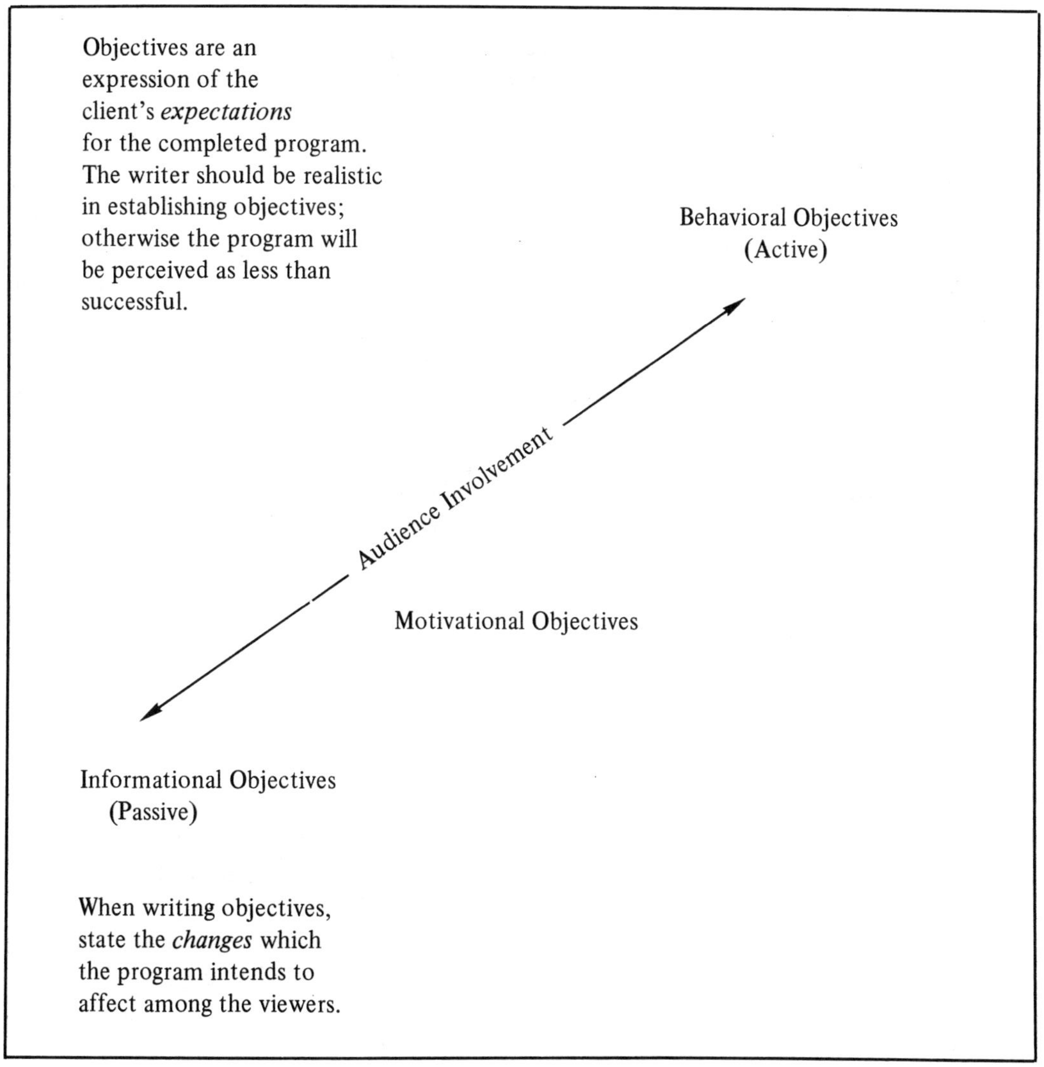

Objectives are an
expression of the
client's *expectations*
for the completed program.
The writer should be realistic
in establishing objectives;
otherwise the program will
be perceived as less than
successful.

Behavioral Objectives
(Active)

Audience Involvement

Motivational Objectives

Informational Objectives
(Passive)

When writing objectives,
state the *changes* which
the program intends to
affect among the viewers.

To show how the test kitchens are organized to support divisional
development and marketing activities for new food products.

These objectives simply imply that information will be presented to the viewer.
How the audience is expected to respond or act upon this new information is un-
specified.

Behavioral Objectives

On the opposite end of the continuum, however, is programming with behavioral objectives. In these instances, the audience's post-viewing actions are spelled out quite specifically. Since behavioral changes are observable, they can be measured through pre- and post-test devices. Changing behavior generally requires training. In fact, the behavioral objective is synonymous with the instructional objective. Media presentations intended to teach or instruct should be described with behavioral objectives. As Robert Mager points out in *Preparing Instructional Objectives,* in order to instruct successfully, the program designer must state the terminal behavior expected of the learner: ". . .an objective always states a performance, describing what the learner will be DOING when demonstrating mastery of the objective."[1]

Here are examples of behavioral objectives for two video-based training programs:

> Upon completion of the program, the trainee will be able to type, store, recall and modify correspondence, reports, forms and other materials, using features of the WP201 Word Processing program.

> At the conclusion of this instructional unit, participants will be able to identify and classify epileptic seizures, using the International Classification System based on patient observation and analysis of brain wave recordings.

Different as the two program topics and objectives are, each contains the phrase "will be able to." By stating what the viewer or learner will be able to do after completing the program, you identify the expected terminal behavior.

Of course, the behavioral objectives above are overall course objectives. To reach the overall objective, the student must master a multitude of limited and specific sub-objectives that function as necessary component building blocks. Here are several sub-objectives taken from a video-based training program for gas turbine operators and maintenance personnel:

> To achieve the overall objective, content and exercises will be structured so that participants *will be able to*:

> Identify basic turbine components: gas generator, HP compressor drive unit, LP turbine, load.

> Demonstrate an understanding of the use of control parameters to protect gas turbine parts.

Identify various control systems used to overcome compressor stall.

Select an appropriate course of action when high temperatures are present.

In all, there are 36 sub-objectives for this particular training module. Each is stated in behavioral terms and contributes to mastery of the overall course objective.

Behavioral or instructional objectives require the viewer to become sufficiently involved in the content of training programs to learn the desired behavior. Instructional programming, therefore, often uses interactive techniques, allowing the learner to stop the audiovisual presentation for "hands on" learning experiences with workbook exercises, simulations, role playing, quizzes and other activities.

The ultimate experience in this vein, of course, is interactive video. By combining television with the capabilities of the videodisc and computer-assisted instructional technology, a whole new world opens up to the instructional designer, as we see in Chapter 11. For now, the key point is that objectives for instructional programming must be stated in behavioral terms, describing *how* the learner will demonstrate mastery of the content.

Motivational Objectives

The motivational objective stands between the two extremes of informational and behavioral objectives. The terminal behavior for motivational objectives is less specific than for instructional objectives, yet a definite response to subject matter is sought. For instance, take a typical corporate video communication topic: the annual report to employees. When the company has a good year, the report may be purely informational, stressing positive developments in sales, operations and markets. In a year of poor performance, however, the emphasis may shift to more motivational objectives, such as:

To stress the need for budgetary restraint in all areas of operations.

To improve manufacturing productivity by reducing material waste and manufacturing defects.

To create a greater awareness of the role of interdepartmental communication in improving customer service.

Here the audience must be persuaded to adopt an attitude that in turn will lead to more specific behaviors as conditions dictate.

A common motivational objective can be found in communications to sales representatives. These can take the form of major multi-image national sales meetings or video communications on specific products or market opportunities. In either case, getting the sales force "pumped up" and enthusiastic about the sales opportunities ahead requires a strong motivational message. Here are two examples from the pharmaceutical industry:

> To motivate the district sales organizations to make a commitment to the detailing effort required to surpass competitive detailing activity.

> To motivate and mobilize the sales force to provide a winning product information sales effort. Reinforce the need for effective, professional detailing and a high degree of personal productivity throughout the sales force.

Such audiovisual presentations are intended to change the behavior of the viewing audience. However, unlike the instructional objective, there is no clearcut way of observing and measuring on-the-job performance. This makes the motivational program more difficult to conceive and execute than either the informational or training program. How does one measure subjective attitudes such as "greater awareness of the role of interdepartmental communication in improving customer services?" How does one know when a sales force is "motivated and mobilized?"

Motivational objectives often lack definitive criteria. How *much* budgetary restraint is needed, for instance? Or *how* can production workers reduce waste and manufacturing defects? These objectives are wide open to individual interpretation.

When the scriptwriter tackles a program with motivational objectives, good judgment is needed to ensure that the objectives are realistic. Management may expect too much from a single motivational communication. In setting objectives, the writer should clarify what the audiovisual presentation can and cannot accomplish. An audiovisual presentation may create awareness and raise issues in exploring the role of interdepartmental communication in improving customer service. But to generate an actual effect on customer service, management may need to streamline work flow procedures, improve productivity through a computerized order system, or tap employee creativity through quality circles. Raising unrealistic expectations for an audiovisual presentation is a disservice to all involved—the client, the production team, the medium itself.

Of course, media presentations are often asked to be motivational, because a well-designed presentation can communicate with an audience on an emotional as well as intellectual level. Even programs with informational or instructional objectives usually require certain emotional appeals. Often, you must motivate a viewing audience on the value of specific training in order to engage them in the subject matter. To hold an audience's attention during an informational program may require built-in emotional appeals.

Motivational objectives appeal to emotions. And emotional communication is a key strength of audiovisual media. The synergy between sight and sound unfolding in time can be used to create strong emotional appeals. Study the psychology of selling and you'll find it's commonly accepted that people buy on emotion, then justify their purchase with logic. Consider the role emotion plays in our daily lives.

Calculate the amount of discretionary income you spend on emotion. Each time you go to the movies, you're paying for an emotional experience. Each time you purchase records or tapes, you're buying one of the purest of all emotional experiences—music. Our purchases of novels and tickets to concerts, live theater and sports events are investments in our emotional lives.

Audiovisual writers can learn a lot from sales people. That's because we're essentially "selling" something with every script we write. To appeal to the emotional core of our audience, we must consider their response to the subject matter and script accordingly.

Entertainment Objectives

Because audiovisual media can move people and touch their hearts as well as inform their minds, we should not overlook the role of entertainment in developing presentations. Writers for the movies and commercial television have entertainment as their primary goal. Entertainment may not appear often on the list of objectives for business, medical or educational presentations, but the role of entertainment values in such programs has long been recognized by the top producers, directors and writers.

For starters, the argument is made that viewers on the job or in the classroom come to a media experience with thousands of hours of conditioning watching commercial television and seeing Hollywood movies. As viewers gain more control over their options through cable and VCR use, they become increasingly demanding of the fare they see in relation to work or study.

Second, the tools of entertainment and commercials have proven invaluable as learning aids through such programming as *Sesame Street*. In watching such a show, it's almost impossible to say where entertainment leaves off and instruction begins.

When striving to meet motivational objectives and move an audience to think or behave in a certain fashion, the emotional strength of a message is often carried largely through the entertainment values inherent in the chosen medium. Put another way, successful audiovisual programming makes interesting use of the chosen medium's strengths in dealing with the content at hand.

In summary, then, whatever the subject, most audiovisual projects revolve around the three generic types of objectives. Moving from informational to behavioral objectives requires greater audience involvement in program content. Consequently, it's easier to measure the results of programming with behavioral objectives than with motivational and informational programming. When defining program objectives, the writer must be aware of the category of generic objective involved.

All objectives direct effort toward an end result. Use of the word "to" is a convenient way to insure objectives are goal oriented. Read through the sample objectives in this chapter and note how the directive "to" functions in each. Finally, to achieve an overall program objective, several sub-objectives must be accomplished. It's not unusual for a single program to contain several informational, motivational and. behavioral objectives. After all, one must impart information to instruct; and one must often motivate a learner to become actively involved.

Whatever the writing assignment, take the time to state the program's objectives with clarity and precision. Remember, you're establishing expectations for the program. As Mager advises: "What we are searching for is that group of words or symbols that will communicate your intent exactly as YOU understand it."[2]

CRITICAL CONTENT FOCUSING

In his book, *Adventures in the Screen Trade,* William Goldman describes a discussion with investigative reporter Bob Woodward:

> "I fiddled with the rest of the narrative. . .then Woodward came to my office. I asked him to list the *crucial* events—not the most dramatic but the essentials—that enabled the story eventually to be told.

> "I think there were thirteen of them and he named them in order. I looked at what I'd written and saw that I'd included every one. So even if the screenplay stunk, at least the structure would be sound."[3]

The quote is instructive on several counts. First, it shows the screenwriter's keen awareness of the crucial essentials involved in telling his story. Woodward and Goldman can identify thirteen critical content points—elements which must be communicated in order to tell the story.

Second, it points up the importance of the relationship between content and structure in a work that many would consider primarily a dramatic piece with strong commercial entertainment values.

The audiovisual scriptwriter must also forge a strong identity between self and the crucial content of a communication. As Edel put it, we are "allowed the imagination of form, but not of fact." So what facts does the writer select to focus on at the conclusion of the research phase? If your research has been thorough, you probably have more facts at your disposal than you have screen time. So what guides you in deciding which facts are crucial to the telling of your story and which are extraneous?

The answer can be found by examining content in light of the program's objectives and the analytical audience profile. What does your audience absolutely need to know in order for the communication or learning experience to reach the objectives? Answering that question will aid in identifying the *critical* content points—the thirteen, or ten, or maybe even three points that are absolutely crucial to telling your story.

When you can identify these critical content points with the confidence of Woodward and Goldman, you are well on your way toward crafting a content outline—the third writing product which results from the Assimilation phase. The outline excerpt in Figure 4.2 presents content points for a video program on the importance of protecting proprietary information and building security. It is for an internal audience of employees and contractor personnel. The outline serves as another important checkpoint between writer and client. Look for clues to how the writer intends to treat this material as an audiovisual presentation.

If you failed to pick up on anything which characterizes this outline as specifically written for television, that's good. There is nothing that distinguishes a content outline for a videotape or multi-image presentation from an outline for print media. The function of the content outline is to focus attention solely on what the program is going to be about. It should intentionally avoid matters of style, format, creative strategy, and use of media techniques and effects.

Given identical audience descriptions, objectives and research findings, five different writers should arrive at quite similar content outlines. In treating the material for the screen, however, these five writers are likely to be totally different and distinctive in style, tone, and approach to the medium. One might employ humor, another, dramatization, still a third, an elaborate stage setting to present identical content.

That's why the content outline should be written *after* the writer has formulated the audience profile and the objectives and prior to writing a screen treatment. The audience profile and the statement of objectives form a matrix that helps the writer identify what content needs to be communicated to the audience in order to reach the stated objectives. In reviewing research findings, begin by relating the content

Figure 4.2: Excerpt: Key Content Points

Overview:

The video communication will focus on the role employees and contract suppliers should play in safeguarding intellectual products, protecting access to buildings and information, and security guidelines for visitors, resident visitors and resident contractors. The umbrella-like theme is that securing information and property is a matter of *common-sense* principles.

I.   Communicate basic principles involved in protection of proprietary information.

    A.   Definition of proprietary information.
    B.   The three levels of proprietary information:
       1.   proprietary
       2.   confidential
       3.   classified
    C.   How proprietary information is protected.
    D.   Employee/non-employee responsibilities for protecting proprietary information.

II. Inform employees about common-sense security procedures.

    A.   Need for procedures to admit visitors.
    B.   Need to safeguard identification cards.
    C.   Need to protect proprietary information, including computer software.

III. Case Study Facts relating to specific security breaches in the past and the resulting legal/marketing problems created. (Specifics to be determined.)

IV. Need for procedures to take equipment in and out of buildings.

    A.   Use of Personal Property Tag for bringing personal equipment in and removing the same equipment.
    B.   Process used to remove and return company property with a Property Removal Pass.

Figure 4.2: Excerpt: Key Content Points (Cont.)

V. The concept behind and need for common-sense computer security guidelines.

    A. For employees.
    B. For non-employees.

VI. General philosophies, summary and conclusion.

    A. Intent of company security policy and procedures is to make *intentional theft* more difficult.
    B. Employees need to follow common-sense security practices, but should not "cry wolf" at every opportunity.

to the audience and objectives. Try to focus on those points that are absolutely essential in communicating the intended message to the audience. Information, facts and data which help achieve an objective should be included in the content outline.

Use traditional formatting and organizational techniques to express what the program is all about. If the subject matter lends itself to a chronological ordering, use that sequence. If a topical or cause-and-effect structure makes sense, then go that route. This does not mean that the content will follow in identical order in the first draft script. That decision will be made in the Rehearsal phase of the script development process.

Often, the writer's perception of the communication climate has an impact on the relative emphasis given to the subject matter. For example, when research reveals morale is down, you are most likely facing a negative communication environment. In that event, your critical content focus for a new product introduction may need to be placed on topics such as techniques to maximize time and territory management, the competitive viability of the product, or the long-term potential of the product and its role in returning the company to a level of profitability that supports an expanded sales force.

In short, get the critical content points down on paper in a logical sequence. That way, client, writer and subject matter experts can focus attention strictly on content without becoming diverted on matters of form or style. With a content outline, missing points or extraneous material can be more easily identified. Shifts in emphasis on significant points can also be worked out. And it's all accomplished without the intrusion of creative concerns.

SUMMARY

Together, the three elements of the action plan—the analytical audience profile, the statement of objectives and the content outline—give the client a comprehensive report on your research findings. If there are problems or misconceptions they can be ironed out before the script is generated. And with these elements formulated, the writer is now ready to shift gears and move fully into the creative process. As William Goldman put it:

> "In any case, before you begin, you must have everything clear in your head and you must be comfortable with the story you're trying to tell. Once you start writing, go like hell—but don't fire 'till you're ready. . ."[4]

By generating the items of the action plan, everything should be clear in your head; you should be comfortable with the story you're trying to tell.

FOOTNOTES

1. Robert Mager, *Preparing Instructional Objectives,* 2d ed. (Belmont, CA: Pitman Learning, Inc., 1975), p. 48.
2. *Ibid.,* p. 19.
3. William Goldman, *Adventures in the Screen Trade* (New York, NY: Warner Books, Inc., 1983), pp. 235–236.
4. *Ibid.,* p. 124.

Step 2: Rehearsal

5 Idea Development

INTRODUCTION

In the Assimilation phase of the scriptwriting process, you functioned as an explorer, collecting raw material and sifting through it, seeking the critical content of your media presentation. Now comes the most creative phase—Rehearsal.

Rehearsal sounds like an odd activity for a writer—actors and musicians rehearse, writers put words on paper. But the creative process invariably involves an experimental stage—a time to play with unusual combinations, make serendipitous connections. It's like the painter who begins a massive work by making small, informal sketches. That's a form of rehearsal.

We mentally rehearse what we will say in the "big scenes" of our lives: how to ask the boss for a raise or explain to a spouse how the fender got bashed in. Why not also mentally rehearse the big scenes of the emerging script? The writer brainstorming with the program's director, willing for the moment to consider any option, is like an actor in the early stages of creating a character, trying out lines with various interpretations.

Rehearsal is also a time to set the subconscious mind to work on the material. Often, rehearsal means setting the research results aside and turning to other activities, giving the creative child residing in your subconscious time to toy with germinating ideas. Consider, for example, Mozart's approach to writing music. . .

Composing in Your Mind

It was natural for Mozart to "compose" when he was traveling in a carriage or strolling after a hearty meal. Psychologist Howard Gardner, in his book *Art, Mind & Brain,* interprets the meaning of Mozart's letter describing his composing methods. Mozart describes what happens inside his head. . .

> ". . .and the whole, though it be long, stands almost complete
> and finished in my mind, so that I can survey it like a fine

picture or a beautiful statue, at a glance. Nor do I hear in my
imagination the parts successively, but I hear them, as it were,
all at once."[1]

Gardner strives to answer the question: "How can one hear something, as it were, in
the mind's ear?"

The question is worth pondering by scriptwriters. Before setting down "a
chronological sequence of events" as words on a page, the scriptwriter must
mentally conjure up the sights and sounds that will appear on-screen. In this context,
the embryonic compositional processes of writing music and media scripts pose
similar problems.

Gardner draws an analogy between methods used to compose music and more
common activities we can all relate to: planning a dinner party or writing a letter of
recommendation. There are certain mental processes you go through prior to taking
physical action. The host or letter writer works from general "schemas—abstract
mental representations of what a party or a letter should be like. These schemas are
sufficiently general and abstract to apply to a variety of parties, a series of letters."[2]

In Mozart's day rules for composition were clearly spelled out, with definite
formulas for writing a symphony. Gardner suggests that when Mozart decided to
write a symphony, many important decisions had been made in advance. Mozart's
challenge was to invent promising themes for each movement: to "play" these
themes in his mind against the backdrop of the compositional form he knew and
then "to fashion those exciting departures and deviations that made each symphony
different from the others. . . ."[3]

In a similar vein, Gardner cites a conversation involving twentieth-century
American composer Walter Piston who reported to a friend a piece he'd been working on was almost completed:

> " 'Can I hear it then?' his friend asked. 'Oh, no,' Piston retorted,
> 'I haven't yet selected the notes.' "[4]

In Gardner's analysis, Mozart did not actually hear all the "notes" in a second
or two. Mozart meant that crucial decisions about where sections of a piece would
begin and end, where instruments would enter, when themes would recur, could all
be grasped at once.

Scriptwriters employ a similar process: creating the structure of a work in the
mind's eye, envisioning a beginning, middle and end and the principal media storytelling techniques while leaving detailed content to be filled in at the time of actual
composition.

The writer makes many choices, such as use of formats and placement of content from beginning to end, before embarking on a first draft. The writer must lock

into a narrative voice with a tone and style ideally suited to the material at hand. Decisions must be made over what visual materials to use—a studio set, location footage, computer graphics, special effects, chroma-key artwork, etc.

Such decisions should be made now—in the Rehearsal phase. Like Mozart prior to writing down a detailed musical score, the material and its treatment should be vivid in your mind. Then, you proceed to Drafting confident that details can be worked out.

Most of Your Time Is Spent Planning

Professional writer and teacher of writing Donald Murray once agreed to become a "laboratory rat" in a writing study conducted by a colleague. Over two-and-a-half months, Dr. Carol Berkenkotter studied Murray's writing methodology. Murray consented to tape record everything he did during that period and to save every note and draft. Then Dr. Berkenkotter studied the tapes and notes and interviewed Murray and observed him at work.

Murray cites the most important discovery: ". . .I spent three-fifths of my time, or more, collecting information and *planning* my writing. Most of my rewriting turned out to be, in fact, planning. On occasion, I spent 90% of my writing time planning."[5]

Murray sums up the payoff: "Inexperienced writers often write too soon. . . . Much of the bad writing we read from inexperienced writers is the direct result of writing before they are ready to write."

In my introductory scriptwriting workshop, I take writers through the scripwriting process from Assimilation to Editing. About three-fifths of our time is spent in Assimilation and Rehearsal. I warn participants they will begin to feel "stuck forever in the Rehearsal phase." That's because it is the most crucial period for the media writer.

Resist the urge to begin Drafting immediately following research. Much work remains to be done. The problems inherent in using the medium of film, television or multi-image to reach your objectives for the audience will be wrestled to the mat in Rehearsal.

The Creative Concept

The creative concept for any script represents the underlying rationale for the entire narrative and visual experience. It's akin to what Henry James called "the germ" for a story or novel.

To arrive at the concept for an audiovisual program, the writer must make decisions about style, format and structure, evolving a creative strategy for the work which unifies those elements. In this chapter, we'll examine those creative elements one at a time, placing them under the microscope for analysis. We will see how the creative concept shapes those elements into a unified, aesthetically pleasing whole.

STIMULATING A VISION WITH PROGRAM FORMATS

Sometimes the shape and form of a program literally spring fully developed into the writer's consciousness, as though the concept has been incubating in the subconscious through the entire research period. Very little Rehearsal time is required. But those creative concepts are usually a gift. Good concepts are usually hard to come by (for reasons we'll explore). More often, concepts evolve in a writer's mind through a combination of conscious effort and subconscious playfulness.

Despite the seemingly endless ways to treat a subject, when writing for audio-visual media there are only a handful of well-worn formats—generic methods of presenting material—used over and over to convey varying content. A format is simply a generic method of presenting information in an audiovisual medium and therefore is distinct from both content, style and structure. Content can be dealt with in any format the writer wishes, although generally some formats will be more suited to the content than others.

It's often a useful Rehearsal technique to visualize your material in the following five generic formats. Some will strike you as totally inappropriate and you can dismiss those formats for the particular content at hand. Whenever a format holds promise, focus on those content points that it seems to suit best. It's not unusual for a presentation to contain a carefully balanced mix of several program formats, each designed to carry a specific portion of the message.

The Talking Head

Imagine a speaker, put words in his or her mouth and you have a talking head. Over the years, the talking head format has taken considerable abuse from media professionals; some is deserved, some not.

On the negative side, the talking head makes minimal use of any audiovisual medium's strong suit—the capability to *show* while telling. As one corporate communicator put it, "Why not send me an audio tape and a photograph?" But think of a one-man show such as Bill Cosby's HBO Specials. That's nothing more than 90-minutes of a great talking head—but we don't find it visually or narratively boring. The talking head format is "talent" dependent.

Obviously, the talking head lives on because, in many communications, *who* delivers the content is as important as what is said. When the message comes from the chairman of the board, the chancellor of the university or the physician who pioneered a new surgical technique, what is said carries the added weight of authority and credibility.

Unfortunately, executives and experts called on to deliver talking head messages rarely have the aptitude for such work or the time and patience to prepare and rehearse.

Nevertheless, there are times when the talking head is a necessary program element. When words you hear in Rehearsal belong only in the mouth of the chairman, president or acknowledged expert, then the talking head is justified. In that case, brevity is the operative word.

Seek direct input from the person who's going before the cameras. Talking head remarks should be written in the style of the speaker—not the writer.

As a pure format, the talking head should be used judiciously, never running more than three to five minutes. (Think about it—five minutes is a long time to watch the same visual image.) Limit content to those things that only the president or an authority can say. Reserve other content points for more visual formats.

The Talking Head with Props

Give a talking head props to work with and greater visual content results. Julia Child's cooking programs are classic examples: an enthusiastic, animated talking head demonstrates the fine points of souffles for a viewing audience. This format is ideal for many corporate, educational and medical subjects—particularly for certain kinds of training applications. The props can literally be anything—a house as is the case with "This Old House"; a real object, such as a computer terminal, or artwork such as diagrams of the cardiovascular system. Set pieces and staging areas can be designed and propped to serve as functional visual elements.

Don't confine your thinking to the studio. A narrator strolling through a manufacturing plant and pointing out stages in an assembly line or touring the facility of a medical center is simply using a life-size prop to illustrate content. A training program on financial services shows a narrator in a park with two kids on a teeter-totter to illustrate the ups and downs of bond pricing.

There are, however, inherent dangers in this format. If the props used are unsuited to the aspect ratio or resolution requirements for the chosen medium, visual content will suffer. Julia Child's kitchen was laid out for optimum camera angles as well as the chef's convenience. The set included a special mirror for looking down on the range. Another problem may arise when a sequence of events is not structured for screen time. Consider how Julia Child chops, mixes or bakes stages of a recipe in advance to condense the screen time. Audiovisual media need to keep unfolding content at a rather brisk clip compared to "real time."

Visuals and Voices

With visuals and voices the narrator is heard but not seen. A sequence of visuals fills the screen while narration comments on the action. The visual material may be quite varied: product footage, animation, slides or photographs, artwork, charts, symbols and other graphics—literally anything the eye can see and a camera shoot.

The writer's goal is to structure sequences where the combined effect of picture and sound equals more than the sum of its parts. Synergistic use of pictures and sound makes the most of the informational capacity of all audiovisual media. Although we call this "visuals and voices," don't overlook "visuals and music" or "visuals and sound effects." The combination of music and pictures is potent for establishing a mood or reaching an audience on an emotional level. Visuals, voices and music/sound effects can be mixed for great emotional impact in multi-media or multi-image presentations.

The visuals and voices format also offers tremendous flexibility for manipulating time and space. It's possible to leap from London to Manila to Los Angeles, or to make visual comparisons between Henry Ford's first assembly line and today's high-tech robotic assembly lines in 10-second sequences.

Yet for all the apparent flexibility, this is a demanding format, requiring discipline and control in scripting. Visual information must be sufficiently varied and move from image to image and scene to scene with sufficient pacing to sustain interest. At the same time, stylistic integrity is necessary to avoid a haphazard effect. Motion within the frame and/or changes in perspective or visual content must be frequent to keep the presentation from becoming static.

On the other hand, although a writer may envision a flood of images, sooner or later the practical production realities of shooting or gathering that footage within time and budgetary restraints must be faced.

One final point on visuals and voices. Because the narrator goes unseen, this format tends to be impersonal. Personal messages, subjects that focus on human interaction or topics where expert analysis is needed do not lend themselves to the impersonal, disembodied voice that characterizes this format.

Interviews

What distinguishes the interview from other formats is that, essentially, it is half scripted. Interview shows are often referred to as unscripted, but good interviews don't just happen. The interviewer must prepare probing questions and discussion points. The strength of the interview format is that it allows people to be themselves on camera. Interviews convey (for better or worse) personality as well as content. The subject's reaction to a question, the smile that crosses the face during an answer, the pause that telegraphs thought processes—all communicate as much as words themselves by placing the content in the context of character.

This program format contains two distinct sub-categories: the on-camera and the off-camera interview. As the name implies, the on-camera interview features the interviewer as an active participant in the program, à la Barbara Walters or David Frost. On-camera interviews usually give the appearance of proceeding from beginning to end.

In the off-camera format, the interviewer is unseen and generally unheard. The off-camera interview results in a less structured, more documentary style, lending itself to juxtaposing several interviews in order to organize content topically rather than chronologically.

The writer's role is to structure interview sequences (and questions when necessary) so that predetermined content comes out naturally and spontaneously from the subject. Note that scripting answers is asking for trouble. The only rationale for interviews in the first place is to allow subjects to choose their own words, to be themselves. While interview topics can be discussed in advance, specific questions and answers should allow for maximum spontaneity.

Dramatizations

On first perception, dramatization would appear to have much in common with the talking head and interview formats—people talking to one another. Dramatization, however, involves the assumption of character. Put two or more characters in conflict and you have the essence of all good dramatic writing.

As such, dramatizations are most useful when subject matter focuses on the dynamics of interpersonal relationships: selling techniques, employment interviewing, counselling and other situations that emphasize human interaction. Here, the strength of the dramatization is that it can demonstrate predictable behaviors and provide role models, i.e., how to handle customer complaints, how to conduct performance appraisals, how to overcome objections from prospective buyers.

Dramatizations can also be used to surprise an audience that may be expecting a more traditional treatment of the subject. In this regard, I've seen highly effective dramatizations of subjects such as anti-trust law, computer accounting systems, employee benefits, and financial services. This format is a good way to build audience interest or empathy or put an entertaining twist on a subject.

The skills of bringing a character to life can also serve the audiovisual writer in creating character narrations. One example of this technique is the use of a historical person to convey content—the founder of the company describing how the business was started, for instance.

From the writer's viewpoint, two critical skills are needed to construct dramatizations. First, drama involves characters in conflict. This doesn't mean all dramatizations should contain the melodrama of soap opera (though I sometimes refer to this format as the "industrial soap"). For a dramatic scene, however, two or more characters must be motivated by objectives that are at cross-purposes. Second, drama requires dialog—not narration. Playwrights and motion picture writers are known for having "good ears." Media writers who adapt this format to their own purposes must also develop an ear for dialog. Chapter 8 covers the subject in depth.

Mixing Formats

An advertising friend's retort to the old adage "You can't mix apples and oranges" has always stuck in my mind. "Sure you can. It's done every day," he'd say. "It's called a fruit salad." Just like apples and oranges these five basic formats can be mixed, matched and combined in infinite variety to fit the content and goals of any given communication. In fact, most subjects don't fall neatly into a single, uniform format unless they are very short, five minutes or less in length. (Multi-image modules are often done solely in the visuals and voice format.)

More frequently, the content of corporate, medical or educational A/V programming is too complex and varied to fit categorically into a single format, and a typical shooting script involves mixing several formats, as shown in Figure 5.1.

A multitude of combinations is possible. The writer's mental imaging of various formats should always link format to a critical content point. Determine which format will be most effective in communicating the message.

Figure 5.1: Examples of Mixed Formats

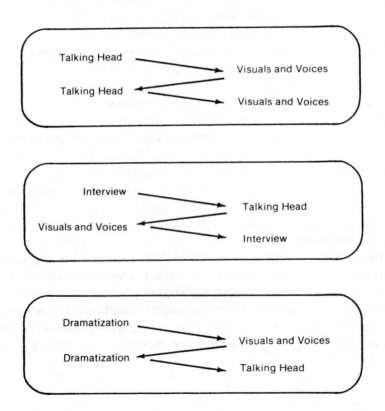

STRUCTURE

All writing has structure, and audiovisual scripts are no exception. Structure is the "chronological sequence of events" that comprise your script. It begins with an opening scene and marches resolutely through the middle and on to a concluding scene. The ultimate viewing experience will unfold in time for the viewing audience.

The structure of a script is dictated by the critical content points. Your big scenes should be built around the critical content. They will become the memorable moments of your script. As William Goldman put it:

> "The essential opening labor a screenwriter must execute is, of course, deciding what the proper structure should be for the particular screenplay you are writing. And to do that, you have to know what is absolutely crucial in the telling of your story—what is the spine.
>
> "Whatever it is, you must protect it to the death."[6]

That opening labor consists of three decisions:

1. What material to include.
2. What material to exclude.
3. The placement of that material from beginning to end.

The first two decisions have already been made. The content outline prepared in the Assimilation phase determines what material is included and excluded. Through that outline, you've identified what the program is about. Now, you have the opportunity to explore the best placement of that material within the emerging script.

You can choose between two methods of structuring the content:

> The scriptwriter can *advertise* structure as a means of gaining clarity. . .
>
> or,
>
> The scriptwriter's aims lead him/her to *conceal* the structure.

Structure prepares the audience for what comes next. Sometimes you want the audience to be able to predict quite accurately what comes next; other times you want the element of surprise to work for you, letting subject matter unfold in a seemingly random way.

Advertising the Structure

When would the scriptwriter want to advertise structure? Generally, when writing training material. In order to reach behavioral objectives, most training content needs to be presented and mastered by the learner in a specific sequence. Before you can understand what happens when a centrifugal gas compressor surges, you have to understand how a centrifugal compressor is supposed to work under normal circumstances. Before you can learn to operate a computer keyboard, you have to become familiar with functions of special keys. Often the writer finds it helpful to summarize what's been learned up to now and preview what's coming later in the program—a way of advertising the structure. This is shown in the first part of Figure 5.2, an excerpt from an insurance sales training videotape on objection handling.

The track and field analogy provides a way of visualizing the abstract concept of handling objections. The subject matter experts use this analogy to "billboard" what will happen:

> "*In the next few minutes, we're going to* provide you with techniques for running a sales track which has the hurdles in place. . . ."

> "*Before getting into specific techniques* for objection handling— *let's define* what we mean by sales resistance and objections. . . ."

The most basic way of advertising structure comes from the old military training maxim: "First you tell 'em what you're gonna tell 'em; then you tell 'em; then you tell 'em what you told 'em."

Of course, there are many other ways to advertise the structure than simply to billboard what's coming next. Read through the second section of the sales training script in Figure 5.2.

The organization of visual material as indicated in the VIDEO column is all designed to reinforce the distinction between insincere and genuine objections. It's achieved through the use of set pieces, graphics, titles and a special wipe effect. In the program, the viewer can predict quite specifically what will happen next.

When you want to advertise the structure of your script, consider adopting these writing strategies:

1. Billboard content and tell the viewers what they're expected to get from the program.
2. Incorporate the logic of your content outline in the structure of the program.
3. Review what has gone before and set up what will come later.
4. Share the objectives or critical content points with your audience prior to in-depth development.

Figure 5.2: Structure in a Script

VIDEO	AUDIO
Section 1	
MS on Jack by the chroma-key screen. It contains a freeze frame of a track and field event—runners going around a track.	JACK: WE CAN LEARN A LOT ABOUT HANDLING OBJECTIONS FROM SPORTS. CONSIDER, FOR INSTANCE, TRACK AND FIELD EVENTS.
CLOSE UP on screen as action of race begins.	GARRY AND I HAVE ALWAYS BEEN PROPONENTS OF HAVING A SALES TRACK TO RUN ON. WHEN YOU'RE PREPARED; WHEN YOU KNOW YOUR LINES SO THEY'RE NATURAL AS BREATHING– THEN YOU'RE LIKE THE TRACK STAR WHO'S PREPARED AND CONDITIONED FOR RUNNING THE BIG RACE.
MS on Garry, who is now seen in main stage area. Abstract style artwork suggests a stadium or arena. Several hurdles away from cyc provide an area for Jack and Garry to move from point to point. In this establishing shot, Garry refers to hurdles behind him.	GARRY: BUT WHAT HAPPENS TO THE RUNNER WHO SUDDENLY FACES AN UNEXPECTED OBSTACLE— SUCH AS A HURDLE? IF THAT RUNNER HAS NEVER TRAINED FOR HURDLES—HE OR SHE WILL BE THROWN OFF STRIDE. THEIR RHYTHM AND CONFIDENCE WOULD BE BROKEN.
MS on Jack by chroma-key screen. It shows freeze frame of race featuring hurdles. Footage rolls as Jack speaks.	JACK: BUT—SUPPOSE THAT SAME RUNNER HAS TRAINED INTENTLY TO RUN A RACE INVOLVING HURDLES. THEN, EACH AND EVERY HURDLE HAS BEEN ANTICIPATED— PREPARED FOR IN ADVANCE THROUGH HOURS OF PRACTICE AT TAKING THE HURDLE WITHOUT BREAKING STRIDE.
MS on Garry by hurdles.	GARRY: IN THE NEXT FEW MINUTES, WE'RE GOING TO PROVIDE YOU WITH TECHNIQUES FOR RUNNING A SALES TRACK WHICH HAS THE

Figure 5.2: Structure in a Script (Cont.)

VIDEO	AUDIO
	HURDLES IN PLACE. THOSE HURDLES STAND FOR THE SALES RESISTANCE AND INEVITABLE OBJECTIONS YOU SHOULD ANTICIPATE DURING EACH AND EVERY SALES PRESENTATION. BY TRAINING TO RUN ON THIS SALES TRACK—YOU'LL BE CONDITIONED TO THE RESISTANCE AND TAKE OBJECTIONS RIGHT IN YOUR STRIDE.
Different angle, featuring Jack as he walks into main stage area, joining Garry.	JACK: BY DEVELOPING TECHNIQUES FOR TAKING OBJECTIONS IN STRIDE, YOU'LL BEGIN TO DEVELOP THE CONFIDENCE WHICH WILL LEAD TO AN ATTITUDE THAT WELCOMES OBJECTIONS AS VALUABLE FEED-BACK FROM YOUR PROSPECT. BEFORE GETTING INTO SPECIFIC TECHNIQUES FOR OBJECTION HANDLING—LET'S DEFINE WHAT WE MEAN BY SALES RESISTANCE AND OBJECTIONS.

Section 2

VIDEO	AUDIO
Different angle on Jack with two hurdles behind him. SUPER: 　Insincere 　Genuine Text appears over each hurdle.	TO HANDLE AN OBJECTION EFFECTIVELY, YOU MUST UNDER-STAND WHAT KIND OF OBJECTION YOU'RE FACING. OBJECTIONS FALL INTO TWO GENERAL CLASSIFICA-TIONS: INSINCERE OBJECTIONS AND GENUINE OBJECTIONS.
Isolate Garry by a single hurdle. SUPER: 　Insincere Objection 　(Sales Resistance) Copy block is placed above hurdle.	GARRY: THE INSINCERE OBJECTION IS KNOWN AS SALES RESISTANCE, SINCE IT IS NOT REALLY AN OBJECTION WHICH CAN BE ANSWERED. GENERALLY, THE

Figure 5.2: Structure in a Script (Cont.)

VIDEO	AUDIO
	INSINCERE OBJECTION IS ILLOGICAL. IT'S EXPRESSED THROUGH ALIBIS, EXCUSES OR STALLS. THE PROSPECT GIVES FICTITIOUS REASONS TO HIDE THE REAL, GENUINE OBJECTIONS.
DISSOLVE TO:	HERE ARE SOME EXAMPLES OF INSINCERE OBJECTIONS:
Special wipe effect matting the close-ups in black and positioning lips in various portions of the screen.	**VOICE I:** I'M REALLY TIED UP AT THE OFFICE RIGHT NOW—I JUST DON'T HAVE TIME TO TALK ABOUT INSURANCE NOW...
	VOICE II: YOUR PLAN HAS A LOT OF MERIT—BUT I'D LIKE TO SLEEP ON IT...
DISSOLVE TO:	**VOICE III:** I'M INSURANCE POOR AS IT IS—I CAN'T IMAGINE NEEDING MORE...
CU on Jack.	**JACK:** THE INSINCERE OBJECTION, OR SALES RESISTANCE, IS NOT MOTIVATED BY LOGIC. THE PROSPECT OFFERS FICTITIOUS REASONS OR EXCUSES. QUITE OFTEN, THE INSINCERE OBJECTION MASKS OR HIDES THE REAL, GENUINE OBJECTION.

Source: *How You Handle Objections,* from the Kinder Brothers & Associates Professional Profile Video Series, written by William Van Nostran, directed by John P. Kenlon, created and produced by Kinder Brothers & Associates and The Prudential Audiovisual Communications Division. Used by permission.

Concealing the Structure

Surprise is a hallmark of vivid writing. The skilled media writer can employ surprise to good advantage in programming intended to inform or motivate. There are many ways to achieve surprise and the uniqueness of the subject matter generally suggests possibilities to the writer.

The unadvertised structure usually drops the viewer right into the action of scene one with no explanation or stage-setting, as the excerpt in Figure 5.3 shows.

Just as fiction writers surprise by manipulating time and place, audiovisual scriptwriters have similar opportunities, using media capabilities for great effects. The program in Figure 5.4, designed to motivate employees to take the time to analyze their options under a new flexible benefits plan, moves directly into a series of dramatic vignettes, changing locations fluidly—without giving the audience any preview of the specific content or structure.

The program illustrates the choices each of these four must make based on their personal needs and situation. But the program does not follow a predictable structure. The salesman we meet first, for example, does not reappear until the final scenes of the program.

Programs using an unadvertised structure must still have an inner skeleton on which to hang the content. It doesn't mean the script lacks structure. This type of organization is as consciously crafted as the advertised structure. It simply means you don't want the audience to be aware of the underlying framework or readily predict what happens next.

When your subject matter and audience suggest concealing the structure, your script will probably not follow the logical order in your content outline. Instead, experiment with different ways of ordering the flow of events. Play with the material to create a sequence of events that keeps the audience involved in the presentation.

STYLE

Style is the writer's point of view toward the subject matter. It is expressed in everything the viewer will see and hear—narration, dialog, music, sound effects, on-camera talent, sets, props, graphics, transitions and special effects. Scriptwriters may adopt any point of view toward the subject matter; writers can be playful, humorous, serious, solemn, angry, analytical, theatrical—the whole range of human emotions is available to the scriptwriter.

Often, however, corporate A/V writers are so "buttoned-down" they churn out script after script in what looks like "corporate Helvetica." The result invariably lacks a distinctive voice. Scriptwriters should consciously select a style and voice appropriate for each project and write accordingly. The Rehearsal phase is your

Figure 5.3: Unadvertised Structure

VIDEO	AUDIO
FADE UP ON: The program opens in a hallway by an elevator door. We see a male [Hank Conroy] in his mid-thirties dressed in shirt and tie, carrying a lot of computer printout paperwork, pacing back and forth and hitting the call button impatiently. As the doors open, he gets in and briefly acknowledges a female employee [Liz Talbot] who also carries a handfull of papers. The doors close. . . SUPER: The Ups and Downs of Materials Management DISSOLVE TO: Angle from inside elevator as doors open. Two additional male employees get on. One of these is an installer [Phil Fisher] in shirt and tie, carrying a briefcase with his tools. In his fifties, he's a cigar-chomping type. The second is a locker person [Jeff Collins] in casual, functional clothes. The door closes again on these faces. SUPER: . . .An Orientation to Materials Management Operations.	MUSIC: (Vamp theme plays under, creating a ryhthmic cadence to punctuate the action.) PHIL FISHER: GOIN' UP? HANK CONROY: C'MON IN.

Figure 5.3: Unadvertised Structure (Cont.)

VIDEO	AUDIO
MS outside elevator doors as a warehousing person [Larry Nichols] is waiting for the elevator.	
He goes in and the doors close behind him. Before the doors open again, however, the lights flicker and the elevator bounces up and down. The riders look to one another in awe. . .	**MUSIC & SOUND EFFX:** (The music screeches to an abrupt conclusion. Elevator noise goes off. There's a brief moment of silence.)
	LARRY NICHOLS: (Winces.) OOH. . . I DON'T LIKE THE FEEL OF THAT. . .
They try hitting the floor buttons again in a futile attempt to make the elevator continue on—up or down.	**HANK CONROY:** . . .DOOR DOESN'T WANNA OPEN. . .
	LIZ TALBOT: I THINK WE'RE BETWEEN FLOORS.
	HANK CONROY: IT'S NOT GONNA BUDGE, IS IT?
	JEFF COLLINS: (Checks his watch,) GREAT—I'VE GOT AN HOUR 'TIL I'M DUE BACK TO MY LOCKER.
	HANK CONROY: LET'S EVERYBODY STAY CALM AND WE'LL BE O.K.
	PHIL COLLINS: IF I MIGHT MAKE A SUGGESTION—GIVE THAT EMERGENCY PHONE A TRY. . .
SPECIAL EFFECT	
Page turn or wipe to indicate passage of time.	**BUILDING SUPER:** (Off-camera and filtered.) I'LL GET RIGHT ON THE CASE—BUT YOU'D BEST SIT

Figure 5.3: Unadvertised Structure (Cont.)

VIDEO	AUDIO
Hank is listening to the building superintendant's voice over the elevator intercom.	TIGHT IN THERE. NO TELLIN' HOW LONG IT MIGHT TAKE TO FIX THE PROBLEM. **JEFF COLLINS:** (Checking his watch.) NOW I'VE GOTTA BE BACK TO MY LOCKER IN FIFTY-FIVE MINUTES. **LIZ TALBOT:** (Not really believing it.) HEY—THEY'LL HAVE US OUTTA HERE IN NO TIME. **PHIL FISHER:** DON'T JUMP TO CONCLUSIONS. TAKE IT FROM ME— YOU CAN NEVER PREDICT EXACTLY HOW LONG IT'S GONNA TAKE TO MAKE REPAIRS. **LARRY NICHOLS:** WELL... IF THAT'S THE CASE, MIGHT AS WELL GET TO KNOW ONE ANOTHER. I'M LARRY NICHOLS FROM MATERIALS MANAGEMENT...
At this point, they begin to introduce themselves. . . Montage of shots on mouths and hands intercut with wider shot of group as they all try to shake hands reaching across one another, hampered by the lack of space.	**MONTAGE OF VOICES:** (They all start talking at once, shaking hands, and introducing themselves. With the lack of space in the elevator, it becomes a hub-bub of conversation and takes on a comedic air. We hear only snatches of the interchanges. . .) I THOUGHT YOU LOOKED FAMILIAR. . . YOU MEAN YOU WORK IN THE MATERIALS MANAGEMENT WARE-HOUSE?

Figure 5.3: Unadvertised Structure (Cont.)

VIDEO	AUDIO
	THAT'S A REAL COINCIDENCE, ISN'T IT?
	HANK CONROY: WELL, ALL I'VE GOT TO SAY IS THEY'D BETTER GET US OUTTA HERE OR THEY'RE GONNA HAVE A WORK SLOW DOWN IN MATERIALS MANAGEMENT.
	PHIL FISHER: I DON'T BELIEVE THIS. OF ALL THE DEPARTMENTS TO GET STUCK WITH, I HAVE TO PUT UP WITH YOU MATERIALS MANAGEMENT PEOPLE.
	LARRY NICHOLS: WE ALL TRY TO DO THE BEST JOB WE CAN.
	PHIL FISHER: (Full of self-righteousness.) YOU MATERIALS MANAGEMENT PEOPLE SURE CAN MAKE OR BREAK MY DAY. IF I DON'T GET THE RIGHT MATERIALS EVERY SINGLE MORNING, I WIND UP TAKIN' THE HEAT FROM THE CUSTOMER.
	LIZ TALBOT: LOOK—THERE'S A LOT THAT GOES INTO GETTING MATERIALS AND EQUIPMENT TO EVERY LOCKER AROUND THE STATE DAY AFTER DAY...
	HANK CONROY: WHILE WE'RE STUCK HERE TOGETHER, MIGHT BE WORTH WHILE TO FIND OUT WHAT WE ALL DO IN MATERIALS MANAGEMENT.
	PHIL FISCHER: I DON'T HAVE ALL DAY, YOU KNOW.

Figure 5.3: Unadvertised Structure (Cont.)

VIDEO	AUDIO
The men react outwardly to this admission.	**LIZ TALBOT:** HOWEVER LONG WE'RE STUCK HERE, I SHOULD WARN YOU. I'M A LITTLE CLAUSTROPHOBIC.

Source: From "The Ups & Downs of Materials Management," written by William Van Nostran, produced and directed by Kim Cloutman, for SNET Corporate TV Center. Used by permission.

opportunity to try out a range of styles and select the one that seems most effective, given the needs of the project.

The next two sample scripts are different treatments of the identical subject: sexual harrassment in the workplace (Figures 5.5 and 5.6). Read through them looking for cues that reveal differing attitudes toward the subject matter.

In putting forth stereotypes of sexual harassment, the writer of the script in Figure 5.5 chose a comedic and presentational style. The music and visual transition are intended to telegraph to the audience that they are entering a fantasy world. The stylized set, exaggerated costumes, dialog and acting style all combine to convey a comedic tone.

The lines "to camera" in which Miss Penneypinch breaks character are a theatrical device to heighten the presentational tone.

Contrast this style to the different treatment in Figure 5.6 in which sexual harassment is depicted in more subtle, realistic terms.

The dialog and action in these scenes reflect a "slice-of-life" style and tone. The writer strives for realism and this should be reflected in the acting, costuming and staging.

CONCEPT DEVELOPMENT

In his book *Writing with Power,* Peter Elbow states the dilemma all writers face: "Writing calls on two skills that are so different they usually conflict with each other: creating and criticizing."[7] Nowhere are these two polar skills more in evidence than in the process of concept development.

Figure 5.4: Unpredictable Structure

VIDEO	AUDIO
Open with wide shot on highway early in the morning. A few cars go by. Then, as soundtrack comes up, isolate on mid-size sedan. We follow it as the car goes by camera position. Then. . .	**RADIO SOUNDTRACK:** (Mix sounds of highway traffic going by with sound of Ray Charles Maxwell House commercial growing louder. As car passes by, lyric is filtered to simulate automobile radio sound.)
Cut to interior of car as Rich Sullivan sips coffee from styrofoam cup while humming along.	(Mix sound of Rich Sullivan chiming in with Ray Charles, followed by typical morning drive time chatter, such as:) . . .COMIN' UP ON EIGHT-FIFTEEN HERE AT KTZ. IF YOU'RE JUST LEAVIN' FOR WORK—BETTER GRAB THAT UMBRELLA. . .CHANCE OF AFTERNOON SHOWERS. (Pull under.) IN A MINUTE HERE, WE'LL GO TO THE PHONES AND SEE IF WE CAN GIVE AWAY FREE TICKETS FOR THE EDDIE RABBIT CONCERT. KTZ WANTS TO MAKE YOU A WINNER—BUT FIRST, YOU GOTTA LISTEN FOR OUR COUNTRY QUIZ PERFORMER OF THE DAY. AND HERE HE IS NOW. . . (etc., as song continues under.)
During Narrator's speech, insert ECU on open briefcase beside Rich in car. Show special promotion materials covering unopened Benechoice booklet mailing. Different angle, from back seat as Rich pulls into supermarket lot.	**NARRATOR:** (Voice-over.) MEET RICH SULLIVAN—A MAXWELL HOUSE SALES REP. RICH'LL BE IN AND OUT OF MORE SUPERMARKETS IN THE NEXT EIGHT HOURS THAN MOST OF US SEE IN A MONTH. MAXWELL HOUSE INSTANT'S GOT A SPECIAL PROMOTION COMING UP. SO YOU CAN BET RICH SPENT A FEW HOURS OVER THE WEEKEND GETTING READY TO PERSUADE STORE MANAGERS TO STOCK UP IN ADVANCE. RICH ALSO *INTENDED* TO SPEND TIME WITH HIS GF BENECHOICE BOOKLET THIS WEEK-END—DIDN'T YOU RICH?

Figure 5.4: Unpredictable Structure (Cont.)

VIDEO	AUDIO
Rich addresses Narrator from rear view mirror.	**RICH SULLIVAN:** (To camera.) LISTEN. . .I PLANNED TO SKIM IT. BUT WHEN I GOT ASKED TO GO SAILING. . .WELL, MY PRIORITIES GOT REARRANGED.
Rich gets out of car with briefcase and goes to trunk for sample case.	**NARRATOR:** FOR A GUY IN RICH'S SHOES, IT'S EASY TO PUT BENEFIT PLANNING ON THE "BACK BURNER." HE'S TWENTY-EIGHT AND SINGLE. NOT A SOUL TO LOOK AFTER EXCEPT HIMSELF—AND A LONG LIST OF SUPERMARKET MANAGERS.
Closes trunk and walks toward supermarket.	**RICH SULLIVAN:** (To camera.) MAYBE I'LL LOOK THIS BENECHOICE STUFF OVER WHEN I GRAB A SANDWICH AT NOON. . .
DISSOLVE to. . .	**NARRATOR:** (Skeptically.) SURE, RICH. WE'LL CATCH UP TO YOU LATER. . .
Howard Richardson in office. He stands at desk, getting items out of briefcase and arranging stacks of papers. We catch a glimpse of Benechoice book and worksheet with penciled entries.	NOW *THIS* GUY'S A COMPLETELY DIFFERENT STORY: HOWARD RICHARDSON. HE'S A MANAGER IN THE PET FOODS DIVISION. HE'S IN HIS MID-FORTIES. . .
	HOWARD RICHARDSON: (To camera.) HEY, THAT'S NOT SO BAD. I STAY IN SHAPE.
	NARRATOR: (Continuing right on.) . . .AND HE AND HIS WIFE HAVE *THREE* TEENAGERS. . .
	HOWARD RICHARDSON: (Points finger to camera lens.) NOW YOU'RE TALKIN' MAJOR PROBLEMS. . .

Figure 5.4: Unpredictable Structure (Cont.)

VIDEO	AUDIO
Howard puts suit coat on and gathers up materials to take with him. Follow as Howard exits office and moves to area where Roberta Scott, a young black, is organizing for the day ahead. Roberta puts bag on desk and we see Benechoice booklet in a side pocket.	**NARRATOR:** NEED I SAY MORE? HOWARD'S SPENT HOURS ANALYZING *HIS* CHOICES UNDER GF'S NEW FLEXIBLE BENECHOICE PROGRAM. HOWARD'S SECRETARY, ROBERTA SCOTT, IS ALSO TRYING TO REACH A DECISION ON HER OPTIONS. LIKE HOWARD, ROBERTA'S MARRIED. SHE'S IN HER LATE TWENTIES WITH NO CHILDREN.
Howard starts to exit, then turns back for line about glasses.	**HOWARD RICHARDSON:** HERE'S THE ADDITION TO THE PACKAGING STUDY. I'M OFF TO HENRY'S STAFF MEETING. SEE YOU LATER. SAY— YOU GET NEW GLASSES?
Different angle as Roberta calls after Howard as he is heading down corridor.	**ROBERTA SCOTT:** HARDLY. THESE ARE *OLD* GLASSES. LENS FELL OUT OF MY GOOD ONES ON THE BEACH THIS WEEKEND. GOOD THING I HUNG ON TO THESE. . .(She blinks.) I THINK. BEFORE YOU GO—MR. HORNBEIN ASKED IF I COULD SCHEDULE YOU FOR A MEETING TOMORROW AT TWO-THIRTY. THAT'S O.K. ISN'T IT?
	HOWARD RICHARDSON: SHOULD BE. BOOK IT.
MS on Roberta working at desk.	**NARRATOR:** ROBERTA—DON'T FORGET TO SCHEDULE SOME TIME FOR *YOURSELF* TODAY.
	ROBERTA SCOTT: (To camera.) TIME FOR *MYSELF?* IN THIS DEPARTMENT? YOU'RE A REAL BLUE-EYED OPTIMIST, AREN'T YOU?

Figure 5.4: Unpredictable Structure (Cont.)

VIDEO	AUDIO
	NARRATOR: (A little bit of a nag.) YOU REACH ANY DECISIONS ON BENECHOICE? YOU'RE RUNNING OUT OF TIME.
	ROBERTA SCOTT: HONEY, I'M RUNNIN' OUTTA *MOTIVATION* TO READ ABOUT BENEFITS. DOESN'T QUITE HOLD YOUR ATTENTION LIKE STEPHEN KING'S LATEST SPELLBINDER.
	NARRATOR: WELL, THE LUCK YOU'VE HAD WITH EYEGLASSES LATELY—YOU OUGHTA BE SPELL-BOUND BY THE SECTION ON REIM-BURSEMENT ACCOUNTS'
	ROBERTA SCOTT: (Resigned.) O.K. I HEAR YOU. LET ME GET THROUGH MY MORNING COFFEE, FIRST.
DISSOLVE to shot of Terri Felton walking through entrance to Dover Plant. Condense action to pick her up at desk, on phone. We see photo of her son displayed in work area.	**NARRATOR:** FINE—GIVES ME A CHANCE TO INTRODUCE ONE MORE PERSON—TERRI FELTON. SHE'S A CUSTOMER SERVICE REPRESENTA-TIVE IN HER MID-TWENTIES. SHE'S RECENTLY GONE THROUGH A DIVORCE. GOT HER HANDS FULL RAISING HER YOUNG SON, BEN. THINK THAT'S BENNY ON THE PHONE NOW. . .
CU on Terri.	**TERRI FELTON:** (Delivered a la Bob Newhart. Terri has a slight edge to her voice.) . . .BENNY, YOU PUT *WHAT* IN THE GOLDFISH TANK? (Beat.) THAT'S WHAT I THOUGHT YOU SAID. BENNY, WHERE'S MRS. LEVITT? (Beat.) CLEANING OUT THE GOLDFISH TANK. BENNY, I'VE TOLD YOU PLEASE NOT TO CALL MOMMY AT WORK UNLESS IT'S A

Figure 5.4: Unpredictable Structure (Cont.)

VIDEO	AUDIO
	REAL EMERGENCY. NOW TELL MRS. LEVITT I'LL CALL AROUND LUNCH-TIME. AND, PLEASE, NO MORE EXPERIMENTS. . .
Puts phone down, starts to go about her business. . .	**NARRATOR:** TERRI—YOU REALIZE YOU COULD NOW BE PAYING MRS. LEVITT WITH TAX-*FREE* DOLLARS?
then turns to camera.	**TERRI FELTON:** TAX-*FREE* DOLLARS? SOUNDS LIKE SOME-THING FOR THE "HIGH ROLLERS."
Camera moves closer.	(Leans forward, and delivers next line half confidently, half jokingly. With a twinkle in the eye.) JUST BETWEEN THE TWO OF US—I'M NOT EXACTLY IN THE FIFTY-PERCENT TAX BRACKET.
Now she listens to Narrator.	**NARRATOR:** LET ME PUT IT THIS WAY—RECENT CHANGES IN TAX LAWS, COMBINED WITH GF'S NEW BENECHOICE PROGRAM, MAKE IT POSSIBLE FOR YOU TO STRETCH YOUR DOLLAR FURTHER—NO MATTER WHAT YOUR SALARY.
Cut to shot of Rich Sullivan eating a burger in diner. His Benechoice book's propped up in front of him by a Coke glass.	**RICH SULLIVAN:** (Interior monologue.) IF I UNDERSTAND THIS RIGHT—USING BEFORE-TAX DOLLARS FOR THE LONG-TERM FEATURE OF THE THRIFT-INVESTMENT PLAN'S A LOT LIKE AN I.R.A. . .
	NARRATOR: I'VE BEEN LOOKIN' ALL OVER TOWN FOR YOU. WHERE'VE YOU BEEN?
	RICH SULLIVAN: (To camera.) HEY— I'VE BEEN OUT WHERE THE RUBBER MEETS THE ROAD, YOU KNOW? NOW,

Figure 5.4: Unpredictable Structure (Cont.)

VIDEO	AUDIO
	I WAS THINKING ABOUT OPENING AN I.R.A. AT MY BANK. MAYBE THE LONG-TERM FEATURE OF THE THRIFT-INVESTMENT PLAN'S A LOT LIKE AN I.R.A. . . .
	NARRATOR: YES, IT CAN BE BETTER THAN AN I.R.A. IT'S ALL THERE IN YOUR BOOKLET.
	RICH SULLIVAN: HIT ME WITH THE HIGHLIGHTS.
Rich looks to placard advertising dessert special.	**NARRATOR:** SEE THAT PLACARD?
	RICH SULLIVAN: STRAWBERRY SHORTCAKE?
The card rotates to become graphic display area for TIP highlights.	**SOUND EFFX:** (As placard rotates magically.)

Source: From "Benechoice," written by William Van Nostran,
directed by James G. Libby, produced by William Hoppe, for
General Foods Corp. Used by permission.

There are several ways of describing the creative concept and illustrating its function. First, a range of definitions, then some examples:

> **Concept:** A single idea or premise which shapes style, format, content and structure into a unified, aesthetically pleasing whole. Once a concept is set, parameters for aesthetic and production considerations are established.

> **Concept:** The creative vehicle for conveying content.

> **Concept:** A unique, involving method of delivering content to the target audience.

Figure 5.5:   From "Sexual Harassment:
**   Fact or Fiction"**

TWO SHOT on both.	**FEMALE NARRATOR:** GOOD REASONS TO TAKE THE ENTIRE ISSUE OF SEXUAL HARASSMENT SERIOUSLY. BUT THEN THE QUESTION BECOMES: "WHAT CONSTITUTES SEXUAL HARASS-MENT AT WORK?"
	MALE NARRATOR: NOW WE'RE GETTING TO THE CRUX OF THE PROBLEM. SURE, THERE'S A TYPE OF BEHAVIOR WHICH IS BLATANT HARASSMENT. FOR INSTANCE, I CAN ENVISION THE SORT OF GUY WHO MIGHT...
	FEMALE NARRATOR: THIS I WANT TO SEE!
	MALE NARRATOR: OH, YOU NOT ONLY GET TO SEE IT, JENNIFER— YOU GET TO *LIVE* IT...
Special video effect, similar to transition to dream or other imagined event. It should be an obvious television "convention."	**MUSIC & SOUND EFFX:** (Theme and effects to clearly establish transition to fantasy sequence.)
Effect takes us through to scene set in office done in same "pop-up" art style.	
ECU—On cover of Wall Street Journal. ZOOM out to reveal Male Narrator reading it at desk. His dress parodies the well-heeled executive: three-piece pin stripe suit, flower in lapel, gold cuff links and tie tack. He's also given a bit of grey at the temples. Both Narrators obviously "play-act" these scenes.	

**Figure 5.5: From "Sexual Harassment:
Fact or Fiction" (Cont.)**

MALE NARRATOR: (To himself, after a groan.) WHY DO I ALWAYS LISTEN TO THAT IDIOT BROKER? (He puts the newspaper down in disgust. Then speaks through his intercom.) MISS PENNEY-PINCH.

VOICE OF FEMALE NARRATOR: (Off camera.) YES, MR. LETCHWORTH?

MALE NARRATOR: (With a leer and unabashed lilt in his voice.) DICTATION TIME, MISS PENNEYPINCH!

MS—On entrance of Female Narrator. She is attired in a tight fitting sweater dress; giving her a buxom appearance. She is overly made up, sports a blonde wig and cracks chewing gum. She plays this scene as a cross between Loni Anderson and Marilyn Monroe. She moves to chair in front of desk. . .

FEMALE NARRATOR: (Entering through doorway with steno pad.) IS THIS TO BE INTERCOMPANY CORRESPONDENCE OR A LETTER TO THE OUTSIDE WORLD?

MALE NARRATOR: THE DOOR, MISS PENNEYPINCH. . .I CAN'T CONCEN-TRATE WITH THE DOOR OPEN.

FEMALE NARRATOR: BUT YOU KNOW WE GET SO MUCH MORE DONE WITH THE DOOR OPEN, MR. LETCHWORTH. . .MAYBE JUST AJAR A BIT?

MALE NARRATOR: (Fixated on her.) MY DEAR, YOU'RE LOOKING TOO GOOD TODAY TO EVEN THINK OF LEAVING THE "JAR" "ADOOR". . . (realizing his flub.) UH. . .DOOR AJAR. (He closes the door firmly. Then stalks about her as he begins to dictate.) THIS MEMO GOES TO R.O. HAMILTON. . .

**Figure 5.5:   From "Sexual Harassment:
Fact or Fiction" (Cont.)**

SUBJECT: SEVERE INVENTORY SHORTAGES. . .THE RECENT RASH OF INVENTORY SHORTAGES, COMMA. . .(He loses train of thought, fixating on her again. She looks up.) READ BACK WHAT YOU HAVE SO FAR. . .

Different angle—As she reads, he leans over her and places arm around her. He's obviously not listening.

FEMALE NARRATOR: TO: R.O. HAMILTON. . .SUBJECT: SEVERE INVENTORY SHORTAGES. . .THE RECENT RASH OF INVENTORY SHORTAGES, COMMA. . .

MALE NARRATOR: (Fondling her shoulder.) MISS PENNEYPINCH, THAT PERFUME. . .YOU KNOW WHAT IT DOES TO ME? (He nuzzles.)

FEMALE NARRATOR: (To the audience, breaking into her Narrator persona.) JEEZ, WHAT A TRITE COME-ON. . .(She rises, and refers to steno pad.) I THINK YOU LEFT OFF IN THE MIDDLE OF A SENTENCE, MR. LETCHWORTH. . .

MALE NARRATOR: (Trying to compose himself.) I DID? OH YES. . .I WAS SAYING THAT YOUR PERFUME BRINGS OUT THE BEAST IN ME. . . (He pursues, she moves away, but it puts her in front of sofa.)

FEMALE NARRATOR: (Reading from pad.) YOU REALLY WANT MR. HAMILTON TO KNOW: "THE RECENT RASH OF INVENTORY SHORTAGES, COMMA, BRINGS OUT THE BEAST IN ME?

MALE NARRATOR: PUT THAT ASIDE. (Taking pad and pencil from her.) I'M TALKING ABOUT YOU AND ME, MISS

Figure 5.5: From "Sexual Harassment: Fact or Fiction" (Cont.)

PENNEYPINCH. WE CAN MAKE SUCH BEAUTIFUL MUSIC TOGETHER. (He leans into her, forcing her to plop onto the sofa.)

FEMALE NARRATOR: BUT WHAT ABOUT THE DUET YOU HAVE WITH— *MRS.* LETCHWORTH?

MALE NARRATOR: (He leans over her and kisses her neck.) COMPARED TO YOUR LOVELINESS, MRS. LETCHWORTH'S A WORN-OUT TUNE. . .AN OLD REFRAIN. . .

FEMALE NARRATOR: (To camera.) I JUST HOPE MOTHER NEVER SEES THIS. . .(She breaks free of him, rises, gathers her composure and emphatically says:) MR. LETCHWORTH! SHOULDN'T WE GET DOWN TO BUSINESS?

MALE NARRATOR: WELL PUT, MISS PENNEYPINCH. (With a sense of intimidation.) I HOPE YOU REALIZE YOUR CONTINUED EMPLOYMENT HERE DEPENDS ON *MY* PERSONAL ESTIMATE OF YOUR PERFORMANCE?

FEMALE NARRATOR: (Intimidated.) YES, I'M WELL AWARE OF THAT, MR. LETCHWORTH.

MALE NARRATOR: GOOD. BECAUSE IF YOU'RE GOING TO PLAY IN MY ORCHESTRA—YOU'D BETTER PICK UP THE TEMPO!

FEMALE NARRATOR: MR. LETCHWORTH. . .I DON'T KNOW WHAT TO SAY. . .

**Figure 5.5:   From "Sexual Harassment:
Fact or Fiction" (Cont.)**

	MALE NARRATOR: ACTIONS SPEAK LOUDER THAN WORDS, MISS PENNEYPINCH. . .(He pursues with renewed vigor.)
Special video effect to highlight the transition. . .	**MUSIC AND SOUND EFFX:** (Transitional theme to reality.)
DISSOLVE THROUGH TO:	
MS—On Narrators in studio setting, seated on stools in foreground. They are dressed as seen at the outset.	

Source: From "Sexual Harassment: Fact or Fiction," written by
William Van Nostran, directed by James G. Libby and produced by
William J. Benham for AT&T Corporate Television. Used by
permission.

> **Concept**: A storytelling theme used to provide a warm, human
> touch to the cold facts which constitute the content.

William Hoppe, a veteran corporate video producer, once used this analogy: "The concept is like a hook which takes the viewer straight through the program. It's like when you go to a car wash—once your car is hooked up, it's out of your control. But it's pulled effortlessly through each stage of the process."

A good concept functions the same way. It's not simply a catchy opening. Those are easy to come by. Strong, creative concepts serve the viewer well from the first FADE UP to the final FADE TO BLACK.

The concept also functions to humanize the message:

> **Concept**: A storytelling theme used to provide a warm, human
> touch to the cold facts which constitute the content.

Up to this point, the writer has "rehearsed" the content mentally—imagining critical content in various formats, deciding whether or not to advertise the structure, and so on. In the process, perhaps the writer has already had one or more concepts pop into consciousness. (In fact, the scriptwriter may have already experienced the

Figure 5.6: Excerpt from "Sexual Harassment: Fact or Fiction"

Scene in open office area where Cindy works with other programmers. Cindy is wrapping up a phone conversation at her desk as George comes over to her.

GEORGE: (Quite sincere.) CINDY. . . . JUST WANT TO LET YOU KNOW THAT FOR THE NEW KID ON THE BLOCK, YOU'RE DOING JUST FINE. THIS PROGRAMMING'S FIRST-RATE.

CINDY: WHAT A RELIEF. I SURE SPENT ENOUGH TIME ON IT. . . RUINED LAST WEEKEND, IN FACT.

GEORGE: JUST ONE LITTLE AREA NEEDS TO BE REWORKED SOME. . .

CINDY: OH, WONDERFUL—HOW BADLY DID I REALLY MESS UP?

He pulls up a chair and places an arm around her as they pour over her work.

GEORGE: IT'S NOT A MISTAKE, ACTUALLY. JUST A LITTLE PECULIARITY IN OUR APPROACH TO DATA TRANSFER. YOU SEE. . . OUR COMPUTERS ARE SET UP TO PROCESS INCOMING SERVICE REQUESTS LIKE THIS. . .

CLOCK WIPE EFFECT:

Different Angle on Cindy's area. Shot features Jack in foreground, straightening his desk before going home. Cindy is bent over stack of computer print outs.

CINDY: FIVE O'CLOCK ALREADY? WHAT A WEEK!

JACK: YOU'RE NOT KIDDIN'. I'M GETTIN' OUTTA HERE ON TIME FOR ONCE. I'M GONNA CRASH IN FRONT OF THE TV—DON'T CARE WHAT'S ON. YOU READY TO LEAVE?

CINDY: I'M JUST GOING TO FINISH UP A FEW THINGS.

Figure 5.6: Excerpt from "Sexual Harassment: Fact or Fiction" (Cont.)

	JACK: O.K. HAVE A GOOD WEEK-END. . .
Jack exits as George enters. His tie is undone and his vest unbuttoned.	**GEORGE:** CINDY, YOU LOOK AS BEAT AS I FELL. SOME WEEK, HUH?
	CINDY: WELL, AT LEAST IT MAKES YOU APPRECIATE THE WEEKENDS.
	GEORGE: AT THIS MOMENT, I'M JUST LOOKING FORWARD TO GETTING OVER TO RYAN'S. HEY. . . WHY DON'T YOU C'MON OVER AND I'LL BUY YOU A COCKTAIL?
	CINDY: THANKS. . .BUT NOT TONIGHT, GEORGE. . .
	GEORGE: C'MON. . .YOU DESERVE A LITTLE HAPPY HOUR IN YOUR LIFE. . .
	CINDY: NO, REALLY. I'VE GOT TO GET HOME. . .
	GEORGE: HEAVY DATE, OR WHAT?
	CINDY: A LOT LESS EXCITING, I'M AFRAID. . .
Hand on her arm; trying to be sympathetic.	**GEORGE:** LOOK, JUST 'CAUSE ONE GUY TURNS OUT TO BE A LOUSE DOESN'T MEAN WE'RE ALL BUMS. . . ONE DRINK. . .IT'LL MAKE MY WEEK. . .
	CINDY: (Relenting: but not enthusiastic.) OH, ALL RIGHT. BUT JUST FOR A FEW MINUTES. THEN I'VE GOT TO GET GOING. SERIOUSLY, I DO HAVE SOMETHING PLANNED. . .

Source: From "Sexual Harassment: Fact or Fiction," written by William Van Nostran, directed by James G. Libby and produced by William J. Benham for AT&T Corporate Television. Used by permission.

lightning bolt of inspiration described by Mozart wherein ". . .the whole, though it be long, stands almost complete and finished in my mind, so that I can survey it like a fine picture or a beautiful statue, at a glance.")

The strong creative concept is usually deceptively simple; seemingly obvious once expressed. Good concepts take only a line or two to describe:

> "We'll use a doll house and chroma-key hands wearing white gloves and a suggestive piece of clothing to visualize key points about preventing burglary."[8]

> "Let's go inside the computer and demonstrate how it works by making an analogy to how a director orchestrates action on a feature film set."[9]

> "Let's get five characters from different Materials Management departments stuck on elevator forcing them to interact (reinforcing the theme 'we're all in this together') and letting them become multiple narrators."[10]

> "We can shoot the presentation from subjective camera point of view to heighten audience awareness of the importance of vision and threat of glaucoma."[11].

Basically, all you're after is an interesting way to communicate the content, using a specific A/V medium. It usually takes lots of brainstorming. Sometimes the writer is able to brainstorm with the producer or director. Other times, the writer must brainstorm solo.

This is where Elbow's dichotomy between creating and criticizing is most apparent. To generate as many interesting, whacky, off-the-wall, playful and potentially useful ideas as possible, you need to banish the critical "judge" who resides within, giving your creative child a safe haven for playfulness.

Only after you feel you've exhausted the creative possibilities should you enter a more analytical mode. First, look over the doodles, notes, clusters and scraps of paper you probably generated. Look for relationships. Connections. Circle and join ideas that have the most promise.

At this point, one of two things will happen. First, you may strike upon a creative concept so compelling that it dominates your thinking on how to write the script. The concept comes to you "full-blown"; you envision the various parts of the program fitting together like movements of a symphony. The experience is Mozartean.

Or, your movement toward a concept will have been more evolutionary. You may take various approaches, combining or refining them into that single idea which "shapes style, format, content and structure into a unified, aesthetically pleasing whole."

Whichever way you generated the concept, you've been in the creative mode—giving freedom and encouragement to your playful side. Now don the judge's robes—putting your concept on trial to identify any weaknesses. You shift gears from the creative to the critiquing mode. A useful tool for making such judgments is the "Concept Evaluation Matrix," (Figure 5.7).

Concept Evaluation Matrix

This is nothing more than a series of questions you should ask yourself to evaluate the validity of your concept. The answers will reveal if your approach merits full-blown development, some modification, or sends you "back to the drawing board." There are seven criteria you must apply to the concept.

1. *Content Origination:* Does the concept spring from careful consideration of the subject matter or is it arbitrarily imposed upon the subject? The decision to write a script encouraging eye check-ups for glaucoma from a subjective camera point of view arises from consideration of the content. The notion of

Figure 5.7: Concept Evaluation Matrix

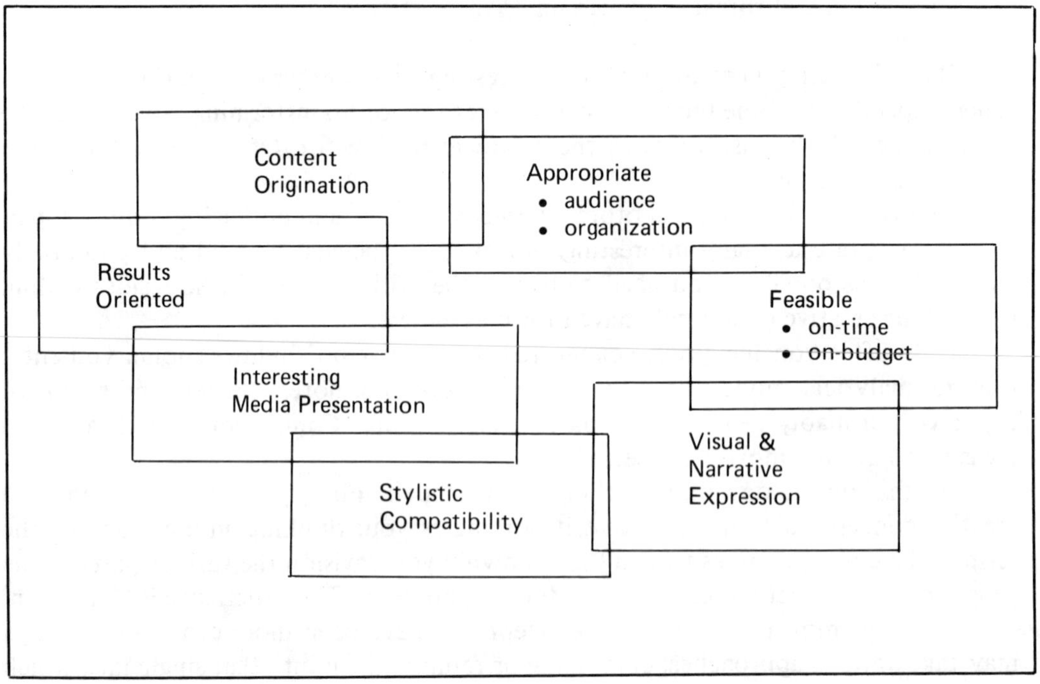

doing a Star Trek take-off to communicate key features of a 401K Investment Plan is arbitrary and indulgent. Originality involves finding the "hook" inherent in your material, not coming up with an idea and then forcing the material to fit. To return to Rachel Carson: "...the discipline of the writer is to learn to be still and listen to what his subject has to say to him."

2. *Appropriateness:* Your concept must be appropriate for both the organization and the audience. The sleek and handsome set made from polished plexiglass may be quite appropriate for the high-tech electronics company but totally off-key for the Wall Street international banking firm. The approach you take to reach an audience of sales people will be quite different from your appeal to unemployed blue-collar job seekers.

3. *Feasibility:* If a good concept cannot be properly executed within the "givens" of the assignment—time, money and talent—you must either refine the concept accordingly or explore other options.

4. *Visual and Narrative Expression:* Your concept should allow for a synergistic use of the chosen medium's capabilities. Inexperienced media writers often begin by scripting the audio side of the page first—totally ignoring the visual potential. Good A/V writing links words with images.

5. *Stylistic Compatibility:* All the elements of your concept (mix of formats, structure, style, use of talent, etc.) must be organically integrated. Do all your "main themes" work together?

6. *Interesting Media Presentation:* Your concept should be intrinsically interesting. Whether working in film, video, multi-image or audiocassette you have at your disposal media which have been used imaginatively to plumb the depths of almost any subject known to man. If you can't think of an interesting way to use the medium for your material—you're either in the wrong business or you haven't worked at it hard enough.

7. *Results Oriented:* Go back to your objectives and ask honestly whether your concept will successfully achieve results that match the client's expectations.

Remember that to generate intriguing concepts you must be in a receptive, creative state of mind. To test the validity of your concepts, you must examine them critically, according to the criteria of the matrix.

Award-winning writer Donna Matrazzo adds one more question you must answer: "Can I write this well?" The most challenging concepts often stretch a writer to the outer limits of his or her capabilities. If you're up for the challenge—go for it. But if you honestly think a concept is beyond your ability to carry off, it's only prudent to go on to another idea. In a year or two, you may feel that you're ready for a similar challenge.

WRITING THE TREATMENT

At the end of the Rehearsal phase, you're ready to generate the next writing product: the treatment.

The treatment expresses the writer's emerging vision of the viewing experience in simple narrative prose form. To write a treatment, you simply transcribe the sights and sounds imagined during Rehearsal. The treatment describes the eventual viewing experience from beginning to end, indicating format, hinting at style and revealing structure.

Inexperienced writers often skip over treatments, leap-frogging directly to a first-draft shooting script. A descriptive treatment, however, is a valuable tool with many benefits at this stage of the writing process.

A well-crafted treatment can serve the following functions: help to overcome script "illiteracy" on the part of your client, content experts and other non-media people involved in the script development cycle; identify issues relating to production requirements; develop a rough budget; and the scriptwriter uses the treatment as a road map during the Drafting phase to produce a first-draft script.

Guidelines for Writing Treatments

Bear in mind that the treatment is a narrative description of the program you see and hear in your mind's eye and ear. Keep the prose simple and uncluttered. Follow these guidelines:

1. Develop the treatment according to the chronological sequence of events you imagine unfolding on the screen.
2. Describe the location and principal on-screen participant for each major scene.
3. Describe "sights" and "sounds" that will appear in the script.
4. Indicate major transitions.
5. Describe important sets, graphics, special effects and titles.
6. Don't overwrite—the treatment is a *general* description of how the program will unfold. Keep it simple. Leave flexibility for the drafting phase.

Like composer Walter Piston who reported a piece he'd been working on was almost finished but he "hadn't yet selected the notes," the scriptwriter will not hear every word of narration nor see each visual in the program. Whereas a script contains detailed instructions on how to produce the program, the treatment is a tool for communicating and discussing the creative concept you are proposing as a solution to the training or communication problems of the project.

To illustrate these guidelines, three annotated excerpts from treatments prepared for informational programs are included in Figure 5.8. The excerpts depict a variety of formats and visual/narrative styles and techniques. Numbers in parentheses in the text correspond to the comments that follow each excerpt and point out how the writer follows the basic guidelines for writing treatments. You should be able to visualize a viewing experience from each treatment.

THE COMPLETE ACTION PLAN

Combine the writing products generated in the Assimilation and Rehearsal phases of the process and you have the elements for presenting a complete project proposal to clients or management. These documents not only illuminate the need for the project and demonstrate the merits of the writer's recommendations, they also function as guidelines for budgeting and scheduling the production.

The complete action plan—including objectives, audience profile, content outline and audiovisual treatment—marks the end of the research and conceptual phase of a project. Once the client and producer/director approve the action plan, the writer turns to execution and the detailed work of constructing a comprehensive shooting script.

The importance of the preliminary work cannot be overemphasized. Although some things will evolve and change on the road to a final shooting script, the essentials of form and style are established through the treatment. Those with the most at stake in the project have agreed to pursue a specific course of action. If a decision maker or the writer has reservations or doubts about the direction the project is taking, now is the time to retreat and regroup. If that means returning to the drawing board and developing an entirely new approach, so be it. Usually, clear thinking and sound conceptual work up to this point will result in an approach that is greeted enthusiastically by all involved.

A creative concept that is on target will result in a good production even in the face of some calculated budgetary, production and time limitations. By contrast, no amount of cosmetic production value can compensate for a presentation based on a bankrupt creative concept. Spend $100,000 or more producing a fifty-cent concept and you still end up with a fifty-cent concept! And as for the old saying "we'll fix it in post-production"—that's a little like trying to clean up an oil spill.

Figure 5.8: Sample Television Treatment.

---

1. PROGRAM: Ohaus Toploader
MEDIUM: Videotape

We FADE UP on an extreme wide angle shot of the Ohaus GT Toploader balance in a stark studio environment. The GT Toploader is bathed in a white light with a hard cyc sweeping behind and around it. Lighting gels give the cyc a diffuse color wash. **(1)**

The camera begins a slow PUSH IN. The MUSIC is an electronic-style theme, slightly active and growing, but not too fast. **(2)** The off-camera narrator sets the stage. . .

> "Introducing the GT Series: affordable, versatile state-of-the-art electronic toploaders from Ohaus. The GT Series balances combine all the high-tech features you want with the solid, sensible design you expect from Ohaus. . ." **(3)**

As this opening narration continues, highlighting key features, the long PUSH IN to the balance continues. At the same time, we INTERCUT near subliminal shots showing the GT Toploader in the same studio environment with a wide range of items appearing on the scale. **(4)**

When the PUSH IN finally concludes, the camera settles on a shot of the GT balance framed to the right of the screen. The lighting is quite dramatic, giving the scale a handsome, high-tech look. **(5)**

Now we begin a short sequence in which the narration highlights the diverse environments in which the GT Series of toploaders can perform.

> "The GT Series of toploaders is equally at home in the scientific lab. . . the electronic lab. . .the school lab. . .the manufacturing plant. . .the test kitchen. . .or the medical lab.
>
> "Ohaus GT balances will prove themselves time and again, no matter where you use them. . . ." **(6)**

During this segment, the screen shows a series of carefully timed DISSOLVES in which various props appear beside the balance to visually depict the differing environments. For instance, when we mention scientific lab, a group of test tubes and beakers appears next to the balance. (One of the beakers might contain dry ice to animate the frame with rising vapors.) **(7)**

When we mention electronic lab, the test tubes will DISSOLVE off as the picture is transformed into a tableau featuring the balance with various electronic components. **(7)**

The narrator mentions "school lab" and the scene DISSOLVES into a shot featuring the scale with a grouping of text books and slide rule. When we talk about the manufacturing plant, a miniature conveyor belt appears by the GT balance with small cartons moving along the belt and off the lower left frame. In

Figure 5.7: Sample Television Treatment (Cont.)

each instance, the transition includes a change in the colored gels used to illuminate the cyc to intensify the effect of the same scale appearing in different environments.**(7)**

Next, we transition to a segment which demonstrates key features and benefits of the Ohaus GT Series precision toploaders. For this sequence, the GT balance is positioned in the center of the frame, the CAMERA looking down on the scale at a slight angle. **(8)** Once again we use a series of slow DISSOLVES as a variety of objects magically appears on the scale, each chosen to demonstrate a specific application—from taring and basic weighing to batching, check weighing, parts counting and animal weighing. **(9)**

The narration provides commentary on the GT balance's performance in each application. Through these diverse applications we also demonstrate the function of key features:

> the easy-to-use FillGuide. . .
> the Over/Under Indicator. . .
> the Movable FineRange. . .
> the Metric, Non-Metric and three custom units. . .
> and Parts Counting.

Throughout, the large digital display read outs appear as an INSET **(10)** in the picture showing the interaction between the item being weighed and the functional display. During this segment, some shots of the GT precision balance will be taken from overhead, looking directly down on the balance. Once again, each change in the item being weighed will be accompanied by a change in the lighting effect on the background cyc. **(11)**

For the close of the program, the electronic MUSICAL **(17)** bed picks up in tempo. The narration provides additional general information about the Ohaus GT Series—stressing versatility, quality, accessories, cost effectiveness and the company's warranty and service commitment.

During this narrative segment, the screen will now go to a series of fast-paced cuts in sharp contrast to the DISSOLVES the audience has been seeing. Each cut will feature the GT balance weighing various items as seen previously and shots of the balance with the props symbolizing the many environments the GT balance can call "home." **(13)**

The final shot of the program is a reverse of the slow PUSH IN used to open the presentation. During this shot, the Narrator is telling the viewer. . .

> "For a closer look at the Ohaus GT Series of balances, contact your local dealer representative or call Ohaus direct. Ask for a demonstration. Or, let an Ohaus specialist help you select the right balance for your needs."

Figure 5.8: Sample Television Treatments (Cont.)

Final titles and credits appear over the slow PULL BACK to the opening shot. Then, we. . . **(14)**

FADE TO BLACK

Notes

In this visuals and voice treatment, the writer must describe the sights and sounds which will unfold on the screen as a chronological sequence of events. This is a stylized treatment for a short program depending largely on staging, lighting, camera angles, and lensing to create the visual look of the concept. At the same time, it is a relatively simple concept: using a limbo studio space to showcase the product as props symbolizing a variety of applications appear "magically" on cue. (The GT "Toploader" happens to be a precision scale used for accurate weighing of small items.)

(1)   The writer begins by describing the opening shot, clearly placing the action in a studio setting, while describing the visual "look" in terms of light and texture.

(2)   The writer describes camera action in non-technical terms and suggests how music accompanies the action.

(3)   Sample narration establishes the tone or "voice" which is slightly on the "clinical" side.

(4)   The use of a subliminal editing technique is described as a component of the unfolding action.

(5)   Again, the writer not only describes the action, but the visual style in terms of staging and lighting.

(6)   The narration for these scenes can be conveyed quite succinctly. . .

(7)   . . .the accompanying visuals, however, require more detail to flesh out. Notice that although the treatment is specific, it's also suggestive. (The reference to dry ice to create vapors, for example.)   From a technical point of view, the effect of various props appearing beside the balance requires a "locked off" camera shot so the scale and background remain in the identical position with only the props changing around it. The director will understand this is what's required. Less technical script readers would only be baffled by more technical descriptions of a "locked off shot."

(8)   Here, the specific framing of a shot is important in visualizing the action which follows, so the writer includes this specific information in the treatment.

(9)   Details relating to the specific content of this segment should be provided in the content outline. Here, the writer condenses screen time since we are focusing primarily on the function of the visuals in an overall way.

(10)   Information about read-outs is an important element, so the writer describes how this will be integrated into the action.

Figure 5.8: Sample Television Treatments (Cont.)

(11)   Since this is a highly staged and orchestrated concept, the writer suggests how lighting might heighten visual impact.

(12)   Music plays a functional role in establishing a faster pace as the short program draws to a close.

(13)   Not all content points need detailed narrative description in the treatment. Here, content is alluded to, as well as a change in the overall pacing of the program.

(14)   The writer has given thought to closing the program by reversing the camera action and visualization described in the opening.

From "Ohaus Toploader," written by William Van Nostran for the Ohaus Company.

---

2. PROGRAM: *You're Hired! The Nuts and Bolts of Job Hunting*
MEDIUM: VIDEOTAPE

Open on shot of female TV News Reporter outside plant with field report. "So, as of next week, employees at this 60-year old plant will be looking for new jobs. As the gates close for good, one has to wonder, where will the new jobs come from? This is Brenda Devlin—Channel 6 News."

Seque to groups of employees coming out of the plant. We catch bits and pieces of their conversation. Their glib joking masks the inner emotions. **(1)** "Hey, Bobby—there's your chance to be on TV."

"Well. . .I don't know about the rest o' you. But I feel like I've earned a good, long vacation." **(2)**

"Yeah—we paid into unemployment all these years. 'Bout time we took a little somethin' out. . ." **(2)**

Follow two of these employees to a car as they share a ride. One, Nick Conti, is in his mid-thirties. The other, somewhat older, looks around, shakes his head and comments. "I can remember the first time I came through these gates." **(2)**

"Guess we all do, Manny."

"Somewhere along the way, I got the notion I might just work here 'til I won the lottery, kicked the bucket or retired. Never dreamed it would all just end like this." **(2)**

They commiserate, talking about how all the rumors have come to pass.

They're about to drive off when Manny asks Nick: "You worried about gettin' work, Nick?" **(2)**

"Why worry? Like my dad used to say—anyone willing to work can find work. Simple as that." **(2)**

They drive off as opening titles and credits appear over a dinner scene in the Conti's home. Nick's wife Linda is seen fussing at the kids: "Stacey, put some of those brussel sprouts on your plate. . ."

There's tension in the air. Nick is trying too hard to act as though everything's normal. But around the table—there's this feeling a bomb might go off. The kids

Figure 5.8: Sample Television Treatments (Cont.)

are eager to finish and be dismissed. (3) Left alone, Nick and his wife Linda talk. Nick still seems overly confident about finding work. **(4)**

Cut to **(5)** television station as the News Reporter, Brenda Devlin, talks with her News Director.

"I want to follow the story beyond the plant closing. Look at the people-side of the story. Report on how their lives are affected. What obstacles they encounter looking for work. Some are going to pick themselves up, go out and find work. Others will flounder. What'll make the difference? I want to see just what it takes to find a job in today's economy." **(6)**

The News Director expresses concern over her workload, but gives her a go-ahead to follow the story.

Cut to a Job Search Group in classroom. A woman is leading the discussion. She's a dynamic speaker, very much in charge. "Looking for a job *is* a full-time job. . . ." As she delivers her "pep talk," we pan around the room at faces listening intently. Many are familiar from the opening scene—including Manny. But Nick is not among them. "It's just like selling a product—only *you're* the product. Now, before we get into your workbook, let's talk a little about what you and your families will experience emotionally. . . ." **(7)**

Her speech continues voice-over, while the action shifts to scenes at the local Unemployment Office. We focus on shots of various individuals waiting on lines and completing the paperwork needed to collect compensation. Here, Nick is among the group. We see him with some cronies. Many were among those in the Job Search audience. The segment ends with a brief exchange between Nick and another laid-off worker: "You sign up for that Job Search program, Nick?"

"Aw, who needs it?" Nick responds. "They're just tryin' to make us feel better about being on the street. I didn't need help findin' my last job. I know what I'm doin'."

Cut to the Reporter interviewing the Job Search Group Leader as background for her story. "So what will make the difference between those who get good jobs quickly and those who don't?"

"Attitude and technique."

"Technique? I don't follow?"

"Basic job-hunting skills. Think about it. Nobody teaches you how to organize and conduct a job campaign. Most people are rank amateurs at it. And I'm talking about simple little things—like knowing how to use the phone to your advantage. . . ." **(7)**

Cut to shot of Nick at pay phone in coffee shop. We listen in as he makes the cardinal sin of asking bluntly, "Do you have any openings?" We see him react as the voice on the other end responds, "Sorry. We're just not hiring now." (7)

Cut back to Reporter and Group Leader as she continues making points about job-hunting skills. "You have to use a system so you know how many phone calls you should be making each day. You've gotta keep records for follow-ups and referrals. Of course, before you even begin looking, you should know how you're going to sell yourself to an employer. . . ."

Figure 5.8: Sample Television Treatments (Cont.)

We segue to classroom shot as the Group Leader is now working with the class. "So you're going to start by taking an inventory of your skills. Things you know how to do well. From this, we'll develop a way to present yourself to an employer positively. You'll learn to capitalize on your strengths and minimize weaknesses." **(7)**

As the group begins to work, we dissolve to Nick in an office being interviewed by a rather intimidating supervisor, a real no-nonsense type. "So just what makes you think you'd be able to do a good job for us?"

Nick's thrown off-balance by the question. He responds tentatively, "Well—I really need this job. . . ." After a few seconds of silence, the interviewer comes back with another question. "It's a lot less money than what you're used to making. How do I know you won't stay here a couple of months and then up and quit when you find something better?" **(7)**

Cut back to classroom as Group Leader is going around the room for responses. "OK. Marilyn—how would you answer that question? **(7)**

We hear Marilyn give her structured response. "Well, one way of handling that is to say, 'In my old job, I had to travel a lot farther. Since this is closer to home—I'm willing to work for slightly less to begin with since I'll be paying less to commute.' " **(7)**

We cut back to Nick, still floundering. "Well. . .you see. . .if I come to work here. . .I wouldn't really be looking anymore. . . ." **(7)**

We cut back to the Reporter talking with the Group Leader as she makes another point: "The folks who don't go about it right, often find themselves dead in the water. They're depressed to begin with—then they start facing a lot of rejection. . . ." **(7)**

Cut to another shot of Nick on phone in his kitchen. We watch his reaction as the voice on the other end says, "I'm sorry Mr. Conti. The position's been filled already. You should've called about that interview on Monday. But we'll keep your application on file. . . ." **(7)**

He hangs up. His wife, making a sandwich, knows without asking that it's another blind alley.

Cut back to Reporter and Group Leader as she continues on. "They're not prepared for the depression. Pretty soon, it affects them at home. . . ." **(7)**

Cut to tight shot of Nick. His wife is clipping his hair. **(8)**
"Hold still, Nick."
"How can I hold still when you keep askin' questions?"
"I just wanna know if they said when they'd get back to you?"
"They didn't say much of anything definite."
"Well, didn't you ask 'em?"

Figure 5.8: Sample Television Treatments (Cont.)

Nick jumps up and throws down the sports section of the newspaper. "Dammit—
you know so much about gettin' a job, why don't *you* go out and get one and I'll
stay home with the kids. Cook and wash and gossip with Corrine." **(9)**

Notes

This illustrates a treatment for a dramatization—a program designed to motivate
displaced blue-collar workers to take job search skill-training seriously. In addition
to describing action in each scene, a treatment for a dramatization should suggest
character and dialog.

(1)   Here the writer sets the scene and describes the action involved on the day
of a plant closing. A TV reporter serves as the main narrative device.

(2)   Some sample dialog conveys a sense of style and communicates character.
From the beginning, it is clear this production involves a "slice of life"
reality style much in the vein of a docudrama.

(3)   In just a few sentences, the writer conveys the sense of tension among
family members, which is the sole function of the scene.

(4)   It's not necessary to flesh out each and every scene in a treatment. Here,
the writer describes the action with broad brush strokes. (In the actual
draft script, this scene seemed superfluous and was eliminated.)

(5)   Reference to transitions suggests a fast-paced, docudrama style.

(6)   We begin to see that the TV reporter in the opening scene will become
an important character and storytelling device.

(7)   Juxtaposition of Job Search Group Leader scenes with vignettes of Nick
committing job search mistakes provides a structural framework for contrasting right and wrong job search techniques.

(8)   Action of haircut provides a context for the dialog that follows. The
writer had to defend this stage business in a production planning meeting.
Is the wife giving the husband a haircut simply a bit of stage action? No,
the haircut has symbolic value. Is the wife doing the haircut because
they're trying to live on a tight budget or has she always done this? Is
Nick more concerned about his appearance because he's on a job search?
The action has symbolic value and was kept in the production. Here is a
perfect example of how visuals communicate in ways which narration and
dialog cannot.

(9)   Conflict is the essence of dramatic action. Here the stress of job hunting
begins to tell on family relationships.

Figure 5.8: Sample Television Treatments (Cont.)

From "You're Hired. . .The Nuts and Bolts of Job Hunting,"[TM] written by
William Van Nostran, created and produced by Karli & Associates and The
Prudential, Audio Visual Communications Division. Used by permission.

- -

3. PROGRAM: Product X Launch[10]
MEDIUM: Multi-image

In this module, we use audiovisual capabilities to dramatize major trends in the
marketplace (aging of U.S. population, trend to once-a-day dosing and competitive
environment). The module culminates in the arrival of Product X as the superior
product for treatment of chronic arthritis.

The module begins with multiple images of kids at a birthday party. The sound
track features children's voices singing "Happy Birthday" as images of party
balloons and hats, candles on a cake, children opening presents and playing typical
party games such as pin the tail on the donkey flicker across the screen. . . **(1)**

Slowly, almost imperceptibly, the chorus of voices singing "Happy Birthday"
appears older and more adult sounding. The party images likewise transition to
show activities at a party for people in their twenties and thirties. . . **(1)**

The voices singing "Happy Birthday" continue to age creating an almost eerie
effect as the chorus soon evolves into the off-key "pipes and whistles" of an elderly
group. The images likewise change to depict old people celebrating a birthday with
their cronies. We see a cake with many candles. **(1)**

A line or two of narration puts the action into context: "The average age of the
U.S. population is growing older everyday. And as people live longer, arthritis becomes an increasingly widespread medical problem. . ." **(2)**

The "Happy Birthday" chorus is pulled under as a variety of images showing
people in their 50s, 60s and 70s appear in various frames of the screen. **(3)** We
now hear a montage of voices dramatizing arthritic conditions. "This damp spell
we're havin' sure makes my arthritis flare up. . . ." And another voice comes in
with "Doctor, I'm taking more and more aspirins everyday. Isn't there something
stronger you can give me?" **(2)**

We transition to sequence of visuals showing doctors in their offices—at first
consulting with patients. We hear voices of physicians: "There's several different
compounds on the market. I'm going to put you on a once-a-day prescription
drug. . . . We'll start you at a moderate dose. . . ." **(2)** Prescription pads with the
notation "Take one tablet daily" appear almost subliminally during this sequence.
(3)

The montage picks up in tempo as we shift to see images of pharmaceutical
representatives detailing physicians. The audio contains a mix of various presenta-

Figure 5.8: Sample Television Treatments (Cont.)

tions, dramatizing that almost every pharmaceutical company has a product in the category and many are new entries. **(4)** Occasionally, lines like "Doctor I'm here today to tell you about our new therapy for relieving the pain and inflammation of arthritis. . ." are heard above the din. Names of competing compounds and the companies making them appear almost subliminally as this sequence builds to a crescendo—a cacophony of sales reps all vying for the physicians' attention. **(4)**

Slowly but surely a new musical theme **(5)** comes to the fore, eventually drowning out the voices of competing sales reps—it is our theme song. Beauty shots of Product X packaging, pills and displays of product literature, journal ads and detail aids featuring the superior to aspirin claim and once-a-day dosing. The sequence ends with the self-confident, assured voice of a sales rep saying, "Doctor, I'm here today to tell you about Product X, an exciting breakthrough in the treatment of chronic arthritis. . . ." **(6)**

Notes

This treatment describes a short multi-image module highlighting the aging of the American population in relation to a new anti-arthritic compound.

(1)   Notice the reliance on music and visuals to establish the theme.
(2)   Narration and dialog is minimal.
(3)   Throughout, there is a sense of the impressionistic effect of a multi-image presentation. The writer is thinking in terms of visuals appearing in various screen areas.
(4)   The audio mix of voices to symbolize the competitive din is reinforced with a visual montage.
(5)   The transition to a musical theme provides the backdrop for showing the new product visually. So within a relatively short period of time, several points have been made without heavy reliance on narration.
(6)   The closing tag line provides a strong closer to the module.

From "Happy Birthday," written by William Van Nostran for the O'Hara Company.

FOOTNOTES

1. Howard Gardner. *Art, Mind and Brain* (New York, NY: Basic Books, Inc., 1982), p. 358.
2. *Ibid.*, p. 362.
3. *Ibid.*, p. 363.
4. *Ibid.*, p. 360.
5. Donald Murray. *A Writer Teaches Writing*, 2d. ed. (Boston, MA: Houghton Mifflin Company, 1985), p. 17.

6. William Goldman. *Adventures in the Screen Trade* (New York, NY: Warner Books, Inc., 1983), p. 196.

7. Peter Elbow. *Writing with Power* (New York, NY: Oxford University Press, Inc., 1981), p. 7.

8. A concept of scriptwriter Ed Schultz for a Citicorp project.

9. A concept of scriptwriter Kevin Cole for a Hewlett-Packard project.

10. A concept of scriptwriter William Van Nostran for producer/director Kim Cloutman and the SNET Corporate TV Center.

11. A concept of writer/director Jack Pignatello for a Crum & Forster project.

Step 3: Drafting

6 Drafting the Shooting Script

FROM TREATMENT TO SCRIPT

Rarely do clients and subject matter experts understand the jargon of film, television and multi-image production. When they see a script in the dual column format (as shown in Figure 6.2) they tend to focus solely on the narration, mistakenly thinking that's where all the content is to be found. When such "visually impaired" readers do venture into the left side of the page, intimidated or put off by the production shorthand, they're often unable to respond constructively. (How many times have you met for client feedback to have someone start by asking, "What does ECU mean?")

That's what makes treatments invaluable. They communicate the intended viewing experience in narrative prose form: no columns to deal with, minimal technical jargon, and only a hint of what the final narration will sound like. Making a treatment the first creative "checkpoint" in the development process, objections to format, structure, style, visualization and graphics or special effects should surface at the conclusion of the rehearsal phase—well *before* beginning the first-draft shooting script.

In the drafting phase, however, the writer must now confront the specifics of the viewing experience in "real time," crafting each moment of the unfolding experience sentence by sentence, image by image. In this chapter, we'll focus first on shooting script formats and their relationship to the script reading/viewing experience; then we'll discuss the process of moving from content outline and treatment to first draft shooting script.

Where are we in the creative process? The writer has collected and digested the information needed to identify and address the challenges inherent in the assignment. Several writing products have been generated, including a content outline and treatment. In writing the treatment, the writer chose a specific creative strategy to capitalize on the strengths of the audiovisual medium, then described the general chronological sequence of events which will unfold on the screen. Now comes a turning point in the process—that period when the complete shooting script is first fleshed out in painstaking detail, resulting in a full, second-by-second description of the viewing experience. The initial result, or first draft, is often crude and unpolished.

The Drafting Process

Drafting the shooting script differs from writing the treatment in the following ways. The shooting script. . .

1. uses language of media production terminology;
2. uses one of two generally accepted shooting script formats;
3. contains detailed, specific and complete narration/dialog;
4. contains adequate and appropriate description of visuals that will appear on screen; and
5. links visual and narrative cues in time, indicating a precise chronological sequence of events.

In doing the above, the scriptwriter crafts detailed, specific instructions for the production team to follow in producing the program.

Sight and Sound in Time

When watching an audiovisual program, you see a continuous evolution of spatial relationships between the camera (film, television or still camera) and the subject. Concurrently you hear a continuous mix of music, voices, and sound effects. To describe this chronological sequence of events and the relationship between sight and sound cues, the writer uses a special vocabulary—the language of media production terminology.

Some terms describe the spatial relationship between camera and subject: long shot (LS), medium shot (MS), close-up (CU) and extreme close-up (ECU). (Figure 6.1 illustrates each.) For motion media, other terms define the movement of the camera in relation to the subject: pan left or right; zoom in or out; dolly in or truck right. (See Glossary.) In multi-media scripts, the writer often describes the action that takes place within the screen area (such as a "Pop-on," a visual effect in which succeeding elements of a visual appear from nowhere while the rest of the image remains static). In television and film, even when the camera remains still, the writer often describes evolving spatial relationships within the frame:

MS—on female nar-
rator in park set-
ting. Background
action consists of

teenage boys tossing
football or frisbee.

Such terms and descriptions are the basic vocabulary of television, film and multi-image production. The terminology is a functional shorthand; a way of communicating instructions on how to "make" the audiovisual production. (The shorthand codes in a shooting script function in a way similar to the abbreviations used in recipes to communicate quickly and efficiently what the cook must do to move from printed page to hot dish.)

The writer also sets down copy to be spoken with visuals; music to establish mood, time or locale; and sound effects to punctuate on-screen action.

Space and sound, then, are two of three dimensions audiovisual scriptwriters shape. Stripped of content (the substance of a presentation), film, TV and multi-image shows are *three*-dimensional media consisting of sights and sounds occurring in *time.* Skilled, experienced media writers develop a keen sense of sculpting time with words on paper, knowing that the words themselves are not as important as the *events* they describe.

The words on paper always become translated into space and sound, in time. Thus, a ten-minute presentation always takes ten minutes to watch. (Disregard random access, interactive videodisc programming for the moment.) The writer's use of time is known as "pacing." In most audiovisual presentations, time is

Figure 6.1: Camera Shots

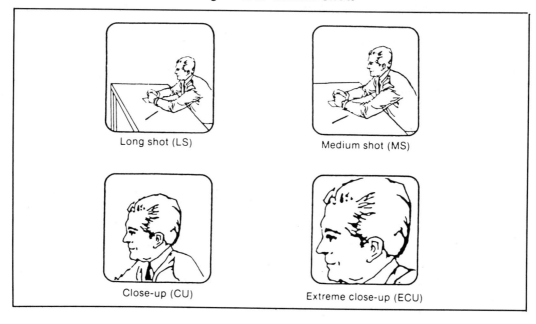

Long shot (LS)

Medium shot (MS)

Close-up (CU)

Extreme close-up (ECU)

generally measured by the duration of audio events. A segment of narration takes ten seconds to read; a musical interlude lasts 45 seconds; a sound effect occurs for three seconds. (You might even script 11 seconds of silence to achieve a specific effect.)

THE SPLIT-PAGE FORMAT

The audiovisual writer is continually orchestrating three raw materials. A shooting script simultaneously shows. . .

spatial events, which describe the visual content of specific scenes and shots,	and	auditory information, which includes narrative copy, music and sound effects.

If we orchestrate visual and auditory cues side by side as shown above, we have the classic split-page format generally used for television, multi-image and multi-media shooting scripts (see Figure 6.2).

Time is the glue that binds the two events together. Why this emphasis on time? In the pragmatic business of corporate and industrial video, film and tape documentaries, and, to a lesser extent, multi-image slide shows, the subject matter is highly specialized. Inexperienced writers often become entangled in the spider web of subject matter expertise, placing far too little emphasis on the ultimate *viewing experience.*

When scripting chunks of informational copy, the writer must consider how the duration of audio events establishes the pacing of the visual content. One full page of narration, typed double-spaced on the right side of the page, equals about 60 seconds of screen time. For every page of narration, the viewer must also *see* something for 60 seconds!

The left side of the page must be synchronized to the auditory cues on the right side of the page. Look again at Figure 6.2.

Using a fundamental progression of long shot to medium shot to close-up, the writer first establishes the scene with a wide angle view, then calls for close-ups to illustrate specific copy points in greater detail. In this sequence of about 90 seconds, the writer calls for 12 different shots. Furthermore, there's an integral relationship between the shooting instructions on the left and the narrator's copy on the right. For instance, the writer clearly wants to see a "CU of hands on keyboard" at the precise moment when the narrator says, "It's as simple as a typewriter." Or, when the narrator states "all kinds of information," the writer calls for a "quick change" in the "info on the CRT screen."

Figure 6.2: Sample of Split-Page Format

VIDEO	AUDIO
LS—Wide angle view of model office. Narrator moves towards TRIPS terminal.	**NARRATOR:** OUR NEW TRAVEL SERVICE OFFICE—MODERN, COMFORTABLE, SPACIOUS. THE OFFICE ITSELF SAYS "PRESTIGE, INTEGRITY, SECURITY AND SERVICE."
ZOOM in to MS of Narrator and terminal.	THIS IS THE TRIPS TERMINAL, AND AS YOU CAN SEE, IT'S RIGHT AT HOME IN OUR NEW ENVIRONMENT.
CU—On Narrator.	BUT WHAT IS TRIPS? TRIPS IS A MULTI-ACCESS RETAIL RESERVA-TIONS, ACCOUNTING AND COM-MUNICATIONS SYSTEM. . .AND TO CALL IT REVOLUTIONARY IS AN UNDERSTATEMENT. THE TRIPS COMPUTER SYSTEM PUTS THE WHOLE WORLD OF TRAVEL INFOR-MATION *LITERALLY* AT YOUR FINGERTIPS.
ECU—Of hands on terminal keyboard.	IT'S AS SIMPLE AS A TYPEWRITER. . . AND AS NEW AS TOMORROW.
ECU—On CRT screen displaying information.	IT'S A NEW WAY OF HANDLING INFORMATION. . .
Info on CRT screen changes rapidly two or three times. Screen now shows the artwork graphic of globe with animated network.	ALL KINDS OF INFORMATION. IT'S A NEW METHOD TO ENHANCE OUR WORLD-WIDE DISTRIBUTION NETWORK. . .OUR WHOLE MARKETING EFFORT.
MS—On Narrator and terminal.	IT'S A NEW TECHNIQUE TO EXPAND OUR CUSTOMER SERVICE CAPABILITIES. TRIPS MAKES AVAIL-ABLE, FOR THE FIRST TIME ANY-WHERE, *ALL* OF OUR TRAVEL RESOURCES ON A MULTI-ACCESS TERMINAL:

Figure 6.2: Sample of Split-Page Format (Cont.)

VIDEO	AUDIO
Cut to MS on jet liner taking off.	. . . . . .AIRLINES. . . . . .
Cut to MS on exterior of famous hotel.	. . . . . .HOTELS. . . . . .
Cut to MS of tour bus or group tour.	. . . . . .TOURS. . . . . .
Cut to MS of car rental area in airport terminal.	. . . . . .CAR RENTALS. . . . . .
ECU—On terminal with display.	. . . . . .OTHER TRS SYSTEMS. . . . . .
MS—On Narrator by terminal.	EVERYTHING—RIGHT HERE ON THIS ONE SCREEN.

Source: From "TRIPS: Your Selling and Servicing Partner,"
written by Allen Neil, directed by James G. Libby, produced by
Video Marketing Group for American Express Travel Services.
Used by permission.

The format is known as a shooting script because it provides sufficient detail for a production crew to execute the program from the written instructions describing what happens on the screen moment by moment. This script format links the synchronization between visual and auditory events occurring in time.

Cues for visual events need not be limited to narration or dialog. The script excerpt in Figure 6.3 shows how specific visual elements are linked to a music track.

This event-driven writing style distinguishes professional scriptwriters from the amateurs. Whenever the left side of the page lacks shot-by-shot detail, it's a dead giveaway the writer focused on narrative copy at the expense of visualization. This makes for neither good pictures nor good narration.

Too many audiovisual scripts are created by writing narration first, then returning to fill in the visuals as an afterthought. As a result, narrative copy tends to be wordy and lengthy, more like a speech than audiovisual commentary on pictures. Skilled scriptwriters search for the potential synergy between pictures and sound.

Words and Pictures

In *Philosophy in a New Key,* aesthetician Susanne Langer describes the difference between what she calls a "discursive symbol" (such as language) and a "presen-

**Figure 6.3:   Linking Visual Elements to a
                Music Track**

VISUALS	AUDIO
Multiple images of party fade in and out in various screen areas. Close-ups of activities such as a kid ripping open a present; playing pin the tail on the donkey; and hitting a pinata.	**MUSIC & SOUND EFFX:** (Children's voices singing "Happy Birthday" mixed with party sounds and laughter.)
Sequence culminates with fullframe shot of birthday cake holding four candles.	
Use SPECIAL EFFECT to simulate flicker of candles.	
MATCH DISSOLVE	CROSS-FADE AUDIO
Cake remains the same, but there are now more candles—twenty to thirty.	**MUSIC & SOUND EFFX:** ("Happy Birthday" lyrics sung by more adult, middle-aged voices.)
MATCH DISSOLVE	CROSS-FADE AUDIO
Cake remains the same, but is now ringed with candles—it is clearly the cake of a septuagenarion.	**MUSIC & SOUND EFFX:** ("Happy Birthday" lyrics are now voiced by an elderly group of senior citizens....
	. . .as the lyric comes to its conclusion, we hear the sound effects of the celebration. . .)
SPECIAL EFFECT as candles on cake flicker, extinguish and the screen FADES momentarily to BLACK. As music establishes, shots of mature adults fade in and out of various screen areas.	**VOICE I:** BE SURE TO MAKE A WISH! **VOICE II:** YOU'RE GONNA NEED SOME HELP BLOWING OUT ALL THOSE CANDLES. . . **SOUND EFFX:** (Of breath blowing out candles followed by cheers, clapping and birthday salutations.)

**Figure 6.3: Linking Visual Elements to a
            Music Track (Cont.)**

VISUALS	AUDIO
As opening lyrics hit, images show mature men and women engaged in semi-athletic endeavors—biking, strolling in a park, playing golf and tennis, pitching ball to young-ster with a bat, walking a dog, sailing a yacht. These are not decrepit senior citizens, but successful, up-scale men and women who are still leading vibrant, active lives and would not want to be slowed by arthritic conditions. (Initially, the screen pattern should mirror that used for toddlers in opening sequence.)	**MUSIC:** (While screen is in black, we hear the first strains of the show's theme song reprised. . .)

Source: From "Happy Birthday," multi-image module written by
William Van Nostran for The O'Hara Company. Used by permission.

tational symbol" (such as a painting). Words communicate through "a linear, discrete, successive order; they are strung one after another like beads on a rosary." In this sense, all language has a "form which requires us to string out our ideas even though their objects rest one within the other; as pieces of clothing that are actually worn one over the other have to be strung side by side on the clothesline."[1] Langer calls this property of verbal symbolism *discursiveness.*

The laws that govern visual communication are totally different from the laws of syntax governing language. The most radical difference is that *visual forms are not discursive.* They communicate their meaning *simultaneously* (rather than successively, like language), so the relations determining a visual structure are grasped in a single "act of vision." In this way, visual symbols are *presentational* rather than discursive. (This distinction may partially explain why inexperienced scriptwriters, especially those with print backgrounds, overwrite narration and underwrite the visuals. By training, writers are more comfortable with discursive symbols.)

Narration, unfolding in linear form, takes more *time* to comprehend than a picture, which can be grasped almost instantaneously. Incredible detail is conveyed by a portrait, for instance, because we do not have to stop to construe verbal meanings. Says Langer, "That is why we use a photograph rather than a description on a passport. . . ."[2] This is simply a variation on the theme that a picture is worth a thousand words. It is also why effective visualization in an audiovisual presentation generally reduces the need for explanatory verbalization.

Print writers use discursive symbols to express their ideas and emotions. Photographers and graphic artists use presentational symbols to express their visions and emotions. The audiovisual scriptwriter uses *both* discursive and presentational symbols *simultaneously* to express ideas, visions and emotions.

THE FIRST DRAFT—GETTING "BLACK ON WHITE"

Passion Hot vs. Critic Cold

Doing the first-draft shooting script is the time to be in your creative, artistic mode; "passion hot" rather than "critic cold." "It helps to separate the creating and criticizing processes so they don't interfere with each other," advises Peter Elbow in *Writing with Power*. "First write freely and uncritically so that you can generate as many words and ideas as possible without worrying about whether they are good. . . ."[3] Actually, you've already organized your ideas—conceptually, structurally and stylistically—through the treatment. So all you're trying to do now is capture on the fly the energy of the emerging text as you move from the generalized treatment to the specific shooting script.

You want to set down specific visual and narrative cues as they come second by second, minute by minute and page by page. Elbow is a big proponent of what he calls "free writing." "Free writing makes writing easier," he says, "by helping you with the root psychological or existential difficulty in writing: finding words in your head and getting them down on paper."[4]

Here's a trick for getting your emerging shooting script underway. I compose on a word processor. To initiate a first draft script, I often go back to my treatment and electronically "dump" everything relating to the visuals in the left-hand column. Then I "dump" everything relating to narration, dialog or sound in the right-hand side. Then I begin fleshing them out in greater detail, working down *both* sides of the page simultaneously.

Sometimes it's difficult to get going on the opening scene of a script. (The opening of an A/V show is analogous to the journalist's lead writing task—it's a vital, demanding type of writing which often requires a marshaling of energies, concentration and focus.) If you don't feel up to tackling the opening right away, start with a section of the program you feel mentally prepared to commit to paper. Do some "free writing." Then work from that starting point.

At this stage in the writing process, try to remove the critical side of your writer's persona from the scene. Don't fret over spelling. Don't ponder whether a semicolon or comma is proper. If you can't quite find the word to convey your precise meaning, leave a blank space and go back later with a thesaurus. Right now, you want to exploit the speed inherent in the keyboards of word processors and electronic typewriters. Go like lightning. Feel yourself energized by the seconds and minutes, the chronological sequence of events in your mind unfolding in time.

Pacing

As you move in tandem down the dual columns, be conscious of the "pacing" of the emerging text. All audiovisual programs involve a continuous evolution of spatial relationships between camera and subject, coordinated with a sequence of audio events. The rate at which those spatial relationships change is known as pacing. Using our rule of thumb (one full page of narration, typed double-spaced on the right side of the page, equals about 60 seconds of screen time) when you've written a quarter page of narration, you know 15 seconds have elapsed. At the top of page 12, you know you're about 11 minutes into the program. Are you where you should be in terms of communicating critical content points? If your goal is a 15-minute script, are you about ready to "round third and head home?"

This sense of time and energy is vital when generating a first draft. Writing is totally involving. It takes energy (some writers work on first rising and the night owls write after midnight, when their energy level peaks). I work in the downstairs portion of our house, which gets quite cool in winter. Until the woodburning stove kicks in, I'm usually chilled on January and February mornings. But after an hour of writing, I can feel perspiration building up. That's a sign of the energy and focus writing demands. That's the kind of energy to aim for when generating a first draft.

Visual Pacing

Ideally, each page of a shooting script is constructed shot by shot, so the writer describes visual images or action on the left side of the page and the copy, dialog or other auditory material on the right. Scriptwriters must see pictures and hear speech simultaneously—just as the viewing audience ultimately will.

The shot, with accompanying text, music or sound, becomes the basic building block of the audiovisual writer. As a general rule, you should script new visual information at least every 15 seconds for motion media such as film and video. Multi-image slide shows, video walls and the like need far more visual action. Relate that to the time equation of the split-page shooting script format (or the film-style format) and it works out to at least four shots per page—sometimes many more. This isn't to say your shots will be evenly distributed, one every quarter page. The frequency and duration of a shot depends on several factors: visual content and complexity, the action taking place within the frame, and camera movement in relation to the subject.

More complex, visually dense compositions require more screen time than a static shot containing minimal visual detail. In the next chapter, we analyze visualization as a separate entity. For now, we're focusing on correlations between sight and sound.

The general mood, tone and energy of a segment also influence pacing. A series of quick cuts in which the viewer is unlikely to absorb all visual detail is suitable for an up-tempo, emotional segment with an energetic, fast-paced mood. A series of long shots where the camera lingers over details of a scene is more appropriate to pacing designed to create an air of tranquility and reflection.

Audiovisual Transitions

Just as individual shots create a scene, a complete audiovisual presentation consists of many interrelated scenes. Obviously, scene changes occur whenever action moves from one location to another. Additionally, major shifts in subject matter, introduction of new faces or voices, or the passage of time also correspond to scene changes. Sometimes, scenes are delineated by a significant change in program format, such as moving from an interview segment to visuals and voices. Scene changes may even by cued by introducing a new style, mood, tone or tempo.

Bridges linking one scene to another are also written using audiovisual production language. Here are commonly used terms for describing visual transitions:

> FADE TO BLACK/FADE UP
> CUT
> DISSOLVE
> WIPE
> SPECIAL EFFECT TRANSITION
> CUSTOM TRANSITIONAL DEVICE

For a detailed explanation of these terms, see Chapter 7.

Audio Transitions

The method used to bridge audio between one scene and the next is as important as visual transitions. Not all transitions need trumpets blaring. Often, a simple, slow dissolve with no sound at all ideally suits the writer's stylistic intent. (Think of silence as a functional element in the sound track, just as white space plays a functional role in an advertising layout.)

One straightforward way to bridge the aural transition between two scenes is by "cross-fading" the two sound tracks. The audio in Scene A goes under as Scene

Figure 6.4:   Using Visual and Audio Transitions

VIDEO	AUDIO
HISTORICAL photos of Clarence Birdseye doing early experimentation with quick-freezing foods.	**MALE NARRATOR:** (V.O.) HE CONCLUDED THE SECRET LAY IN *RAPID* FREEZING AT EXTREMELY LOW TEMPERATURES. HE RETURNED TO THE U.S. A MAN POSSESSED BY A DREAM: TO MAKE QUICK FROZEN FISH, MEAT AND VEGETABLES A COMMERCIALLY VIABLE BUSINESS.
	FEMALE NARRATOR: (V.O.) THE MAN? OUR OWN CLARENCE BIRDSEYE. TODAY, CLARENCE BIRDSEYE'S DREAM IS A 14 *BILLION* DOLLAR INDUSTRY...
MONTAGE of full-color shots showing busy frozen food aisles in supermarket.	**MUSIC:** (Up tempo, rock style theme to punctuate facts.)
SUPER: 6% Total Supermarket Volume	**MALE NARRATOR:** (V.O.) A BUSINESS WHICH ACCOUNTS FOR MORE THAN SIX PERCENT OF TOTAL SUPERMARKET VOLUME....

Source: From "Focusing on the Fundamentals," written by William Van Nostran, produced and directed by Jack Gagliardo, for General Foods Corp. Used by permission.

B's audio is brought up. Cross-fading often accompanies a visual dissolve. A related bridging technique, "L cutting," brings in the audio from Scene B as the Scene A picture continues for a few seconds. (This is a technique often used in feature films. Listen for it.) The change in the sound track cues the audience to expect a visual transition.

Appropriate music and sound effects do much to support, punctuate and enhance the effectiveness of visual transitions. The excerpt in Figure 6.4 illustrates how both visual and audio transitions work in tandem.

As you're drafting the shooting script, be aware of your major transitional moments and how they relate to the pacing of the overall program. Have you spent eight pages explaining a content point that merits only four pages? Consider whether you're striving for fluid symmetry and balance in the relative pacing of each program segment as opposed to a rhythmic, staccato-like effect where quick cuts give viewers a sense of momentary disorientation.

THE MOTION PICTURE FORMAT

The split-page format has evolved as a standard for many professional audio-visual productions. Most video and slide show scripts employ this format. Film productions can be scripted in the dual column format, but many film producers are more comfortable with the motion picture format.

Although this page layout still relies upon the use of production terminology (LS, MS, CU, etc.), the relationship between picture and sound is expressed differently in the draft script. We've recast the American Express excerpt, shown in split-page format in Figure 6.2, in a motion picture format in Figure 6.5.

Relationships between picture and sound in the motion picture format are also delineated by typography and margin settings. Each camera shot is numbered. Narration, music and sound effects are described below and within each shot. Changes in location are indicated by the shot description—INT. for interior shots, EXT. for exteriors.

As we said earlier, clients and subject matter experts often cannot visualize a program. With the split-page format, the client and subject matter expert may simply ignore the left side of the page, thinking the "important" material appears in narration or dialog.

The motion picture format does make it more difficult to ignore visuals. However, it is probably no less bewildering to readers with little or no media background. Both script formats require visualization skills to "translate" words on the page into sights and sounds on the "mental" screen.

STORYBOARDS AND RENDERINGS

When you want absolute certainty that the client's perception of visual images matches your intent, the surest technique is to storyboard.

In advertising agencies, storyboards are standard practice for television commercials. Storyboarding is an ideal way to communicate the storyline and flow of a 15-, 30- or 60-second message. The shot-by-shot illustrations make quite clear when and how the sponsor's product is seen on screen or in action. Most multi-image modules are committed to storyboards. (These are usually short pieces—three to five minutes typically.) The advantage is obvious: visual content is communicated in a presentational form rather than through discursive verbal descriptions. The American Express project is storyboarded in Figure 6.6 as an example.

For lengthy television or film presentations (20 to 30 minutes or more), storyboarding may prove impractical. If the creative concept involves dramatic vignettes

Figure 6.5: Sample of Motion Picture Format

1. INT. WIDE ANGLE SHOT OF TRAVEL OFFICE. NARRATOR ENTERS AND MOVES TOWARD TRIPS TERMINAL.

NARRATOR
(Addressing camera.) Our new Travel Service Office—modern, comfortable, spacious. The office itself says "prestige, integrity, security and service."

2. ZOOM IN TO TWO-SHOT OF NARRATOR AND TERMINAL.

NARRATOR
This is the TRIPS terminal. And, as you can see, it's right at home in our new environment.

3. CLOSE-UP ON NARRATOR.

NARRATOR
But what is TRIPS? TRIPS is a multi-access retail reservations, accounting and communications system. . .and to call it revolutionary is an understatement. The TRIPS computer system puts the whole world of travel information *literally* at your fingertips.

4. EXTREME CLOSE-UP OF HANDS OPERATING KEYBOARD TERMINAL.

NARRATOR
It's as simple as a typewriter. . .and as new as tomorrow.

5. EXTREME CLOSE-UP ON CRT SCREEN DISPLAYING INFORMATION.

NARRATOR
It's a new way of handling information. . .

6. INFO ON CRT SCREEN CHANGES RAPIDLY TWO OR THREE TIMES.

NARRATOR
all kinds of information. It's a new method to enhance our world-wide distribution network. . .

Figure 6.5: Sample of Motion Picture Format (Cont.)

7. MEDIUM SHOT ON NARRATOR AND TERMINAL.

NARRATOR
It's a new technique to expand our customer
service capabilities. TRIPS makes available,
for the first time anywhere, *all* of our travel
resources on a multi-access terminal:

8. EXT. CLOSE-UP SHOT OF JET LINER TAKING OFF.

NARRATOR
Airlines. . .

9. EXT. MEDIUM SHOT OF FAMOUS HOTEL ENTRANCE.

NARRATOR
Hotels. . .

10. EXT. MEDIUM SHOT OF TOUR BUS OR TOUR GROUP.

NARRATOR
Tours. . .

11. EXT. MEDIUM SHOT OF CAR RENTAL AREA IN AIRPORT TERMINAL.

NARRATOR
Car rentals. . .

12. INT. EXTREME CLOSE-UP ON TERMINAL WITH DISPLAY.

NARRATOR
Other TRS systems. . .

13. INT. MEDIUM SHOT OF NARRATOR BY TERMINAL.

NARRATOR
Everything—right here on this one screen.

Source: From ''Trips: Your Selling and Servicing Partner,'' written
by Allen Neil, directed by James G. Libby, produced by Video
Marketing Group for American Express Travel Services. Used by
permission.

Figure 6.6: Sample Production Storyboard

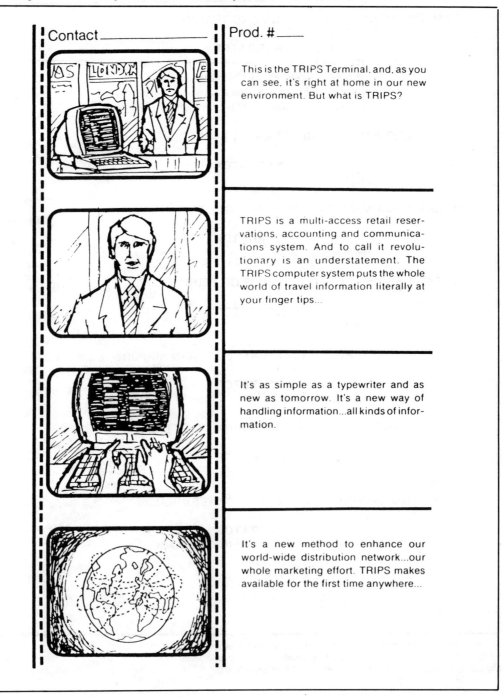

Contact _____   Prod. # _____

This is the TRIPS Terminal, and, as you can see, it's right at home in our new environment. But what is TRIPS?

TRIPS is a multi-access retail reservations, accounting and communications system. And to call it revolutionary is an understatement. The TRIPS computer system puts the whole world of travel information literally at your finger tips...

It's as simple as a typewriter and as new as tomorrow. It's a new way of handling information...all kinds of information.

It's a new method to enhance our world-wide distribution network...our whole marketing effort. TRIPS makes available for the first time anywhere...

Figure 6.6: Sample Production Storyboard (Cont.)

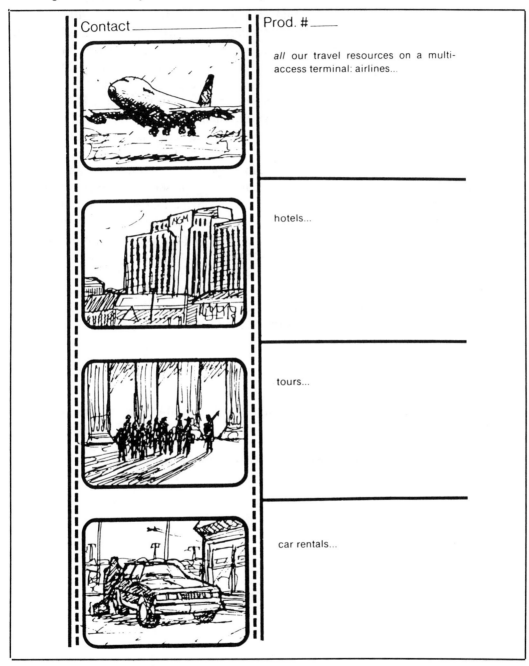

Contact _____   Prod. # ____

all our travel resources on a multi-access terminal: airlines...

hotels...

tours...

car rentals...

Source: Drawings by John Onuschak.

or documentary-style interview or action footage, the relationship between what the storyboard shows and what the actual footage offers may be quite different. A lengthy talking head scene of four minutes doesn't really require a storyboard to present the gist of the visual content. Or, when the visual material is familiar to everyone and consists of real-life objects, it's sufficient to write "CU—On hands operating keyboard." It doesn't take great imaginative powers to visualize the shot.

However, there may be selected scenes or passages in a script which do cry out for some form of visualization. For many audiovisual scripts, a selection of sketches, illustrations, or "renderings" to augment the shooting script is an effective way to help clients, subject matter experts, producers and directors visualize key elements.

If your script involves a stylized studio stage set, which changes and evolves throughout the program, then an artist's rendering of the set and its main variants is quite useful. If your program involves abstract subject matter (such as financial information or certain scientific concepts) you may wish to have an artist storyboard symbols or graphics treatments of key content points. If computer graphics or animated scenes will play a role in the script, the artist may want to storyboard the sequence.

As a basic rule, then, use the split-page format for multi-image scripts and for most video projects. Use the motion picture format when you're scripting a film project or when you feel it will be more useful in the review process than a split-page draft.

FOOTNOTES

1. Susanne K. Langer, *Philosophy in a New Key* (Cambridge, MA: Harvard University Press, 1956), pp. 80–81.
2. *Ibid.*, p. 95.
3. Peter Elbow, *Writing with Power* (New York, NY: Oxford University Press, Inc., 1981), p. 7.
4. *Ibid.*, p. 14.

7 The Imaginative Eye

"Even today, I feel in myself the nervous excitement of childhood when I realize that I am actually an illusionist, since cinema exists only because of an imperfection in the human eye. . . ."

Ingmar Bergman[1]

"The core of creation is to summon an image and the power to work with the image."

Anais Nin[2]

"To draw is to put down your thoughts visually."

Fritz Scholder, Native American painter[3]

Writers for audiovisual media need to become "audiovisual thinkers." In Langer's terminology (see Chapter 6), scriptwriters must communicate by constructing and juxtaposing *both* discursive and presentational symbols. To get maximum "bang for the bucks" from audiovisual media, scriptwriters must leverage the potential synergy between two different, distinctive symbol systems. Painters or sculptors focus solely on visual modes of thinking, rehearsing and creating. Novelists and essayists rely primarily on the effect of words on paper. But media writers must be adept at thinking visually, verbally and aurally in a simultaneous, synchronous mode.

It's like being a switch-hitter in baseball. Most players are only comfortable swinging from one side of the plate. But switch-hitters are ambidextrous. Media writers need to develop this facility to work with so called right and left brain symbol systems, switching gears and moving smoothly from one mode to the other. Often, beginning scriptwriters find either the verbal or visual symbol predominates.

My initial writing jobs were in print-oriented public relations departments. I wrote news releases and features. Although I had done graduate work in TV and film, the daily print-oriented writing strengthened my verbal muscles while the visual ones atrophied. As a result, when I began working in nonbroadcast television, I had to concentrate on exercising my visualization muscles. It took a lot of work.

Only recently have I felt some sense of balance between my verbal and visual skills—like the switch-hitter whose left-right batting averages are about equal.

VISUAL AND VERBAL FRAMES OF MIND

All of us have been taught, with varying degrees of skill and success, to use language. (And, as with any skill, in putting what has been learned into practice, we may develop bad habits along with the good.) Childhood socialization and formal education places heavy emphasis on developing and refining verbal thought and expression. After the primary grades, development of visual modes of thinking and expression is left largely to chance.

How do communication theorists and aestheticians distinguish between verbal and visual thinking? Allan Paivio writes:

> "While language is a socially constructed and conventionalized mode of expression, no corresponding single visual language exists. . . . This is one of the classical behaviorist arguments—imagery is subjective and inferential, words are objective and manageable."[4]

In some ways, this contradicts popular wisdom. A picture is supposed to be worth a thousand words, implying that pictures communicate with greater precision or clarity than words. In truth, however, pictures and words can function as either highly precise or highly ambiguous symbols.

In college freshman communications courses, students learn that "meanings are in people, not in words." The same can be said of visual images. "Meanings are in people, not in visuals." What is obvious and clear to one viewer may be loaded with ambiguity to another. (What does the burning candle flame symbolize in the motion picture *Blue Velvet*? Who knows the significance of the woman's apartment building being on Lincoln Street? Why is the robin at the end of the movie a mechanical bird?) What is provocative to one audience is offensive to another. A comforting message to one group patronizes the next.

Scriptwriters face other unusual creative paradoxes. Painters, sculptors and potters create visual works which are tangible expressions of themselves and direct by-products of their craft. They paint, draw, shape clay on a revolving wheel. A potter can set a bowl on the table and say to those around, "This is what I made today."

Scriptwriters also communicate through visual imagery but must trust to collaborative craftspeople—directors, set designers, graphic artists, computer animators—to realize their images on screen.

Another paradox. Even though working toward a visual mode of expression, the scriptwriter communicates function, style and pacing of visual material through words on paper. And, as Vera John-Steiner points out, there is a dichotomy between language and imagery:

> "Language is a highly conventionalized form of expression, but images—the constituent forms of visual thought—are hard to standardize or to define. There is no dictionary of images, or thesaurus of photographs and paintings. . . ."[5]

Ironically, then, scriptwriters must use a highly conventionalized form of expression (words) to describe forms of visual thought (images on a screen) intrinsically difficult to standardize or define. However, our clients expect us, as professional communicators, to deliver content to the target audience with absolute clarity every time out of the chute. The client expects every member of the target audience to walk away from a viewing with identical messages. Indeed, consistency and uniformity of the communication are often cited as prime management benefits of media presentations. Every member of an organization, all across the country, sees and hears the same message. How can there possibly be room for individual interpretation? How could communication breakdown happen? Quite easily. And more frequently than professional communicators would like to admit.

In writing workshops, I use a series of slides displaying minimal graphic symbols like those in Figure 7.1 and ask participants to jot down what the image means to *them*. Since these symbols are taken directly from the *Symbol Sourcebook*,[6] each has a precise "conventional" meaning. Yet few participants are familiar with the coded meaning of each symbol—so, when asked to generate a meaning or association on the spot, their spontaneous responses vary widely.

The teaching point is that each visual elicited a powerful response from each individual—and the meanings are valid from each one's frame of reference. But those responses are never *uniform*. "Meanings are in people, not in *visuals*."

The Scriptwriter's Code

The essence of all this is summed up by screenwriter Paul Schrader:

> "I am not a writer. I am a screenwriter, which is half a film-maker. I can't be a writer because words are not my code; words and sentences and punctuation. My code is far more elaborate. It has to deal with images. Montage. Cinematography. Editing. Sound. Music."[7]

Figure 7.1: Selected Symbols

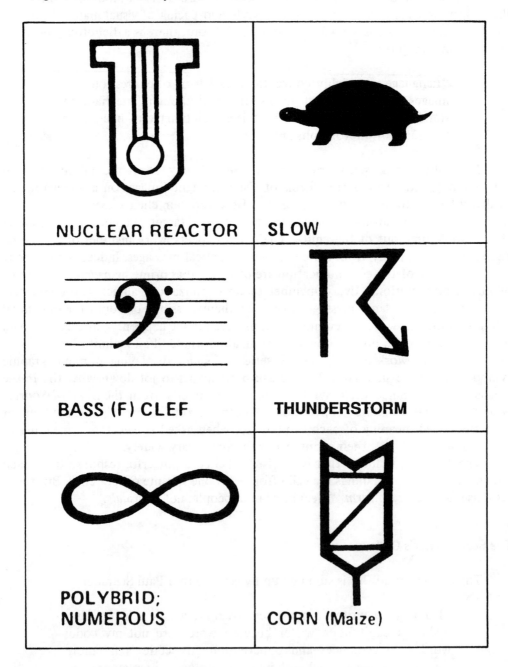

Source: Adapted from the *Symbol Sourcebook,* by Henry Dreyfuss
(New York: McGraw-Hill, 1972).

Schrader brings us full circle—he does not think of screenwriting as putting words on paper. He views scriptwriting as constructing a viewing experience from a "chronological sequence of events."

The following description of the genesis of an idea for a documentary film shows how powerfully visual subject matter can spark a seasoned filmmaker's imagination:

> "One example of a highly pictorial 'birth of an idea,'" writes Vera John-Steiner in her book *Notebooks of the Mind,* "was described to me by Andrew Ferguson, who was one of the producers of the Childrens' Television Workshop. He is a man whose imagination is thoroughly visual, but who can translate his inner processes into clear and well-formulated language. He described the beginnings of one of his favorite documentaries in the following way:

> "'One day I was up very early, and saw a group of [black] kids waiting for a bus. I went over to them and saw that they were carrying their breakfast. They were being bussed to a white suburban community. Just seeing them there—standing—started me thinking about bussing. . . .Then I saw the kids as part of a film; I first saw them in a tight little frame, like portraits. You don't know where they are going because they are just cute little faces. And, then you are beginning to pull them around, you present them and what they are waiting for. . . . The film never starts with an idea. It never happens that way to me.'"[8]

The "code" Schrader and all screenwriters employ to describe their visual images and events is the code of audiovisual production terminology. In this chapter, we'll focus on practical aspects of using audiovisual production terminology when drafting the "chronological sequence of events" that describes the intended viewing experience.

TIME AND SPACE: THE AUDIOVISUAL CONTINUUM

Within the confines of a motion picture screen, TV set, or multi-image screen, any media program is a continuous evolution of spatial relationships between camera and subject, coordinated with a sequence of audio events. To describe those spatial relationships and their synchronization with audio events, the writer uses the language of film, television or multi-image production.

The visual "language" of audiovisual communications is rife with descriptions of spatial relationships. Most describe spatial relations between camera and subject, such as the classic progression from Long Shot (LS) to Medium Shot (MS) to Close-Up (CU) to Extreme Close-up (ECU) illustrated in Chapter 6.

Camera movements such as PAN, TILT, DOLLY, TRUCK and ZOOM (see Glossary for definitions) describe movements of the camera over, across or in and out on the subject.

Terms to describe transitions from shot to shot or scene to scene imply spatial juxtapositions between two images: CUT, DISSOLVE, WIPE, PAGE TURN, etc.

In multi-image production, many of the same terms have similar meanings. In addition, this medium employs visual codes peculiar to creating visual images through multiple-projector computerized programming.

The term FRAGMENTATION, for instance, refers to the use of multiple screen areas to project any number of related and/or repeated images. Each image is cropped and masked to fit the desired screen mosaic. (Video walls also lend themselves to creation of multiple screen action.) MIXED FORMAT refers to use of more than one slide format in a show, i.e., mixing horizontal with vertical or vertical with square, etc. These terms represent verbal descriptions of visual spatial relationships.

Write Down What You Visualize

All writing is problem solving, and the problem of which pictures and images should accompany which words is the essence of media writing. So let's look first at typical pitfalls in writing the visual portion of a shooting script, then we will explore techniques to improve and clarify descriptions of what viewers should see.

TYPICAL VISUALIZATION PROBLEMS

Verbal Dominance

Too often, audiovisual scripts are visually weak because the communication is driven by verbal expression. Visual expression is considered only as an afterthought, or not at all. This is not to say that all programming must be highly visual. When the purpose of the communication is to reveal the chairman or president's thinking on a critical issue facing the organization, there may be little need for visualization. Too often, however, wall-to-wall text is scripted for a narrator while only the most cursory consideration is given to what will be on the screen throughout the recitation. Strong visualization never results when the left side of the page is treated as an afterthought.

Figure 7.2: Using a Visual Analogy

Metaphors, analogies and similes are useful ways of making abstract subject matter more concrete. This sales training program likens handling objections to track and field events. Runners who train with hurdles (buyer objections) take those hurdles without breaking stride. Likewise, the sales person who prepares and practices overcoming sales resistance and objections raised by the prospect will also take them in stride.

The analogy is carried out visually in the studio set design which incorporates hurdles as a way of illustrating specific types of objections.

Photo courtesy of The Prudential and Kinder Bros. & Associates.

The Kitchen Sink Syndrome

The kitchen sink syndrome is just the opposite. In the writer's zeal to visualize, every narrative point has an accompanying illustration. While each visual element may be appropriate for that particular moment, there is no underlying stylistic framework or visual theme.

This problem is always compounded when the client wishes to integrate a variety of existing visuals into the program. The writer may be faced with old film footage, videotape from a previous presentation, slides from the photo library and artwork used in a promotional print piece. Each element, of course, will have been produced by different people, at different times, with no thought of the project at hand. Inexperienced writers may embrace this material and begin plugging it all into the left side of the page. Unless this is done with extreme sensitivity and skill, however, the result will be a hodgepodge of visuals lacking clarity and unity.

Inappropriate Visualization

Some scripts suffer from use of visual material which is totally inappropriate. Some visual material may not be suitable for the audiovisual medium you are writing for. Detailed charts or graphs may contain too much information and detail for resolution on the TV screen but may work as projected slides. Writers cannot assume that the director and crew will find a way around technical problems. It's the writer's responsibility to develop a shooting script that is practical, pragmatic and "do-able." Whenever the writer paints production personnel into a corner, a disservice is done to all—especially the client.

Another form of inappropriate visualization is more stylistic. Earlier, directors were characterized by their fondness of the verb "to see." Another word directors like is "look"—used as a noun. The look of a program describes its visual style, a "documentary look," for instance, or a "high-tech look." Every audiovisual program is characterized by its own individual look. Writers should feel confident the look they are describing is appropriate for the specific content, audience and objectives of a project.

A serious corporate awareness program on issues relating to productivity is probably not the place for whimsical, cartoon style artwork. Nor would abstract, computer-generated graphics be appropriate for a presentation that focuses on the history and heritage of an organization or institution. The writer must develop a degree of visual literacy and taste. In a studio set, for example, the distinction between wood-paneled backdrops with leather chairs versus plexiglass panels with contemporary furniture makes a definite statement about the style and culture of an organization. The typeface selected for theme titles in a multi-image sales meeting slide show should fit the organization's image and purposes of the meeting. In describing locations, studio settings, graphics, photography, film footage, animation, special effects or any visual element, the writer should strive for a look that is compatible with the overall tone, purpose and stylistic integrity of the presentation. Avoid visual incongruity.

GUIDELINES FOR EFFECTIVE VISUALIZATION

Make Stylistic Decisions Early

Problems like verbal dominance or inappropriate visuals generally result from inattention to the visual style of the program in the concept stage. The writer can avoid many visualization problems by thinking through the visual style of the program before doing any narrative writing. In fact, if you follow the process described in Chapter 5, you are forced to deal with what the viewer will be seeing, as well as hearing, long before you script narrative copy. For preliminary visualization, you don't need to have every single graphic slide change, camera angle or special effect clearly in mind. Rather, focus on the potential for visualization in the overall context of the program. What look and style will serve your communication goals?

If you envision a studio set, what elements should the set contain? What function do they perform? How are they integrated with the narrator or other on-screen participants? If you're combining a variety of visual inputs, how will they be integrated so that the resulting look is unified, aesthetically whole? If you envision multiple locations or sets, what is the rationale for using each location? How are they linked together? Don't forget the relationship between visuals and voices. Is your talent on or off camera? If on camera, what environment will talent appear in? If you're suggesting totally off-camera narration, do you have sufficient visual material to engage the viewer's eye?

Often, there's no simple answer to these questions. Your decisions will be influenced by content, budget considerations, production and logistical constraints, client needs—and the audience. By giving early consideration to the style of your visuals, you ensure that individual shots, graphics and titles fit into the overall visual framework.

Determine the Function of Visual Material

Visuals serve many purposes in audiovisual presentations. On the most literal level, you may be using the television camera to show how a task is performed, for example, in a training program on unloading liquid hydrogen. In that instance you will be quite literal in describing graphic elements. To explain the inner workings of an internal combustion engine, a program might use simple animation or a sequence of diagrams or a cutaway scale model. Such visuals serve a specific tutorial function,

Figure 7.3: : Use of Setting and Backdrop

The writer's description and handling of settings and backdrops should be as well conceived as narrative copy. The
oversized typewriter functions as a display area for writing
samples in a business correspondence course. Courtesy
Crum & Forster Corp.

leading the viewer to focus on concepts, not the artwork itself. The function in these
cases is straightforward illustration.

Given other subject matter, however, visuals may be meant to create interest,
establish need or stimulate the imagination, calling attention to the style of the
visual material. When content is abstract, you may want visuals to serve a more presentational function. In such instances, artistic elements can be emphasized and
broadly executed. Cartoon style artwork conveys an air of whimsy or humor. Computer animation, by contrast, has a high-tech quality. Similarly, sets or other backdrops can range across the spectrum in terms of function. For a training program on
writing the business letter, the oversized, stylized typewriter shown in Figure 7.3
provides a functional way for the narrator to refer to writing samples. But it's also a
staging device means to be impressive and attention-getting. In a humorous training
program designed to serve as a discussion starter on the importance of strategic
planning in business, off-beat painted backdrops and set pieces convey the slightly
surrealistic tone of the piece. Symbols, abstractions, even "magical" computer-
generated animation video effects offer still other methods of making striking visual
statements.

Documentary style footage, on the other hand, may be the most functional when you seek to establish credibility. Media often serve as windows on the world, giving your audience a glimpse of unfamiliar realities. To illustrate the world of a youthful prison inmate making a new start through a special parole program, for instance, documentary footage serves the writer's purposes.

By considering carefully the *function* your visuals should perform, you will arrive at valid decisions about the *form* visual material should take. Form should evolve naturally from function. Answer the question: "What do I want visuals to *do* for the viewing audience in this program?"

Identify the Big Building Blocks

When toddlers construct with building blocks of different sizes, they learn to select big ones first, put those in place, then add smaller ones as the structure grows more complex. Scripting is somewhat the same. Once you have the component building blocks in mind, it's simple to write "ZOOM in for ECU on Block C. CUT to TWO SHOT of Blocks K and F. . . ." If you've thoroughly identified the functions of your visuals, this step is simply an extension of that process.

If, for instance, you've pictured a set with multi-level staging areas as the functional method of visualizing a program on writing business letters, you next need to clarify precisely how many staging areas are needed. What is the individual purpose and function of each? How often will each area be used? How will transitions from one area to the next be accomplished? The writer should answer these questions before writing details of the shooting script.

Or suppose you've determined that an animation sequence is a functional way to illustrate the action of a new drug. Now you need to identify how many different content points will use animation. How many animated scenes does that require? How will the scenes fit together? If you will be visualizing principles of medical malpractice law with a sequence of short dramatic vignettes, you must determine how many vignettes the content requires, what settings are needed (emergency room, a delivery room, etc.) and what action takes place in each locale.

At this point, it's helpful to construct lists of such elements or sketch them out roughly, if you're one of those fortunate writers who can draw. You're still not down to writing shot-by-shot descriptions or sketching a complex storyboard. But like the toddler, play with the big blocks first, arranging them until they fit together well.

In addition to helping the writer identify specific visual elements, this activity has definite practical value. If you plan to illustrate a historical narrative with still photos and period artwork, for instance, you must determine that there is sufficient source material available to sustain the piece visually. Granted, you may not know yet the sequence of these visuals, or the specific camera moves you'll script. But if you anticipate a five-minute narrative and can locate only six relevant photos or pieces of art, you're still in search of a visual solution. If the multi-level staging area set you envisioned will cost $30,000 to construct for a project budgeted at $38,000 total, you'll need to rethink the set and its elements. Again, the basis for this work should have been reflected in your treatment.

CAMERA AND STAGING

When you've arrived at a clear perception of the style and purpose of your visuals and have the big building blocks in place, you can get down to the nitty-gritty of writing camera directions. Many beginning writers are uncertain as to just what to include and how detailed a description is needed when writing the visual portion of a script. Screenplay writers simply indicate locations and time of day or night in their scripts—detailed camera directions are considered amateurish.

In audiovisual writing, however, where the subject matter is highly specialized and the purpose of programming goes beyond entertainment, it is imperative that the writer specify shots, camera angles and transitions. This doesn't mean the director will always follow the directions slavishly, or that production logistics won't alter the writer's suggested visualization. But since almost every audiovisual program requires a one-of-a-kind format and visualization, it's up to the writer to include sufficient detail for the script to function as legitimate instructions on how to make the program—a blueprint for the production team.

Set the Stage

By all means, describe the overall function, style and look you wish to establish. Usually, this kind of video description occurs on the first page or two of a script. In the excerpt in Figure 7.4, for instance, the writer devoted nearly an entire page to describing the style, function and component elements of a studio environment.

The writer has a specific style clearly in mind and shapes that vision through text such as: ". . .executed in a sketchy, minimal, free-style form. . .not intended to be realistic. . .monochromatic shades. . . ." Additionally, the writer explains how certain building blocks will be used throughout the presentation: ". . .the Narrators refer to these charts as Supers appear in handwritten style to highlight key points. These flipcharts also serve as display areas for getting in and out of vignettes."

The initial descriptions of the visual content of a program are extremely important in conveying the images in the writer's mind to the client and the director. These descriptions help those all important readers of scripts to visualize the viewing experience as you intend.

Figure 7.4: Excerpt Describing Video

VIDEO
FADE UP ON:
CU—Camera pans across studio backdrop, which consists of flats painted with free-style renderings of an office setting and perhaps an AT&T truck parked by telephone pole. This artwork is executed in a sketchy, minimal, free-style form. It is not intended to be realistic.
The art is done in monochromatic shades, grey and black or tan and dark brown, for instance.
These flats are cut out and arranged in front of a plain studio cyc [cyclorama; see Glossary]. The appearance is like a life-size children's "pop-up" art book.
The same style is used to represent two classroom flipcharts. Throughout the program, the Narrators refer to these charts as Supers appear in handwritten style to highlight key points. These

Figure 7.4: Excerpt Describing Video (Cont.)

VIDEO
flipcharts also serve as display areas for getting in and out of case study vignettes. For this opening, the main titles. . . **SEXUAL HARRASSMENT: FACT OR FICTION** appear over shots of these backdrops. Then. . . Cut to TWO SHOT on male and female Narrators. They sit on simple stools in foreground area.

Source: From "Sexual Harrassment: Fact or Fiction?," written by William Van Nostran, directed by James G. Libby, produced by William J. Benham for AT&T Corporate Television. Used by permission.

Describe Action

The writer is the first member of the production team to stage action. Although the writer's imagined actions are modified and refined as the production takes on its own life, the writer's initial indications of on-screen activity are essential. Figure 7.5, for instance, shows the opening shots for an employee orientation to the Maxwell House Division of General Foods.

The writer uses television production terminology to describe the activity. "P.O.V." (an abbreviation for point of view) indicates that the camera should assume the vantage point of a shopper entering the store. "Truck" tells the director the camera should physically move down supermarket aisles. The writer also describes actions the on-camera participants will be performing and calls for close-up shots as insert material. Notice that directions are specific enough that the script

Figure 7.5: Excerpt Showing Action

VIDEO
FADE UP ON:

Montage of shots in
supermarket
environment. (Could
be shot from P.O.V.
of shopper entering
store.) We pass by
check-out counter
and ZOOM to can of
Maxwell House being
rung up. Action
moves into
supermarket aisles as
we truck down coffee
aisle.

[SUPER opening
titles.]

Establish Maxwell
House Sales Rep
putting up display.

Feature "The Best
Coffee Company"
slogan.

Different angle as
Narrator enters scene
and addresses camera.

Narrator strolls down
aisle, referring to shelf
facings.

Insert CLOSE-UPS
on cans and jars.

Source: From "The Best Coffee Company," written by William Van
Nostran, directed by Robert Shewchuk and James G. Libby,
produced by William Hoppe, General Foods Corp. Used by
permission.

readers have an understanding of what shots are needed to construct the scene; at the same time, the directions provide sufficient latitude for adjusting to the logistics of the shooting environment.

Later, this same script (Figure 7.6) calls for an actor to portray Joel Cheek, originator of the Maxwell House blend. He describes how he went from wholesale grocery representative, working his territory on horseback in 1873, to founder of the Cheek-Neal Coffee Company, which first marketed Maxwell House. The left side of the television script contains these descriptions.

Much of this is stage business for the actor to perform. More detailed camera directions are not necessary since camera placement is the director's perogative, dictated by physical environment and practical blocking of stage business.

Script the Camera Directions

A functional shooting script provides camera directions to the extent that they are necessary. This does not mean each and every shot will be described in the shooting script. Camera directions should correlate to the specificity required by the subject matter.

A training tape for anesthesiologists on how to administer an injection anesthetic, for instance, would call for many more specific camera directions than a dramatic vignette of an employment interview. In the case of the anesthesiology traing tape, the writer will call for specific close-ups on action relating to the induction and maintenance of the anesthetic during surgery.

CU as nitrous oxide is
administered.

CU as oxygen is
administered. . .

and airway protection
provided.

ECU as muscle
relaxant injection is
administered.

Insert ECU on hand
adjusting rate of
micro-drip anesthetic.

Figure 7.6: Excerpt Describing Stage Business

VIDEO
Action begins as actor portrays Joel Cheek. Cheek moves about in office with turn-of-the-century memorabilia. He uses props and photo album to illustrate his story. He goes to map on wall. ZOOM to CU on map: follow route of Cumberland River. MS on Cheek as he moves to saddlebags slung over chair. INSERT close-ups as he pulls coffee bean samples from the bag. Moves to copper kettle and empties samples into kettle. INSERT close-ups of beans as appropriate. MS as Cheek moves to photo album. Begins to leaf through. ZOOM CU on photos or art of Maxwell House Hotel.

Source: From "The Best Coffee Company," written by William Van Nostran, produced by William Hoppe, directed by Robert Shewchuk and James G. Libby for General Foods Corp. Used by permission.

All such specific action would be detailed in the shooting script and keyed to narrative text. In the case of a dramatic vignette, however, specific camera directions may be minimal unless there is a key bit of action or reaction that is important for the viewing audience to see at a given moment. For example:

CU on job applicant;
her face registers
confusion in response
to the interviewer's
question.

Usually, however, the blocking and staging of dramatic scenes determine camera angles and cuts. As a general rule, if you want the viewing audience to see a specific image on the screen at a precise moment in the script, then describe the shot accordingly.

Indicate Titles and Supers

When you want the viewing audience to see text or other types of special graphic or visual effects, write it in the visual descriptions column. The superimposition of text over a scene should always be indicated by the word "SUPER." A sales training program in which track hurdles are used to symbolize the prospect's objections would be written as follows:

MS on two sales
trainees by two
hurdles.

SUPER: (Above each
hurdle)

Genuine Objection
Insincere Objection

The appearance of arrows, to draw the viewer's attention to a portion of the image, or other graphic superimpositions should be written out in a similar manner.

CU on map.

SUPER:

(Concentric circles to
indicate possible
customer service
driving routes.)

When describing superimpositions, the parentheses indicate that you are describing a visual effect as opposed to text which appears on the screen. Program titles, directions to pause or stop the program, indentification of a speaker's name and job title are typically indicated as supers.

Describe Visual Transitions

Just as a series of individual shots creates a scene, a total program consists of a series of interrelated scenes. Obviously, scene changes occur whenever action moves from one location to another. Additionally, major shifts in subject matter, the introduction of new faces or voices or the passage of time may also correspond to scene changes. Sometimes, scenes are delineated by a significant change in program format—say, moving from an interview segment to a section containing visuals and voices. Scene changes may even be cued by introducing a new style, mood, tone or tempo. In multi-media productions, a change from a slide sequence to motion picture footage corresponds to a scene change.

The writer's bridges linking one scene to the next are also written using media production language. Let's look at the terms most frequently used to describe transitions.

Fade Up/Fade to Black

All television and film programs begin and end in "black." The very first image fades up from a black screen, and the final image returns to black. In addition, a momentary fade to black (sometimes referred to as touching black) then fading in the next scene can also be used as a transitional device to bridge program segments. Generally, this transitional effect is too interruptive to serve as a frequent transition between one scene and another. However, training programs designed for group discussion, workbook activities or other interactions often use as much as 8 to 10 seconds of black to allow for the mechanics of stopping and restarting playback equipment.

Cut

A cut is nothing more than an instantaneous change between two shots or images. The final frame of Scene A is followed by the first frame of Scene B. (The term "cut" originates from motion picture editing, where one piece of film is literally cut and butt-spliced to the preceding shot. Later, in the heyday of live television, the cut or "take" from one camera to another became a standard transition.) Although a writer may use a cut to go from one scene to the next, it doesn't mean every cut is a transitional device. The simple cut from one camera angle to another, from one image to the next is the normal method of going from shot to shot. A cut between one shot and the next is always implied in a shooting script unless the writer indicates otherwise.

Dissolve

Since the cut is so common, it usually does not signal shifts in locale, time or content as vividly as the writer might like. The dissolve is an extremely functional way of joining two scenes. In a dissolve, the tail end of Scene A fades out while the first frames of Scene B simultaneously fade in. The two images overlap for a period of time. It's a fluid transition, and since the effect itself requires screen time to occur, it telegraphs to the viewer that a change is taking place.

Wipe

The wipe is sometimes described as a hard-edged dissolve. It looks as though Scene A is being wiped off the screen by the appearance of Scene B. A hard line separates the new scene from the previous scene. The mid-point of a wipe is like a split screen with half of Scene A on one side and half of Scene B on the other. (Like most visual effects, a verbal description sounds more complex than it really is.) A wipe between scenes can move from screen left to screen right, or vice versa. A vertical wipe moves up or down the screen; a diagonal wipe starts out in one of the four corners of the frame. A series of wipes between relatively short but closely related scenes can be an effective, up-beat way of going from one to the next. Stylistically, the wipe calls attention to itself more than the dissolve. Always be certain the transitional effect is appropriate to the style and tone of the program.

Special Effect Transitions

When a writer feels the need for a still more pronounced stylistic transitional device, a variety of special effect transitions may be written into the script. Here's where a good grasp of the chosen medium's capabilities, editing equipment and techniques helps express visual continuity on the printed page in practical production terminology. In TV, effects are generated electronically: in film, through optical printing effects; and in multi-image, through computer programming capabilities.

A new television post-production editing tool, the Quantel or digital effects generator, gives videotape editors unusual flexibility in manipulating the size and perspective of a single image. Using digital effects, transitions such as simulated page turns, flip-flopping pictures, infinity zooms and other types of optical magic can be created within the editing suite. The relative ease with which these striking effects can be created makes video post-production ideal for many situations, even for material shot on film.

Custom Transitional Devices

Sometimes the writer will even customize a unique transitional device as part of the overall visualization. A custom-tailored transitional effect should, however, be genuinely motivated by content. In the case of the American Express script excerpted earlier, part of the intended message was to dramatize the worldwide application of the new computerized TRavel Information Processing System (TRIPS). In that instance, the writer magically transported the narrator to American Express travel offices around the globe through a specially devised three-dimensional cube which appeared initially as the American Express logo. (See Figure 7.8.) shows how the transitional effect was described in the shooting script.

Such a unique and technically complex transition was justified in this instance because of the importance of the communication, overall production values and substantial budget. Effect for the sake of effect, however, is invariably self-defeating. Ninety percent of the time, you will be well served by cuts, dissolves and simple fades. Special effects and digital effects transitions should be the exception, not the rule. Otherwise, they become unspecial effects.

Describe Special Effects

When the writer feels an electronic video effect is critical to telling the story, the effect should be described in the left hand column. Effects such as chroma-key, squeeze zooms, halls of mirrors and tumbling pictures should be described vividly so that the production team can execute the effects precisely.

Graphic simulating
aperture of a camera
lens. Matte title
graphic, "Focus on
Research" in center.

Figure 7.7: Using a Custom Transitional Device

For a project on the American Express TRIPS system, the
writer suggested a custom transitional device: a cube that
reveals upcoming scenes as it rotates. Courtesy American
Express Travel Services Division.

Figure 7.8: Excerpt Describing Transition

VIDEO	AUDIO
MS—On Narrator by terminal.	**NARRATOR:**...TO SEE THE RESULTS OF THAT PLANNING AND DESIGN-ING, LET'S LOOK AT TRIPS IN ACTION AND SEE ALL THE THINGS IT CAN DO FOR THE CUSTOMER... AND FOR US!
On his final word, the picture FREEZES and the camera pulls back to reveal frozen image on one face of blue American Express cube. The cube begins to rotate...	OUR FIRST STOP IS OUR PARK AVENUE OFFICE IN NEW YORK CITY. **MUSIC:** (transitional "tag" theme comes up to accompany scene change.)
it continues to turn until the new face, containing a frozen image of Narrator outside Park Avenue office is full-front and the preceding scene is gone. Camera moves in, losing the box, as the scene comes alive.	
MS—On Narrator. Follow as he enters office.	**NARRATOR:** WHEN AMERICAN EXPRESS ENTERED THE TRAVEL BUSINESS BACK IN 1915, PROVIDING TRAVEL SERVICES AND MAKING TRAVEL ARRANGEMENTS WAS RELATIVELY SIMPLE...

Source: From "Trips: Your Selling and Servicing Partner," written by Allen Neil, directed by James G. Libby, produced by Video Marketing Group for American Express Travel Services. Used by permission.

Simulate closing and opening shutter. Scene of new R and D con-struction is now matted into the shutter area.

Often visual effects are difficult to describe since they have the characteristics of presentational symbols. For this reason, writers should make a point of discussing the function and substance of an effect with the director and technicians who are required to execute the effect. (I have often been surprised at a first screening of a program for which I wrote the script but had no hand in the production process. Sometimes the surprises are pleasant—other times, not. In these cases, I regret not being more emphatic in describing ideas for sets, staging, style of artwork, etc.)

COMPUTER GRAPHICS

In many areas of production for slides and videotape, the computer has taken the place of the artist's table, photographer's copy stand, the animator's cell art and even live action shoots. Figure 7.9 shows six examples.

In slide production, computer graphics are ideal for the typical business slide: bar charts, graphs, trend lines, etc. Text is easily integrated with artwork or graphic symbols. Such slides can be readily created by an artist working at a computer console. There is a wide palette of vivid colors to choose from and the excellent resolution characteristics of 35mm slides. (Computer generated slides are easily updated or changed, since the original artwork is stored on disk. When it's time for an update, only the changed data needs to be re-entered into the computer.) See examples in Figure 7.9.

Computer generated art is not limited to the business data slide, however. In the hands of a skilled computer graphics operator these systems can be used to generate imaginative graphics and three-dimensional objects. The most sophisticated computer graphics generators allow for subtle shading, modeling and texturing, giving artists the capability to produce quite complex and/or realistic images. The more sophisticated artwork usually requires more computer time to create—and that can make for a very expensive slide. It's safe to say, however, that a large percentage of business, medical and industrial slides used in presentations today are generated by a computer.

Computer Animation

Likewise, computer-generated graphics have also become routine in television production. The output of the computer can be recorded directly onto videotape, providing opportunities for a wide range of graphics and animated effects from rudimentary pop-on style animation to highly sophisticated three-dimensional creations limited only by the computer animator's imagination, time and budget. (Network news, sports, program openings and local TV station I.D.s are replete with examples of the most glitzy computer animation.)

Additionally, many of these systems do not necessarily require an artist to generate images. The most sophisticated can take direct input from a video camera or videotape, capture and store that image and then allow the animator to move, colorize, position and modify or combine the image with others.

Whether developing a slide or video presentation, media writers should be familiar with the potential, as well as the limitations, of computer-generated graphics systems. Since this field changes so rapidly, I'll offer broad guidelines rather than mention specific hardware or software.

Figure 7.9: Sample

Computer-Generated Slides

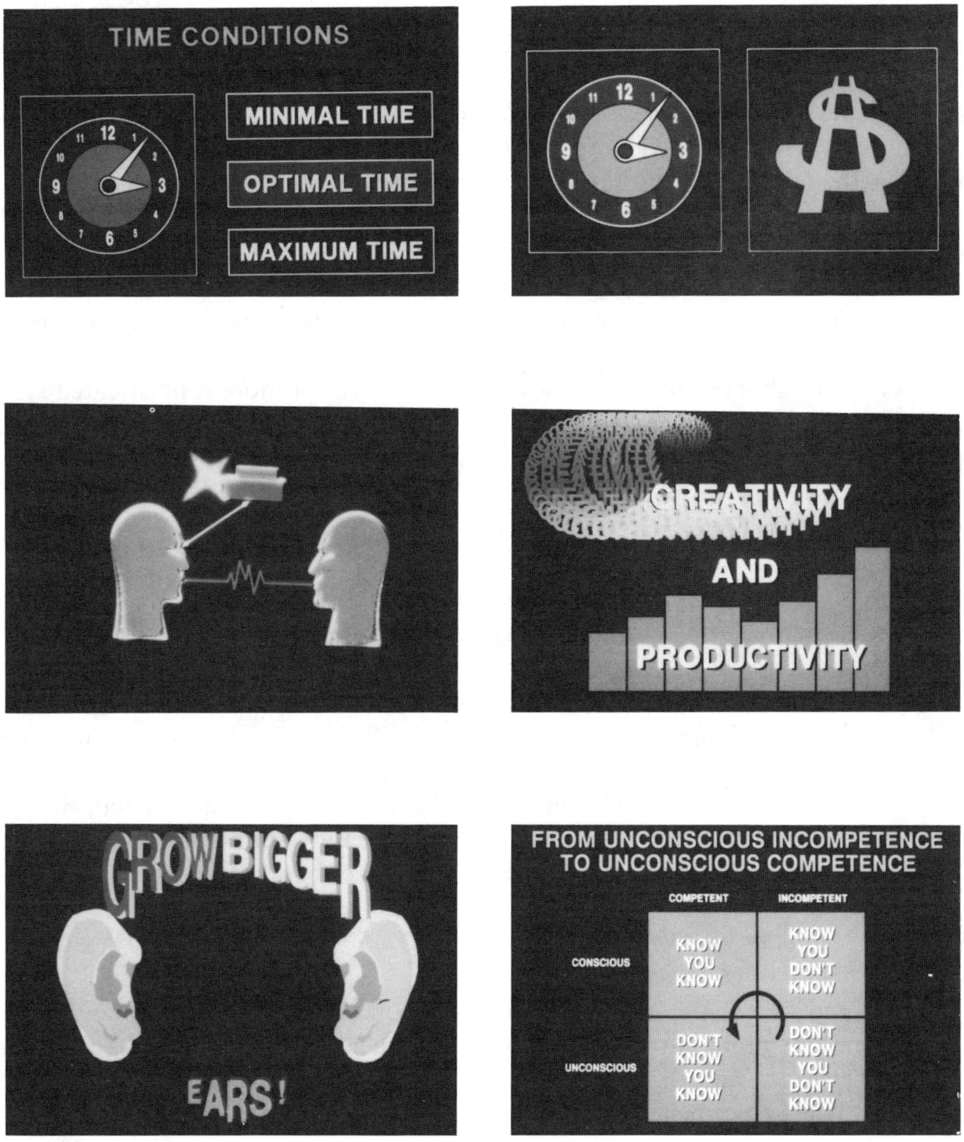

Source: Van Nostran Associates, Inc. Used with permission.

Low End Systems

Graphics generated on personal computers are generally grouped together as "low end" graphics production systems. Such hardware and/or software generally has limitations in terms of the artistic sophistication that can be achieved as well as the potential for video animation effects. In many cases, PC-generated graphics are quite suitable for the bar charts, graphs and other one-dimensional symbolic art that is the staple of the business presentation. They can often be generated in slide format or transferred to videotape for use as visual aids in a live presentation. (In this case, the tape can be displayed on a monitor or a video projection system.)

Another useful function of PC graphics systems is for storyboarding. Some software programs designed specifically for scriptwriting formats incorporate computer graphics storyboarding as a key feature. Using standard figures, icons and other simple artwork, these can be quite useful to the scriptwriter in communicating the visual side of the page to literal-minded clients.

As a rule, PC-generated graphics lack the power of more sophisticated systems to create subtle shadings, texture and modeling. They also have restricted capability for moving objects, transforming them or animating a sequence.

Mid-range System Features

For those capabilities, the middle-range computer systems offer greater artistic and animation freedom. First, these systems are designed specifically for slide or video production. They provide higher resolution than most PC programs and offer greater opportunity for creating more complex, realistic artwork and greater capability for frame-by-frame animation techniques. Some of these systems may take a video input from camera or tape sources, store it and then allow the artist to refine or embellish the image and combine it with text or other inputs. Often, these mid-range systems are used in video production to create the base artwork which then becomes electronically manipulated through digital effects switchers.

High-end "Turnkey" Systems

High-end video graphics generators are sometimes called "turnkey" systems because they combine all the flexibility (and then some) of both a sophisticated graphics generator and digital electronic effects generator. It's expensive, state-of-the-art hardware combined with powerful software. Many of these systems owe their genesis to Computer Aided Design (CAD) equipment which gave engineers the capability to design on a computer terminal instead of the traditional drafting table.

These systems, therefore, feature an array of three-dimensional possibilities. Objects can be rotated, tumbled, and explored in dynamic three-dimensional fashion.

In several instances, the programmer's commands parallel those of television production, i.e., "zoom," "pan," "dolly" and "truck." These systems also incorporate the sophisticated modeling, shading and texturing capabilities of the mid-range systems, giving the artist/animator tremendous flexibility. With this level of sophistication, however, the time and money involved to create even a short segment of animation (30 to 60 seconds) means these capabilities are not going to be available for most projects.

Implications for Media Writers

As with any type of visual or special effect, computer-generated graphics and animation should be used because they play a functional role in the communication, not for the sake of glitz. Media writers need not become experts on these systems to script imaginative graphics or animation effects. But it is imperative to define the graphics/animation needs of the project and match these to the capabilities of the specific systems available to the production team. Medical and engineering programming often cries out for computer-generated animation—but frame by frame pop-ons, arrows and titles may suffice instead of full-fledged animation.

Whatever the application, the writer should meet with the computer graphics artist and explore the capabilities of a specific system prior to writing such programming. Detailed storyboarding is usually a required step in developing computer graphics.

As with any production tool, scriptwriters should know the capabilities, limitations and practical realities entailed in executing a specific computer graphics sequence. By consulting and collaborating with the director and computer graphics artist, the writer can develop scripts that are appropriate for the application and feasible given the production logistics and budget.

SUMMARY: KEEP IT FUNCTIONAL

Visual descriptions in a shooting script communicate the sequence of visual events that will comprise the viewing experience. The writer must think visually, conjuring up appropriate, purposeful imagery in the mind's eye. Communicating visual ideas with words on paper is complicated by the contrasting nature of presentational and discursive symbol systems.

You need to supply sufficient instructions so that client and crew understand how the content will be visualized. You must also use the language of audiovisual production as a shorthand to communicate how visuals should be executed. Descriptions of screen action, camera shots and video effects represent a practical, pragmatic kind of writing. Keep video instructions functional and realistic. If you have a clear perception of visual style and content before writing detailed shot descriptions, you should find the writing flowing logically from image to image. As you gain experience anticipating and solving visualization problems before they develop, you'll find first-draft shooting scripts will have an inherent cohesiveness and unity that stamp them as the work of a professional scriptwriter.

FOOTNOTES

1. Vera John-Steiner, *Notebooks of the Mind* (New York, NY: Harper & Row, Publishers, 1985), p. 38.
2. *Ibid.,* p. 28.
3. *Ibid.,* p. 83.
4. *Ibid.,* pp. 82–86.
5. *Ibid.,* p. 83.
6. Henry Dreyfuss, *Symbol Sourcebook* (New York, NY: McGraw-Hill Book Company, 1972), pp. 39, 56, 80, 123, 157, 212.
7. John Joseph Brady, *The Craft of the Screenwriter* (New York, NY: Simon & Schuster, Publishers, 1981).
8. Vera John-Steiner, pp. 23–24.

8 The Imaginative Ear

"Sentences are not different enough to hold the attention unless they are dramatic. No ingenuity of varying structure will do. All that can save them is *the speaking tone of voice somehow entangled in the words* and fastened to the page for the *ear of the imagination.* That is all that can save poetry from sing-song, all that can save prose from itself." [Author: Italics mine]

Robert Frost[1]

A "speaking tone of voice" written for the "ear of the imagination" is all that can save narration from the listless, bland corporate style. Read annual reports. They seem to be composed in sterile rooms. The prose contains no surprises. The anonymous writer (more likely, committee of writers) hides from view. Neutered, the resulting text lies on the page like T.S. Elliot's evening sky: "a patient etherised upon a table."

Donald Murray, the writing coach mentioned earlier in this book, describes "voice" in the context of newspaper writing:

"Voice, the way the story *sounds,* is the distinctive element. . .that gives the illusion of individual writer *speaking* to individual reader. [Italics mine.] It is the element of the story that carries its emotional force. The story may be detached, angry, humorous, caring, sarcastic, ironic, sad, amused. The whole range of human emotions is available to the writer using voice."[2]

Frost and Murray attribute the aural qualities of language as the key to unlocking secrets of style. With audiovisual narration, the way the story *sounds* is paramount. Your audience reads nothing on paper. Their viewing experience consists solely of sights and sounds unfolding in time. Usually, viewers hear your words one

167

time only at a predetermined pace. Media writers must become proficient at sculpting vivid narrative copy that communicates ideas with verbal and *aural* clarity.

WRITING FOR THE HUMAN VOICE

Narration is the workhorse of audiovisual programming. In writing for the ear, one fact is paramount: a living, breathing human voice brings words on paper to life. Good scriptwriters develop skill creating vivid narrative copy that communicates ideas with verbal *and* aural clarity. Writing for the ear is really not so dificult. Often, it's just a matter of common sense—don't write sentences so long and complex that they cannot be spoken in a single breath.

Usually, narrative copy will fall into one of four general categories:

- On-Camera Narration
- Off-Camera Narration
- Executive Message/Subject Matter Expert Commentary
- Character Narrations

We'll deal with the first three now, saving character narrations for Chapter 10, "Wearing the Instructional Dramatist's Two Hats." A fifth type of narrative material, the interview, is not dealt with here because it is unscripted. (For more on developing interview content and integrating documentary style interviews into audiovisual programming, see Chapter 11.)

Narration written for a professional spokesperson is either delivered on camera (talking head/talking head with props format) or delivered off camera to be synchronized with visuals (visuals and voice format). The two may also be mixed so blocks of on- and off-camera narration are juxtaposed.

The medium also influences selection of a narrative technique. On-camera narrators appear in both films and videotapes. But television's live presence creates greater intimacy and immediacy between audience and on-camera personalities. Many documentary films, by contrast, consist solely of visual and voice off-camera narration. (Interviews are also more frequently seen on television than on flim, again owing to the "live" look of videotape and the medium's reliance on close-ups.) Multi-image programs consisting totally of slides, however, almost always use off-screen narration. Multi-media presentations, mixing slides and motion picture footage, frequently combine an on-camera narrator appearing in motion picture segments with off-camera narration and voices.

Multi-media presentations staged as part of live national sales meetings are invariably high on motivational copy and often incorporate a live host or hostess—sometimes even a cast of singers and dancers—integrated with multi-image presentations.

Professional or Non-Professional Narration

Off-camera copy is almost always delivered by a professional narrator. Non-professionals, especially content experts and organization leaders, are usually included to lend credibility or authority. Generally, such non-professional on-camera appearances need to be brief and to the point. When detailed content points must be delivered precisely, or when copy is motivational in tone, the professional narrator is the best choice. Despite being outsiders in presentations designed to communicate inside information, professional voices have the distinct advantage of being able to read narration conversationally. And for off-camera commentary, where the voice is disembodied, expression must come solely from vocal inflection, timing and pacing. This requires performing and interpretive abilities.

Writing informational copy for the on- or off-camera professional, the writer must settle into an appropriate narrative "voice." Donald Murray describes the range of styles or "voices" available to journalists (or scriptwriters, for that matter):

> "Journalism once attempted to achieve a single voice as if an in-stitution were speaking. Today, journalism not only allows increasingly diverse voices, it encourages them so that the reader hears writers speaking. *It is our responsibility as writers to develop a range of voices* with which we feel comfortable, and then to try them out by drafting leads to see which one will work best on a story. If we discover the voice then we usually have the lead."[3] [Italics mine.]

Corporations and organizations, too, often attempt to speak as if an institution were speaking. But most audiovisual communications need more humanity, more drama and interest. Interest results, as Frost observed, from dramatic sentences. A distinct narrative voice is one way to achieve such drama.

Try this experiment. Think of a talking head or visuals and voice presentation that you know well. Perhaps it's the script you just completed. Maybe it's a TV commercial you know all too well. Perhaps it's a message from the chairman of the board that you edited. Whatever narrative thread you select, make a "mental loop" of the audio track about a minute in length. Keep playing the words and content of that loop over and over in your head. (In workshops, I have participants close their eyes and go into a trance-like state until the narrative copy becomes a mantra.) Then, as this narrative copy plays on and on, start changing the narrator. First, make your narrator Barbara Walters, then, change to Bill Cosby. Next, make your narrator Johnny Cash. Then Woody Allen. And finally, make the narrator Kermit the Frog.

Do this exercise with a group of people and you'll notice them grinning and giggling at different voice/content combinations. Certainly for some choices the incongruity between narrative voice and content is sufficient to create laughter. More significantly, however, when you ask how many people began to *change the copy* with change of narrator, at least half the class usually raises their hand. This is the power of finding a voice—it will dictate the words, sentences and pace of the narration.

The secret to writing in distinctive, yet appropriate, narrative voices lies in discovering a suitable voice in your inner ear, then locking into it as you draft narration or dialog.

Presently, I'm writing a training program for a frozen foods broker's sales representatives. These men and women go into local supermarkets and compete for freezer space, shelf positioning and merchandising programs for frozen food products made by big companies like General Foods. It's a shirt-sleeve kind of job, in and out of supermarkets all day. In writing narrative copy, I want to establish a real down-to-earth voice. Lots of short, simple sentences but very action-oriented. When I began writing, I had to strive consciously to achieve the desired tone. But once I "locked into it," the inner ear took over; the voice became second nature.

This desire to achieve diverse narrative voices contradicts my previous views expressed in *The Nonbroadcast Television Writer's Handbook.* There, I urged an objective, factual, transparent voice—the institutional approach to writing. The skilled media writer, however, should be able to call upon a range of narrative voices to meet the needs of varying scriptwriting assignments.

Communication takes place on many levels in audiovisual presentations. Establishing emotional rapport with viewers is often overlooked in the mechanics of nailing down content. Setting just the right narrative tone is one way to connect with your audience on an emotional level.

Executive Messages and Subject Matter Expert Commentary

The third type of narrative writing also calls for a personal style and voice, not the writer's, but the *speaker's*. The in-house spokesperson should be used when *who* delivers the message carries as much weight as the specific content. When the recog nized expert on centrifugal gas compressors speaks, other engineers listen. When the president of the company talks, employees take the content to heart.

In drafting on-camera comments for such speakers, the scriptwriter's search for a voice begins with the executive or subject matter expert. The speaker's attitude toward the content, management style, speech patterns and rhythms all influence the writer's task. As in more traditional speech writing, the writer "ghosts" for the busy executive or expert. Sufficient personal knowledge and insight into the speaker's character lead naturally to a voice compatible with the individual's own style. Later in the chapter you'll find specific suggestions for doing this.

With these narrative types in mind, let's discuss techniques for achieving clarity using a conversational writing style—no matter what the voice.

OBSERVE *THE ELEMENTS OF STYLE*

Strunk and White's *The Elements of Style* remains the accepted standard on brevity and clarity for writing with vigor and authority. Its principles certainly apply to scripting narration. My advice: commit *The Elements of Style* to memory; it's a model of brevity in its own right. (More practically, at least read Strunk and White about twice a year to keep its principles of English usage fresh in your mind.)

Three of Professor Strunk's stylistic rules have special relevance for writers of narration. First. . .

> **Use the active voice.**
> The active voice is usually more direct and vigorous than the passive.[4]

Direct, vigorous writing has greater impact on the ear than vague, indefinite passive constructions. The active voice gives the writer of narration a better shot at aural clarity.

Second. . .

> **Put statements in positive form.**
> Make definite assertions. If your every sentence admits a doubt, your writing will lack authority.[5]

Media presentations play to captive audiences who expect to recieve useful information or learn new skills. The more positive and forceful your narration, the more likely the viewing audiences will feel they are receiving a positive, worthwhile communication. Writing that lacks authority is not worth the expense of mounting a media production. It also places the narrator—your flesh and blood transmitter—in the awkward position of sounding wishy-washy. As Murray says, "Good writing is always based on a firm foundation of authority—there is a significant relationship between the word 'author' and 'authority'."[6]

Finally. . .

> **Omit needless words.**
> Vigorous writing is concise. A sentence should contain no un-

> necessary words. . . . This requires not that the writer make all his sentences short, or that he avoid all detail and treat his subjects only in outline, but that every word tell.[7]

When you are writing narration, words translate into screen time, which in turn translates into money. In media that can gobble up time and money, the writer owes it to audience and producer to be economical in every sense. Become ruthless, and "omit needless words."

Observe these three principles, and you've taken a big step toward ensuring that your own narration can be spoken easily and will be clear to the listening audience.

KEEP IT CONVERSATIONAL

Narrators in voice-over sessions are often directed: "Keep it conversational." The admonition should be applied first to the scriptwriter. Conversational tone begins with the writing. A narrator can't take convoluted, formal text and make it sound like a chat over the back fence simply by reading with a big smile and sounding friendly. The following principles characterize a conversational style.

Conversational Writing Is Informal and Personal

Unlike a speech, which addresses a group using rhetorical and declamatory conventions, good media narration is written as a conversation directed to an audience of one. So write the way people speak. That doesn't mean narration should be riddled with slang or take on the random structure of a spontaneous conversation. But it should convey informality and have a personal tone, as though the narrator is speaking to an individual.

As an example, here are two versions of the same information. The copy on the left contains legal jargon, which often crops up in corporate projects. While this may be marginally acceptable in print, it becomes totally sterile and impersonal when read aloud. (Go ahead—try to read that copy aloud and sound friendly and personal.) The version on the right, by contrast, is written as one person might express the thought in conversation with another person.

To qualify for an allowance, all advertising must be prepared in accordance with the terms and conditions of the current Cooperative Advertising Allowance Agreement. . .	To receive your allowance, make sure ads conform to requirements spelled out in the current Co-Op Ad Allowance Agreement. . .

Several factors make the right-hand version more appropriate for a narrator to read conversationally. First, it uses personal pronouns, "you" and "your," acknowledging that the comment is directed to individuals. Words, such as "advertising" and cooperative," are shortened to a conversational form, "ad" and "co-op." The legal jargon such as "in accordance with" or "terms and conditions" is simplified through a less threatening vocabulary: "conform to requirements." Notice also the conversational version "omits needless words."

Develop an ear for the simplicity which characterizes spoken conversation. Contractions and simplified word forms, for instance, lend informality to narrative copy.

Instead of	Write
we will	we'll
cannot	can't
automobile	auto (car)
due to the fact that	because

Write With Pictures in Mind

Words without pictures are just a speech. You can't make your narration functional by writing in a vacuum. Once again, don't write anything on the right side of the page without knowing what's taking place on the left side. The most obvious reason for this is to avoid audiovisual redundancy—describing through narration what is perfectly obvious visually. Narrative copy should enhance the visual portion of the presentation, adding perspective and interpretive viewpoints.

Use the Langauge of the Audience

On the surface, this suggestion seems to contradict earlier advice to use the simplified, straightforward word form. In reality, however, it recognizes that audiences of insiders often have their own trade or professional shorthand. The writer's initial research should include developing a working knowledge of that professional or industry lingo. For instance, in the insurance industry, otherwise common words such as "risk," "exposures" or "surplus" have unique connotations. In the pharmaceutical/medical community, words and phrases like "efficacy," "indications," "over-the-counter," "well tolerated" and "mode of action" all carry specific meanings.

However, when the communication is directed to an outside audience—the general public, opinion leaders or other industry outsiders—then special terminology should be avoided or properly explained. The conversational standard, then, is determined not by the writer or the client but by the audience.

Avoid Hyperbole and Hype

Bold claims and superlatives belong to the advertising copywriter. When your audience consists of employees, stockholders, a student body, faculty, physicians, lawyers, nurses or other specialists, straight talk and logic make for the most credible message. If you want a narrator to sound sincere, knowledgeable and convincing, then write narration that is sincere, knowledgeable and convincing.

This doesn't mean you can't tout a product or generate enthusiasm for a new policy or program. But substantiate positive sentences and claims by offering proof that a product or program is the "best on the market." Sales representatives need real features and benefits and hard data to make a good sales presentation. They also need to be prepared for marketplace realities. Selling the sizzle in place of the steak usually leaves the audience hungry for more. Honesty of purpose always shines through the glitter of media presentations and touches the audience directly.

Don't Over-write

The audio column is not just for words. It also includes music and sound effects. When writing for the ear, keep in mind that, at certain strategic points, it's most effective to allow the narrator to step aside for a musical or sound effect interlude. Some of the best accompaniment to a visual is nothing more than silence.

Test Your Copy

The acid test for narrative copy is foolproof: read it aloud. This is the quickest, surest way to detect narrative problems and fix them. If you, the writer, can't read the copy comfortably, something's wrong. For instance, read this copy aloud right now.

> OUR NEW "SNEEZE" COMMERCIAL
> WILL BURST INTO THE HOMES OF
> MILLIONS OF AMERICANS
> STARTING THE WEEK OF
> NOVEMBER SECOND AND WILL
> IMPACT ON THE COLD AND FLU
> TARGET AUDIENCE THROUGH A
> MIX OF PRIME TIME, LATE NIGHT
> AND DAYTIME EXPOSURE AT THE

> ONSET OF THE COLD AND FLU
> SEASON.

A third of the way through it leaves one gasping for breath. It also makes two references to a specific time frame: "November second" and the "cold and flu season." Here's one possible rewrite.

> OUR NEW "SNEEZE" COMMERCIAL
> WILL BURST INTO THE HOMES OF
> MILLIONS OF AMERICANS
> STARTING THE WEEK OF
> NOVEMBER SECOND. AT THE ONSET
> OF THE COLD AND FLU SEASON,
> THE COMMERCIAL WILL REACH
> THE TARGET AUDIENCE THROUGH
> A MIX OF PRIME TIME, LATE NIGHT
> AND DAYTIME EXPOSURE.

Now, see if that isn't easier to read conversationally. Also, the connection between "November second" and the "cold and flu" season is now clarified—yet we've omitted the duplication of the phrase.

Even better than reading to yourself, sit down with the producer or director to read your first draft aloud, making notes about what needs improvement.

COPY FOR THE NONPROFESSIONAL NARRATOR

Certainly, the same stylistic elements that guide the writing of narration apply when writing for the executive or other nonprofessionals. In fact, it's even more important to ensure that the copy is written to be spoken. The trained professional can adapt to an unusually long sentence or successfully navigate a tongue-twisting phrase. But the nonprofessional must have copy that can be spoken in a normal, conversational manner and that suits the style of the speaker.

When scripting for an executive, then, the writer must learn about the personality and style of the executive and adopt a fitting tone. Find out whether you're dealing with an executive who's strong and forceful, a captain of industry, or one who comes across as one of the boys, folksy and down-to-earth. Is the executive one who takes a rational, reasoned approach to the business or a highly motivational leader who appeals to the emotions? The staff writer usually has advantages over the free-lancer in these cases. Yet even in-house writers are often isolated from busy executives. Both staff and freelance writers should try to review an executive's past speeches and video appearances to get a feel for rhetorical style. It's also important to meet with the executive, if only for 15 to 20 minutes, to hear firsthand what the executive would like to accomplish.

If you're scripting for a content expert, your role is to help that person express his or her knowledge through the chosen medium. In addition to gaining insights into personality, consider what visual support will help convey content. Will the person work best with physical props, or will cutaway graphics prove more functional?

Two or More Narrator Voices

Sometimes, you may choose to use two or more narrators—male/female duos are most popular in this affirmative action era. The technique is often used in lengthy scripts containing blocks of narrative copy. Alternating two voices, especially the male/female combination, helps delineate transitions and changes in subject matter.

When writers produce a single, lengthy narration, then simply assign every other paragraph to each of the two narrators, they miss an opportunity to make two voices play functional roles in the script. A more imaginative solution is to identify a specific role and voice for each narrator, then script copy accordingly.

For instance, the frozen foods broker's training program I referred to involves a male and a female narrator. They play different roles in the delivery of the content. The male narrator serves as a studio-based anchorman, while the female narrator always appears on location, delivering reports from the frozen food aisle of a local supermarket. The male narrator's tone is more matter-of-fact than the female narrator, who is down-to-earth but warmer and more personal in tone.

MUSIC AND SOUND EFFECTS

The right side of a dual column script is labeled "AUDIO." For most informational and educational programs, narration and dialog usually dominate the AUDIO column. As a result, scriptwriters often fail to take full advantage of the power of music and sound effects to establish mood, stir the audience, fulfill motivational objectives and raise the spirit.

In *Philosophy in a New Key,* Langer traces musical aesthetics from a historical perspective, then offers this insight into music's appeal:

"Another kind of reaction to music, however, is more striking and seems more significant: that is the *emotional* response it is commonly supposed to evoke. The belief that music arouses emotions goes back even to the Greek philosophers. It led Plato to demand, for his ideal state, a strict censorship of modes and tunes, lest his citizens be tempted by weak or voluptuous airs to indulge in demoralizing emotions."[8]

Music can provide an injection of emotional appeal to your audience. Consider how important emotion is in nearly every human communication or enterprise. While doing a series of sales training scripts one summer, I was confronted with the assertion that "people buy on emotion, then justify their purchase with logic." I kept resisting that notion, putting more credence in rational behavior. Then, the course designer made this observation: "Think how much of your disposable income you spend to purchase 'emotional experiences.' When you buy tickets on the fifty yard line or behind the dugout, you're buying the emotional experience of being part of the crowd, yelling and screaming for your team. Or consider the money you spend on books, theater tickets, concert tickets, art work, compact discs, the movies, the TV. . .the list goes on and on."

In almost every project and assignment, scriptwriters are overtly or covertly playing on the audience's emotions, trying to sell them the benefits of new products or employee benefit programs, the importance of learning procedures for operating centrifugal gas compressors, or the need for following procedures during an armed robbery. Hospitals use video on the day before surgery to reassure anxious patients. Corporations sell stockholders and security analysts on the company's accomplishments and performance through image pieces.

Music offers a direct path to the emotional heart and soul of an audience. Why, then, is music used inappropriately or even totally ignored in some A/V productions? For starters, scriptwriters often fail to envision and assign a specific communication function for music.

Recently, my wife and I accompanied our daughter to her Freshman orientation weekend at college. Among the evening activities was an illustrated lecture on "Dying and Death in Alfred Hitchcock's Films." The professor was provocative and witty (in a macabre manner), introducing themes about Hitchcock's depiction of murder on the screen.

While showing scenes, he made comments to the darkened audience: "look at his use of quick cuts here. . .see? The villain's screen left, the hero screen right. . . ." At one point, he intoned, "listen to his use of music right here. . . ."

During the post-mortem (pun intended), a parent raised the issue: "Why did you make so much fuss over music? I was taught the best movie music was in the background. You're not supposed to be aware of it."

"Why not?" crackled the greying prof. "You make a conscious effort to notice editing. You're aware of composition, lighting, action within the frame, special effects—and the more sophisticated the viewer, the greater the appreciation of such cinematic elements. Why not pay attention to the music? How is it playing against picture? What's its storytelling function?"

I realized then why I've always disliked most stock library music. The pieces are intended to serve as "background" music. That's why I'm burned out on insipid, synthesized music played by unskilled, uncaring anonymous musicians. So let's bring music to the *fore*ground and see how it can improve our media communications.

Foreground music says, "Pay attention! I have a role to play in this communication. I've been carefully placed in this script by the writer to serve a purpose."

O.K. So music should be functional. What are some roles music can play in audiovisual scripts? For starters, music and sound effects can:

- Establish mood
- Cue a transition
- Emphasize a point
- Support the pictures
- Play "against" the pictures
- Provide a rhythmic tempo for editing
- Communicate an emotion
- Provide a change of pace
- Surprise the audience

Notice what is conspicuous by its absence on this list: "open the program," "close the program," "provide background music." The misuse of "background" music is most in evidence in programs that begin with music, end with music, and have "background" music running under the entire narrative track.

Admittedly, certain programs and viewing situations do call for "wall-to-wall" music. Programs used in booths at conventions and trade shows may need a sustained music track to gain attention. Most audiovisual communications, however, require more subtle, intelligent uses of music. It all starts with a writer identifying the function of music and making it an integral element of the script, as the excerpt in Figure 8.1 shows.

Music and sound effects can play highly specific, functional roles in telling a story. To use music functionally, writers need a range of musical listening experience to draw on: classical, pop, rock, folk, hillbilly, jazz, avant garde, show tunes, blues, film scores, etc. The scriptwriter is probably not a musician, but the complete scriptwriter will be conversant with music in many forms to envision imaginative uses of music within the structure and content of a script.

Today, the rapidly changing technological developments in creating and recording music should make media producers less dependent on pre-recorded library music. Although bewildering, such things as composing by computer, synthesizers, and digital sound manipulation have brought the practicality and cost of original

Figure 8.1: Integrating Music in the Script

VIDEO	AUDIO
	SHIRLEY COOPER/INSTRUCTOR: MAKING THE TRANSITION FROM A LONG PERIOD OF UNEMPLOYMENT TO THE WORLD OF WORK IS THE KIND OF MAJOR CHANGE THAT CAN PROVE STRESSFUL.
	WHAT DOES STRESS FEEL LIKE? SOME PEOPLE EXPERIENCE STRESS PHYSICALLY—SOME MENTALLY AND EMOTIONALLY. IN SOME WAYS, IT'S A LITTLE LIKE A ROLLER COASTER RIDE. . . .
MOS FOOTAGE OF ROLLER COASTER RIDE. BEGIN WITH SEQUENCE OF ROLLER COASTER GOING SLOWLY TOWARD THE TOP.	**SOUND EFFX & MUSIC:** (Mix of carnival music and sounds of roller coaster and riders.)
	SHIRLEY COOPER/INSTRUCTOR: FIRST, THERE'S THE ANTICIPATION OF THE SLOW, STEEP CLIMB UPWARD. . .
SLO-MO OF ROLLER COASTER REACHING THE PEAK. . .	THEN THERE'S THAT BRIEF MOMENT WHEN YOU SEEM SUSPENDED IN TIME AT THE VERY TOP—STOMACH FULL OF KNOTS.
THEN NORMAL ACTION AS IT DESCENDS. INTERCUT REACTIONS OF RIDERS.	AND THEN, THE EXCITEMENT OF FREE FALL—THE FORCE OF GRAVITY TAKES OVER.
	AND FINALLY, THE EXHILARATION OF MAKING IT SAFELY TO THE END OF THE RIDE.
CU ON SHIRLEY COOPER.	SOME OF THE STRESSES YOU EXPERIENCE TRAVELING TO THE WORLD OF WORK MAY MAKE YOU FEEL LIKE YOU'RE ON A ROLLER COASTER.

Figure 8.1: Integrating Music in the Script (Cont.)

VIDEO	AUDIO
INTERCUT MOS FOOTAGE OF ROLLER COASTER WITH ALMOST SUBLIMINAL SHOTS OF LAURA, EDUARDO AND JAMES SCOTT AS SEEN PREVIOUSLY.	USUALLY, THE PERIODS *CLOSEST* TO THE ACTUAL CHANGE ARE THE MOST STRESSFUL, LIKE THAT FIRST DAY OF CLASS. . . THE FIRST INTERVIEW. . . THE FIRST DAY ON THE JOB. ANTICIPATING THE CHANGE IS LIKE GOING UP THE ROLLER COASTER— THE CLOSER YOU ARE TO THE MOMENT OF CHANGE—THE GREATER THE FEAR.

Source: From "The Choice is Yours,"TM written by William Van Nostran, directed by Walter Schoenknecht, created and produced by Karli & Associates and The Prudential-Audio Visual Communications Division. Used by permission.

scores within the range of many media producers. But it all starts with a writer whose "imaginative ear" hears *where* music would be effective and explains *how* in the script.

SCRIPTING AUDIO PROGRAMS

When I bought my word processor years ago, the equipment came with a stack of manuals and a package of audiocassette tapes to "talk you through" each lesson. That's one example of an "audio only" application. Here are others. Many lengthy video-based classroom training programs make extensive use of audio-cassette segments to convey specific, detailed and non-visual content. Sales managers, recognizing their sales force spends hours every day strapped into an automobile, commission informational and motivational audiocassette messages to reinforce previous training, sales meeting themes and home office direction. And, there's a whole industry built around the seeming insatiable appetite for self-improvement material. Do not underestimate the power of writing for the human ear.

Even though I'd written several "audio only" scripts, it wasn't until I was asked to conduct a workshop for writers forming a team to turn out an extensive series of training-oriented audiocassettes on high-tech information that I began formulating my thinking on the topic.

Pebbles of Meaning

Fortuitously, I was researching American Indian myths for a personal writing project. Digging into this oral-based culture provided insight into the nature of verbal storytelling. I discovered that the oral traditions and experiences of American Indians are quite different from those of our written culture.

Each culture responds to language in different ways. For us, a word consists of highly abstract symbols (called the alphabet) such as those you are reading now. These symbols occupy *visual* space on pages. Because of our deeply ingrained literacy, words are largely (but not exclusively) visual entities.

For a non-literate culture, however, the word is *totally* experienced as an oral/aural entity. There is no visual alphabet. No words and sentences and punctuation on paper. The non-literate is more comfortable than the literate with the sense of language as a flow of sound (just like narration) because that is how the ear perceives language. With the image of written language cues, we have "no difficulty imagining what the aural poet means if he says that words are pebbles of meaning, but that very image of written language makes us see as a metaphor what he may mean as a literal statement. . ."[9]

All of which brings us full circle to Frost! Writing for the ear requires the "speaking tone of voice," that sense of language as a *flow of sound.* To craft good audio scripts, develop your appreciation for the full, rich potential of the aural medium at your disposal—not only speech, music, and sound effects but also the *visual* potential. What struck me reading American Indian literature was its vivid, imaginative visual imagery.

Like our grandparents sitting around the first radios, Indians around the campfire under an evening sky were free to let their imagination take whatever flights of fancy the night's storyteller could invent. And so Indian tales are full of images of animals who take on human form or humans who become birds or insects as an integral part of the plot.

An Audiovisual Medium?

Radio writers used to refer to the medium as "theater of the imagination" and wrote vividly in all manner of genre—soap operas, westerns, cops and robbers, science fiction, comedy. They challenged their audiences to use their imagination and "see" literally anything possible to envision in the mind. (In this sense, television takes something away from a viewer's participation.)

As Robert Hilliard says in his book on writing for TV and radio, radio allows writers "complete freedom of time and place. There is no limitation on the setting or on movement in time or in space. The wrtier can create unlimited forms of physical action and can bypass in the twinkling of a musical bridge minutes or centuries of time." Hilliard cites Orson Welles' radio treatment of H.G. Wells' *War of the Worlds.* He refers to a similar but unsuccessful televised version of the story. "Limiting the action to what one can present visually restricts the imaginative potentials of word and sound,"[10] concludes Hilliard.

So, in a very real sense, radio and audiocassettes are visual media; media where the audience plays an active role envisioning what the writer suggests the listener *see.*

Another potential for expression in audio-only media is the non-linear counterpoint and overlaying achieved by mixing several auditory sources: music, sound effects, dialog, narration or interview comments interwoven to create a collage of sound.

It is what the late, eccentric Canadian pianist Glenn Gould called his polyphonic radio documentaries: contrapuntal radio.

> "...We tried to have situations arise cogently from within the framework of the program in which two, or three or four voices could be overlapped, talking essentially about the same thing... treating those voices as characters—as all the material...was gained through interviews. It was documentary material treated as drama."[11]

The audiocassette scriptwriter works in a similar imaginative realm. Anything is possible: talking electronic typewriters, a sales representative in heaven or hell, a radio call-in show about the fine points of zero-based budgeting—give your mind free rein.

For inspiration, turn to the spoken arts section of the library record collection. Check out old Mel Brooks/Carl Reiner bits. Listen to Bob and Ray's fictitious interviews. Go even more theatrical with the Fireside Theatre creations. Get hold of old Stan Freberg radio spots. Check out early Woody Allen monologues. And read some American Indian myths. They will set your aural imagination on fire with the visual possibilities.

The script excerpts in Figure 8.2 illustrate imaginative approaches to informational or instructional subject matter delivered through the audiocassettte medium.

Sales people spend lots of time in their car. Audiocassette programs are an efficient way to reach them with informational or sales training material. Excerpt "A" in Figure 8.2, from a General Foods sales training audiocassettte series, uses take-offs on familiar radio broadcast formats as a way of developing a fast-paced style that gets the message across entertainingly.

In this introductory module, the audience is introduced to the concept through a mock traffic report and call-in show (Excerpt A).

Figure 8.2: Imaginative Approaches to Audio Programs

A

MUSIC: ENERGETIC UPBEAT ROCK LOGO THEME HITS IN FULL FOR FIVE SECONDS AND IS GONE.

ANNOUNCER: W–K–G–F! All Sales Radio! One Hundred Percent on your dial and serving the worlds of. . . (ECHO) GENERAL FOODS (ECHO OUT). . . with information and entertainment that *sells* it like it is!

MUSIC: MUSICAL NOTES G–F–F–G A, LA NBC CHIMES.
SOUND: HOVERING HELICOPTER, INTERIOR PERSPECTIVE; FADE UP AND UNDER

HOST: (SPEAKING OVER COPTER EFFECT) Welcome to WKGF. I am your host, (ACTOR'S NAME), and I'll be bringing you the (AHEM) overview to help you profit from this series of six programs designed to help you go far on the road to sales professionalism.

SOUND: COPTER UP BRIEFLY THEN UNDER.

HOST: Today, on WKGF, you'll be tuning in to Charlie "The Cold" Call's Call-In Show to get some reactions from out there on the road. . .Dr. Ruth will be advising you on "Good Sales". . .you'll hear the latest chapter in the adventures of America's favorite sales rep on WKGF's award-winning soap opera, "As The World Sells". . .followed by exciting sports action as John McEnroe faces Ivan Lendl at the GF Open. . .and, closing WKGF's broadcast day, Dr. Fairleigh Lucid with some thoughts to reflect on.

SOUND: COPTER UP AND UNDER.

HOST: Now, from up here, your situation looks very good. Up ahead, just over the horizon I can see an even brighter future. There is some competing traffic along the way. . .a possible road block or two, but let's see if we can help you get ahead of the one and steer clear of the other. You're doing fine, and we're going to keep you on the move!

SOUND: COPTER UP

Figure 8.2: Imaginative Approaches to Audio Programs (Cont.)

HOST:	Oh, I see it's time now for your favorite call-in show. Over to you, Charlie!
SOUND:	**COPTER UP AND OUT.** **BRIGHT, STRIDENT PHONE RING.**
CHARLIE:	(NASAL, SNIFFILY, CHRONIC COLD) Thanks, (HOST'S NAME). Charlie "The Cold" Call here, ready to pop open a can of worms. Whadda you say we take a couple of quick calls, okay? You're live.
REP ONE:	(FILTER) No offense, but if you really want to help me find a brighter future. . .
CHARLIE:	Yeah?
REP ONE:	(FILTER). . .tell me how to get my customers to listen to me. One won't hear me out, another just walks away, or they make up their minds before I finish! And one other thing. . .
CHARLIE:	Talk to me.
REP ONE:	(FILTER) What do you do with customers who give preferential treatment to the competition in return for premiums and free tickets and stuff like that, huh?
CHARLIE:	How about giving them better sevice than the competition?

B

SOUND:	**PHONE RINGS.**
CHARLIE:	Think we hit a nerve here, all right, all right. You're on the air. What's bugging you, pal?
Rep. TWO:	(FILTER) While the job can be fun and exciting. . .
CHARLIE:	Here it comes!
Rep. TWO:	(FILTER) Well, let's face it, we do have our share of uncooperative customers and tough volume objectives to meet. We have to sell more and faster, and now *you're* going to tell us something else we should be doing?! Gimme a break.

Figure 8.2: Imaginative Approaches to Audio Programs (Cont.)

CHARLIE:	Okay, okay. This is your can of worms. (HOST'S FIRST NAME), so it's back to you.
	SOUND: COPTER UP AND UNDER.
HOST:	I hear you, Charlie. And you down there—I can see that you're caught between the proverbial rock and a hard place, but I think we can ease that situation, too. Oh—wait a minute—I can see there are some GF customers heading for their telephones. Could there be another side to this story, Charlie?
	SOUND: COPTER UP AND OUT.

PHONES RINGING MADLY FADE IN AND UNDER

CHARLIE:	Can you hear those phones, (HOST)? The switchboard's turned into a Christmas tree. (ON PHONE) You're live.
CUST. ONE:	(FILTER) You want the other side of the story? Talk about not listening—you salespeople never listen to my objections, never answer my questions—just keep talking, talking, talking. . . .
	SOUND: PHONE RINGS.
CHARLIE:	Get it off your chest.
CUST. TWO:	(FILTER) Can't you teach them something besides those worn-out prepared speeches? I got enough canned goods already. When are they going to talk to ME—about MY store? On top of that, they cost me time and money trying to sell me stuff I can't use.

C

ANNOUNCE:	Now, here to answer those embarrassing questions and put your mind at ease is Sales Therapist Dr. Ruth Besttiming with her prize-winning program, "Good Sales!" What's up, Dr. Ruth?
DR. RUTH:	Your sales, I hope. (GIGGLES)
	MUSIC: THEME OUT.
ANNOUNCE:	You heard, Dr. Ruth, the conflicting positions of the sales reps and their customers?
DR. RUTH:	Sure. It's a very natural conflict—very natural.

Figure 8.2: Imaginative Approaches to Audio Programs (Cont.)

ANNOUNCE:	So, who's right and who's wrong?
DR. RUTH:	As usual in these cases, everyone is a little bit right and a little bit wrong. But, realistically, since the sales rep typically initiates the contact, he or she sets the tone. And, in my experience, an overly aggressive "selling" tone often stimulates the problem.
ANNOUNCE:	But a sales representative has to be aggressive, take charge, make things happen.
DR. RUTH:	There are as many ways to make a sale as to make love—maybe more. And what we are trying to do here on Good Sales is help all you sales representatives out there discover that you have more alternatives than you maybe think. But you will have to think about what motivates you to sell. . .examine your attitudes towards your customers. . .and ask yourself what is your role as a sales representative.
ANNOUNCE:	Do tell, Doctor.
DR. RUTH:	First of all, sometimes the perception of "selling" can contribute to our difficulties.
ANNOUNCE:	Really?
DR. RUTH:	Think about it. "Sell!" can be considered a confrontational word. One human being inducing another human being to buy something, sometimes with no regard as to whether they need it or not. Do you like that?
ANNOUNCE:	No.
DR. RUTH:	What do *you* do if you feel someone is manipulating you like that?
ANNOUNCE:	I resist.
DR. RUTH:	Ah! You see? Automatically a hostile environment is created and a hostile environment is conducive neither to love nor good sales.
ANNOUNCE:	Oh, too bad. But stay tuned for today's episode of "As the World Sells." I think you'll find it very much attuned to our discussion. Goodbye for now and Good Sales!

Figure 8.2: Imaginative Approaches to Audio Programs (Cont.)

MUSIC:	**THEME UP TO CONCLUSION.**

D

MUSIC:	**"SOAP" THEME ON ORGAN IN AND UNDER.**
SOAP ANN;	And now, "As The World Sells" . . .
MUSIC:	**THEME UP FULL AND UNDER.**
SOAP ANN:	On our last episode, Andy Dooley, up and coming young sales rep, demonstrated his ability to grasp even the most technical aspects of the theory of selling. But could he put theory into action? We join him now on his first call of the day. . . .
SOUND:	**SUPERMARKET BGD; CHECKOUT COUNTER DOMINANT; BAGS BEING PACKED. FOOTSTEPS APPROACH.**
ANDY:	(FADING IN) Ah, there you are, Mr. Canon. Have I got some good news for you today!
CANON:	(HURRIED & HASSLED) You're taking early retirement? (CALLING OUT) Open up Number Six! (NORMAL) Excuse me, I'm busy.
SOUND:	**TWO PAIRS FOOTSTEPS WALKING, ONE TRYING TO KEEP UP WITH THE OTHER.**
ANDY:	You'll want to know what's new about Frosty Fudge.
CANON:	I know what's new about Frosty Fudge. . .when did *you* find out? (OFF MIKE) Ursula, don't stack the paper towels more than four levels high, please. Only you can help prevent avalanches.
CANON:	James, leave the bottles and bag for a while at Number Six. Thank you.
ANDY:	So you know we've added two new flavors?
CANON:	Yes. Your competition told me.
SOUND:	**SHOPPING CART WHEELS IN; FOOTSTEPS STOP.**
CUSTOMER:	Are you the Manager, sir?

Figure 8.2: Imaginative Approaches to Audio Programs (Cont.)

CANON:	Yes ma'am, can I help you?
CUSTOMER:	I certainly hope so. There's no more Sanka!
CANON:	Aisle Two, ma'am. . .the end opposite the checkout.
CUSTOMER:	That's where it *used* to be.
ANDY:	There's room in your freezer for two facings of the straw-berry. . . .
CANON:	There's no room. I'll find it for you, ma'am.
	SOUND: CART WHEELS AWAY; FOOTSTEPS FADE.
CUSTOMER:	(FADING) I should hope so! I can't drink anything else! Imagine being out of Sanka!

E

	SOUND: COPTER UP THEN UNDER.
HOST:	The traffic on The Road to Success is pretty heavy now. To stay on this road and keep up to speed calls for top notch skills in following The Sales Motion. You've heard about The Sales Motion and are probably wondering what it's all about. Well, let's switch you now to courtly Forest Hills and colorful Billie Jean Pavlova covering the McEnroe-Lendl match at Parallel Park in Westchester.
	SOUND: COPTER UP AND OUT; CROSSFADING TO TENNIS HITS, POLITE "AWWW" FROM CROWD, FOLLOWED BY DECOROUS APPLAUSE. GAME CONTINUES.
FOREST:	(WHISPERING SO AS NOT TO DISTURB THE PLAYERS) Thank you for joinging us, tennis fans. The match is just underway and already McEnroe is exhibiting the. . .err. . . *aggressive* game he's well-known for. Wouldn't you say, Billie Jean?
BILLIE:	Oh, I don't know—he hasn't hit the referee.
	SOUND: LOUD, ANGRY, BUT INDISTINGUISHABLE SHOUTS IN THE DISTANCE.
BILLIE:	Yet.

Figure 8.2: Imaginative Approaches to Audio Programs (Cont.)

FOREST: McEnroe takes the first game and the serve goes to Lendl. What should we be looking for in this match, Billie Jean?

BILLIE: The Sales Motion.

FOREST: Pardon?

BILLIE: Yep. To me, tennis is the almost perfect metaphor for The Sales Motion.

FOREST: (NOT INTERESTED) Really.

BILLIE: The Sales Motion, as you know, Forest, is the basic dynamic of the sales situation.

FOREST: But, tennis. . .

BILLIE: . . .is a constant flow of unpredictable action—and although it always follows the same rules, it never happens exactly the same twice, right?

FOREST: Well, yes. . .

BILLIE: Just like the Pro out there, the Sales Rep has to be flexible, ready for anything. . .prepared to respond. That's The Sales Motion.

FOREST: Tennis is different. . .

BILLIE: Oh, yes, Forest. There's a *big* difference. In The Sales Motion, the other party is not your opponent but your partner. You have to win together.

FOREST: Still, Billie Jean. . .

BILLIE: Still-motion studies have shown there are four distinct stages to The Sales Motion. Did you know that, Forest?

FOREST: No. (LOWERING VOICE) Ah, Lendl's about to serve.

BILLIE: (LOWERING VOICE) The serve is like the first step—The Attention stage of The Sales Motion in which the sales rep captures the customer's attention.

Source: From "The Sales Motion," written by Ed Schultz, produced by Jack Gagliardo, directed by William Rogers for General Foods Corp. Used with permission.

Figure 8.3: Additional Approaches to Audio Programs

F

MUSIC: (An up-tempo Dixieland jazz theme hits full. We let the infectious rhythm play full for a few seconds, then drop to background.)

NARRATOR: THAT'S A MUSICAL THEME SET TO THE BEAT OF A NATURAL RHYTHM. . .

AND HERE'S ANOTHER NATURAL RHYTHM WITH A STRONG BEAT. . .

SOUND EFFX: (Musical theme segues into the steady pulsing of a strong, regular heartbeat.)

NARRATOR: AND HERE'S ANOTHER NATURAL RHYTHM—THE FLOW OF THE PROCAINAMIDE DETAIL. . .

SALES REPRESENTATIVE:. . .PROCAINAMIDE IS A NATURAL CHOICE AS FIRST-LINE THERAPY SINCE IT OFFERS: VERSATILITY BY TREATING BOTH VENTRICULAR AND ATRIAL ARRHYTHMIAS; COMPATIBILITY WITH DIGOXIN; (Pull under.) DEPENDABILITY OF MAINTAINING THERAPEUTIC DOSING LEVELS ALL DAY AND ALL NIGHT. . .

NARRATOR: RECENTLY, HOWEVER, THE NATURAL RHYTHMS OF THIS DETAIL ARE NOT BEING HEARD ON A REGULAR BASIS IN DOCTOR'S OFFICE AND HOSPITALS ACROSS THE COUNTRY.

G

WE'RE GIVING COMPETITION THE OPPORTUNITY TO DROWN OUT OUR MESSAGE BY PLAYING INFERIOR THEMES. . .

SALES REPRESENTATIVE: . . .DOCTOR, FOR YOUR PATIENT WITH EITHER ATRIAL OR VENTRICULAR ARRHYTHMIAS, WILL

Figure 8.3: Additional Approaches to Audio Programs (Cont.)

YOU PRESCRIBE PROCAINAMIDE AS
FIRST-LINE THERAPY?

AUDIO MIX: (Mix of voices detailing competitive
products comes in on top of Sales Representative.
The resulting babble drowns out the company
Representative: "QUINIDINE FREQUENTLY
RESULTS IN GREATER THAN 90 PERCENT
REDUCTION IN VENTRICULAR ECTOPY. . . "

". . .DISOPYRAMIDE HAS PROVEN
EXTREMELY EFFICACIOUS IN STABILIZING
VENTRICULAR ARRHYTHMIAS. . ."

". . .THIS DRUG'S RELATIVELY LONG 13-
HOUR HALF-LIFE MAKES IT SUITABLE FOR
TWICE-A-DAY DOSAGE, IMPROVING
PATIENT COMPLIANCE. . ."

". . .PROPRANOLOL IS INDICATED FOR
TREATING BOTH SUPRAVENTRICULAR AND
VENTRICULAR ARRHYTHMIAS. . ."

(At this point, a cacophony of dissonant themes,
with audio effects to simulate wow and flutter
overpowers the company detail.)

MUSIC: (Establish bossa-nova or other rhythmic
beat, then pull under Narrator.)

NARRATOR: IN THIS PROGRAM, WE'LL
PRACTICE THE NATURAL RHYTHMS OF
THE PROCAINAMIDE DETAIL TO GENERATE
THE STRONG, STEADY BEAT OF CONTINUED
MARKET SHARE FOR THE PRODUCT. . .IT'S
A BEAT THAT'S IRRESISTIBLE WHEN THE
ENTIRE SALES FORCE PLAYS THE SAME
THEME TO PERFECTION. . . .

MUSIC: (Return to Dixieland main theme.)

NARRATOR: WE ASKED BOB TOBIN,
PROCAINAMIDE PRODUCT MANAGER, TO
PUT THE NEED FOR INCREASED
DETAILING INTO PERSPECTIVE.

Figure 8.3: Additional Approaches to Audio Programs (Cont.)

> **BOB TOBIN:** (Key points: Introduction of generics and new products have created a more competitive environment. The fact remains, however, that when you analyze features and benefits in comparison to competitive strengths and weaknesses, procainamide still merits market leadership position.)
>
> **NARRATOR:** WHAT IS THE GOAL OF INCREASED DETAILING?
>
> **BOB TOBIN:** (Key points: Important to make certain the cardiologist is fully aware of the competitive benefits procainamide offers. One-on-one detailing is critical because only the sales representative can address the specific concerns or issues which might make cardiologists or internists prescribe a competitive product.)

Source: From "The Beat," written by William Van Nostran, directed by David P. Emmerling for The O'Hara Company. Used by permission.

Within minutes, other callers give the flip side of the coin—the customer's viewpoint (Excerpt B).

Shortly, a Dr. Ruth parody introduces the sales therapist for the series (Excerpt C).

The overview and format parodies continue with a soap opera spoof, "As the World Sells" (Excerpt D). Notice the use of sound effects to create visual imagery in the listener's mind.

A sports event offers yet another familiar radio format and an opportunity to allow the imaginative listener to participate in an active way (Excerpt E).

Next, review another audiocassette script aimed at sales people, in this case pharmaceutical sales representatives. (See Figure 8.3.) The topic involves a prescription product to treat irregular heartbeats known as arrhythmias. In this case, the writer takes a more traditional narrative approach. However, the writer still integrates music and sound effects into the narrative text as a means of illustrating and reinforcing key copy points (Excerpt F).

Then, a mix of voices, additional music cues and an audio interview are used to convey content while generating a sense of pace and vivid listening experience (Excerpt G).

Although radically different in style and tone, these two sales training excerpts illustrate the potential for creating interesting, informative and involving listening experiences when writing for that singular sense: the human ear.

SUMMARY

Writing for the ear is easy to underestimate in both what the combination of narration, dialog, music and sound effects can achieve and the craft and technical finesse necessary to fully capitalize on such potential.

The key lies in realizing that viewers never see words on paper—they hear words unfold in time as "pebbles of meaning." Achieving aural clarity with dramatic sentences a narrator can easily articulate comes from the "speaking tone of voice" writers are encouraged to seek through the "imaginative ear."

FOOTNOTES

1. From liner notes to "Robert Frost Reads His Poetry" (New York, Caedmon).
2. Donald Murray, *Writing for Your Readers:* Notes on the writer's craft from the Boston Globe (Boston, MA: Globe Pequot, 1983).
3. *Ibid.*
4. William Strunk, Jr. and E. B. White, *The Elements of Style,* 3rd Ed. (New York, NY: Macmillan Publishing Co., Inc., 1979), p. 18.
5. *Ibid.,* pp. 19-20.
6. Murray, *Writing for Your Readers.*
7. Strunk and White, *The Elements of Style,* p. 23.
8. Langer, *Philosophy in a New Key,* p. 211.
9. Brian Swann, ed. *Smoothing the Ground, Essays on Native American Oral Literature* (Berkeley, CA: University of California Press, 1983).
10. Robert L. Hilliard, *Writing for Television and Radio,* 3rd. Ed. (New York, NY: Hasting House, Publishers, 1976), p. 13.
11. "Glenn Gould: Concert Dropout, a Conversation with John McClure" (New York, NY: a Columbia Records Masterworks recording, stereo BS 15).

Step 4: Revision

9 Making the Most of Feedback

It's an old story I heard, supposedly about Mel Brooks. It's a re-write session during the so-called "golden age" of television. A large group is gathered around a table to provide feedback on Brooks' efforts for the week. One by one, they go around the table—each offering, in turn, their analysis of what was wrong with each and every sketch. "O.K., O.K.," said Brooks. "But where were all you guys when the pages were *blank*?"

"Re-vision: to see again." There are many ways to see our first draft scripts "again." One is through the eyes of others—client, content expert, producer, director, boss, writing buddy, wife or husband. That's called "feedback."

Another way of seeing first draft scripts "again" is through the eyes of the writer. Only the writer relates to the shooting script as both *creator* and *critic*. It is "whole-brain thinking" epitomized. A response from both the artist and the judge.

Yet overall, revision is the phase in the scriptwriting process when we are at our most critical. As von Oech would put it—this is the time to don the "judge's wig" with all its authoritarian associations.

Reactions to scripts come in many guises—and sometimes disguises. What does the perturbed chairman of the board mean when he says, "It misses the mark. It just misses the mark!"? What does the content expert mean when she says, "You don't seem to be focusing on the real core of our problem"? What does the hurried client mean when he says, "I don't know, it's just not what I had in mind somehow"?

At this turning point, the scriptwriter must sometimes play the dual roles of sales person and psychotherapist, gently questioning and probing to clarify what the buyer or patient really means. Is the script in need of major surgery? Or are the problems largely a matter of style and voice? Did the writer's creative boldness push the producer farther out on the "creativity/risk" limb than he/she's comfortable with?

Or, most depressing scenario of all to the writer, has something in the overall nature of the project *changed*? Perhaps the target audience has been expanded; or

197

maybe some new, unforeseen objectives have crept into the parameters defining a project's scope and boundaries.

Whatever the nature or significance of feedback, the scriptwriter must now work to understand each script "reader's" perception then determine how to accommodate that perspective into a second draft script.

Unfortunately, some writers attach negative meanings to words like "revision," "re-write" and the like. Perhaps it's a carry-over from high school English teachers or torturous college term papers. But strong, vivid narrative media writing does not spring full blown in one draft. Often directors are literally forced to rip the pages from a scriptwriter intent on polishing and re-working up until, and even past, the final hour. (I think that's why many directors don't like writers hanging around on shoots.) As one director, Jim Libby, aptly puts it, "Scripts are never finished; they're simply abandoned." Prior to abandonment, however, there should be a period of studied, analytical and skillful rewriting incorporating relevant feedback and reactions from all involved—including the writer.

Scriptwriters walking into the meeting following circulation of a first-draft script have cause for trepidation. The handful of select "scriptreaders" have read and re-read. Now, they gather (like vultures?) around a table to offer feedback. Each responds from their own, usually highly focused perspective. (Content experts focus on content, clients on objectives, producers on dollars, directors on logistics, etc.). Depending on the size of the group, it's easy to feel lonely—and a tad defensive. "Just *where were* all you folks when the pages were blank?"

Feedback plays an integral role in each phase of the scriptwriting process. We write content outlines and treatments for the express purpose of soliciting feedback before spending the time and energy a first-draft script demands. In evaluating such feedback, the scriptwriter needs to consider three related factors:

> *When* does it occur in the writing process?
> *Who* does the feedback come from?
> *What* is the substance of the feedback?

WHEN DOES IT OCCUR IN THE WRITING PROCESS?

With experience, you come to expect certain types of critical reaction at different stages of a project. Discussions about the creative concept should be flushed out and resolved at the treatment stage. "If it's not working at the treatment and outline stage," says scriptwriter Donna Matrazzo, "then it won't work as part of the script."

So, if the scriptwriter begins to hear feedback relating to the premise of the entire creative treatment on a *first draft,* serious problems are afoot. These concerns should have surfaced long ago and been addressed head on before writing a first-draft shooting script.

Hearing such feedback at this stage of the project indicates one of several possible problems:

1. The treatment did not fully indicate to the client, content expert, or producer the full ramifications of the creative direction and its implications.
2. Or, some new element relating to objectives, content, style, budget or use of the program has been injected into the project without the writer's knowledge. In other wrods, the parameters or "givens" of the project are being changed.
3. Or, it *is* also possible that the writer strayed significantly from the original content/treatment rationale in executing a first draft.

WHO DOES THE FEEDBACK COME FROM?

Feedback relating to content most often comes from subject matter experts. Writers should realize that significant content revisions can and often do occur at the first-draft stage. Although the content outline performs a function similar to that of the treatment by communicating what the program is about prior to a first draft, considerable detail is added to the content outline in a first draft—especially for technical or complex subjects with training objectives.

Often, when expanding content in the first draft, technical errors, omissions and ambiguities surface. Conscientious content experts are sticklers for getting it down right. Depending on the topic and situation, clients may also have a significant amount of input relating to content. I've even participated in script sessions where differences between content experts and clients arise. This is great fun; an opportunity for writers to sit back, relax, and watch how the differences will be resolved.

Who feedback comes from is important in a larger context. Various industries, businesses, educational and medical subjects have languages of their own. Often the writer may have a good grasp of the subject but fail to use the precise words or "jargon" the intended audience would relate to. (I experienced this problem in a project for the United States Golf Association. I wrote, for instance: "from tee to putting green." It was changed to "from tee to green." Obviously, I don't spend enough time on the "links.")

I do lots of scripts for pharmaceutical and insurance companies. Each industry has a unique vocabulary. In time, that vocabulary becomes second nature to the scriptwriter. But when you're new to a specific field, your first draft often requires some reworking to capture the nuances.

At a first-draft reading, feedback from producers and directors is likely to fall into two areas: style, and budgetary or logistical issues. For the most part, major questions of style would certainly surface in the treatment. But while the treatment conveys the conceptual "germ" and creative schema, the first draft reflects a precise working out of this approach—scene by scene and shot by shot.

Perhaps a disturbing inconsistency in style or voice crept into narration. Maybe the balance between formats appears differently in the first-draft script than it did in the breezy, abbreviated style of a treatment. Producers and directors expect the script to be technically accurate and meet the client's objectives, but they expect the script to stand on its own merits as an audio presentation, film, TV or slide show. So producers and directors may have a lot of input when everyone gathers to dissect the first draft.

Their comments tend to be more general on content, but quite specific on style, narrative voice, visualization, the function of each scene, format, pacing and length, use of graphics, music and sound effects—those elements which comprise the "production terminology" of an audiovisual script. Comments on technical or stylistic aspects of the first draft from clients and SMEs, on the other hand, can sometimes be taken with a grain of salt.

So scriptwriters at a first-draft meeting not only need to listen to the substantive message of the feedback, but should also consider *who* is offering the comment. This helps in judging the nature and interrelationship of various responses to the script from the differing perspectives of each script reader.

WHAT IS THE SUBSTANCE OF THE FEEDBACK?

Initially, the scriptwriter must "type" and catalog the responses. The most terrifying feedback comes in the form of information that clearly indicates the *parameters* of the project have *changed*. Somehow, the givens are different now than at prior meetings on content and objectives. Another equally frightening form of feedback occurs when the content expert says, "I don't think you really understand what we're trying to teach about how a centrifugal gas compressor works." If you get a sinking feeling in the pit of your stomach, the SME's probably right. Often, such comments result from clients hoping to expand on the uses of the audiovisual program:

> "We'd not only like to show the tape to our dealer sales reps—we want a shorter, edited version aimed at consumers for dealer reps to play at point-of-purchase."

Or. . .

> "This script isn't 'meaty' enough. We not only want to use it to *introduce* the product—we wanna build some *training* sessions around it."

> Or the producer explains. . ."The budget has changed and we're
> gonna have to come up with a less expensive approach."

In each case, the feedback indicates the scriptwriter may have to rethink the project—take one step forward and two back by returning to the concept development stage. If a client wants to change the audience or objectives, it's up to writer and producer to explain the consequences on scripting and production. When told they cannot meet all their needs without developing two distinct versions of the A/V presentation, resulting in additional production costs, clients may reconsider and return to a more limited approach.

If not, then the writer will have to assess how the new parameters affect the existing first draft. The impact usually cannot be fully assessed right on the spot. Reaching two distinct audiences may require more research with the content expert. It might mean shaping *two* versions of the script using a common concept, format, and production elements. That's a conceptual matter requiring problem identification, analysis and solution. It's more than a rewrite; we're talking a "rethink" and that calls for "time out" to regroup. (Changes in the original specifications usually impact the total production schedule. It's not "kosher" to expect the writer and production team to stick to initial commitments without some give-and-take in the schedule. If that's not possible, the writer, at least, is facing overtime. Clients should pay for such overtime.)

Sometimes feedback coming from different sources has multiple effects on the script. Often only the writer is fully aware of the significance of such changes. For instance, I once used dramatization and a concealed structure for a program on employee benefit changes. For reasons having to do with the company's policies and commitment to equal opportunity employment, the actions and motivations of two characters (a black female clerical employee and a white female professional employee) were reversed. On the surface, that doesn't seem like much of a rewrite— simply switching names and a few lines of dialog should easily respond to the client's concern. In this instance, though, I had to do major surgery on the highly fluid and flexible concealed structural spine to accommodate the change. Sometimes, only the writer can fully appreciate the scope and consequences of the feedback. And only the writer can go off to sift through it all and fix problems.

In short, whenever the writer hears feedback which indicates a major problem with the concept, content or structure—the revision process is likely to go beyond the adding, deleting or editing normally associated with revision.

HANDLING OBJECTIONS

For a time, all my projects were on the same subject: sales training. I'd never had much respect for selling and salespeople. (Most consumers don't. We're usually distrustful and wary of salespeople, sometimes even adversarial, especially when buying an intangible product like insurance.) Not only was I writing a lot of training material, it all related to selling *insurance*!

So, of course, I learned a lot about the sales process. And sales training courses place considerable emphasis on objection handling. Once I dug into the content and spent time discussing selling skills with the subject matter experts, I began to realize that objection handling is exactly what *writers* do during script conferences. So the skills used to handle objections can be readily adapted to make the script conference more productive and less traumatic for writers. For instance, one of the first objection-handling rules is to *anticipate* the objection.

I met to discuss feedback on the United States Golf Association script mentioned earlier in this book. The objective was to illustrate the causes and cures of slow play, golf's most serious "disease." Two pros, Fuzzy Zoeller and Amy Alcott, were to be the spokespersons. The treatment proposed a solution for the major scripting problem: how to demonstrate the wrong way causes of slow play. Here is a portion of that treatment.[2]

CREATIVE STRATEGY

The Challenge

There is an inherent challenge in communicating this content via film or television. On the one hand, these media are ideally suited to capturing and demonstrating both the causes and cures of slow play. The challenge, however, lies in developing a stylistic approach to ensure on-screen demos of slow play don't result in a viewing experience which is also slow and protracted.

A Solution

The following treatment addresses this problem head-on with a creative concept designed to "speed up" the action and viewer interest of slow play scenes while illustrating negative behaviors.

The solution involves what we call the "Home Movie" effect:

TELEVISION TREATMENT

Home movies—even home videos, for that matter—have a characteristic, amateur look (hand held shooting, overuse of zooms, scratchy prints, etc.) which often makes the action mildly

> humorous. At the same time, home movies appear slightly
> speeded up when transferred to video. Our concept is to shoot
> "wrong way" scenes in the style of a home movie or videotape.

> Basically, here's how the program would unfold. . .

The producer/director and I were both comfortable with the "home movie" device for illustrating slow play. But prior to the client meeting, we tried to anticipate potential objections, confusions or questions. Other than total rejection, we could come up with only one objection: the treatment focused on describing the "home movie" technique for illustrating wrong way examples. On reading the complete treatment, however, one might assume the majority of screen time and emphasis went to the "home movie" segments, leaving our professional golfers a minimal role.

The treatment appropriately explained what was most difficult to envision: how the home movie technique would be executed and integrated into the body of the program. Scripting the "right way" commentary of the pros required little explanation. However, should the client raise the objection that the "stars" might be overshadowed by the wrong way hackers we had a response in our hip pockets. No "think on your feet" adlibbing would be necessary.

So, begin by considering the script or treatment, the players and politics involved and then anticipate areas most likely to raise questions or concerns.

Next, salespeople are tutored to "hear the objection out. Keep your mouth shut. Let the buyer get the full objection on the table." Usually, the "buyer" (client, producer or SME) feels better simply for having voiced their objection. And the salesperson (writer) has not short-circuited the process by jumping in and answering an objection too quickly. After all, without hearing the objection out, we may miss vital information—the key to unlocking "the sale."

Now it's the writer's turn to speak, but it's still too early to answer the objection head on. Instead, use the salesperson's technique of analyzing and clarifying the objection. You do this by asking a question or two in return to make certain you understand. . .

> "Let me make certain I follow. Are you saying you're not com-
> fortable with the home movie technique itself—or are you con-
> cerned about upstaging the pros?"

It's the salesperson's technique of making the buyer answer an "either. . .or" question. The real objective may lie beneath the surface. Also, listening to a client's feedback (or anyone's feedback on your writing) requires "third-ear" listening skills. Often what's *not* spoken, but implied or buried in rhetoric, carries the heart of the issue.

Remember—people buy on emotion, then justify their purchase with logic. The same applies to scripts and clients. Their most important reactions are emotional and affective. Often they're *trying* to like the script, but they need help. Sometimes, all that's needed is for the writer and producer to bolster the client's confidence by saying they know what they're doing and the resulting program will work with the target audience.

Once the objection has been clarified and you feel you understand the client's genuine point of view, the writer needs to decide, "Do I *want* to answer this objection?" And if "yes," do you "want to answer it *now*?" Not every objection requires an answer. Some objections (known to sales types as "minor point objections") are simply too picayune to bother with. Others point to additional problems the client or content experts need to get off their chest. So allow them to "hold court." Give them the floor. Listen carefully. Listen for what they do and *don't* say. Are you hearing objections you expected to hear and have ready answers for? Are you hearing minor points which can be fixed through rewrites? Is the client/content expert having trouble with the concept? Or, do they find the treatment or script lacks effectiveness and impact?

Classifying Objections

Answers to these questions determine your response. New salespeople are taught to classify objections according to type. The most dismaying is the hopeless objection:

"I just don't like this script at all."

"I was dubious of this as a treatment. Now I'm convinced humor is the wrong approach for our audience."

"I think we should go back to my idea for opening the program."

Such statements are big, bold oral rejection slips. Just as salespeople are cautioned not to take rejection personally, writers need to steel themselves against such criticism. If you've done your best work, adopt a Zen-like attitude. So they didn't like your script. The sun still rises in the east tomorrow morning. Or try this mental self-talk: "If the client can't see the merits of my work, that's his/her problem, not mine. I'll complete the assignment as best as I can and move on to more appreciative clients who believe in my work."

But what to do after the mental pep talk? David Lyman, founder and director of the Maine Photographic Workshops, says that sometimes "creativity is knowing when to let go. . .to know you're in a no-win situation and that it's a waste of your creative energies to swim upstream any further."

So you have to write it the way the client dictates. They wear you down. When you know the resulting program will be a dull, lifeless, ineffective use of the A/V medium, with little audience appeal, it's like rubbing salt in the wound. But take the most businesslike, professional approach possible under the circumstances. That's what you're paid for. There will be other clients, other opportunities for scripting the award-winning program. And even recalcitrant clients can wise up in a hurry when the jury of audience opinion votes.

To sum up, the various types of objections and the appropriate responses are listed below:

1. Hopeless objection: requires no defense. It's time to retrench.
2. Minor objection: usually needs little discussion. When facing only minor objections, you're home free.
3. Genuine objection: the client raises relevant shortcomings in the first draft. This is the most important objection to overcome or address through revision. You must overcome this sales resistance; or, agree to make changes to resolve the issue.

Handling Genuine Objections

When you hear the client pose a genuine objection, you may have one of several initial responses:

Total disagreement
Total agreement
Uncertainty—you're not totally sure whether to agree or disagree
Confusion

If you disagree with the client's point, your instinct will be to do battle for your work. Standing your ground. . .

CLIENT: "I don't know. Seems to me like the 'home movie' stuff is upstaging the pros who are supposed to be the stars."

WRITER: "I'm glad you brought that up. You're right. In the treatment, the 'home movie' action seems to predominate. But that's primarily because the technique is difficult to visualize and we wanted to flesh it out for you. Believe me, in the first-draft script, the home movie action will be about twenty-five percent of the screen time, the pros will be in the spotlight for three-quarters of the time. . ."

Often, when you answer an objection head-on and do so convincingly and professionally, the client will acquiesce. After all, they've said earlier they like the concept, they're simply voicing concerns. If you allay their fears, they will trust your judgment. (However, if the first-draft script of our slow play golf program comes in with *fifty* percent of the screen time devoted to the "wrong way" home movie content and fifty percent on Fuzzy and Amy, the client has a legitimate beef at the script session.)

Next, suppose you agree with the client's feedback? Does this happen often? Yes. Sometimes, especially at the treatment or first-draft stage, a section of the script may bother you as writer, but you don't know quite how to put it right. If the client points to the same concern, you both know the problem needs fixing. Now it's time to talk openly and honestly to the client, seeking their thoughts and ideas. Try to avoid being defensive or having guilt feelings that your writing's fallen short. Writing is not a discipline with right and wrong answers to problems. Rather, there is a range of solutions, some better than others, to most writing problems. Sometimes it helps to share with the client why you find the section difficult to write. Verbalizing and discussing the difficulty may help solve the problem itself.

Sometimes, though, feedback on your work may come in shades of gray. This occurs when the client's comments relate to a topic you had not considered before. Or, perhaps your client expresses a viewpoint in an insightful way, forcing you to see the script or writing problem in a different light. An idea has merit, but it also may mean changing tone or structure or some other aspect of the draft. Will the new approach pay off, or simply lead you down a sidetrack?

Responding to this type of feedback, you're not necessarily prepared to don the warrior's helmet and rush in to defend what's presently on paper. Neither do you want to dismiss the comments as irrelevant. Generally, a positive, yet noncommittal response is most appropriate: "Gee, that's an interesting idea. I never thought about it that way. Let me mull that one over for awhile." It's short, honest, and leaves all doors open.

There really are a number of ways in which to respond to feedback on your work at any stage of the writing process. Understanding and rapport with the client, producer, director and subject matter experts (as well as plain old tact) create a climate in which you can accept feedback in positive, constructive ways.

For more insight into adapting objection-handling skills to the writing process, delve into some sales training books. There are plenty around; one that I recommend, is *A Motivational Approach to Selling* by James F. Evered (AMACOM, 1982).

THE MOST IMPORTANT READER

Earlier, we introduced the concept of the scriptwriter as one of the handful of select individuals to actually function as a *reader* of shooting scripts and participate in review sessions. Yet novice writers are not always aware of their role in the review process.

Granted, we participate as readers during the physical drafting of the script, moving from what Lucy McCormick Caulkins calls "passion hot" (when we're writing freely and easily) to "critic cold" (when we allow the "judge" to peer over our shoulder and critique the emerging text). And, we often read first-draft scripts aloud when presenting them to clients and content experts, commenting on relationships between visual and narrative copy.

But I'm talking about something different. The idea can be found in the roots of the word revision (see again). Caulkins and other writing teachers describe the writer's function in revision as one of distancing yourself from the drafting process so that you can read and respond to the script from several perspectives. Time provides the necessary distancing. Set your emerging manuscript aside for a period. Then return to it later with fresh eyes and renewed enthusiasm.

Put yourself in the shoes of your target audience. Then, read your draft. How do *you* like it? How do you *feel* about it? Something I've learned over the years is that your writing is never as brilliant, insightful and inspired as you think it is when created in the fever of inspiration. Neither is it ever as dreadful and ineffective as you believe when the writing was difficult and painstaking or you felt totally uninspired. With a little distancing (sometimes as brief as a day or two for short scripts; weeks or even months for longer works) you find yourself responding more normally to the work.

So how *do* you like it? Anything *you* want to change? After a first draft, you invariably find things to improve. Maybe it's simply a matter of wordsmithing; or perhaps you see how a simple structural change might make the program more effective. Do you feel the script is too long? (I *always* have that problem.) How about the balance between two chosen formats? Happy with how that worked out?

You can ask yourself innumerable questions about your emerging text. Figure 9.1 is a list of "revision strategies" I adapted for A/V writers from Lucy McCormick Calkins' book.

Obviously, you'll probably never undertake all these strategies on a single project. Use it as a checklist to decide what you wish to focus on as a reader of your own script. As you read and re-read with fresh eyes, you'll find yourself responding alternately as "artist, judge, even warrior and explorer" on occasion.

So drive around the "race track shifting from gear to gear" as Roger van Oech would say, depending on the nature of the project and your response to what you've written. You'll find things you want to change. Oddly enough, one of the most

Figure 9.1: Twelve Revision Strategies

1. Change a section from one format to another.
2. Rework a confused section—the ending, the open, a key point, an important transition, etc.
3. Reconsider tone or voice. Try on a different voice. See if it improves the script.
4. Make a long script shorter.
5. Take a short script and expand it into a more detailed version.
6. Try different openings.
7. Predict the viewer's questions, then revise in order to be sure they are answered, ideally in the order in which they are asked.
8. Read the script aloud—listening to how it sounds. Revise accordingly.
9. Reread the draft, evaluating what works and what doesn't. After identifying what works, write another draft or portion of a draft, building on that strength. Decide whether to delete, repair, or ignore what does not work.
10. Put the draft aside and return to it another day.
11. Talk with someone about the subject. Then rewrite the draft without looking back at the previous versions.
12. Read the script looking at only one aspect, e.g.:

    Narrative style and voice
    Visualization
    Structure and pacing
    Formats
    Transitions
    Music and sound effects
    Visual effects, etc.

Source: Adapted from Lucy McCormick Calkins, *The Art of Teaching Writing*. Portsmouth, NH: Heinemann Educational Books, Inc., 1986.

frustrating and unusual experiences of my scriptwriting career resulted from a client who liked my first draft so much that he wanted to proceed directly into production—no revision necessary. I told him there were things I really wanted to change, but he was content. He didn't feel a rewrite was necessary! Believe me, don't expect this to happen often.

FOOTNOTES

1. Peter Elbow, *Writing With Power, Techniques for Mastering the Writing Process* (New York, NY: Oxford University Press, 1981), p. 7.
2. From a proposal by William Van Nostran for a United States Golf Association project.

Step 5: Editing

Editing

If you return to the diagram of the media writing process you'll see we're pulling into the last stop. After you revise the first-draft script, the client, content experts and production team all get another crack at reviewing the script.

If you've done your work well and painstakingly, you should now be home free. The major objections to content, style, voice, visualization or other first-draft problems will have been addressed in developing a second-draft shooting script. At that time, you either added, deleted or changed a portion or all of the script. Now, the content expert and client should be down to nit-picks. If the project has been on track to this point, the production team may even begin the early stages of the production process, from pre-production planning to execution.

As a reader of your own work, you, too, will have played a role in shaping the substance and style of the second-draft shooting script. By now, you should be comfortable with the story you've told and how you've used the strengths of the chosen medium to convey that story. You, too, should be entering the nit-picking stage.

You may or may not have another roundtable meeting with all the principal players. If your first draft was well received, the team is probably confident that any major changes have been incorporated, and they may opt to read the second draft and submit comments through notes or phone calls.

At this point, if you're working on other projects and the production schedule is tight, you may simply coordinate the final input and hand the script over to someone for copying and final distribution. If you have the luxury of time, however, now is your final crack at responding to the soon-to-be-abandoned script. Maybe you take it along on an airplane flight for an objective reading. Maybe you sit with the director and read the copy aloud for the last time. Maybe you go through the script page by page on your word processor and incorporate other people's comments while reacting yourself.

Now's the time to ask these simple questions:

- Did the first revision remain true to the concept, structure, style and tone of the original script?

- Do any changes made by client, SME, producer or director stand out like a sore thumb or clash? (Perhaps it's only a word or two, but those words matter. A quality all creative individuals share is persistence coupled with a drive for perfection. Writers may be sloppy in other parts of their lives, but they must be ruthlessly honest, self-critical and meticulous in the editorial stage.)
- Has everything in the visual portion of the script been appropriately described?
- Does the voice remain constant throughout the entire script? (The longer the work, the more critical this becomes. The more narrators, speakers or characters, the more complex this becomes.)
- Do *you* still like the script? If not, you at least say it is a craftsman-like solution to the writing problems, given the compromises you were forced to make?

This last question is tough. After living with a project day and night for weeks or even months, it's only natural for a certain weariness to set in. In the corporate and organizational media world, you rarely reach the end of a project without having made some compromises along the way, usually due to budget and time limits, or client relations.

In short, you often feel ready and willing to "abandon" this child, turn it over to the production crew and let them wrestle with it and all its shortcomings. Resist. Give yourself the luxury of one last, long, careful re-reading of the material. Don't go *looking* for things to fix: "if it ain't broke, don't monkey with it." But experience has shown that just as the client, SME and production team want to make last-minute, subtle changes, the writer will also see small things that can be fixed in the process of moving from the second (or third or fourth) substantive revision to finished production script.

You may want to use the thesaurus and search for a more precise meaning. Maybe you find a section of narration that can be made more conversational simply by using more contractions. Maybe you suddenly have a great idea for a transition. Go ahead and incorporate the notion as long as it remains within the practical realities of production.

Once these types of detailed revisions are made—you can lean back, kick your feet up on the desk and say, "Well, by God, we did it! Created something out of nothing. We made ourselves an audiovisual script!" It's a good feeling.

Introduction to Part II

Part I presented a generic writing process which can be applied to any media writing project, including print assignments.

The remaining chapters provide more detailed material related to specific media writing challenges such as instructional dramas, interactive video, teleconferencing and multi-image.

Building on the foundation of the basic scriptwriting process, these chapters may be read and studied in more random fashion. Focusing on those subjects that are relevant to your writing assignments will provide additional insights and script-writing techniques for mastering these media or genres.

10 Wearing the Instructional Dramatist's Two Hats

When Fitzgerald, Faulkner and Ferber ruled the literary roost, serious writers viewed Hollywood with disdain, looking east to Manhattan as the mecca for literary fame celebrated over dry martinis at the Algonquin. Today, however, aspiring writers show no such aversion. From Alaska to Maine, we toil on word processors retrofitted with the latest scriptwriting software while sipping Perrier. Screenwriting is more than respectable today—look how seriously William Goldman, Lawrence Kasdan, Stephen King or Leonard Elmore are taken. (The Writer's Guild of America registers nearly 1500 screenplays a *month*. Yet Hollywood produces only about 80 to 90 features in a full year!)

INSTRUCTIONAL DRAMAS

These days, however, corporate, educational and medical television churn out thousands of hours of drama. These are plotlines with a twist, however. They must *inform* or *instruct* through characters and dramatic action. Entertainment value, though important, is not the driving force.

An instructional drama is usually (though not always) shorter than a screenplay. Typically, an instructional drama takes 15 to 30 minutes of screen time. Like screenplays, these dramas depend on characters in dramatic situations to communicate ideas. But the audience for an instructional drama, unlike the audience for screenplays, is usually narrow, specific and homogeneous—such as a company's sales force. And, the content of an instructional drama is equally specific, geared toward meeting well-defined instructional or informational objectives.

With increasing frequency, corporate communicators and trainers recognize the value of dramatic action as a way to meet varied communication objectives. There's a greater demand than ever for scriptwriters capable of working in the dramatic form. (My own assignments now come at the rate of about two dramatic scripts for every one straight narrative or documentary program.)

Nor is this boon limited to the nonbroadcast arena. Look at the burgeoning number of religious programs on cable. I know one writer who landed a contract to

215

write six scripts on the lives of saints. The project, commissioned by Santa Fe Communications and the Archdiocese of New York, is intended to reach children. "In trying to make something entertaining for kids, we struck on the concept of dramatizing the lives of such people as Joan of Arc and St. Patrick, using a cast of child actors," says the writer, Hal Walker. "The scripts incorporated humor and anachronisms for entertainment value while illustrating specific moral principles."

College and university video and film departments and PBS stations are another outlet for dramatic fare that aims to instruct.

In writing workshops, I refer to such programming as the "industrial soap" genre. Though tongue-in-cheek, the description by no means implies disdain. In fact, you must be totally professional in order to write instructional dramas successfully. Still more important, you must be comfortable wearing *two* hats: that of dramatist and that of trainer/educator.

What Instructional Dramas Teach

Instructional dramas fall into three major categories based on their purpose:

1. *Behavior Modeling*

Many dramas that teach show viewers how to behave in given situations. One of my clients, General Foods, produced a program to illustrate how sales managers should conduct interviews with potential job applicants. (At the opposite end of the spectrum, a corporate giant undergoing a major reorganization commissioned me to script a program on how to dismiss employees.) The most socially significant project I've had the fortune to work on provided welfare recipients with role models on how to conduct a job search.

In each instance, dramatic vignettes illustrate positive behaviors that conform to a step-by-step process. Learners observe and assimilate the process to apply in their own interactions. The excerpt in Figure 10.1, from a script by Kevin Cole on dismissing an employee for unsatisfactory performance, provides a role model which is taught one step at a time.

2. *Hooking an Audience*

Drama can add new twists to otherwise predictable films and video tapes. "Sesame Street" and "The Electric Company" are wonderful examples of how colorful characters fulfill educational objectives while entertaining.

I recently asked a corporate media producer his opinion on how entertaining industrial television needs to be. His answer: "Corporate video *always* needs to be entertaining. You've got a very sophisticated audience and now you've got sophis-

Figure 10.1: Use of Role Models

NARRATOR: WHAT DO YOU DO THEN?

SMITH turns away from George and looks at camera.

SMITH: (To us, sheepishly) "What do I *DO*?—I wish I had a PLAN."

IMMEDIATELY FREEZE FRAME

SQUEEZE ZOOM BACK:

(OR CUT TO:)

22.0 SMITH and NARRATOR with our CHROMA-KEYED FREEZE FRAMES in place behind them.

NARRATOR: (On cam)

A PLAN IS RIGHT. WITH GOOD PREPARATION—

He points to "Do's" box.

—AND BY FOLLOWING THE 'DO'S', YOU'LL MAKE THE MEETING GO MORE SMOOTHLY.

SQUEEZE ZOOM OUT:
(OR CUT TO:)

23.0 FREEZE FRAME SHOT.

We're in a CONFERENCE ROOM, we see termination meeting with SMITH and GEORGE, opposite angle from previous vignette. FREEZE FRAME begins action.

SUPER TITLE: "DO'S"

NARRATOR: (Voice over)

EXAMPLE: *DO* GET QUICKLY TO THE POINT. AND HAVE YOUR POINTS WELL REHEARSED. . .

SMITH: "George, you and I have had a lot of conversations about problems in

Figure 10.1: Use of Role Models (Cont.)

> this department, and the fact is that we don't see the same solutions.''
>
> (CUT back and forth as needed.)
>
> GEORGE: ''Oh, I know we don't always agree, Smitty, but I *have* made some changes. . .''
>
> SMITH: ''Yes, but it's obvious the changes haven't been enough.''
>
> NARRATOR: (Voice over)
>
> NOW, BRIEFLY DESCRIBE WHAT LED TO THE TERMINATION. STICK TO THE FACTS. . .
>
> SMITH: ''I've concluded that our differences are just too many. I need people who are team players, who have a vision for this organization.
>
> You do have excellent qualities, George, but for this job, and for the corporation's needs, those qualities don't match. . . .''
>
> NARRATOR:
>
> CLEARLY STATE THAT THE EMPLOYEE IS TERMINATED, AND LEAVE NO ROOM FOR DOUBT.
>
> SMITH: ''As of today, you're terminated. You're no longer with the company.''
>
> George's reaction is disbelief and some shock. But Smith stays calm and focused. (*SOME DIALOGUE UNDER*)
>
> NARRATOR:
>
> EXPECT DISBELIEF. SOME PEOPLE JUST WON'T ACCEPT RESPONSIBILITY, AND MAY TRY TO PUT *YOU* ON THE DEFENSIVE.

Figure 10.1: Use of Role Models (Cont.)

	GEORGE: (Dialog FADING UP) "... This is really just a personal thing, isn't it. You never liked me. Maybe I'm a threat to you, isn't that it?"
NARRATOR:	DON'T FALL FOR IT. STAY FOCUSED, AND FOLLOW YOUR OUTLINE.
	SMITH: "The issue is performance, George. We've had lots of taoks about it, verbal and written warnings. . . we've *had* our differences, but they've been strictly business."

Source: From "Terminations," written by Kevin Cole, produced by Nell Newberry, directed by Ron Rinella for U.S. BanCorp. Used by permission.

ticated people working in corporate TV, people who know that, to communicate an idea, you've got to do it in a professional way. It's like telling a story. If it's interesting and captures your attention, the information behind that story's going to come across."

Even with a subject as serious as job readiness training for welfare recipients, entertainment has a place; for instance, a comedic retelling of Aesop's grasshopper and ant fable. "The 'welfare cycle' is no fairy tale," says Keith Manning, one of the clients and executive producers on the series, "but the lessons learned from the ant and grasshopper fable are germane in teaching those caught in the public assistance maze.... We also believe that a training program for the economically disadvantaged needs to be not only effective but *entertaining* as well."

Increasingly, corporations recognize that entertainment helps "sell" ideas. When the president of a major health and beauty care company wanted to dramatize the importance of goal setting, planning and controlling all business functions, the resulting script was a farce featuring pirates, jugglers and a genuine management "guru." The theater-of-the-absurd piece made points broadly and boldly while serving as a discussion-starter for shirt-sleeve training sessions.

The opening scenes in Kevin Cole's otherwise serious script on dismissing employees begins with comedic vignettes designed to create empathy, disarm and capture the audience's attention, as Figure 10.2 shows.

Figure 10.2: Use of Comedy

PART ONE:
"Termination for Cause"

FADE UP TITLES, THEN:

FADE IN ON:

1.0   **OFFICE OF A U.S. BANCORP MANAGER**

We see "SMITH," a middle-aged manager sitting at his desk. He's in shirt-sleeves, reading through a file folder with the name "C. Jones" on it. As the narrator speaks, Smith shakes his head, and looks off into the distance imagining. . .

> **NARRATOR** (VOICE OVER:)
>
> IT'S A FACT OF LIFE FOR ANY MANAGER—OCCASIONALLY, YOU'LL HAVE TO TERMINATE AN EMPLOYEE.
>
> WHEN YOU DO, IT'S ONLY NATURAL TO IMAGINE THE WORST. . .

(IMAGINATION MUSIC UP, THEN UNDER)

WAVY "IMAGINATION" DISSOLVE TAKES US TO:

2.0   CONFERENCE ROOM. We see Smith, now in a suit, with folder in front of him, leaning in toward camera.

> (*NOTE:* All imagination scenes could be shot with soft borders)

> **(NARRATOR (VOICE OVER:))**
>
> . . .YOU DREAD HOW IT WILL AFFECT THE OTHER PERSON.
>
> **SMITH:** "I'm sorry, Miss Jones, but it's all over."

CUT TO REVERSE ANGLE, we see "MISS JONES," a 30-ish teller. She has gone rigid with shock. She sits stone stiff and stares blankly ahead.

Figure 10.2: Use of Comedy (Cont.)

                                   SMITH: (Snapping his fingers)
                                   "Miss Jones? Miss Jones?"

                    (BRIEF IMAGINATION MUSIC UP)

WIPE TO:

3.0   EXT. BUILDING LEDGE. "HARTMAN," a middle-aged man, is edging
      along it. He's backing away from SMITH who leans out a window, imploring
      him to come back.

      (SFX car horns)

                                   SMITH: "Hartman, I feel just terrible
                                   about this. . ."

                                   HARTMAN: (Hysterically)
                                   "Sure you do—you've destroyed my life!"

            They both look down and up in exaggerated terror, then:

WIPE TO:

4.0   SAME CONFERENCE ROOM, another angle. We see Smith and "GORDON,"
      a rather large young man.

                                   SMITH: "Gordon, c'est la vie. . ."

                                   GORDON: (He growls)
                                   "Oh yeah? Well c'est la fist, boss. . .

QUICK CUT TO CLOSE UP, wide angle, of GORDON'S FACE and HUGE
THREATENING FIST.

                    (IMAGINATION MUSIC UP)

LONG DISSOLVE TO:

                                   NARRATOR (VOICE OVER:)

                                   CHANCES ARE YOU'LL ALSO
                                   FANTASIZE HOW THE TERMINATION
                                   WILL AFFECT *YOU*. . .

5.0   CONFERENCE ROOM DOOR AREA. Smith is watching Miss Jones being
      wheeled out in a straight jacket.

Figure 10.2: Use of Comedy (Cont.)

SMITH: (Distraught) "I've ruined her!"

QUICK CUT TO:

6.0   EXT. BUILDING LEDGE. Smith is peering down helplessly.

SMITH: (More distraught)
"I've killed him!"

QUICK CUT TO:

7.0   CONFERENCE ROOM WALL AREA. Smith is being choked by Gordon.

SMITH: (The words come out choked)
"He's killing *me*!"

(IMAGINATION MUSIC WILL END AFTER:)

Source: From "Terminations," written by Kevin Cole, produced by
Nell Newberry, directed by Ron Rinella for U.S. BanCorp. Used by
permission.

3.   *Audience Identification*

Dramatic vignettes allow target audiences to identify with specific characters. In an award-winning script introducing a new flexible benefits program to current employees, the dramatic action centered on how four employees—a young unmarried salesman, a middle-aged executive with three kids, a secretary providing a second income, and a newly divorced middle manager and mother—went about making choices under the new flexible benefits package. In preliminary script sessions, great attention was given to selecting the mix of employee "types," based on the demographic characteristics of the target audience. The opening scenes served to introduce and establish each character's situation (see Figure 5.4).

Dramatic Formats

In Chapter 5, we analyzed six generic media formats, drama being one. Within dramatic form are three variations of the generic format. I call them pure dramatization, character narration, and dramatization with narration.

Pure Dramatization

Any situation in which there is conflict and the resolution of that conflict involves the assumption of character. Dialog and dramatic action are expected to

Figure 10.3: Use of Character Types

In a program on employee benefits, characters represent a cross section of the audience—in this case, a young unmarried sales representative.

Source: Photo courtesy of General Foods. JVC.

convey *all* content as well as establish character, create mood and style, etc. The excerpt in Figure 10.4, from a motivational docudrama aimed at out-of-work blue-collar workers, tells the story purely through dramatization.

Character Narration

In this format, narrative information is communicated through a monologue in which the narrator assumes the identity of a character. Character narrations involve a single character (performing the traditional narrator's function) who addresses the audience directly. They are often useful for historical subjects. (Here is where the scriptwriter's ability to create a variety of "voices" and assume different personae proves invaluable.) The script in Figure 10.5 for instance, brings the founder of the Maxwell House Coffee Co. to life as a way of telling company history in an orienta-

Figure 10.4: Use of Pure Dramatization

VIDEO	AUDIO
FADE UP ON: Establishing shot of TV Reporter outside plant gate.	**TV REPORTER:** SO AS OF NEXT WEEK, EMPLOYEES AT THIS MEDICAL INSTRUMENT PLANT WILL LOOK FOR NEW JOBS. AS THE GATES CLOSE FOR GOOD, ONE HAS TO WONDER: WHERE WILL THOSE NEW JOBS COME FROM? THIS IS BRENDA DEVLIN—CHANNEL SIX NEWS.
CUT TO shots of ENG crew as technician rewinds tape for playback.	**TECHNICIAN:** SOUNDS GOOD, BRENDA. LET'S JUST CHECK THE PLAYBACK.
DIFFERENT ANGLE, featuring group of employees. Their glib joking masks the inner emotions. [NOTE: Casting should include minorities.]	**EMPLOYEE 1:** LOOK LIKE WE MADE THE EVENING NEWS. . . **EMPLOYEE 2:** HEY, MARILYN— THERE'S YOUR CHANCE TO GET ON THE TUBE. SAY "HI" TO MOM. **MARILYN:** VERY FUNNY, ROCKY— YOU GONNA APPLY FOR WORK AS THE PLANT CLOWN? **EMPLOYEE 2:** WELL—I DON'T KNOW ABOUT THE REST O' YOU. BUT I FEEL I'VE EARNED A GOOD LONG VACATION. **EMPLOYEE 1:** YEAH—WE PAID INTO UNEMPLOYMENT ALL THESE YEARS. 'BOUT TIME WE TOOK A LITTLE SOMETHIN' OUT. **EMPLOYEE 2:** I HEAR THE FISH ARE BITIN' REAL GOOD UP AT THE LAKE. . .
CUT BACK to news crew looking at playback.	**TV REPORTER:** (Appears as play- back.). . .AFTER WEEKS OF RUMORS,

Figure 10.4: Use of Pure Dramatization (Cont.)

VIDEO	AUDIO
	A TOP MANAGEMENT TEAM FLEW IN TO ANNOUNCE THEIR DECISION. THE PLANT IS NO LONGER PROFITABLE IN TODAY'S HIGHLY COMPETITIVE MEDICAL TECHNOLOGY MARKETPLACE.
CUT TO Nick Conti, in his mid-thirties, and Manny Esposito, somewhat older, as they reach their cars in the parking lot.	**MANNY ESPOSITO:** I REMEMBER THE FIRST TIME I CAME THROUGH THOSE GATES LOOKIN' FOR A JOB.
	NICK CONTI: GUESS WE ALL DO, MANNY.
	MANNY ESPOSITO: SOMEWHERE ALONG THE LINE, I FIGURED I'D WORK HERE 'TIL I WON THE LOTTERY, KICKED THE BUCKET OR RETIRED. NEVER DREAMED IT WOULD JUST—END.
	NICK CONTI: GUESS THE HAND-WRITING HAD BEEN ON THE WALL FOR A WHILE.
	MANNY ESPOSITO: TELL YOU WHAT THE HANDWRITING SAYS NOW—I GOTTA FIND WORK. YOU WORRIED ABOUT THAT, NICK?
	NICK CONTI: WHY WORRY? MY DAD USED TO SAY—ANYONE WILLING TO WORK CAN *FIND* WORK. SIMPLE AS THAT.
	MANNY ESPOSITO: I SURE HOPE SO, NICK. HOPE IT *IS* THAT SIMPLE.
	NICK CONTI: WELL—WE'RE ABOUT TO FIND OUT, AREN'T WE?

Figure 10.4: Use of Pure Dramatization (Cont.)

VIDEO	AUDIO
	MANNY ESPOSITO: WANNA STOP AT RYAN'S? THE GANG'LL PROBABLY BE CHEWIN' THE FAT.
	NICK CONTI: I DON'T FEEL MUCH LIKE IT. BESIDES, LINDA'S PROBABLY GOT SUPPER ON.
	MANNY ESPOSITO: I DON'T EXACTLY RELISH FACING THE "MUSIC" ON THE HOME FRONT.
CUT TO close-ups as dinner is being served up to kids around the kitchen table. Nick's two girls are about eight and ten years old. Laurie is the youngest.	**LINDA CONTI:** STACEY—PUT SOME O' THOSE LIMA BEANS ON YOUR PLATE. . .
	STACEY: AW, MOM. . .
	LINDA: THEY'RE YOUR FATHER'S FAVORITE. HE DESERVES A GOOD MEAL AFTER HIS DAY.
	NICK: NOT REALLY HUNGRY, ACTUALLY. YOU SEE ANYTHING ABOUT THE PLANT ON TV?
	LAURIE: YEAH—WE WATCHED OVER AT DARLENE'S. SHE SAW HER DAD LEAVING THE PLANT.
	STACEY: WE LOOKED FOR YOU ON TV, DADDY. . .
	LINDA: SUPPOSED TO HAVE A FULL STORY ON THE LATE NEWS. . .
	LAURIE: CAN WE STAY UP?
	NICK: (Snapping at her.) NO YOU CAN'T STAY UP. (Trying to soften the blow.) BESIDES—IT'S ONE HECK OF A WAY TO GET ON TV.

Figure 10.4: Use of Pure Dramatization (Cont.)

VIDEO	AUDIO
	LINDA: THE KIDS JUST WANTED TO LOOK FOR YOU—THAT'S ALL. OH, BY THE WAY, JIM WANTS YOU TO CALL AFTER SUPPER.
	NICK: OH, GREAT. HE DIDN'T WASTE ANY TIME CALLIN' TO CONGRATULATE ME BEIN' ON THE STREET.
	LINDA: NICK—PLEASE DON'T TALK LIKE THAT. HE WAS REALLY CONCERNED.
	NICK: AND I'M SURE HE'S GOT ALL KINDS OF FREE ADVICE ABOUT HOW TO GO ABOUT GETTIN' A JOB.
	LINDA: SAID HE HAD A LEAD OR TWO FOR YOU—THAT'S ALL.
	NICK: WHEN I NEED YOUR BROTHER'S HELP GETTIN' WORK— I'LL ASK FOR IT. STACEY, HOW 'BOUT SOME BUTTER DOWN AT THIS END O' THE TABLE.
DISSOLVE TO:	

Source: From "You're Hired! The Nuts and Bolts of Job Hunting,"™
written by William Van Nostran, directed by Walter Schoenknecht,
created and produced by Karli & Associates and The Prudential-Audio
Visual Communications Division. Used by permission.

tion program for new sales representatives. Figure 10.6 is an illustration from that program.

Dramatization with Narration

In this form, dramatic vignettes are freely interspersed with a traditional spokesperson who provides narrative commentary or interpretation. The writer, as dramatist,

Figure 10.5: Use of Character Narration

VIDEO	AUDIO
SPECIAL EFFECT as FREEZE-FRAME image of Joel Cheek ZOOMS forward to fill the frame. Action begins as actor portrays Joel Cheek.	
Cheek moves about in office with turn-of-the-century memorabilia. He uses props and photo album to illustrate his story.	**JOEL CHEEK:** [To camera] AS A YOUNG MAN, FRESH FROM KENTUCKY FARM LIFE, MY CAREER BEGAN WITH A JOB REMARKABLY SIMILAR TO YOURS. I STARTED OUT REPRESENTING A NASHVILLE WHOLESALE GROCERY FIRM. THAT WAS BACK IN 1873.
He goes to map on wall. ZOOM to CU on map; follow route of Cumberland River.	I HAVE QUITE VIVID RECOLLEC-TIONS OF THAT FIRST JOB. MY TERRITORY STRETCHED ALONG THE BANKS OF THE CUMBERLAND RIVER IN TENNESSEE.
MS on Cheek as he moves to saddle-bags slung over chair. INSERT close-ups as he pulls coffee bean samples from the bag.	IN THOSE DAYS THERE WAS NO SUCH THING AS A COMPANY CAR. SADDLEBAGS SERVED AS MY SAMPLE KIT. FROM THE BEGINNING, COFFEE HELD A SPECIAL FASCINA-TION FOR ME.
Moves to copper kettle and empties sample into kettle.	NOW SOME FOLKS THINK COFFEE BEANS ARE ALL PRETTY MUCH THE SAME. TAKE IT FROM ME—COFFEE BEANS HAVE QUITE DISTINCT AROMAS AND FLAVORS.
INSERT close-ups of beans as appropriate.	A COFFEE EXPERT CAN PRETTY MUCH TELL YOU WHAT PART OF THE WORLD A TYPE OF BEAN COMES FROM. THE MOST SATISFY-ING BREW RESULTS FROM PRECISE ROASTING AND BLENDING. YOU MIGHT SAY, I WAS A MAN OBSESSED WITH FINDING MY OWN PERFECT BLEND OF MATCHLESS FLAVOR.

Figure 10.5: Use of Character Narration (Cont.)

VIDEO	AUDIO
	SO, ONCE I GOT A PROMOTION AND SETTLED IN NASHVILLE—I SPENT NIGHTS TRYING MY OWN HAND AT BLENDING BEANS IN THIS COPPER KETTLE. SOME OF THOSE CONCOCTIONS WERE DARNED FLAVORFUL.
MS—As Cheek moves to photo album. Begins to leaf through.	BUT IT WASN'T 'TIL 1892 THAT I FELT I HAD THE BLEND WHICH FIRED MY IMAGINATION. I WAS READY TO PUT THIS BLEND TO THE TEST.
ZOOM to CU on photos or art of the Maxwell House Hotel.	I TOOK IT TO ONE OF THE SOUTH'S FINEST HOTELS—THE ELEGANT MAXWELL HOUSE RIGHT HERE IN NASHVILLE. THEIR GUEST BOOK READ LIKE A WHO'S WHO OF THE DAY—DIPLOMATS, GENERALS, EVEN PRESIDENTS STAYED THERE. THESE PATRONS SOON BEGAN TO COMMENT QUITE FAVORABLY ON THE MELLOW FLAVOR OF MY SPECIAL BLEND. 'FOR LONG, THE MAXWELL HOUSE SERVED NO OTHER BLEND.
Art or photo of first Nashville plant. Show Cheek with fellow workers.	THAT ENDORSEMENT GAVE ME THE IMPETUS TO MANUFACTURE THE BLEND IN THIS NASHVILLE PLANT. WE STARTED OUT WITH A SINGLE 150-POUND ROASTER.
MS on Joel Cheek.	AND, AS I'M SURE YOU CAN GUESS, WE NAMED THIS COFFEE AFTER THE MAXWELL HOUSE HOTEL. . .

Source: From "The Best Coffee Company," written by William Van Nostran, produced by William Hoppe, directed by Robert Shewchuk and James G. Libby for General Foods Corp. Used by permission.

Figure 10.6: Actor Playing Role of Joel Cheek

In this historical introduction to Maxwell House Coffee, an actor plays the role of Joel Cheek, who originated the blend and founded the company. It's an example of how mixing formats can add interest to the subject matter. On the surface, it's simply a "talking head with props." Simultaneously, however, the writer uses dramatic technique (a character narration) to give the subject matter more human interest. The character narration also allows the writer to develop a "voice" which departs from more predictable corporate narration.

Source: From "The Best Coffee Company," written by William Van Nostran, produced by William Hoppe, directed by Robert Shewchuk and James G. Libby for General Foods Corp. Used by permission.

does not have to work so hard, since the narrator can "set up" a scene, even tell the audience what to look for in the dramatic vignette. These functional narrative segments can be written as straightforward descriptive narration or through the voice of a character narrator. Figure 10.7 shows an off-camera, first-person character narration followed by a scene from the same training program in which an on-camera narrator introduces and comments on the dramatic action.

This dramatic segment is followed by 13 instructional units in which the character of Shirley Cooper also functions as an on-camera narrator—setting up additional dramatic vignettes. Figure 10.8 shows part of one unit.

Wearing the Two Hats

Wearing the dramatist's hat, your attention will focus on creating believable characters and setting them in action through conflict. Under the trainer's hat, you will be responding wholeheartedly to your client's instructional/educational objectives, seeing to it that the dramatic material delivers content and key learning points.

Figure 10.7: Use of Dramatization with Off-Camera Narration

VIDEO	AUDIO
ESTABLISHING shot of two men out for a business lunch. The waiter brings their dishes.	**WAITER:** . . .HERE YOU ARE. SORRY IT TOOK A BIT LONGER THAN USUAL.
	CUSTOMER 1: WE'RE IN NO RUSH TODAY.
	WAITER: AN ASSISTANT IN THE KITCHEN'S LEAVING US TODAY. WE'RE HAVING A LITTLE "GOOD BYE" CELEBRATION. BEEN WITH US ALMOST THREE YEARS.
	CUSTOMER 2: MUST'VE MADE A GOOD IMPRESSION TO RATE A FAREWELL PARTY.
	WAITER: SHE'S VERY SPECIAL— CAME IN HERE AND LEARNED THE BUSINESS FROM THE GROUND UP. TOOK SOME CLASSES AT THE COMMUNITY COLLEGE. AND GUESS WHERE SHE'S GOING?
	CUSTOMER 1: WHERE?
	WAITER: SHE'LL BE ONE OF THE ASSISTANT CHEFS AT THE TIMBERS. WE'RE GONNA MISS HER. SHE'S BECOME ONE OF THE "GANG."
As MUSIC hits we DISSOLVE TO shots of LAURA opening cards from other staff members in kitchen.	**MUSIC:** (Instrumental version of original song up full establishing theme, then under.)
TIGHT on LAURA's face intercut with reaction shots of those around her as she opens cards and a present or two.	**LAURA:** (Interior monologue.) FUNNY HOW LIFE WORKS OUT. I CAN STILL REMEMBER THE FIRST DAY I WALKED IN HERE—SCARED STIFF. COULD NEVER'VE GOTTEN THROUGH THE INTERVIEW IF IT HADN'T BEEN FOR MRS. COOPER.

Figure 10.7: Use of Dramatization with Off-Camera Narration (Cont.)

VIDEO	AUDIO
	HER CLASS GAVE ME THE ENERGY TO BE AMBITIOUS. . .
DISSOLVE TO:	
TIGHT SHOT on Laura tentatively asking directions to classroom.	AND YET, I SHOWED UP AT THAT JOB TRAINING CLASS BOUND AND DETERMINED I WOULDN'T GET A THING OUT OF IT. I'D NEVER WORKED OUTTA THE HOUSE IN MY LIFE. WHAT COULD THEY TEACH ME THAT WOULD DO ANY GOOD?
Then SHOT of her and others filing in.	MRS. COOPER STARTED BY MAKIN' EVERYONE INTRODUCE THEM- SELVES. I WAS SO NERVOUS OVER WHAT TO SAY I DIDN'T LISTEN TO NO ONE ELSE. . .
TIGHT SHOT on JAMES SCOTT, obviously uncomfortable among the group. . .	**JAMES SCOTT:** (Obviously uncomfortable.) MY NAME'S JAMES SCOTT AND I'M FROM RIGHT HERE IN CLARKSVILLE. I'VE BEEN OUTTA WORK FOR MOST'UVA YEAR NOW.
Begin slow pan right from center of table, showing REACTIONS of others. Some are listening, some stare out the window, EDUARDO is doodling on a pad.	
TIGHT on SHIRLEY COOPER.	**SHIRLEY COOPER:** WHAT WAS YOUR LAST JOB?
BACK to JAMES, etc.	**JAMES SCOTT:** CONSTRUCTION WORK. THAT'S MOSTLY WHAT I'VE DONE.
	SHIRLEY COOPER: AND WHY DID YOU LEAVE, JAMES?
	JAMES SCOTT: GOT HURT PRETTY BAD IN AN ACCIDENT. LEG STILL ACTS UP ON ME.

Figure 10.7: Use of Dramatization with Off-Camera Narration (Cont.)

VIDEO	AUDIO
	SHIRLEY COOPER: O.K. LET'S GO ON TO MARTHA. . .
TIGHT on MARTHA, very unkempt.	**MARTHA:** MY NAME'S MARTHA HOWARD. I'M THE MOTHER OF ONE CHILD. I LIVE OVER IN PHIPPSBURG. I'VE BEEN ON WELFARE NOW FOR ABOUT. . .I GUESS IT'S GOING ONTO THREE YEARS. . .
CAMERA roams around room, in hand-held cinema verite style showing varied expressions of the class members.	**MUSIC AND DIALOG:** (Cross-fade MARTHA'S speech with crescendo in musical theme. MUSIC dominates as another PARTICIPANT introduces self. The DIALOG is too low to be heard distinctly. On CUE, pull MUSIC under LAURA'S speech. MUSIC OUT on SHIRLEY COOPER'S next line.)
DISSOLVE TO:	
TIGHT SHOT on LAURA in class with head down, avoiding eye contact.	**LAURA:** (Interior monologue.) FUNNY THING WAS, ONCE IT GOT TO BE MY TURN—I DIDN'T HAVE A THING TO SAY. EVERYONE ELSE HAD *DONE* SOMETHIN' BEFORE. NOT ME.
CUT to SHIRLEY in front of the class, addressing question to LAURA.	**SHIRLEY COOPER:** SO, LAURA, WILL YOU TELL US SOMETHING ABOUT YOURSELF?
	LAURA: (Seemingly disinterested. She looks off into the distance.) I DON'T HAVE NOTHIN' TO SAY.
	SHIRLEY COOPER: EVER HAD A JOB OUTSIDE THE HOUSE, LAURA? (Laura sits in stony silence.) YOU KNOW, LAURA, WE'VE HAD PEOPLE COME THROUGH HERE WITH NO WORK EXPERIENCE AT ALL AND

Figure 10.7: Use of Dramatization with Off-Camera Narration (Cont.)

VIDEO	AUDIO
	THEY'VE GOTTEN JOBS. YOU'VE GOT SKILLS YOU PROBABLY DON'T REALIZE. (Laura remains unresponsive. Turns to the next subject.) O.K. GROUP—BEFORE WE GET INTO THE FIRST SUBJECT, WE'VE GOT SOME PAPERWORK TO DO. . .
DISSOLVE TO:	

Source: From "The Choice is Yours,"^{TM} written by William Van Nostran, directed by Walter Schoenknecht, created and produced by Karli & Associates and The Prudential-Audio Visual Communications Division. Used by permission.

It's likely you'll be more comfortable in one of those roles. But as with the "whole-brain" approach characterizing the writing process in general, success in this genre is achieved by striking a balance. First, we'll consider each role separately—then explore the tug-of-war which takes place between writer as dramatist and writer as trainer.

WEARING THE DRAMATIST'S HAT

Dramatization is the narrative technique of telling a story through characters. Sounds simple. But dramatic formats pose demanding problems for any writer:

1. You must create imaginary persons so credible they exist for the viewer as real within the context of the program.
2. You must put your characters in conflict.
3. Dialog, not prose or narration, is the chief means for advancing the story, revealing character and communicating content.

In a drama you tell your story through characters interacting. The tough part goes back to ancient Greek theater: your characters must be in *conflict*. Characters pursuing contradictory goals make the most interesting, viable dramatic situations. (When Cookie Monster tries to dupe an unsuspecting person into giving him a cookie, for example, the situation contains built-in conflict.) Characters sitting around chatting, with no undercurrent of tension or conflict, are undramatic. If Romeo and Juliet had both been Capulets, there would be no drama. They might still be lovers, but the *drama* results from them being *star-crossed* lovers.

Figure 10.8: Use of Dramatization with On-Camera Narration

VIDEO	AUDIO
CU on SHIRLEY COOPER on studio stage. The screen displays a FREEZE FRAME from LAURA'S DREAM. TRANSITION TO. . .	SHIRLEY COOPER/INSTRUCTOR: EACH JOB HUNTER'S WORK HISTORY CONTAINS CERTAIN "BLEMISHES." BUT THERE'S NO REASON THEY CAN'T *LEARN* HOW TO MINIMIZE WEAK POINTS AND ACCENTUATE THE POSITIVE. TAKE LAURA, FOR INSTANCE. . .
Location footage of LAURA during actual interview with RON.	ONCE SHE LEARNED WHAT TO EXPECT, HOW TO PREPARE, BEHAVE AND ANSWER SPECIFIC QUESTIONS— SHE FOUND INTERVIEWING MUCH EASIER THAN ANTICIPATED. . .
TWO SHOT on LAURA at her interview with RON in the restaurant.	LAURA: . . .SO WHEN I FINALLY REALIZED I COULD ACTUALLY TURN SOMETHING I LIKED AND WAS HALF-WAY DECENT AT INTO A CAREER, I MADE UP MY MIND TO GET SERIOUS. SO I SET OUT TO FIND WORK IN FOOD SERVICE. . .
MS on SHIRLEY COOPER with action of LAURA and RON in screen area.	SHIRLEY COOPER/INSTRUCTOR: THIS IS WHAT LAURA'S BEEN WORKING TOWARD—AN OPPORTUNITY TO TELL A PROSPECTIVE EMPLOYER SHE'S THE BEST CANDIDATE FOR THE JOB. . .
ACTION of LAURA and RON goes full frame again.	LAURA: . . .SO I'M WILLIN' TO START AT THE BOTTOM AND LEARN THE BUSINESS. I THINK MY WILLINGNESS TO WORK AND DESIRE TO SUCCEED ARE MY BIG STRENGTHS. . .
MS on SHIRLEY COOPER with action of LAURA and RON in screen area. . .	SHIRLEY COOPER/INSTRUCTOR: LAURA TELLS THE INTERVIEWER SHE'S THE BEST PERSON FOR THE JOB IN MANY WAYS. CERTAINLY *WHAT* SHE SAYS GREATLY INFLUENCES THE EMPLOYER'S

Figure 10.8: Use of Dramatization with On-Camera Narration (Cont.)

VIDEO	AUDIO
	DECISION. BUT OTHER THINGS ALSO SHOW SHE'S GENUINELY INTERESTED IN THE JOB.
FULL SCREEN shots showing LAURA getting dressed for interview. . .	HER NEAT DRESS AND APPEARANCE. . .
arriving at the restaurant. . .	HER EARLY ARRIVAL FOR THE INTERVIEW. . .
Her meeting with RON. . .	HER CONFIDENT ENTRANCE TO THE INTERVIEW. . .
answering a question with sincerity and animation. . .	HER ABILITY TO ANSWER THE EMPLOYER'S QUESTIONS WITH CONVICTION AND CREDIBILITY. . .

Source: From "The Choice is Yours,"[TM] written by William Van Nostran, directed by Walter Schoenknecht, created and produced by Karli & Associates and The Prudential-Audio Visual Communications Division. Used by permission.

This doesn't mean every "industrial soap" must be power-packed with the ravings of Oedipus or the intensity of *The Killing Fields*. Conflict is found in commonplace moments of everyday life. Read the excerpt in Figure 10.9 and follow the notations keyed to the dialog to see how many points of conflict result from the two character's changing motivations.

Generally, subject matter suggests a natural conflict. In developing a sales training program, the seeds of conflict lie in the age-old buyer-seller confrontation.

In a fanciful program in which a 20th century genie appears to introduce a new computer system to a secretary, the writer generated conflict in two ways. First there's a conflict because the genie can only grant job-related wishes. (Our young lady believes he's a fake when he can't produce a sports car.) As a result, she doubts he can even deliver the goods on the job-related wishes.

Seek out elements within your content that can lead to conflict. (It's another form of critical content focusing.) Usually, this involves characters with opposing motivations working at cross purposes (buyer/seller; job candidate/employment interviewer, etc.) or it may be an internal conflict within the character (how do

Figure 10.9: Use of Conflict

VIDEO	AUDIO
FREEZE FRAME of conference room as we find Paul, a middle-aged sales manager, concluding a sales meeting. As the action begins, Paul is gathering up overhead transparencies while the sales staff files out. **SUPER:** Case Study 2 Action begins. . .	VIGNETTE 2 **WALTER:** GOOD MEETING, PAUL. I LIKED THAT EXERCISE ON GETTING AT CUSTOMER NEEDS. I'LL MEET YOU OUT IN THE LOBBY. **RICH:** PAUL—YOU GOTTA MINUTE? **PAUL:** (Checking his watch.) WELL, I'VE GOTTA GO WITH WALTER TO VISIT A CUSTOMER OUT IN RIVER-VIEW. CAN YOU MAKE IT BRIEF? **RICH:** IT'LL JUST TAKE A SECOND. I'VE FINALLY GOTTEN A HANDLE ON HOW TO GET SOME BUSINESS AT THE FIBERMOLD ACCOUNT. . .**(1)** **PAUL:** YOU REALLY THINK IT'S WORTH A LOT MORE TIME TRYING TO SELL THEM? I MEAN, YOU JUST DID SOME VERY EXTENSIVE TRIALS THAT WERE QUITE SUCCESSFUL. IF THEY CAN'T SEE WE'VE GOT A SUPERIOR PRODUCT, I DON'T KNOW WHAT MORE YOU CAN DO AT THIS POINT. **(1)** **RICH:** I ADMIT, I WAS A LITTLE STYMIED. BUT NOW I'VE GOT INSIGHT INTO THE *REAL* REASON THEY'RE NOT BUYING FROM US.

Figure 10.9: Use of Conflict (Cont.)

VIDEO	AUDIO
	PAUL: O.K. SHOOT. **(2)**
	RICH: WELL, YOU EVER RUN ACROSS A HANK GRANT?
	PAUL: FROM MID-STATES CHEMICALS?
	RICH: THAT'S THE GUY. A REAL TALKER. I RAN INTO HIM IN THE PARKING LOT WHILE MAKING A CALL THE OTHER DAY.
	PAUL: ONE OF THOSE CALLS WHERE THE COMPETITOR'S COMING *OUT* JUST AS YOU'RE GOING *IN,* HUH?
	RICH: YOU GOT THE PICTURE. WELL, WE GET TO TALKING AND THE CONVERSATION TURNED TO FIBERMOLD. SEEMS GRANT'S NOT GETTIN' ANY BUSINESS FROM THEM EITHER.
	PAUL: RICH, YOU'RE NOT THE FIRST GUY THAT'S RUN INTO A BRICK WALL WITH THOSE FOLKS. THAT'S A TOUGH ACCOUNT TO CRACK. **(3)**
	RICH: MAY BE. BUT HANK GRANT WAS TELLING ME THAT THE COMPANY *GETTING* ALL THEIR BUSINESS IS REALLY LOW-BALLING. I MEAN THEY'RE SELLING AT A SUBSTANTIALLY LOWER PRICE THAN EITHER HE OR I CAN OFFER— EVEN WITH VOLUME DISCOUNTS.
	PAUL: WELL, YOU KNOW WHAT I KEEP PREACHING: YOU'VE ALWAYS GOTTA RELATE YOUR PRICE TO VALUE RECEIVED.

Figure 10.9: Use of Conflict (Cont.)

VIDEO	AUDIO
	RICH: THAT'S GOOD TEXT-BOOK SALES THEORY. BUT WHAT HANK AND I STARTED TALKING ABOUT WAS SEEING IF WE COULDN'T GET OUR MANAGEMENTS TO SHAVE A LITTLE EXTRA OFF OUR FIBER-MOLD QUOTES. THAT WAY WE STAND A CHANCE OF PICKING UP SOME OF THAT BUSINESS.
Paul stops his busy work, reacting to Rich's "solution."	**PAUL:** (Starting to register a bit of concern.) RICH, LET ME MAKE SURE I GET YOUR DRIFT. YOU HAD A DISCUSSION WITH A COMPETITIVE SALESMAN IN WHICH YOU *BOTH* AGREED TO LOWER YOUR PRICE WHEN BIDDING ON FIBERMOLD? **(3)**
	RICH: (Sensing Paul's displeasure.) I WOULDN'T SAY WE ACTUALLY CAME TO AN AGREEMENT. WE JUST DECIDED TO TALK TO OUR MANAGEMENT AND SEE IF AN EXCEPTION COULD BE MADE.
	PAUL: RICH—I CAN'T BELIEVE WHAT I'M HEARING. I MEAN, WHAT'S ONE OF THE TOPICS I BRIEF THE WHOLE SALES FORCE ON AT LEAST TWICE A YEAR?
	RICH: I'M NOT. . .FOLLOWING.
	PAUL: (Getting a bit hot under the collar.) FORGIVE MY BLUNTNESS— BUT DO THE WORDS "PRICE FIXING" RING A BELL FOR YOU? **(4)**
	RICH: (Flustered.) OH—NOW, C'MON, IT WASN'T *THAT* KIND OF DISCUSSION. I MEAN, WE WERE JUST TRYING TO FIND A WAY TO

Figure 10.9: Use of Conflict (Cont.)

VIDEO	AUDIO
	GET A FOOT IN THE DOOR AT FIBERMOLD.
	PAUL: MAY SEEM INNOCENT ENOUGH TO YOU—BUT IF CERTAIN EARS OVERHEARD THAT CONVERSATION, THEY COULD HAUL US ALL INTO COURT ON A PRICE-FIXING CHARGE.
	RICH: PAUL, BELIEVE ME—IT NEVER OCCURRED TO ME THAT. . .
Action FREEZES as Paul turns to camera for soliloquy. . .	**PAUL:** (Quite furious.) WELL, IT *SHOULD* HAVE OCCURRED TO YOU. . . (To camera.) DAYS LIKE THIS I WISH I'D NEVER BECOME A SALES *MANAGER.* LIFE WAS SO MUCH SIMPLER WHEN I WAS ON THE ROAD HANDLING MY OWN ACCOUNTS. WELL. . .I PROBABLY SHOULD TAKE A DEEP BREATH AND COOL DOWN. I'M SURE RICH DIDN'T *PURPOSELY* GET MIXED UP IN SOMETHING THAT SMACKS OF PRICE FIXING. AT LEAST BY TELLING ME THE WHOLE STORY WE KNOW WHAT WE'RE DEALING WITH. I NEED TO HANDLE THIS SO WE MINIMIZE POTENTIAL DAMAGE WITHOUT SQUELCHING THE GUY'S EGO. **(5)**
Action resumes.	(Back to Rich.) RICH, I'M GLAD YOU'VE TOLD ME ALL THE CIRCUMSTANCES. I DON'T MEAN TO ALARM YOU—BUT ON THE SURFACE IT'S A BIT INCRIMINATING. WHEN'D YOU SAY THIS CONVERSATION TOOK PLACE? **(6)**
	RICH: (Subdued.) COUPLE DAYS AGO.

Figure 10.9: Use of Conflict (Cont.)

VIDEO	AUDIO
	PAUL: AND TO THE BEST OF YOUR KNOWLEDGE, WERE THERE ANY WITNESSES? ANYONE WHO MIGHT HAVE HEARD YOUR CONVERSATION?
	RICH: NOT THAT I KNOW OF. WE WERE IN THE PARKING LOT BY OUR CARS. **(4)**
Walter sticks his head into the room.	**WALTER:** EXCUSE ME—BUT WE'RE SUPPOSSED TO BE OUT AT RIVER-VIEW IN HALF AN HOUR. . .
	PAUL: I'LL BE RIGHT WITH YOU, WALTER, NOW, RICH, WHEN I GET BACK THIS AFTERNOON MEET IN MY OFFICE. WHILE I'M GONE, MAKE NOTES ON EXACTLY WHAT WAS SAID BETWEEN YOU AND THIS GUY—HANK. . . **(8)**
	RICH: GRANT. **(9)**
	PAUL: RIGHT, THEN I'LL PUT A CALL THROUGH TO LEGAL—GET SOME PROFESSIONAL COUNSEL.
	RICH: LEGAL? PAUL, REALLY—WE DIDN'T COME TO ANY SPECIFIC AGREEMENT. . .**(10)**
	PAUL: RICH, DON'T GET BENT OUTTA SHAPE. PROBABLY NOTHING'S GOING TO COME OF THIS. BUT TO PROTECT EVERYONE INVOLVED, LET'S DOCUMENT WHAT HAPPENED AND TAKE STEPS TO HEAD OFF TROUBLE. OUR LAWYERS ARE ON *YOUR* SIDE. IF WE TAKE THEIR ADVICE, WE

Figure 10.9: Use of Conflict (Cont.)

VIDEO	AUDIO
	MINIMIZE THE CHANCES OF THIS GETTING BLOWN OUT OF PROPOR- TION. (Begin to pull audio under.) I SHOULD BE BACK AROUND TWO- THIRTY. CAN YOU MEET ME THEN?
DISSOLVE TO:	

Script Notations

(1) Initially, Rich tries convincing Paul to give him his attention. Paul, in a hurry to leave, is dubious over the value of Rich's concern over one, difficult account.

(2) Rich accomplishes his first objective. He gains Paul's attention.

(3) Paul continues to be dubious over Rich's interest in one account—a point of minor conflict.

(4) Paul reacts to Rich's story, begins losing his temper and responds out of anger.

(5) In a moment of internal conflict, punctuated by a SPECIAL EFFECT, Paul tries to regain composure through an internal monologue.

(6) Paul now seeks clarification. He quickly becomes the one leading the con- versation. His motivation is to determine if Rich's discussion could be con- sidered price fixing. Rich wants to downplay the entire incident.

(7) Rich is now trying to defuse the potential damage his conversation with a competing sales person might cause.

(8) Paul, the sales manager, is no longer concerned about leaving immediately. He's motivated by the desire to take appropriate action on Rich's information.

(9) Now, Rich is no longer the talkative one.

(10) Rich does not want Paul to involve the legal department. So as the scene closes, they're still at cross purposes from a dramatic point of view.

Source: Script excerpt from "DuPont Business Ethics," written by
William Van Nostran, Produced by Henry Nason Productions, Inc.,
directed by James G. Libby for the DuPont Co. Used by permission.

these new benefits affect me and my family?). The seeds of drama are sown in conflict. Find the conflict and you've got something to build on.

Character Development

Characterization is the creation of imaginary persons so credible they exist for the viewer as real, within the context of the program. That "within the context of the program" leaves generous room for interpretation. Stylistically, dramatizations range from presentational to realistic.

In a realistic dramatization, character, setting and action resemble a "slice of life." The writer mirrors life through realistic dialog, behavior, settings, situations and sound effects.

In a presentational dramatization, aspects of character, setting or situation are exaggerated to make a point. No attempt is made to create the magical illusion of reality. Characters exist as caricatures.

Both styles have a place in instructional drama. For realistic dramas, your main characters are likely to be fully developed portrayals revealing complex, sometimes contradictory human motivations. A fully developed character's reaction to a situation cannot be easily predicted. In writing seminars, I have participants analyze Miss Piggy. On the surface, one would think of Miss Piggy as a caricature. After analysis Miss Piggy turns out to be a well-drawn, complex, *fully developed* character. (See Figure 10.10.)

By contrast, a caricature focuses on one or two individual qualities of a person and exaggerates or distorts the dominant trait. (Cookie Monster is a one-dimensional caricature.)

What types of characters work best for instructional dramas? The more realistic your style, the more you must depict fully developed characters.

I once wrote a script for a company test marketing an interactive videotext system. To show prospective customers how this system could benefit their family, we dramatized a "day in the life" of a family using the videotext system for banking and shopping from a home terminal. I had to show various family members using the system, and I had to convey a "slice of life" reality. To create a credible family, you have to spend a lot of time developing each character's *subtext:* the information about family members and their relationships which may never appear in the program but gives a richness and fullness. (For more on creating full, rich characters, read Robert Newton Peck's *Fiction Is Folks.)*[1]

For a comedic drama in which a management consultant works with a pirate king and troupe of jugglers, however, broad, one-dimensional caricatures suited the instructional purpose ideally (Figure 10.11).

Scripting Dialog

Dialog is the chief mechanism for revealing character, developing conflict and propelling the story forward. In this respect, an instructional drama is no different from a screenplay. In addition, however, dialog is also the chief mechanism for communicating learning points.

Screenwriters are said to have an "ear for dialog." They've developed sensitivity to the conversational rhythms and speech styles of individual people. Different folks used different words to say the same thing. A character's background age, sex, education and emotional make-up accentuate such differences.

Figure 10.10: Character Analysis—Miss Piggy

Characterization has two components: internal traits and external manifestations of those traits. Internal traits are inherent characteristic qualities associated with an individual's personality. To put flesh and blood characters in motion through conflict, the dramatist must illustrate internal traits through the character's external words, actions and behavior. Notice how Miss Piggy's internal traits become externalized—often through quite visual external characteristics.

INTERNAL TRAITS	EXTERNAL CHARACTERISTICS
Vain	Dress Constant hair primping
Pretentious	"Mock French" Strong celebrity identification
Quick-tempered	Easily provoked to anger (especially over references to pigs and pork)
Violent	Beats up on Kermit Knows karate
Fickle	Quick to dump "Kermmy" when someone more glamorous comes along
Gluttonous	A pig-like corpulence
Flamboyant	High-fashion dress

Read the two scenes in Figures 10.12 and 10.13. Though similar in content and action (one involves an employment interview, the other an employee counseling session), the socio-economic backgrounds of the characters differ (white-collar in contrast to blue-collar). Notice how voice and idioms reflect the varying backgrounds and experiences of each character.

Although easily defined, dialog is not so easily mastered. Here's one definition:

> Dialog: The conversation of two or more people as reproduced in a script.

Figure 10.11: Use of Caricatures

In this farcical management fable the writer makes use of caricatures and types in a comedic vein.

Source: From "My Business Is Different," written by William Van Nostran, directed by James G. Libby for Van Nostran Associates, Inc. Used by permission.

Dialog performs several functions within a script, sometimes simultaneously:

1. Advances action.
2. Reveals character.
3. Gives the impression of naturalness without being a verbatim record (a semblance of reality, not reality itself).
4. Presents an interplay of ideas and personalities among those conversing.
5. Varies in voice, diction, rhythm, phrasing, sentence length, etc., according to character of speakers.

Media scriptwriters are urged to develop a "conversational' narrative voice. Dialog goes a step further. It is more than conversational—it *is* conversation between

Figure 10.12: Scripting White-Collar Dialog

WALTER: WELL, I THINK I'VE GOT A GOOD FEEL FOR WHAT YOU'VE DONE TO THIS POINT IN YOUR CAREER. YOU'VE OBVIOUSLY BEEN A BUSY PERSON.

JACK: I DO GET A LOT OUT OF MY WORK. I DON'T THINK I'D BE HAPPY IN AN ENVIRONMENT WHERE I WASN'T CHALLENGED: UNDER THE GUN.

WALTER: WE'VE GOT PLENTY OF CHALLENGES HERE, I CAN ASSURE YOU. I'D LIKE TO EXPLORE THIS THEME OF JOB SATISFACTION IN A LITTLE MORE DEPTH. A FEW MOMENTS AGO YOU STATED THAT, IN UNDERWRITING SYSTEMS, YOU MUST KNOW AS MUCH OR MORE THAN THE UNDERWRITER HIMSELF. WHAT DID YOU MEAN BY THAT?

JACK: (Very self-assured.) I THOUGHT I DETECTED A RAISED EYEBROW ON THAT COMMENT. LET ME PUT IT THIS WAY. I HAVE TO BE MORE EXACTING THAN AN UNDERWRITER IF AN UNDERWRITER MAKES A MISTAKE. IT AFFECTS ONLY THAT SINGLE RISK. IF I SCREW UP—EVERYTHING THAT'S IN THE COMPUTER SYSTEM IS WRONG. AND THAT MAKES EVERY POLICY IN THE SYSTEM WRONG. THE MAGNITUDE OF THE ERROR IS GREATER—SO THAT'S A NEED TO BE MORE PRECISE.

WALTER: WHAT GIVES YOU SUCH CONFIDENCE ABOUT YOUR ABILITY IN THE AREA OF UNDERWRITING?

JACK: I KNOW INSURANCE—PLAIN AND SIMPLE. WHEN I STARTED IN PERSONAL LINES UNDERWRITING WITH THE NATIONAL INDEMNITY. I SEEMED TO CATCH ON TO BASIC PRINCIPLES QUICKLY.

WALTER: WHAT SORT OF TRAINING DID YOU RECEIVE THERE?

JACK: INITIALLY, I WENT THROUGH SEVERAL SELF-STUDY COURSES IN SHORT ORDER. I FOUND I HAD AN APTITUDE FOR IT—SO THE NEXT STEP WAS CPCU COURSES. I'M STILL INTO THAT. IT TAKES AWHILE. . .

WALTER: DON'T I KNOW IT. . .

JACK: BUT I SHOULD BE ABLE TO COMPLETE THE PROGRAM IN ANOTHER YEAR.

WALTER: OK. THAT ACCOUNTS FOR YOUR GROUNDING IN UNDERWRITING? WHAT ABOUT THE SYSTEMS KNOWLEDGE?

JACK: WELL, WITH MY COLLEGE WORK IN COMPUTER SCIENCE AND MATH—IT ALL WORKS TOGETHER IN DEVELOPING AN AUTOMATED

Figure 10.12: Scripting White-Collar Dialog (Cont.)

COMPUTER SYSTEM FOR A LINE OF BUSINESS. I FEEL AN INTERDIS-CIPLINARY BACKGROUND IS PERHAPS MY GREATEST STRENGTH IN THIS TYPE WORK.

Source: From "Employment Interviewing," written by William Van Nostran and Beverly Beach, directed by James G. Libby. Copyright Crum & Forster Corp., 1982. Used by permission.

two or more characters. In life, people rarely speak in lengthy paragraphs. There's a natural back-and-forth flow (similar in tempo to a long volley in tennis). As William Noble describes it: "In some respects, good dialog writing is a mirage. It *seems* to be realistic, it seems to portray actual people doing actual things. But it doesn't. Not really."[2]

As you read the script excerpts in this chapter, notice how this give-and-take rhythm makes the dialog appear to develop spontaneously, as each line prompts a reaction and, therefore, a related line from the other character. Notice too, that dialog is not necessarily a very *quick* way to convey information, but the forcefulness with which drama makes its points more than compensates.

There's no secret to writing believable dialog. A pro can learn to do it. How? First, get to know your characters. Know them as you know friends and relatives. Develop biographical sketches of principal characters, like the one shown in Figure 10.14.

You may use little of such information specifically in your script (though you'd be surprised how much can surface) but it gives you a subtext for scripting dialog. If you're a novice at dramatic writing, you may want to use the Character Chart (Figure 10.15) as a tool for defining key aspects of your characters and indicating relationships.

Next, work at developing your "ear" and voice. Become conscious of the idioms and accents of people you know. Pattern a dramatic character on someone you know so well your word choice is automatically "flavored" and colored with that person's language. Keep sentences short. Use simple words. (Notice how many one-syllable words Shakespeare uses.) Contractions, slang and regionalisms carry the spice of informal, spontaneous daily conversation. Read plays and screenplays and focus on the dialog. Acting in plays is a great way to develop your ear and voice.

The cardinal rule, however, is you must *always* read your dialog aloud. That simple practice will help you better than anything to spot the false notes and tongue-twisters. Trust your own ear and voice.

Figure 10.13: Scripting Blue-Collar Dialog

BRAD ANDERSON: (Avoiding eye contact; not really relishing the situation he finds himself in.) SO TELL ME, JIM—AND I WANT YOU TO BE HONEST WITH US HERE— HOW D'YOU FEEL YOU'RE DOING RIGHT NOW? AS FAR AS THE JOB'S CONCERNED?

BRAD: WELL, LOOK—I'M NOT OUT TO NAIL A PERSON BECAUSE OF A SINGLE FOUL-UP. . .

BRAD: YEAH, I KNOW, I KNOW, AND IF IT WERE JUST THAT ONE ISOLATED INCIDENT. THERE'D BE NO PROBLEM.

BRAD: JIM—NOW LOOK. I KNOW YOU'RE STILL RELATIVELY NEW WITH THE COMPANY. AND I KNOW THAT WHEN YOU TRANSFERRED INTO OUR SHIFT FROM THE AFTERNOON SHIFT—WELL THAT MADE YOU THE FIRST BLACK GUY ON THE SHIFT. SO I DIDN'T WANNA JUST JUMP ALL OVER YOU. I'VE BEEN TRYING TO GIVE YOU SOME BREATHING ROOM TO GET INTO THE SWING OF THINGS.

BRAD: JIM, LOOK, I APPRECIATED THE FACT YOU'RE TRYING TO DO JOBS QUICKLY. BUT IT'S EQUALLY IMPORTANT— MAYBE EVEN *MORE* IMPORTANT— TO DO THE JOB CORRECTLY.

JIM RIVERS: WELL—BETTER, MUCH BETTER. I MEAN, I KNOW I MESSED UP THAT ONE ASSIGNMENT REAL BAD. BUT THAT WAS JUST NERVOUSNESS—FROM BEING NEW, YOU KNOW? I REALLY THINK I'M GETTING INTO THE GROOVE NOW. . .

JIM: I KNOW THAT, AND, WELL, I REALLY APPRECIATE YOUR SUPPORT. I MEAN, A LOTTA GUYS WOULD'VE HIT THE CEILING WHEN THOSE PULLEYS WENT. I KNOW IT WAS A DUMB MISTAKE. BUT SOME- TIMES THE HARDER YOU TRY, WELL, YOU JUST WIND UP MAKING MORE ERRORS, SORT OF LIKE A BALL CLUB, YOU KNOW?

JIM: WHAT D'YOU MEAN? THAT'S THE ONLY TIME I CAN REMEMBER YOU EVER REALLY HAD A PROBLEM WITH MY WORK.

JIM: HEY, MAN—I KNOW THAT. AND I APPRECIATE IT. WHY DO YOU THINK I GO AROUND ASKING FOR NEW JOBS ALL THE TIME? . . .I'VE BEEN BUSTIN' MY BUTT OUT THERE FOR YOU. I THOUGHT YOU APPRECIATED THAT.

Source: From "Equal Employment Opportunity Case Studies," written by William Van Nostran, directed by Daniel Klugherz, produced by Kenneth B. Wollny. ©1978 Mobil Oil Corporation. Reprinted by permission of Mobil Oil Corporation.

Figure 10.14: Character Sketch

The following description was written to define one of the key characters in a job search training program targeted to people on welfare or other disadvantaged workers. Notice that the style is telegraphic and informal, since this is primarily a writer's tool and not a finished product.

LAURA JOHNSON

Age: 20-22

Ethnic Type: White Female

Character Profile:

Dropped out of high school in the 11th grade because of teenage pregnancy.

Mother of one.

No work experience. Has been a homemaker since dropping out of high school.

Extremely sheltered in terms of life experiences. She is also functionally illiterate. Sub-text implies she could have been wife-beating victim. Initially has a submissive personality—later grows in confidence.

Does not want to be going through Job Search program. Unwilling and non-participative. At first she's seeking a way out of the program.

Career Goal:

Coming into the Job Search class, Laura has no self-confidence, low self-esteem and does not think she is capable of getting work. Eventually decides on restaurant or catering work. Begins to see this kind of work as the start of an actual career. Once she locks into a career goal, she begins to overcome her low self-esteem.

Casting Criteria:

On the plump side. Not very verbal. Seems more disinterested than she really is—probably a lifelong defense mechanism.

Source: From "The Choice Is Yours,"™ written by William Van Nostran, directed by Walter Schoenknecht, created and produced by Karli & Associates and The Prudential Audio Visual Communications Division. Used by permission.

Figure 10.15: Character Chart

One easy way to begin getting acquainted wih your characters (particularly when you must draw fully developed, realistic portrayals) is by filling out a character chart. You can take this basic form, then expand on it to meet your own needs.

	Character	Character	Character
Age			
Appearance			
Personality			
Heritage			
Occupation			
Relationships			
Hobbies			
Health			
Other			

WEARING THE TRAINER'S HAT

Trainers are not interested in Aristotle's *Poetics*. In their world, success or failure depends on what students learn. In a business context, learning is measured by the application of skills, not in the classroom, but back on the job.

The classic tools for evaluating training effectiveness are "pre" and "post" testing. Testing the learner before training establishes each individual's starting point. Retesting after training demonstrates whether change has occurred in the learner's application of knowledge or mastery of job-related skills. *Change* is the key word. Trainers are in business to improve job performance by changing behavior.

Behavioral Objectives

In his classic series of books, Robert Mager outlined steps for developing training to improve job performance. Mager points out the only valid measurement of training is to observe behavior. Does the airline pilot follow procedures for getting clearance for take-off? Does the salesperson analyze and clarify the objection before giving an answer? Does the gas compressor operator perform the proper start-up sequence to avoid damage to parts?

In this context, your dramatic action must be structured to communicate learning points relevant to the specific instructional objectives of the training program. Unlike writers of screenplays, sitcoms and soaps, entertainment is not the only criterion for success. Writers of dramas that teach must focus on effective communication of content and teaching points.

So—before donning your dramatist's hat, be sure you've worn the trainer's hat long enough to grasp the purpose of the content in relation to instructional objectives. Ask yourself these questions. . .

Do I Understand the Role of Video within the Training Environment?

Few instructional video/film presentations are "stand alone" communications. Video is generally one component in a mix of instructional techniques which can include any of the following:

- Lecture/discussion
- Buzz group activities
- Role-playing
- Written exercises
- Audiocassette segments
- Computer learning interactions
- Simulations and case studies

You must know the overall context in which your dramas will be shown. This will help determine the length of vignettes and types of interactions which will take place between video segments.

Do I Know the Instructional Objective of the Video or Film Module?

The videotape to communicate a flexible benefits program, for instance, was strictly motivational. By providing role models of the decision-making process, the program motivated employees to analyze their own family and financial needs with equal thoroughness. The "welfare drama," by contrast, included several specific role models showing how to behave on interviews, use the telephone to track down job leads, etc. Spend time wearing the trainer's hat early in the process so that you know precisely what objectives your client expects you to accomplish.

Do I Know the Key Learning Points?

This goes back to the "critical content focusing" in Chapter 4. Again, identify those key content points which are absolutely crucial to the specific communication. In Goldman's terms, know the "spine of the story you are trying to tell."

Before writing a dramatic scene, identify learning points the scene will convey. If you find a scene functions solely to develop character or establish conflict without conveying "critical content," it may be a "red flag" that the dramatist is indulging at the trainer's expense.

Once you've answered these questions, you'll be in a position to develop dramatic vignettes that teach or fulfill specific communication objectives.

UNDER THE TWO HATS

Who controls the tug-of-war between dramatist and trainer when actually writing? If the dramatist dominates, precious screen time is squandered on clever dialog. Learning points become obscured by the drama. Viewers keen on learning will wonder why they're being forced to watch.

As producer Whit Rummel cautions, ". . .tempering a program to make it entertaining can be dangerous. You can get in so deep that you lose sight of the purpose of the program. . . .We once worked with a client from a big utilities company who was determined to make the sales training program funny. But the material was so intricate and complicated, we soon argued against too much humor because we felt it would prevent, not help, the salespeople from absorbing information."[3] The resulting program used humor to introduce each subject. The core of the program was delivered in straightforward narrative style.

On the other hand, if the trainer takes command, every line of clinking dialog can sound like a barely disguised teaching point. Human interest is wrung dry. The script becomes pedantic, clinical.

Ideally, dramatist and trainer will find "common ground." It's whole-brain writing epitomized—the classic tension between creativity and critical judgment in any creative endeavor.

Develop Dual Talents

The best instructional dramas achieve the balance of a tightrope walker who skillfully but effortlessly performs high above the ground. The resulting script displays the craft of a writer so adept at wearing two hats, you never quite know which he or she has on at any given moment.

For one example, read through Kevin Cole's script in Figure 10.16. It brings the abstract concept of multi-tasking computer software vividly to life through an

Figure 10.16: Bringing an Abstract Concept to Life

FADE UP: H-P LOGO

FADE TO BLACK AND THEN FADE UP TITLE: "The Inside Story. . ."

FADE TO BLACK THEN FADE UP ON:

1.0   OFFICE. We see a MAN sitting at a DESK working on PC.

a)   SLOWLY DOLLY IN over his shoulder and toward the multi-windowed computer screen.

NARRATOR:
(Voice Over throughout program)

"WE TAKE YOU NOW TO THE NEW HEWLETT-PACKARD 'INTEGRAL' PERSONAL COMPUTER. . ."

b)   We begin to hear faint sounds—VOICES and MUSIC—as if coming from inside the computer.

". . .WHERE WE FIND THERE'S MORE GOING ON THAN MEETS THE EYE."

c)   Continue to DOLLY FORWARD as MATTING VISUAL EFFECT takes us "inside" the PC monitor.

FLOATING CRANE-IN SHOT OF:

2.0   "INSIDE" OF COMPUTER, a wide overview. This is an ethereal, orangish place, slightly opaque in appearance (bee smoke) and warm in feel.

FADE UP MUSIC
(It lends an air of happy activity)

a)   As our CRANE SHOT takes us in to and slightly above the scene we see. . .ACTIVITY!! We see a dozen or so 'CARICATURES' working busily at various tasks using ODD MACHINES AND DEVICES (to be explained).

The "PC interior" is bathed in multi-colored SPOTLIGHTS, creating a dazzling array of patterns. In the center on a raised platform is a tall director's chair, where a CURIOUS FIGURE with a MEGAPHONE is shouting directions. This is "UNIX."

Figure 10.16: Bringing an Abstract Concept to Life (Cont.)

UNIX:
(Like a Hollywood director)

"OK NOW, CALCULATOR, CRUNCH THOSE NUMBERS.
GRAPHICS, LET'S MAKE THAT PICTURE BIGGER!
PRINTER, GIVE US A COPY OF OUR LATEST
REPORT. . ." (fade under narrator.)

In the time it takes to hear these lines, we see:

b) CALCULATOR, an old Einstein look-alike in white smock. He's writing
the answer to a vast equation on a huge blackboard.
c) GRAPHICS, an arty type dressed in bohemian beret with brush and
palette. She's painting a beautiful SPACE SHUTTLE, and squints
behind an outstretched thumb.
d) PRINTER, wearing an eyeshade, rolled up shirtsleeves and a great big
leather apron. He's running pages through an old mechanical printer.
e) Also in the vicinity are: SPREADSHEET, a woman with large display
board filled with 3 x 5 cards; DATA BASE MANAGER, a Bob Cratchit-
type accountant sorting 3 x 5 cards; INSTRUMENT CONTROLLER, a
mad-scientist type playing with joystick in front of video monitors;
MEMOMAKER, a prim secretary typing on old-fashioned Underwood.
All characters are symbolic and exaggerated in dress and manner.

NARR:
(No time lapse between Unix's line and his)

"IF YOU COULD PEEK, *INSIDE* H-P'S NEW 'INTEGRAL
PERSONAL COMPUTER,' WHAT YOU'D SEE IS A
DRAMATIC PERFORMANCE—ALL KINDS OF
PROGRAMS ALL RUNNING AT ONCE. . . ."

CRANE-IN stops above UNIX. We see he's a young, hip Hollywood director. He's
perched a chair above and between PAM, a cool-looking assistant director talking
on several phones at once; and WINDOW MANAGER, a rugged back-stage type
operating a big lighting console.

NARR:
(No time lapse between previous line)

"HERE ALSO YOU'D FIND THE MOST ADVANCED
OPERATING SYSTEM ON ANY PC—BELL LAB'S
'UNIX' OPERATING SYSTEM."

Figure 10.16: Bringing an Abstract Concept to Life (Cont.)

CUT TO:

3.0   UNIX CLOSE UP in director's chair.

    a)   He turns to camera, and we see the word "HP-UX" on his megaphone.

UNIX:
(Directly to camera)

"ACTUALLY, I'M HEWLETT-PACKARD'S *ENHANCED*
VERSION OF THE UNIX OPERATING SYSTEM—'HP-UX.'
I DIRECT SOFTWARE LIKE A BYTE-SIZE STEVEN
SPIELBERG."

    b)   He turns back to action and shouts into megaphone:

"SPREADSHEET, HERE COMES YOUR CUE!"

NARR:

THOUGH HP-UX IS A POWERFUL SYSTEMS DIRECTOR
FEW PC'S USE HIM. HE'S KNOW TO BE HARD TO
MANAGE."

    c)   UNIX looks back to camera and waves the idea off.

UNIX:
(Laughs)

"OH, BUT THAT'S HISTORY. THANKS TO HEWLETT-
PACKARD, I'M THE EASIEST-TO-USE UNIX
OPERATING SYSTEM EVER. BUT WAIT— —"

    d)   He gets down off of chair, eager to show us more.

"—AS LONG AS YOU'RE ON THE SET, LET ME GIVE
YOU A PREVIEW OF MY 'FEATURE ATTRACTIONS'."

CRANE Up again gradually to overview as. . .

    e)   UNIX stands and steps off of platform to STAGE CENTER.

MUSIC SEGUE
(To classical "Hallmark Hall of Fame" theme.)

Figure 10.16: Bringing an Abstract Concept to Life (Cont.)

UNIX:

"ANALOGY: WHEN YOU USE ANY COMPUTER, IT'S KIND
OF LIKE MAKING A MOVIE. YOU HAVE YOUR SCRIPT—"

f)   He gestures to PAM who's talking on phone and writing in large ledger.

"—A TASK, ACTUALLY.
YOU HAVE YOUR PERFORMERS — —"

g)   He gestures to players.

"—THE PROGRAMS THAT PERFORM THE ACTION.
AND YOU HAVE YOUR DIRECTOR— —"

h)   He bows.

"—THE OPERATING SYSTEM. NOW, WHERE PLAIN OLD
CPM OR MS-DOS SYSTEMS ALLOW JUST ONE PROGRAM
TO ACT AT A TIME, UNIX-BASED SYSTEMS CAN PUT A
HUGE CAST INTO PRODUCTION— —"

i)   He gestures broadly around.

"—ALL PERFORMING SIMULTANEOUSLY. WE CALL
THIS "MULTI-TASKING'."

CUT TO:

4.0   DATA SORTING STATION. DATA BASE MANAGER is busy filing 3x5
cards in mail-sorting slots.

NARR:

"ARE YOU SAYING THAT WITH HP-UX DIRECTING, THE
INTEGRAL PC CAN SORT DATA EVEN WHILE IT'S
PRINTING A MEMO?"

CUT TO:

5.0   PRINTER. He's still running pages through the old printer.

UNIX:
(Voice Over)

"EXACTLY! AND AS IT'S SORTING AND PRINTING—

Figure 10.16: Bringing an Abstract Concept to Life (Cont.)

CUT TO:

6.0   GRAPHICS, painting on her easel. Crossing behind her is SPREADSHEET
        pushing a giant spreadsheet. This could be a big grid with data cards mounted
        on a mobile office divider.

              "—IT CAN ALSO CREATE GRAPHICS.
              OR MAKE A SPREADSHEET—"

CUT TO:

7.0   INSTRUMENT CONTROLLER. This be-smocked eccentric is working a
        whimsical joystick, with a bank of monitors and instruments showing strange
        video shapes in motion behind him.

              "—OR EVEN ACT AS AN INSTRUMENT CONTROLLER."

CRANE UP and RIDE DOLLY BACK TO:

8.0   REVEAL OVERVIEW, all action going at once.

              "IT MEANS THAT ONCE YOU'VE SET ONE PROGRAM INTO
              ACTION YOU CAN GET A SECOND, AND A THIRD, AND A
              FOURTH TO PERFORM. . .ALL AT THE SAME TIME."

    a)   REVEAL UNIX, stage center.

                     UNIX:
                     (Live)

              "OF COURSE WHAT'S IMPORTANT TO THE AUDIENCE—
              ER, THE USER—IS HOW EASY HEWLETT-PACKARD HAS
              MADE MULTI-TASKING."

    b)   REVEAL PAM and WINDOW MANAGER on either side of him. He
           gestures to them.

              "AND ALL THANKS TO MY TWO TERRIFIC ASSISTANTS."

CUT TO:

9.0   PAM CLOSE-UP at her desk, she's busy answering phones, leafing through
        script and making changes with a pencil.

Figure 10.16: Bringing an Abstract Concept to Life (Cont.)

UNIX:
(Voice Over)

"TO INTERACT WITH THE PROGRAMS, THE USER TALKS
TO PAM OUR 'PERSONAL APPLICATIONS MANAGER.'
PAM TRANSLATES USER REQUESTS INTO HP-UX
TERMINOLOGY."

CUT TO:

10.0 COMPUTER SCREEN, EXTREME CLOSE-UP. We see CURSOR ARROW
traveling along MENU and choosing a PRINT command.

"THAT WAY WE CAN ALL UNDERSTAND EACH OTHER
AND GET THE PRODUCTION DONE—"

CUT TO:

11.0 COMPUTER PRINTER, EXTREME CLOSE-UP.

a)   Boy, is this sucker printing fast! We see a MEMO being printed out, but
at this point we don't yet see that the printer is built-in.

"—ON TIME AND UNDER BUDGET."

Source: From "The Inside Story," written by Kevin Cole, produced
by Robin Garthwait, directed by Ron Rinella for Hewlett-Packard
Inc. Used by permission.

analogy to a director on a movie set. This creative concept provides a springboard
for creating human interest while communicating key points with impact.

And in Figure 10.17, discover how another writer, Nathan J. Sambul, uses drama
to surprise and hook the audience for the script introducing a new telephone system.

Figure 10.17: Surprising the Audience

FADE UP ON FIRST SCENE. IT IS A CAVEMAN SETTING.
SUPER TITLE:

THE DAWN OF TELECOMMUNICATIONS
10,857 B.C.
WEDNESDAY

A GROUP OF CAVEPEOPLE ARE STANDING IN LINE. AT THE HEAD OF
THE LINE IS A CAVEMAN SENDING A MESSAGE BY BEATING A TREE
TRUNK. TWO CAVEMEN ON LINE TALK. THEY TALK IN "CAVEMAN
TALK," AND ON THE SCREEN ARE SUBTITLES.

CAVEMAN #1: [POINTING AT THE CAVEMAN BEATING
THE TREE TRUNK].
How long has he been on?

CAVEMAN #2: [LOOKS AT SUNDIAL ON HIS WRIST].
About 20 minutes.

CAVEMAN #1:
This is ridiculous. I have an important call to make and we have only
one trunk line. We need a whole new communications system.

CAVEMAN #2:
What do you expect. It's only 10,857 B.C.

CAVEMAN #1:
That's the problem with you, Org. You're not a forward thinker.

WE HEAR AN ELEPHANT APPROACHING. IN A PANIC, ALL THE CAVE
PEOPLE RUN OFF. THE CAVEMAN WHO HAS BEEN BEATING THE TRUNK
THROWS HIS BONE INTO THE AIR. THE CAMERA FOLLOWS IT (POSSIBLY
SLOW-MO). FADE UP MUSIC SIMILAR TO *2001, A SPACE ODYSSEY*: "ALSO
SPRACH ZARATHUSTRA". DISSOLVE INTO NIGHT SKY. ZOOM OUT TO
REVEAL CARL SAGAN LOOK-ALIKE IN THE FOREGROUND. CHROMA-KEY
NIGHT SKY BEHIND HIM.

SAGAN:

The universe. Ever expanding. Ever dynamic. With billions upon
billions of galaxies. There, in the backwaters of the western spiral of
the Milky Way, lies a small insignificant yellow sun.

Orbiting it at a distance of approximately 93 million miles is a little
blue-green planet. The life forms there are so amazingly primitive
that they still think CD players are a neat idea.

Figure 10.17: Surprising the Audience (Cont.)

There, long ago and far away, the telephone was invented. The question of the universe, more perplexing than the Big Bang theory, is "Why do people always hang up the phone as soon as you race out of the shower to answer it?"

CUT TO SHOT OF PHONE SLAMMING DOWN ON CRADLE. AS THE CAMERA ZOOMS OUT, WE SEE A GUY IN ANCIENT WARRIOR CLOTHING WITH A SIGN IN THE BACKGROUND THAT SAYS "HANNIBAL INC." SECOND WARRIOR WALKS IN.

WARRIOR #2:
What's wrong?

WARRIOR #1:
What's wrong? I can't get through to the boss. And he said that if I don't get my plans to him by this afternoon, I'm going to spend the rest of my life on the Sahara front sucking sand.

WARRIOR #2:
Plans for what?

WARRIOR #1: (LOWERS VOICE)
You know, WW 0. . .the big one. . .the Roman Conquest. Hannibal is expecting me to come up with how we're going to transport our troops—and I don't have a clue.

WARRIOR #2:
So what seems to be the problem?

WARRIOR #1:
You know our motto here. [HE POINTS TO THE WALL ON WHICH THERE IS A PLAQUE THAT READS: "NON SURPRISUM."] I can't get through to plead my case. (ASIDE) I hate sand and sun. All the trunk lines are busy. We need a new phone system. (PAUSE—TIGHT CLOSE UP) Trunk lines. I think I smell something here.

WARRIOR #2:
Not me, I took my bath this month.

WARRIOR #1 GLOWERS

WARRIOR #2:
Besides, a phone system is a phone system is a phone system.

Figure 10.17: Surprising the Audience (Cont.)

WARRIOR #1:
Husadrar, will you wake up and die right. This is 216 B.C. Get with it.
All the advanced nations are using modern phone systems. It's the
only way to reach customers, vendors, associates. A new system will
give us the tools we need to stay competitive. We need voice mail,
message waiting, multi-party conference calling, tie-line trunks. . .
there's something here.

WARRIOR #2:
I don't know. . .the old system is fine. And where I come from we say,
if it ain't broke, don't fix it.

WARRIOR #1: [A BIT INCREDULOUS]
Husadrar, where do you come from?

CUT TO ANCIENT MAP. DISTINGUISHED VOICE OVER.

NARRATOR:
Husadrar was born in the mountains of Lubbock, a small community
just northeast of Carthage. From an early age, he was taught to speak
in bromides, such as "Have a nice day," "It's not the heat, it's the
humidity," and "If it ain't broke, don't fix it."

CUT TO CU OF OLD 6-BUTTON TELEPHONE SET. SUPER WORDS OVER PIC.
"IF IT AIN'T BROKE, DON'T FIX IT."

CAMERA ZOOMS OUT AND WE SEE BRIAN IN A COWBOY OUTFIT HOLDING
A SIX-SHOOTER. HE AIMS IT AT THE PHONE AND PULLS THE TRIGGER.
IT EXPLODES AND SHATTERS.

BRIAN:
Oh, Mister Fixit Man. Mister Fixit Man.

ON TO THE SET COMES VIVIAN, DRESSED AS REPAIR PERSON.

BRIAN:
You're not a man, ma'am.

VIVIAN [SHE LOOKS AT HERSELF] :
You're very perceptive. Is everyone as sharp as you are in this
company?

BRIAN:
Can you fix this?

Figure 10.17: Surprising the Audience (Cont.)

> **VIVIAN:**
> I can do one better.
>
> CUT TO SPECIAL EFFECT. PHONE REASSEMBLES TO A MODERN NEW PHONE.
>
> **BRIAN:**
> Gee.
>
> **VIVIAN:**
> No, GTE.
>
> SCREEN GETS PUSHED OFF BY DOUG. BOB WALKS BEHIND HIM.
>
> **DOUG:**
> What's going on here?! Is this a commercial?
>
> **BOB:**
> No. It's just that the company and GTE are installing a brand new phone system here, and we'd like everyone to know about it.
>
> **DOUG:**
> I thought GTE was. . .[SHAKES HIS HANDS].
>
> **BOB:**
> No, they're really straight-shooters. And they are a top-notch phone company. . .with lots of experience. They are also very big on service. And they deliver great quality. They're certainly capable of installing a first-rate phone system.
>
> **DOUG:**
> What's wrong with the old system?
>
> **BOB:**
> What's right with the old system?
>
> CUT TO SERIES OF VIGNETTES.
>
> VIGNETTE #1. BOSS TALKING INTO PHONE.
>
> I'm not exactly sure I can transfer. If I lose you, just call back on **2741**, and if that line's busy, try **3936**, and ask for Viola. . . .

Source: From "Titan—Part I," written by Nathan J. Sambul,
produced by NJ Sambul & Company Inc., directed by Jessie Walker
for Texas Instruments. Used by permission.

Figure 10.18: Another Word on Comedy

No matter how broad, humor often has a serious side. Throughout history, writers have used comedy to get audiences to see subjects in a new light. Comedy, however, makes extra demands on scriptwriters, directors, actors—the entire production team. Before using comedy, make certain you have the resources to carry it off. Audiences have little patience with poorly executed comedy.

Source: The Video Marketing Group, Inc. Used by permission.

FOOTNOTES

1. Robert Newton Peck, *Fiction Is Folks* (Cincinnati, OH: Writer's Digest Books, 1983).
2. William Noble, *"Shut Up!" He Explained!* (Middlebury, VT: Paul S. Eriksson, Publisher, 1987), p. 5.
3. "Training as Drama Event—Realistic Goals for Witcom," *Backstage,* 13 January 1989, p. 42.

11 Writing Unscripted Formats

For most clients, there is safety in a fully scripted program. There are no surprises. Every word is down on paper, meticulously approved prior to shooting. Visuals can be checked, revised, perfected. The fully scripted program is also easier on the director and the production team. The director knows precisely how many locations, scenes, set-ups and shots are required. With thorough pre-production planning, shooting and editing can go literally by the numbers. For cut-and-dried factual content, a fully scripted format is probably the most economical.

Such rigidly scripted and produced formats, however, are not always the best way to achieve objectives. For many subjects, the story is best told not by a writer but by "real people," appearing on camera as themselves. Properly executed, the resulting program exudes a reality and credibility unattainable with fully scripted formats. This sincerity is particularly appropriate for issue-oriented programming when the subject involves controversy, when there are shades of grey and room for honest differences of opinion.

THE UNSCRIPTED FORMAT

Perhaps the most common unscripted program is the traditional interview. For example, the chairman of the board's response to questions about the rationale for a new acquisition may be the ideal way to provide information to all employees and clear the air of rumors.

Such interviews can take many forms. The most straightforward approach is a one-on-one interview with someone posing a series of questions to the subject. In the Barbara Walters style of interview, the interviewer has the responsibility of both asking the right questions and ensuring the interview has direction, focus and clarity. Although generally condensed through editing, this type of unscripted programming has an inherent continuity—a definite beginning, middle and end.

In planning the interview format certain fundamental issues need to be addressed. First, who will conduct the interview? Outside professional talent may be ideal in terms of asking prepared questions, but, unless the content is general, the outsider will not have the insight needed for follow-up questioning. If a group of employees can be gathered as a studio audience, questions could come directly from the floor. Instead of a single interview subject, several executives or experts might answer as a panel or executive forum. If representative employees are chosen to ask the questions, however, they may be intimidated and fail to pose hard questions of people in authority.

Slide Shows from Interviews

Generally, unscripted programs are most effective produced on film or video-tape. It is possible, however, to integrate interview "sound bites" into the audio track of slide presentations. To visualize interview content, plan for photography that illustrates key points, shows the speaker engaged in activities relating to the subject or reveals character. (You might also consider the use of art or graphics to illustrate content.)

When integrating interview material into a still-image presentation, make sound bites short so pacing does not suffer. In one sense, not having lip-synched motion footage of the interview subject can have a liberating effect. Created by college students as an orientation to their campus, one of the most intelligently produced two-projector slide shows I've seen used a variety of interview "sound bites."

Finally, interview material is obviously well suited to presentation in the audio-cassette medium and can bring refreshing spontaneity to such programs.

The Documentary-Style Program

Analogous to the classic documentary is a more involved unscripted format for which the writer provides overall structure, narrative and editorial direction. Since most media programs are produced to meet the communication needs of an organization, the objective reporting and editorial aloofness of the pure documentary are usually inappropriate. Also, the strong presence of an on-camera reporter found in commercial documentaries tends to be too obtrusive for the corporate/organizational style. Therefore, this chapter concentrates on an unscripted, documentary-style format that makes use of off-camera narration. While interviews remain the vehicle for telling the story, the focus is always on the *interviewee*—not the interviewer and not the narrator.

For this documentary-style program, diverse viewpoints from a variety of sources are used to tell the story. Questions are phrased so the subject's responses can be selectively edited and combined with the remarks of others on the same topic. Camera angles focus solely on the subject. The interviewer's questions wind up on the cutting room floor. Thirty seconds may be all that's selected from a 20-minute interview. Or a number of short responses from a long interview may be interspersed with other comments or narrative links as appropriate. Continuity derives not from any one interview, but from the selective use of varied interview footage combined with narrative and cutaway footage to illuminate a specific point of view.

The unscripted format analyzed in this chapter, then, has the following characteristics:

- It often uses off-camera narration to establish major themes and provide transitional bridges between subjects.
- The bulk of the content is communicated through interview footage.
- Off-camera interviewer's questions are edited out, permitting random use of interview footage.
- Comments from various individuals are edited together in patchwork fashion.

The Writer's Role

The writer's role in such projects, particularly in the area of pre-production planning, can often prove as intense and demanding as a fully scripted program. This stems from the dynamics of the unscripted production process, in which success requires gaining the confidence of a variety of people. Obviously, interview subjects will not speak freely and informatively unless they feel a sense of trust. Equally important is management's sense of trust. The unscripted production process contradicts management's ingrained approval imperative. Corporate executives or college and hospital administrators find comfort and security in established approval processes for print and fully scripted programs. Producing the unscripted program, however, means management must make an act of faith. The producer seeks approval to spend dollars and expose many individuals to the trauma of appearing on camera in advance of developing a script.

Writers can make an invaluable contribution at this juncture, by instilling a sense of confidence through pre-production planning documents that chart a direction and provide a focus for the project. Beyond that, the writer often functions as a critical ear during interview taping sessions or, in some cases, even performs the interviewing tasks. (Writers should be good interviewers.) Once footage is in the can, the writer should participate in the process of selecting appropriate interview comments and fashioning the viewing experience. In documentary production, writing the narration generally occurs after interviews are shot and the overall structure is fleshed out by interweaving suitable interview comments.

In scripted formats, the writer's role is focused on pre-production. In an unscripted program, the writer may be involved from pre-production through production into post-production. We'll explore the writer's involvement in each of these phases and point out differences from the scripted production process.

PRE-PRODUCTION

To contribute conceptually and creatively to an unscripted program, early involvement is essential. Even though word-for-word narration will not be written until after shooting, the same preliminary research, objective-setting and conceptual work that goes into scripted programs should be undertaken.

Research

The scriptwriter's research agenda for unscripted projects starts with the same content-oriented focus used to research a fully scripted program. In fact, often the writer begins research not knowing whether content and objectives will suggest a scripted or unscripted treatment.

In this chapter, we'll follow an unscripted project from start to finish. The program, produced for the Johnson & Johnson Worldwide Video Network, and subsequently distributed by Films, Inc., focuses on the success story of Quality Circles at Extracorporeal's Tampa Bay plant, one of the Johnson & Johnson family of companies.[1] (Extracorporeal manufactures kidney dialysis machines, including products designed for treatment in the patient's home.) The first research task was to find out what a Quality Circle is and how it works. In fact, a Quality Circle is a form of participatory management; workers meet in small groups and use structured techniques to identify and solve common problems. Its success in Japan prompted interest in the concept among U.S. managers as a way to improve quality and productivity. (See Figure 11.1.)

Once the producer or writer senses an unscripted format may be the optimum way to tell the story, the research focus shifts to pre-interviews with potential on-camera participants. The writer (and often the producer) listens carefully not only to what is said but to how it is said. Does the individual speak with conviction? Does the person communicate with facial expression and gesture as well as words? Is there a sense of personal involvement and experience? How will members of the target audience relate to this individual?

The writer also begins to envision how each individual fits into the fabric of the entire story. What part of the story is *this* person qualified to tell? In the documentary on a Quality Circle success story, the perspectives of the plant manager, middle management, supervisors and production workers are likely to be quite different and distinct. Yet all viewpoints need expression to tell a balanced story. So in this research, the writer is looking for both factual content and the way in which each individual's personal experiences and viewpoints reflect or illuminate content issues. Simultaneously, the writer assesses each individual's ability to communicate candidly and credibly on camera.

Figure 11.1: Showing scenes from real life is one of the
strengths of the documentary-style program. Sheet metal
workers at Extracorporeal meeting in an actual session
illustrate the value of Quality Circles better than could
narration or other scripted material. Courtesy Johnson and
Johnson.

Again, trust must be established with each person who appears before the camera. Aside from those self-proclaimed hams, most people are reluctant to face a camera and talk freely before a group of strangers. Building an atmosphere of trust, mutual respect and camaraderie is initiated with these pre-interviews and must continue throughout the project. Those going on camera, especially non-managerial employees or individuals suffering medical conditions or social problems, must be convinced they have an element of control and will not be exploited. (See Figure 11.2.) With motion media, the dynamics of getting people to talk casually in front of a production crew and assembled equipment are usually more difficult than when recording audio for a slide presentation. Audio taping is a more low-key, personal event.

Preliminary Documents

When research is completed, the writer should produce the documents that follow initial research for any project: objectives, audience profile, content outline and treatment. In addition, the writer should also describe the rationale for producing in a documentary style. The excerpt below is from the writer's initial report on results of Quality Circle research, which included pre-interviews with several potential on-camera participants.

> *Assumption:* Extracorporeal's experiences implementing the Quality Circle concept in Tampa are ideally suited to treatment as a television documentary.
>
> *Rationale:* To fully appreciate the Quality Circle concept, one must experience the group dynamics of a Quality Circle in action. The problem solving and communication that result are most compelling when *told directly by the people involved.*
>
> Documentary footage of actual Quality Circle sessions. . .interviews with management. . .employee demonstrations of specific quality and productivity improvements. . .such location footage could provide vivid insight into the inner workings of Quality Circles. The show-and-tell style of the television documentary offers a perfect format for this type of material.
>
> Location coverage documents the process and the results in a highly credible, believable manner. After all, an employee's enthusiastic identification with management goals is the very essence of your story. What better way to capture that personal commitment than through the personal medium of television?

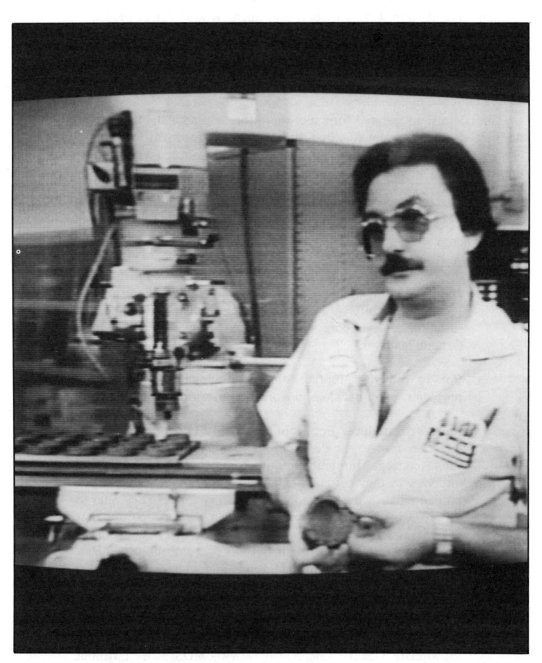

Figure 11.2: Interview subjects often find it easier to talk candidly in their work surroundings. Courtesy Johnson and Johnson.

The writer's recommendation obviously stems from firsthand discussions with those individuals who will participate on camera. Knowledge of the participants and the viewpoints they are able to express on camera is vital to developing detailed pre-production planning documents.

The Treatment

In contrast to scripted formats, where the treatment simply functions as a pre-liminary checkpoint prior to a first-draft script, the treatment for an unscripted pro-gram serves as the basis for the client's approval to proceed with production. Based on research and pre-production interviews, the writer's vision of the finished program should include a sense of how various interview comments will be interwoven to communicate content. To illustrate, look at these excerpts from the Quality Circle treatment. (Although this material is taken from an actual project, fictional names are used here.)

> . . .The scene shifts to the General Manager's area, where we see Jim Kilgore interacting with office staff members. Narration sets the stage for interview comments: "Jim Kilgore describes the situation at Extracorporeal when he became the plant's new General Manager. . ."
>
> Cut to interview footage of Kilgore describing "inherited" problems: order backlogs, rework, absenteeism, etc.
>
> Narrator introduces Ben Robling, Quality Control Manager. In interview footage, he describes his first exposure to the Quality Circle concept. Intercut Robling comments with the Kilgore interview as they recount the initial factors and concerns which influenced their decision to start a Quality Circle. They refer to the role of an outside consultant, and we cut to interview footage of Dr. Richard Hess explaining the involvement of his firm. Rhythmic intercutting between Kilgore, Robling and Hess as they address major considerations and prerequisite training needed for Quality Circle start-up. . .
>
> Transition to describe group dynamics of Quality Circle inter-action. Combine voice-over comments from Hess, Robling, and appropriate Quality Circle leaders with MOS shots [without sound; see Glossary] of Circles in action. Interview comments focus on mechanics of Quality Circle start-up and operation,

> outlining approaches to problem identification, cause-effect analysis, brainstorming and recommendations to management...
>
> Once the Quality Circle modus operandi has been established, focus shifts to exploration of specific case study examples of successful problem solving. . .A terse statement of the problem is voiced by the narrator. . .then, cut to interview footage showing an employee from the Quality Circle explaining how the Circle attacked the problem. . .

The writer not only identifies who will appear on camera, but indicates when they will be introduced and how their comments will be interwoven. The narrator's bridging role is alluded to, as well as a sense of visual materials that will illustrate interview footage.

Content Outline

The treatment, however, is merely a broad-brush overview. Details on what the program will cover and which on-camera participants are expected to make each point are spelled out in the content outline. In developing a content outline for an unscripted program, I prefer a page layout which correlates content points, interview questions and on-camera participants at a glance, as in Figure 11.3. (It's usually easiest to lay out the format horizontally.) Since interview footage of real people provides the source of major content points, this layout clearly links content to specific interviews and shows the extent of each participant's involvement. From this, the writer and the producer/director can evaluate whether the people selected for interviewing are appropriate. Should there be more or fewer interviews? Is there an appropriate mix of individuals to ensure a balanced perspective?

Interview Sheets

Next, the writer develops individual interview sheets, listing specific questions for each person scheduled to appear on camera. Much of this work is already down on paper, since the content outline includes a core list of questions directed toward each person. In the content outline, however, questions are organized by content points, not individuals. The interview sheet is worked up by extracting all questions that pertain to a single individual.

If, for example, we list on a separate piece of paper all questions appearing by the name B. Robling, we have the beginnings of an interviewer's set of questions. Usually, the writer finds those questions need reordering for a more cohesive interview. Also, additional questions, particularly introductory warm-ups or icebreakers,

Figure 11.3: Content Outline for an Unscripted Program

CONTENT POINTS	QUESTIONS	WHO RESPONDS
I. Introduction to Quality Circle concept.	How did you first learn about Quality Circles? What research did you do? What made you think the concept would work at Extracorporeal?	J. Kilgore B. Robling
II. Corporate management's viewpoint.	What was your initial opinion of the Quality Circle concept for the Tampa Plant? How important is top management support to implementing Quality Circles?	B. Elliot D. Whitson
III. "Selling" the Quality Circle concept to middle management and supervisors.	How did you go about introducing this concept to plant management? What was the initial reaction? What groundwork was done to pave the way for a positive response? (For Consultant) How typical was the initial response at Extracorporeal?	J. Kilgore B. Robling T. Sparks R. Hess
IV. Issue—middle management/supervisor's resistance to Quality Circle concept.	What was your initial reaction to the idea of Quality Circles here? What were your "worst fears?" Did they materialize? Why or why not? How much actual problem solving did you think would come from Quality Circles? Have you had to alter your management style to accommodate the Quality Circle concept?	T. Sparks H. Nason G. Brown S. Harris R. Burbick R. Wallach

Figure 11.3: Content Outline for an Unscripted Program (Cont.)

CONTENT POINTS	QUESTIONS	WHO RESPONDS
V. Quality Circles in action A. Definition	Just what is a Quality Circle? Why is a Circle composed of people doing similar work? Why is the size of a Circle important?	R. Hess B. Robling
B. Method of operation	How often do they meet? What distinguishes a Quality Circle from a general "bull session?" What is the rationale behind the frequency and the length of meetings?	R. Hess B. Robling
C. Techniques involved in running a Quality Circle.	How does a team identify problems? How do they select the problems to work on? How do they gather data? What do they do with the data collected? How are suggestions for solving problems evaluated? How are results reported to management?	B. Robling R. Hess Selected circle leaders Actuality footage from circle meetings

as well as potential follow-up probes, may be added. Check to see that all interview questions are left open-ended so they elicit substantive comments, observations and analytical remarks. A string of yes and no answers is death to any interview.

A sample interview sheet for B. Robling is shown in Figure 11.4. Note the use of introductory warm-ups and potential follow-ups to supplement core questions. A list of individual interview questions should be written for each person or each group of individuals. If you'll be asking essentially the same questions of several different supervisors, for instance, then it's probably only necessary to develop a generic Supervisor's Interview Sheet.

Figure 11.4: Interview Sheet for Unscripted Format

PROJECT: Quality Circle Television Presentation INTERVIEW: Mr. Ben Robling	REEL # _____
Questions	**Production Notes**

1) [Warm-up only.] Tell me about your personal background in the field of Quality Control management.

2) How would you assess the plant's performance prior to initiating Quality Circles? What were its strengths and weaknesses?

3) How did you first learn about Quality Circles?

4) What research did you do?

5) What other quality improvement programs or measures did you consider?

6) How did you go about introducing this concept to plant management?

7) What was the initial reaction?

8) What groundwork was done to pave the way for a positive response?

9) Just what is a Quality Circle?

10) Why is a Circle composed of people doing similar work?

11) Why is the size of a Circle important?

12) How often do they meet?

13) What distinguishes a Quality Circle from a general "bull session?"

14) What is the rationale behind the frequency and length of the meetings?

15) How does a team identify problems?

Figure 11.4: Interview Sheet for Unscripted Format (Cont.)

INTERVIEW: Mr. Ben Robling

Questions	Production Notes
16) How do they gather data?	
17) What do they do with the data collected?	
18) How are suggestions for solving problems evaluated?	
19) How are results reported to management?	

So, even though the program is unscripted, those involved in the production have a clear sense of what needs to happen to obtain the footage to tell the story. This is especially important if the writer is not involved in shooting. The treatment provides an overall description of the ultimate viewing experience. The content outline shows how interview questions will yield the substantive comments to cover the subject. Interview sheets provide a framework and plan of attack for each individual's participation. These working documents can be cross-referenced and annotated during production to ensure that spontaneous, candid interviews are resulting in useful footage that can be integrated into the finished program. Though not a word of narration is yet involved, the writer's conceptual framework guides the entire production effort. When it comes time to fashion an edited program, large chunks of material should literally fall into place.

PRODUCTION

A writer's involvement in the actual production can vary. On some projects, the writer may simply observe interviews in progress, offering objective comment on their effectiveness. Sometimes it's appropriate for the writer to perform the interviewer's function. Theoretically, it's also possible for the writer to bow out at this stage and rejoin the staff after all footage is in the can. Whatever the role while shooting, scriptwriters should be sensitive to certain principles of unscripted program production.

Ask Good Questions and You'll Get Good Answers

This is simply a constructive way of saying "Don't put words in people's mouths." The reason for soliciting interviews in the first place is to capture the individual's personal observations. If the interviewer asks good questions, it results, in most cases, in good answers. Absurd as it may sound, I've seen corporate producers *script* answers for people about to be interviewed. That print-oriented mentality always results in a stilted, unconvincing and uninvolving viewing experience. A more common problem, however, is the subject who stays up all night scripting his own answers to anticipated questions. The result usually parallels the former problem: stilted, unconvincing and uninvolving.

It all goes back to trust. Each individual has been asked to participate on camera because he or she has viewpoints and experiences that help tell the full story. To convey that information credibly, participants simply need to converse with the interviewer. The director, the production crew, the interviewer—all are there to create an environment that instills confidence in the interviewee.

Stage for the Subject's Comfort

A non-threatening, relaxed environment is most conducive to a successful interview. Normally, this means conducting the session on the subject's own turf. Camera angles and lighting should be set so the subject and interviewer can make good eye contact, hear one another (an important consideration in factories or computer rooms) and be comfortable. Generally, people are most at ease at their own office or work area. However, if people work in an open office and the topic involves subjective, personal responses, a gaggle of gawking co-workers may inhibit the subject. In this case, a private office or secluded cafeteria area during off-hours might be more conducive. This is another reason for the writer's early involvement and the use of pre-production interview sessions. The writer can gain a sense of the physical environments involved and suggest appropriate areas for each interview. Keep the psychological dynamics of the situation in mind when structuring unscripted formats.

Permit Interviews to Take on Their Own Life

Planning should generate the sense of direction and confidence necessary to allow the documentary-style production to take on a life all its own. Interviewers should not slavishly follow the pre-ordained interview sheets. Optimally, the interview will take on the characteristics of a two-way conversation. It will be a spontaneous and lively exchange, not a carbon copy of the original pre-interview. The interviewer should listen to the answers intently and ask follow-up questions as appropriate. There's always a list of prepared questions to fall back on. But the gems, the candid, utterly believable responses that make for the most compelling on-screen comments, generally spring not from pat interview questions but from the animated give and take of two individuals discussing a subject in depth.

Subjects should also know that with video- or audiotape (and to a lesser extent, film), comments can be taped over, several times if necessary. Answers from various takes can be juxtaposed to make up the edited program. Videotape offers one advantage over film in this situation: if proper technical arrangements are made, taped interviews can be played back on the spot. There's plenty of opportunity to retake the entire interview or selected portions as often as necessary. (All these provisions help build trust.)

Whether the writer acts as interviewer or participates by watching each interview with a critical eye for how well responses can be integrated into the overall structure, it's important to make continual reference to the production planning documents during taping. At the end of each take, jot down responses you find particularly good in the appropriate area of the content outline. Then, halfway through production, when the producer or the director wants to know what content areas need to be explored in more depth, someone has a handle on where the holes or thin spots are. In either case, the writer plays an active role in the production process—and is mentally already working on the post-production phase.

POST-PRODUCTION

Review Footage

The first step in turning individual interviews into a cohesive media presentation is to review interviews in their entirety. If feasible, it's helpful to have transcripts of the interviews at the same time. One experienced producer of corporate unscripted programs has audiocassettes made of each day's videotaping. Those audiocassettes are then sent out for transcription. Shortly after shooting, writer, producer and director all have a complete set of transcripts to work with. Even with transcripts, however, screening of footage is mandatory. Words on paper do not accurately convey the potential of actual footage. Vocal inflection, pacing, gesture, facial expression, even the camera angle may add or detract from a specific comment's usefulness.

In the first review, look for how interview comments play on the screen. If you have a transcript, follow along, making notes to indicate usable comments. If transcripts have not been made, jot down notes and videocassette counter numbers of those interview segments that appear most usable.

Once you have an overall sense of the material available to work with, begin to attack it from an organizational standpoint. Five-by-eight file cards can be quite useful for this preliminary organization. Write down the speaker's name and the general topic, and include the verbatim quote or the in and out cues (the opening and closing words of the quote). The file card should also contain references to help the physical editing process.

The sample card in Figure 11.5 includes the videocassette player counter number (1), which makes it easy to locate the segment on the cassette. At the same time, if the cassette copy includes the SMPTE time code display, make a notation of in and out time codes on the file card (2). The Society of Motion Picture and Television Engineers (SMPTE) electronic time code indicates a specific frame by giving the reel number and the elapsed time on the tape by minutes, seconds and frame number. There are 30 frames per second. Both editor and director will refer to these codes when editing the videotape. The In Cue time code corresponds to the first frame of usable video; the Out Cue to the last frame from the excerpt. The time noted in the lower right-hand corner (3) of the card is the running time or duration of the specific interview comment—26 seconds in this case. (Note: Even when shot on film, it is often most expedient and convenient to transfer footage to videotape for post-production work. This may consist of all footage or only those good takes labeled a "buy" on the production log.)

Develop Continuity

Once you have all relevant interview comments on a given topic logged on file cards, you can identify the people who will carry the freight through their comments and begin to rough out major program segments. The cards are extremely functional for this task. They can be arranged and rearranged in various sequences to see how well certain comments dovetail and play in juxtaposition. One problem the writer usually encounters is redundancy, several people saying essentially the same thing. Eliminate these redundancies by selecting the strongest statements. Discard those

**Figure 11.5: File Card of Interview Comments
                for an Unscripted Format**

JIM KILGORE	TOPIC: Initial Reactions	Reel #: 17
Cassette (1)		Time Code (2)
153	IN: "The initial reaction of the managers, I think. . ."	17:06: 16:25
	OUT: ". . .not going to probably work."	17:06: 42:05
		══════ (3)
		:26

that may lack clarity or believability. Look for the most succinct expressions of an idea; they are generally strongest.

When you find a sequence of comments that covers a given topic with clarity and is likely to play well on screen, the program segment can be transferred from file cards to edit log sheets. Figure 11.6 shows one edit log format that is particularly suited to plotting out unscripted material. These edit log pages are extremely useful, not only to the writer, but to the director and editor as well. First, each page is identified at the top by the general topic being discussed; in this case, initial reactions. These topic headings correspond with main points of the original content outline.

Next, a series of columns provides all information necessary for an editor to physically cut the sequence together on videotape. Column 1 identifies the speaker and the videotape production reel from which the scene is taken. Column 2 gives a videocassette counter reference. Columns 3 and 4 provide a verbatim transcription of the opening and closing words for each specific statement. And Column 5 gives the SMPTE time code number. With both content cues and time code numbers, any editor should be able to piece the sequence together whether familiar with the material or not. Column 6 contains the running time or duration of that specific excerpt. At the bottom, the column is totaled to provide the running time for the complete sequence.

This obsession with time in an unscripted format is important for two reasons. First, the length of individual comments and the sequence in which they're juxtaposed establishes the pace of the program. Second, the screen time given over to various topics says a good deal about the relative importance placed on each.

Scripting Narration

During this process, the writer may begin to enter verbatim sound bites into a word processor and start to assemble a paper edit of the program for reference during post-production. This working script should include page numbers referring back to the transcript pages for each quote. Once the skeleton of the program is on paper, the writer can focus on fleshing it out with the narrative copy. If the writer has been involved in the project from the research phase on, the narrative wrap-arounds should fall into place easily. The narrator's role has been established in the treatment. With intimate knowledge of the interview content available for each segment, the writer should have copy points and voice already in mind.

Generally, narration fulfills three distinct functions in such programming. As an introduction, the copy establishes main themes and content areas as a lead-in to interview footage. Short transitional bridges are usually necessary to link closely related sequences of interview comments. Finally, narration may also be used to convey factual material, condensations of complex interview responses or other

Figure 11.6: Edit Log Sheet for an Unscripted Format

EDIT LOGS—Quality Circles

TOPIC: Initial Reactions

SPEAKER	CASSETTE	IN CUE:	OUT CUE:	TIME CODE	DURATION
J. Kilgore R17	153	"The initial reaction of the managers, I think...	...not going to probably work."	17:06:16:25 17:06:42:05	:26
S. Harris R4	461	"I guess basically, in the back of everybody's mind...	...do your job better than you were doing."	04:24:02:05 04:24:16:17	:14
J. Kilgore R17	163	"I think the initial reaction from the supervisors was that they...	...and that they would lose control on the floor."	17:06:44:01 17:07:01:03	:15
R. Wallach R7	493	"I think the statement I'll have to make...	...the product that actually pays the bills."	07:26:28:18 07:26:58:10	:30
J. Kilgore R17	170	"I would think that the first concern from the engineers...	...from the people on the floor on a timely basis?"	17:07:02:23 17:07:20:18	:18
G. Brown R2	661	"There's always a bit of egotism on the part of engineers...	...does have a better way to do it."	02:39:46:02 02:40:21:21	:35
					2:18

content that is illuminating but not functional or economical to convey in interviews.

Since the writer knows the specific actuality cues that will surround a narrative segment, the narration can be written to segue naturally into interview footage.

Cutaway or MOS Footage

The writer should also have visual footage in mind as cutaway material to cover narrative links. This may range from shots of on-camera participants in daily situations to detailed graphics or action footage. The following lead-in to the subject "Initial Reactions" to Quality Circles at Extracorporeal indicates specific cutaway footage. In addition, the narrator's copy provides a natural bridge to the first interview statement.

VIDEO	AUDIO
Continue MOS footage of Robling and other production workers—highlight footage which shows interaction between management and production worker.	**OFF-CAMERA NARRATOR:** THE NOTION THAT HOURLY EMPLOYEES CAN BEST IDENTIFY AND SOLVE CERTAIN PRODUCTION PROBLEMS IS NEW TO MANY AMERICAN MANAGERS AND SUPERVISORS. THE INITIAL REACTIONS AT EXTRACORPOREAL'S TAMPA PLANT ARE QUITE TYPICAL.
Carry MOS footage featuring Jim Kilgore through a portion of the opening interview statement.	**ACTUALITY INSERT:** Topic—Initial Reactions

The Rough Cut

Once all narrated segments are scripted, the entire program exists on paper for the first time. Although an edited master could be made by simply following cues on paper, usually there is an interim step: a rough-cut version of the program, which serves several functions. It allows the writer and the director to see how specific scenes play as a viewing experience. Almost invariably, both see things they want to change: a particular comment is confusing out of context; a segment bogs down in a lengthy anecdote, which, though interesting, dulls the narrative thrust. Slide shows and multi-image productions can also be put together in rough form and previewed for the client prior to making final art or programming complex sequences.

Additionally, the rough cut gives the producer a vehicle for testing the program with the client or content experts, with management and, if appropriate, even with sample members of the target audience. Comments and reactions from such people are extremely valuable in arriving at final editorial decisions. By this point in the project, writer, producer, director and perhaps even client are too close to the material to be completely objective. Fresh eyes and ears will be quick to sense when the program drags or that a particular statement lacks clarity or that the relative time devoted to a content point seems excessive.

For such input to be constructive, the writer and the producer/director should not be defensive about criticism. You're seeking people's honest reactions to a work in progress, so don't short-circuit the process by resisting suggestions. Hear each person out; then analyze the input you receive objectively and dispassionately. Ultimately, you must trust your own judgment and taste. Every writer needs an editor, and, in an unscripted production, the rough cut is the best tool available for soliciting such input and moving on to the revision phase.

CONCLUSION: STRIVE FOR BALANCE

The key to successfully producing in the unscripted mode is part art, part gamble. Try to strike a balance, consciously controlling through planning yet simultaneously allowing the project to take on a life of its own. Ideally, the final product will be marked by an air of spontaneity that translates into a high degree of believability while covering essential content points concisely and in an organized fashion.

The writer can contribute a great deal to the effort, not so much as a wordsmith but as a conceptual thinker, planner and organizer of content. This can prove as satisfying as seeing 30 pages of original narration translated into a viewing experience. But the writer needs to understand and accept that, by and large, an unscripted program will be *written* by those interviewed for the project.

12 Writing for Multi-Image, Multi-Media and Videowalls

This chapter explores adapting the basic scriptwriting process to media that involve manipulating multiple images simultaneously, usually for display on large screen areas.

The writing process, from assimilation through editing, still provides a basic framework when scripting for these media. Special technical production requirements and specific viewing situations, however, mean the scriptwriter must approach the assignment with special insights and writing "tools." Novice writers will want to have several single-image scripts "under the belt" before tackling multi-image productions.

For simplicity, this chapter focuses on what's *different* about writing for these media.

MULTI-IMAGE, MULTI-MEDIA AND VIDEOWALLS

Since these terms are used indiscriminately, a few defintions may be useful:

- Multi-image: as the term implies, this involves display of two or more *images* simultaneously. The viewing audience must respond to several presentational symbols often presented in rapid sequence.
- Multi-media: here the audience watches two or more *media* simultaneously in the same audiovisual presentation, e.g., a multi-image module that includes a motion picture clip.
- Videowall: use of several video monitors (typically 16 in rows of four) ganged together to create one large video "billboard" for which videotape can be programmed to appear in a number of configurations.

MULTI-IMAGE

These computer-programmed synchronized sound-slide presentations capitalize on the large-screen panoramic dynamics of projected 35mm photographic images.

285

Technically, you can have a multi-image presentation with as few as two projectors and a simple dissolve unit. More typically, multi-image refers to projector configurations which involve at least three projectors and progress in increments of three. You may write for six, nine or more, usually up to fifteen, projector combinations. (See Figure 12.1.)

The more projectors, the more possibilities in terms of multiple images, special visual effects and dramatic impact. In addition, with multiple projectors, the large screen is often subdivided into from two to five discrete areas. These screens may or may not overlap. The writer can call for visuals in a single screen area, can juxtapose images, or write for a "build" (start in one screen area and move across the screen). Another typical effect is to hold a visual in the center screen while simultaneously changing visuals in the two side screens (sometimes called the "outboard" screens).

Generally, large multi-image productions include stereo sound for music, effects and spoken narrative. The combined effect can be wonderfully dramatic in the hands of a skilled writer and production team. Before scripting your first multi-image show, go see several multi-image productions. (Multi-image shows which play to the public can be found across the nation. In New York City, the South Street Seaport includes a theater used exclusively to show a multi-image, multi-media presentation on the seaport's history. If you're on the west coast, take in "The San Francisco Experience" at the Pier 39 theater—where more than 400,000 visitors see a 32-projector presentation each year.)

By contrast, an intelligent script and resourceful production team can also produce highly effective large-screen presentations for two projectors. Even when you are limited to a single screen, it's possible to achieve certain multi-image effects by optically printing 35mm slides so they are cropped to appear in specific screen areas. You might develop certain split screen or quad screen effects, using this technique. (I recently saw a simple, but intelligent and effective use of a two-projector dissolve unit. The presentation was entirely student written and produced as an orientation to their college campus.)

How Multi-Image Differs from Film and Video

If you've been mulling over the pros and cons of various media, the logical question might be: why not simply shoot a 35mm motion picture to achieve the same effect?

First, the requirements and costs of film production and post-production (especially 35mm) mitigates against the type of multi-image effects used in slide shows. Film is almost invariably meant to be edited in linear sequence—scene 2 follows scene 1 and is followed by scene 3, etc. Even the most routine post-production effects (such as adding titles to a photographic image or altering the placement of images in the screen area to be combined with a second moving image) involve

Figure 12.1: 15—Projector Overlapping Screen Configuration

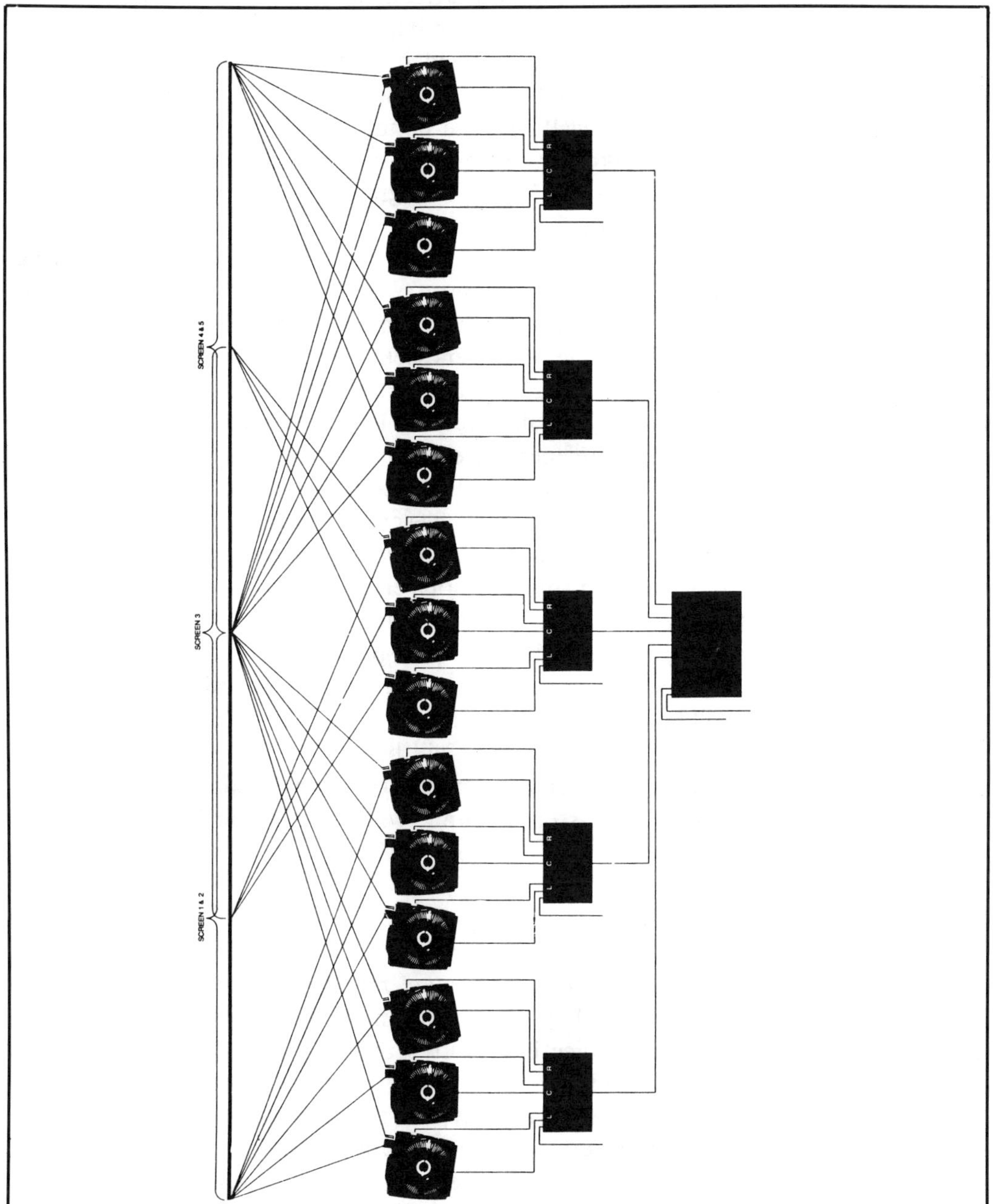

optical printing, which gets expensive and requires a significant amount of laboratory work. Duplicating multi-image production effects and capabilities would soon become prohibitively expensive and time-consuming.

What about video projection? After all, video post-production with its instantaneous digital effects capabilities facilitates multi-screen effects while offering live action. Many TV commercials, as well as some nonbroadcast programs, are shot on film, then "posted" on tape to take advantage of these electronic editing capabilities. And, video can easily incorporate 35mm photographic and computer-generated material as well as live-action video.

Until recently, however, video projection systems were incapable of achieving the large screen panoramic effects of a 35mm slide show. Poor resolution and picture degradation in terms of color and brightness made video less than satisfactory for the impact and drama multi-image producers seek.

Inroads, however, are being made. New video projection systems can be operated in rear-screen configurations. A large sales meeting I scripted recently used a mix of live-action videotape and computer-generated slides produced on a video system.

The most dramatic breakthrough, High-Definition Television (HDTV) (see pg. 7), promises to have enormous impact on large-screen production and projection. In the nineties HDTV will make slow but steady inroads in all phases of the industry. Once an HDTV standard is adopted (by conscious effort or marketplace forces) television's resolution capabilities will equal those of 35mm film or photography. Video-based computer-generated graphics and digital post-production effects will be available for HDTV's 1125-line scanning capability. The resolution and impact of large screen film projection will be combined with the "live" look of videotape.

As that happens, multi-image producers will begin using television as the base medium, transferring film or photographic images to tape as needed. The big-screen impact of HDTV, combined with stereo sound, will provide the large canvas and dramatic effects which are the stock-in-trade of multi-image producers.

Multi-Image/Multi-Media Events

Multi-image or multi-media presentations are rarely used for informational or instructional purposes. They are high-impact, dramatic media, and motivational objectives prevail. Large-screen projection, multi-screen effects and stereo sound for music and narration require a highly emotive style.

The major corporate sales meeting is a typical multi-image application. Largely motivational in nature, these meetings often serve a company's entire field sales organization, perhaps a thousand or more people. They have the ritualistic, tribal feel and the celebratory spirit of high school and college reunions. The auto industry, for instance, holds annual dealer sales meetings to introduce the year's new models. Pharmaceutical and manufacturing companies often hold meetings to introduce new drugs or products to the sales force. Trade associations host conventions with attendees coming from around the country, or even around the world. Short, multi-image modules are often used to kick off the show. They set the tone and often establish a theme for the meeting. Other, shorter modules introduce key speakers or topics and finally provide a "big bank," "send- 'em-home," "feel good" finish. Meetings may last several days and include award dinners, outings, workshops and guest speakers. Sometimes, these meetings even revolve around a custom-designed live revue or stage show (a genre covered in Chapter 14.)

When there are instructional objectives to accomplish, they are usually not done in the general large-audience theater, but in smaller workshop meeting rooms. In those sessions, videotapes may often carry part of the content.

Multi-Image Emphasizes Visuals and Sound

If television is a writer's medium and film a director's medium, then multi-image is the shared medium of the art director and computer slide programmer. Since the objectives are largely motivational, and most modules run from two to five minutes, a module generally revolves around a single idea or concept. The writer's prime contribution is to generate creative concepts which make good use of multi-image capabilities and are targeted to the needs of the client and psyche of a large audience experiencing the presentation in a darkened theater.

In keeping with the emotive nature of multi-image work, music and sound effects play a more significant role than in typical informational/instructional programming. Likewise, narration and dialog are often downplayed. It takes a certain discipline to convey a "big idea" in only three or four pages of copy, maybe half of which is devoted to music and accompanying visual effects.

For example, in a sales meeting conducted to introduce a new anti-arthritic medication to a pharmaceutical sales force, several modules were designed to introduce key speakers. One module introduced a marketing manager to highlight demographic data showing the "aging of America" as baby-boomers matured. (Since many arthritic conditions have their onset in later years, the aging of America also meant market growth for anti-arthritic compounds.) Note how the script shown in Figure 6.3 in Chapter 6 uses almost no narrative copy to establish this theme.

Music and visual imagery work together to demonstrate the key point through suggestive presentational symbols. Narration is purely secondary. (In Langer's terms, multi-image modules are more *presentational* than *discursive*.) In fact, a good way to approach writing multi-image modules is to first try writing a script which tells the story solely through visuals and music/sound effects. (If done well enough, narration may not be necessary.)

Working with Art Directors and Programmers

Storyboarding is a vital step in multi-image production. Writer and art director work together, collaborating on visual flow, use of screen areas and special effects. See Figure 12.2 for an example of a multi-image production script and storyboard.

Just as film or video editors take individual scenes and assemble them into a unified linear presentation, someone has to program multi-image projectors and audiotape machines, synchronizing all effects by using a computer memory program.

The computerized memory allows technicians to input an entire sequence of cues for automatic control of complex projection functions, all cued to the sound track. Individual cues or whole blocks of cues can be added, deleted or altered in a matter of seconds. For synchronizing effects with music, timing between cues can be adjusted by adding or deleting increments of time as small as 1/10th of a second.

The multi-image programmer performs a function similar to a videodisc programmer. The writer does not need to know how to program either a multi-image production or a videodisc, but writers do need insight into the capabilities of the equipment chosen for a project and the requirements of the programmer.

Before describing an animatic-like multi-image sequence, sit down with the programmer and art director to make sure there's a feasible way to achieve the effect in terms of production time and budget. Just as the film/tape director will often suggest better ways to achieve an effect, listen to what your programmer and art director have to say about how to realize your conceptual ideas. It's another way in which audiovisual writing is a collaborative effort.

Show Flow

When writing for a major sales meeting or conference, the writer takes on a larger editorial role. It's not enough to script individual multi-image modules. Scriptwriters must have a vision for the entire meeting and the overall effect of the one-, two- or three-day experience—another way in which multi-image writing may differ from other types of media writing.

Writers often take on an "editorial planning" role, integrating media events (which may include film or video segments as well as multi-image pieces) with speakers, workshop activities, staging and room decor, and special events.

These are high-visibility projects with large budgets. They involve working with the top management of a company or organization, frequently under critical deadline pressures. Often, more than one writer is employed to help with executive speeches or to structure workshop activities. There may be celebrity talent or guest speakers to incorporate into the programs. Clients become absorbed in a myriad of details unrelated to creative excellence, such as the kind of teleprompters to be used, travel arrangements, and the menu for the banquet. Nerves get frayed, tempers flare

Figure 12.2: Multi-Image Production Script and Storyboard

VISUALS	AUDIO
Images of the brain, seen from different perspectives, begin to appear in various areas of the screen.	**MUSIC & SOUND EFFX:** (As lights dim, a solo flute or other wind instrument sets a pensive mood.)
A representation of the brain in center screen dominates.	**NARRATOR:** IT'S BEEN SAID, THE MIND OF MAN IS ONE THING MAN'S MIND WILL NEVER FULLY COMPREHEND.
It comes alive with representations of nerve cells, like twinkling stars. Then, the stars literally explode from the brain. . . the screen becomes a glittering representation of our galaxy.	PHYSICALLY, THE BRAIN IS SIMPLY THREE POUNDS OF TISSUE. YET IT HOLDS ABOUT A HUNDRED BILLION HIGHLY SPECIALIZED NERVE CELLS—EQUAL TO THE NUMBER OF STARS IN OUR GALAXY. . .
The views of the brain reappear in various screen areas, as stars give way to a more neutral background.	. . .UNLIKE STARS IN THE HEAVENS, HOWEVER, NERVE CELLS WITHIN THE BRAIN ARE IN CONSTANT COMMUNICATION. . .
During the next lines of narration, various areas of the brain come alive with animated starburst simulating information passing from one neuron to another.	INFORMATION FLOWS THROUGH ELABORATE NETWORKS. . . INTERACTIONS BETWEEN NEURONS OCCUR CHEMICALLY AND ELECTRICALLY.
The views of the brain give way to shots of computer hardware—twinkling lights, circuit boards and CRT displays.	IN SOME WAYS, THE BRAIN WORKS LIKE A COMPUTER. COMPUTERS MAY "CRUNCH" NUMBERS FASTER THAN THE HUMAN BRAIN. BUT THEY WORK ON A STRICT BINARY CODE.
The computer images are transformed back into depictions of the brain.	BY CONTRAST, OUR BRAIN SIMULTANEOUSLY PROCESSES INFORMATION ON MILLIONS OF CHANNELS OPERATING IN PARALLEL.

Figure 12.2: Multi-Image Production Script and Storyboard (Cont.)

VISUALS	AUDIO
The brain is transformed into a bust of George Frederick Handel. This becomes the focal point for a Monty Python-style sequence: numbers, letters, musical notes, etc., go into Handel's cranium in random fashion. . .	**NARRATOR:** FURTHER, THE BRAIN IS NOT SIMPLY AN INPUT/OUTPUT DEVICE. TAKE CREATIVE THOUGHT. SCIENCE IS UNABLE TO EXPLAIN HOW GREAT COMPOSERS STIR THE SOUL. . .
. . .on cue, the mouth opens as the lyrics and musical notation for the Hallelujah Chorus come floating out of Handel's mouth.	**MUSIC:** (Stirring theme from the Messiah plays full for a moment.)
The musical notation floats across the screen as we hear full chorus and orchestra.	**NARRATOR:** YET FOR EVERY POTENTIAL CREATIVE ACT, MAN'S MIND CAN ALSO FOCUS ON WARLIKE DESTRUCTION.
The bust of Handel is transformed into Napoleon Bonaparte on horseback. All around, the screen comes alive with battle scenes of the time.	**SOUND EFFX:** (Mix of cannon blasts, muskets and sounds of calvary on horseback.)
	NARRATOR: THROUGHOUT HISTORY, THE GREAT MILITARY MINDS WERE THE CLEVEREST TACTICIANS.
During this segment, the bust of Napoleon is transformed into a portrait of Vincent van Gogh. The screen comes alive with visions of Van Gogh's most famous, dramatic paintings.	PERHAPS THIS TENSION BETWEEN CREATIVE AND DESTRUCTIVE IMPULSES DRIVES SOME MINDS TO WITHDRAW INTO A PRIVATE WORLD—CREATING A PERSONAL VISION OF DAILY SCENES. . .
	MUSIC: (Impressionistic theme by Debussy or Ravel.)
Now we see Van Gogh, Handel and Napoleon appear in different areas of the screen.	**NARRATOR:** DESPITE THE DIFFERING ACHIEVEMENTS OF THESE THREE, THEIR MINDS WERE BOUND BY AN IDENTICAL

Figure 12.2: Multi-Image Production Script and Storyboard (Cont.)

VISUALS	AUDIO
	CONDITION. THEY WERE ALL EPILEPTICS.
On this line, the images of Handel, Napoleon and Van Gogh simultaneously dissolve back to clinical views of the brain.	THEIR SEIZURES WERE THE OUTWARD SIGNS OF ELECTRICAL "STORMS" TAKING PLACE IN THE BRAIN. . .
Superimposed over each are lightening bolts depicting the onset of seizure activity.	**SOUND EFFX:** (Sounds of thunder claps on a stormy summer's eve.)

STORYBOARD

IT'S BEEN SAID THE MIND OF MAN IS ONE THING MAN'S MIND WILL NEVER FULLY COMPREHEND.

PHYSICALLY, THE BRAIN IS SIMPLY THREE POUNDS OF TISSUE.

YET IT HOLDS ABOUT A HUNDRED BILLION HIGHLY SPECIALIZED NERVE CELLS.

EQUAL TO THE NUMBER OF STARS IN OUR GALAXY. . .

Figure 12.2: Multi-Image Production Script and Storyboard (Cont.)

STORYBOARD
...UNLIKE STARS IN THE HEAVENS, HOWEVER, NERVE CELLS WITHIN THE BRAIN ARE IN CONSTANT COMMUNICATION... INFORMATION FLOWS THROUGH ELABORATE NETWORKS... INTERACTIONS BETWEEN NEURONS OCCUR CHEMICALLY AND ELECTRICALLY. IN SOME WAYS, THE BRAIN WORKS LIKE A COMPUTER. COMPUTERS MAY "CRUNCH" NUMBERS FASTER THAN THE HUMAN BRAIN. BUT THEY WORK ON A STRICT BINARY CODE. BY CONTRAST, OUR BRAIN SIMULTANEOUSLY PROCESSES INFORMA-TION ON MILLIONS OF CHANNELS OPERATING IN PARALLEL. FURTHER, THE BRAIN IS NOT SIMPLY AN INPUT/OUTPUT DEVICE. TAKE CREATIVE THOUGHT.

Figure 12.2: Multi-Image Production Script and Storyboard (Cont.)

STORYBOARD

	SCIENCE IS UNABLE TO EXPLAIN HOW GREAT COMPOSERS STIR THE SOUL...
	MUSIC: (Stirring theme from the Messiah plays full for a moment.)
	NARRATOR: YET FOR EVERY POTENTIAL CREATIVE ACT, MAN'S MIND CAN ALSO FOCUS ON WARLIKE DESTRUCTION.
	SOUND EFFX: (Mix of cannon blasts, muskets and sounds of calvary on horseback.)
	NARRATOR: THROUGHOUT HISTORY, THE GREAT MILITARY MINDS WERE THE CLEVEREST TACTICIANS.
	PERHAPS THIS TENSION BETWEEN CREATIVE AND DESTRUCTIVE IMPULSES DRIVES SOME MINDS TO

Figure 12.2: Multi-Image Production Script and Storyboard (Cont.)

STORYBOARD

WITHDRAW INTO A
PRIVATE WORLD—
CREATING A PERSONAL
VISION OF DAILY
SCENES. . .

MUSIC:
(Impressionistic
theme by Debussy or Ravel.)

NARRATOR: DESPITE THE
DIFFERING ACHIEVE-
MENTS OF THESE THREE—
THEIR MINDS WERE
BOUND BY AN IDENTICAL
CONDITION—THEY WERE
ALL EPILEPTICS.

THEIR SEIZURES WERE
THE OUTWARD SIGNS OF
ELECTRICAL "STORMS"
TAKING PLACE IN THE
BRAIN. . .

SOUND EFFX: (Sounds of
thunder claps on a stormy
summer's eve.)

Source: From "Every Day for Fifty Years," multi-image module,
written by William Van Nostran, produced by The O'Hara Company
and DD&B Studios. Used by permission.

and last minute changes are inevitable. Producers, writers, slide makers, art directors and multi-image programmers all get tired and cranky. It's great fun—the first time. Needless to say, it takes a certain personality to make a living doing these types of productions.

The excerpts in Figure 12.3 which follow are not from scripts. Rather, they show the type of editorial planning documents which communicate the scope and

Figure 12.3: Sample Multi-Image Planning Documents

The Assignment

As meeting producer, the O'Hara Company will assume responsibility for creating, staging, and executing appropriate product launch sales meetings. Although specific logistics will be developed as part of the assignment, the following guidelines serve to define the scope of the project:

Number of Meetings: 2

Attendance/Meeting: 125 Hospital/Medical Services Sales Representatives, District Managers and home office personnel.

Meeting Dates: Targeted for mid-May launch, pending final FDA approval and availability of meeting sites.

Location: Two sites, one in the Southeast or Midwest and a second in the West. Possible locations include. . .

Orlando	Dallas
Tampa	Phoenix
Atlanta	San Francisco
New Orleans	San Diego

Appropriate meeting and A/V support facilities exist in any of these cities. The O'Hara Company would work closely with Marketing Services to select facilities capable of handling logistical meeting requirements.

Objectives

1) Position the product as the first B.I.D. Beta-2 bronchodilator—a breakthrough product capable of making a vital difference in bronchodilator therapy.
2) Position the product in the competitive marketplace and clearly establish the product's niche in bronchodilator therapy including the long-term potential inherent in line extensions.
3) Maximize market share by providing overall direction and coordination to initial physician detailing activities during the product introduction period.
4) Highlight the key role played by the Hospital and Medical Services sales force in introducing the product to the marketplace and to district sales representatives.
5) Motivate and mobilize the sales force to provide a winning sales effort. Reinforce the need for effective, professional detailing and a high degree of personal productivity throughout the sales force.

Figure 12.3: Sample Multi-Image Planning Documents (Cont.)

Meeting Theme: The Vital Difference

A meeting theme provides overall identity for the content, style and visual elements presented throughout the meeting. It serves as a rallying point, working to unify diverse messages presented by a variety of speakers, as well as workshop activities and related events.

The best meeting themes stimulate the imagination as well as the mind. They stir emotions and create lasting impressions which heighten the intensity of daily sales activity long after the agenda is completed.

The Vital Difference is a meeting theme which can take on a variety of meanings throughout the entire day-and-half. The theme is rich in potential and can be effectively integrated through the meeting agenda, serving as a thematic link sustaining continuity from speaker to speaker.

The opening module will introduce the Vital Difference theme, dramatizing the Vital Difference the company is bringing to the market with this first twice-a-day Oral Beta 2 Bronchodilator.

At the same time, this "umbrella theme" can assume a variety of meanings. . .

The Vital Difference in the company's marketing strategy.

The Vital Difference in our advertising and promotional plans.

The Vital Difference the product will make in patient acceptance and efficacy.

The Vital Difference the entire sales force will make in introducing the product to the marketplace.

In short, this theme is appropriate for the product and can encompass all aspects of the meeting.

Staging the Main Meeting Room

The O'Hara Company will design and produce the necessary theme graphics and elements for a customized stage for the main meeting room.

The Audio/Visual format involves 9 to 12 projectors on one screen surface with an option of going to 9 to 12 projectors wide-screen. We utilize the latest in computer controlled sound, lighting and projection equipment.

Figure 12.3: Sample Multi-Image Planning Documents (Cont.)

Scenically, we propose a stage featuring earth tones with slatted wood columns, multi-level stage and stairs which encompass the screen, podium and matching earth tone side panels. The design will incorporate product or meeting them logos as appropriate. Emphasis will be on creating and executing a functional, clean design which conveys an image of total professionalism.

Sample Agenda

Evening:

6:00– 7:00	General Assembly/Welcome/A/V Module & Keynote Address
7:00– 8:00	Cocktails
8:00– 9:30	Dinner/Entertainment

Morning:

7:45– 8:00	Walk-In/Welcome
8:00– 8:05	Opening Module
8:05– 8:10	Singer
8:10– 8:40	Speaker One
8:40– 9:10	Speaker Two
9:10– 9:15	Module Two
9:15–10:15	Medical Presentation
10:15–10:25	Singer Introduces Coffee Break
10:25–10:45	Coffee Break
10:45–10:50	Introduce Motivational Speaker/Module 3
10:50–11:30	Motivational Speaker
11:30–12:30	Workshops
12:30– 1:30	Lunch
1:30– 3:30	Workshops/Competition
3:30– 3:40	Assembly
3:40– 4:00	Sales Charge
4:00–	Closing Module
6:00–	Cocktails & Dinner

Videotape Role Model

For the "How to Detail" workshop, we recommend a videotape module to provide a role model of the product detail. With simple interactive techniques, this videotape could also be used to simulate physician objections. This allows the participants to interact with the video role model by anticipating how each objection should be handled.

Figure 12.3: Sample Multi-Image Planning Documents (Cont.)

Following screening of the role model, workshop participants will be put into teams for role playing their own product detail. By practicing the detail and dealing with questions and objections which invariably result when detailing a new drug, our workshop participants will sharpen the skills that make the "Vital Difference" when sitting before a physician.

Train-the-Trainer Kit

As a post-launch meeting follow-up, we recommend developing a training kit the Hospital/Medical Services representatives can use to tell the product story in District meetings.

Using A/V materials and audio recordings of major presentations as the basis for this program, we would develop a package to include a video module, slide support and speaker script. A similar approach was used previously and the concept represents productivity in action. The Hospital/Medical Services sales force becomes a vehicle for launching the product in every sales district.

Another potential spin-off of meeting materials to explore is developing an additional speaker kit designed for use in hospital training and in-service programs for pulmonary staff members. Again, the meeting proceedings can become the input for the content and A/V support materials.

Production Schedule

(Based on a launch meeting between November 1 and 15)

Week One:	Research and refine meeting agenda/participants
Week Two:	Script A/V Modules Research with speakers Design Staging and Meeting graphics
Week Three:	Draft Speeches Begin A/V Module Production
Week Four:	Revise and Storyboard Speeches Continue Module Production; set construction, and other production elements (Videotape Detail, etc.)
Week Five:	Preview A/V Modules Begin speaker support slide production Module revisions and final production/programming

Figure 12.3: Sample Multi-Image Planning Documents (Cont.)

Week Six: Prepare logistics and shipping
                   Revisions to speaker support slides

Week Seven/   Rehearse speakers
Week Eight: Revise speaker support materials

Week Nine/   Travel
Week Ten: Site Preparation
                   Dress Rehearsals

Show Equipment List

12 projectors	2 stereo equalizers
3 stackers	1 room analyser
2 eagle programmer computers	2 four-track tape decks
5 doves	1 cassette deck
1 screen 10' x 15'	2 16mm film projectors with rear
10 lenses	projection assembly and lenses
1 12-channel sound mixer	16 stage lights
4 microphones	1 12-channel lighting board
1 lavalier mic	lighting cable
2 amplifiers	2 power trunks and distribution
4 speakers	boxes
4 speaker stands	communications headsets

Source: From a sales meeting proposal by William Van Nostran for
the O'Hara Company. Used by permission.

impact of an entire meeting experience. The multi-image modules are simply threads to stitch the many pieces together.

VIDEOWALLS

It is an over-simplification to think of a videowall as simply another multi-image display format. Comprised of a bank of computer-controlled video monitors that display images in unison or in differing monitors simultaneously, the videowall is a recent technological breakthrough offering distinct user features and benefits.

Typically, several television monitors are placed side by side and on top of one another with only a thin black frame (mullion) separating each monitor. Usually, 16 monitors in rows of four create the videowall. (Monitors in a five-by-five configuration best simulate television's traditional three-by-four aspect ratio.)

Videowall images can be displayed in several different ways:

1.   Portions of a single video image appear in each of the monitors to create one giant image, for example, a space shuttle lift-off. In this configuration, a videowall viewer sees a larger-than-life image. It is like a big screen except for the intersecting moliens.

2.   Each of the 16 monitors can be used to show an identical image over and over in each monitor. In this configuration, the videowall viewer is confronted with a normal-size TV image sixteen times—for example we see a shuttle lift-off repeated as a pattern in sixteen monitors.

3.   Like a large multi-image screen, separate areas of a videowall can be used to display different images. You might show a space shuttle lifting off in the center of the wall with a graphic title appearing in another area and close-ups of the astronauts in remaining monitors. In this configuration, the videowall viewer reacts to multiple images simultaneously.

4.   Computer-controlled video inputs allow a videowall presentation to shift fluidly from one configuration to another at any time during the presentation. This flexibility is one element which makes the videowall medium a challenge for media writers.

Videowall Applications

Videowalls first appeared in Europe in the early 1980s. Initially, the Europeans used videowalls in retail stores, but all types of exhibits, including amusement parks, convention centers and transportation facilities, soon made use of the technology.[2] Thus videowalls are being used in environments different from multi-image big screen presentations.

The videowall is ideally suited for display at point-of-purchase, on convention floors, at museums or other "high-traffic" display areas. In such environments, the videowall presentation is not seen by a single audience, but often runs continuously, showing the same presentation over and over. The audience is comprised of casual viewers with perhaps only modest interest in the message. Due to the size and visual impact of multiple television screens, videowalls are attention-grabbing traffic stoppers.

Videowall versus Multi-Image

There are many distinctions between a videowall and a multi-image program. And, since "the medium is," at least partly, "the message," then writers should clearly appreciate the unique qualities of each:

Figure 12.4: Photo of Videowalls

Source: Attendees at the Presentation Technology Show are greeted
with a menu of events. Photo courtesy of Knowledge Industry
Publications, Inc.

1. The multi-image show consists of projected 35mm *photographic* images.
   The videowall is an electronically created *video* image.
2. Multi-image shows are usually seen by a homogenous, captive audience
   with the lights down. Videowalls are generally encountered in high-traffic
   display environments where their high ambient light output can be seen
   even in daylight.
3. The multi-image presentation presents a panoramic, large-screen "canvas."
   The videowall, even when using all monitors to create a larger-than-life
   image, is still composed of several monitors separated by mullions.

However, programming a videowall is similar to programming a multi-image
slide presentation in that storyboarding is required to assign images on a screen-by-
screen basis. Another interesting phenomenon is that more footage and visual
material is needed than for a single-image TV production. This, in turn, requires
more editing time so that the final production uses both the material and capabilities
of the videowall to the fullest.[3]

One drawback to videowalls relates to the mullions separating each monitor.
Although one would expect them to be distracting, the human brain is superb at
filling in missing data. After a moment or two, the mullions are largely unnoticed.

To see a permanently installed videowall, take a trip to Epcot Center and see AT&T's 32-screen installation. The system has two uses: it's part of a seven-minute information and entertainment program and it's also part of an interactive video system. The walls are configured as two 16-monitor screens, separated by a fiber optics map of AT&T's U.S. network. During the show, the screens duplicate one another; at one moment the program sweeps from one wall to the other.[4]

AT&T's Worldwide Intelligent Network Control Center in Bedminster, NJ, contains a 75-screen videowall. This impressive and enormous installation provides a window to the multiple layers of AT&T's international network, continuously displaying a stream of nerve impulses to network managers. In addition to using the videowall to display real-time network status for AT&T managers, a portion of the wall is also used to show a short presentation on the network for visiting VIPs and potential customers. The wall is part "state-of-the-art data management" and part "show business."

So when it comes to scripting either a multi-image, multi-media or videowall presentation, remember that part of your goal is "show business." We simply can't dodge the entertainment factor in the media scriptwriter's bag of tricks.

FOOTNOTES

1. Ken Burke, "An Evolving Experience from San Francisco," *Multi-Images,* March/April 1987, p. 18.
2. Sammy Danna, Ph.D. "Videowalls Cut the Edge of Corporate Display Technology," *EITV,* July 1987, p. 30.
3. *Ibid.,* p. 30.
4. *Ibid.,* p. 30.

13 Writing for Interactive Video

WHAT TO DO

Interactive video means different things to different people. To determine your need for further information, select the answer that best fits your situation:

A. I have written interactive videodisc programs and am intimately familiar with the concept of tactile viewer involvement and the potential of various branching possibilities.

B. I've followed the development of interactive videodisc in the trade press and seen demos of different programming. I've fooled around with kiosk-type interactive video installations in hotels or public exhibits such as those at Disney World. So, I'm familiar with interactive videodisc on a conceptual level.

C. Don't tell me how the watch is made when all I want to know is the correct time. Can't you summarize what's different about writing scripts for interactive video? If I need to know more later, I'll look it up as needed.

D. Hey, I just got off the boat. Whaddye mean by interactive videodisc instruction?

If you answered A, you can skip this section. Or, at least speed-read for the author's opinions and script excerpts.

If you checked B, go directly to Figure 13.1 and skim through the interactive videodisc reference checklist. If you want to know more about a specific concept, the checklist will refer you to the proper page and section number or additional reference material.

If you checked C or D, fasten your seat belt and welcome to the wonderful world of interactive video. . . .

Figure 13.1: Interactive Videodisc Reference Checklist

MENU SELECTION:

1)   Instructional Benefits . . . .   p.   306, 344

2)   Non-training Applications . . . .   p.   308

3)   Interactive Videodisc Features and Benefits . . . . .   Fig. 13.2

4)   Input Devices . . . .   p.   308

5)   IVD Training Applications . . . .   p.   313

6)   Flowcharting and Key . . . .   Figs. 13.7, 13.8

7)   Implications for Writer . . . .   p.   334

APPLICATIONS

Instructional Benefits

In its most primitive form, "interactive video" is anything on-screen that the user has some relationship with and *appears* to control what happens next. The interactive television viewer is capable of "affecting the outcome of events on the television screen."[1] Each individual user makes the "final cut."

The interactive videodisc (IVD) is a marriage of computer and video technologies. Computers as teaching machines or electronic tutors date back to the 1960s. Computer programs can be written so the learner's responses or choices trigger the computer's next move. In this way, computer-assisted instruction (CAI) and its offspring, interactive videodisc, is a lot like playing chess against a computer. Instruction is nonlinear and individualized, allowing a learner to repeat material that proves difficult or skip information already mastered. Each move of the chessmen the viewer makes is countered by a computer move.

Ironically, the other half of the interactive system—the laser videodisc—was originally conceived as a consumer item. The videodisc performed like an electronic turntable, playing prerecorded movies, plays, sports events, documentaries and other programming for consumer consumption. The videodisc never caught the consumer's fancy, however, for one simple reason. In this original form, it was a "read-only" playback device. And as we know by now, the "time shift" capabilities of videocassette recorders (VCRs) which could tape off-air and play back instantaneously sparked the consumer imagination.

The technical capabilities of the disc, however, quite different from tape, slowly won favor with trainers. Optical disc features and their benefits for the instructional designer are summarized in Figure 13.2.

The most siginficant aspect of interactive videodisc for training is random access. Anyone who's experienced the difference between searching for a song on audio-cassette versus accessing a song on a laser CD player can appreciate the power of immediate random access. In videodisc form, it provides nearly unlimited capabilities for branching.

But random access without "intelligence" would be of little significance. The most revolutionary feature of IVD technology is the direct computer interface: a sophisticated computer can talk to a videodisc player and control its functions. The audiovisual potential of television and special playback features of optical disc (immediate random access to any frame) can be combined with the interactive branching potential and instructional software of CAI.

Figure 13.2: Optical Videodisc Features that Aid Instructional Design

Feature	Benefit
54,000 separate frame locations	The videodisc is an information storage/retrieval system. It permits high-density storage and retrieval of information in various formats: text; videotape; film; artwork; slides or other still images.
Random access	Average access time from frame to frame is 2.5 seconds. This greatly facilitates nonlinear sequencing.
Scan (forward or reverse)	Permits the user to screen program material rapidly to find a specific segment.
Still frame and slow motion controls	Allow the viewer to analyze motion in detail. Could also facilitate note taking or detailed study of a single frame or sequence of frames.
Direct computer interface	A special connector permits access to the disc player's internal microcomputer from an external computer.

Non-training Applications

For example, look at the excerpt in Figure 13.3 from an interactive videodisc program designed to attract passersby at an electronic trade show as a way to enhance Perkin Elmer's image as a leader in high-technology. It illustrates the most basic level of interactivity. As writer Alice Stitleman points out, "Our design was very simple, branching from the main menu (the gypsy offering to read your fortune) to one of the horoscopes and back again."

Now look at a more complex example of interactivity in Figure 13.4. One of my favorite non-training interactive applications, it is shown at the United States Golf Association's museum. It allows visitors to peruse endlessly through golf's golden moments. But it also gives visitors of any age a chance to design their own golf course through interactive techniques, match wits with a partner on a golf quiz, or compare the swings of pros throughout history. (See how Bobby Jones and Arnold Palmer match up, for instance.)

Designed by Digital Techniques, Inc., this award-winning interactive exhibit brings the museum to life by involving the visitor in a "hands-on" way. (If you're in the Bedminster, NJ area, drop in and design a course.)

These two examples of interactive design illustrate how this random access technology can be put to a myriad of specialized, information-dense video applications. Entire product catalogs have been put on videodisc. Videodisc kiosks (like those seen at Epcot Center in Orlando) are often used to put visitor information at a user's fingertips. Computer menus allow users access to the specific video segment, graphics or still frame information they seek.

Another useful application for this technology is in point-of-sale demonstrations and information exchanges. A free-standing kiosk houses the hardware (usually the computer hardware is locked away, hidden from view) while the familiar television screen beckons the shopper to interact and learn more about the product.

Input Devices

In both cases, the power of the videodisc driven by computer software is how it allows the viewer to respond to what's on the screen and affect what appears next. Users must have some method of "talking back" to the TV screen. Technically, this is achieved through input devices such as keyboards, keypads, light pens, touch screens, joy sticks, a mouse, etc. These devices, familiar to most personal computer users, function as the learner's means of communicating with the computer software.

Light pens and touch screens offer certain advantages for teaching subjects requiring parts identification. An automobile engine can be displayed on the screen and mechanics in training can identify components by touching them with a light pen or finger. Or, pharmaceutical sales representatives can receive instruction on the

Figure 13.3: Excerpt from Interactive Videodisc Program

VIDEO	AUDIO
Narrator: (Dressed as a gypsy)	Welcome to "Semi-Signs." I am the Gypsy of the Semi-Zodiac. I help people understand their destinies by reading their circuits.
Looks down into crystal ball.	You have chosen to look into the true nature of things. Let me help you, as together, we pierce the facade of seeming and reach the real world of being.
Camera moves in on ball.	Ah. . .I see, I understand. Be sure you are close to the screen so that you too can see the truth of things.
Narrator: (Dealing out 12 cards one by one on table.) (Emphasize)	We are all guided by the stars and the circuits to fulfill our special destinies. I have here 12 cards which hold many secrets. Come. Pick the card you want, and place your finger on a sign. *Pick-and-place.*
Picture of the Point-Contact Transistor Visual changes	The twelfth House of the Semi-Zodiac is the oldest sign in the semi-universe—the sign of the Point-Contact Transistor. Those born under the magical sign of the Contact Transistor are devoted to serving humanity.
A close-up pan of Point-Contact Transistor	Often creative, they are inventive in their approach toward life. Although they tend to be a bit old-fashioned, their wisdom is evident to all they meet.
Picture of the Junction Transistor Animation of electrical charge overlaid on picture	The eleventh House of the Semi-Zodiac is the Junction Transistor. Those born under this ancient sign are known for their common sense. This practical sign is *charged* with a consistency that makes Junction Transistors stable and reliable. They make wonderful friends.

Figure 13.3: Excerpt from Interactive Videodisc Program (Cont.)

VIDEO	AUDIO
Picture of the First Integrated Circuit. Dissolve "1" on picture	The tenth House of the Semi-Zodiac is the sign of the First Integrated Circuit. The First IC is depicted by a small but powerful rectangle which represents *simplicity,* but not simple-mindedness.
Visual changes. Visual changes again. (Emphasize)	Characterized by an active intelligence, First Integrated Circuits exhibit a commitment to the future. Their strong will enables them to face all earthly challenges. However, they need to exercise caution in their daily affairs. As true children of the modern age, they are not as *discrete* as their parents were.
Picture of the First Planar IC Emphasize spoke section (Pause) Rotate image.	The ninth House of the Semi-Zodiac is the sign of the First Planar IC. The circular symbol of the First Planar IC indicates this sign's wholistic approach to life. Those who are born under the ancient sign of the IC overcome problems by *simplifying* them. Known for their probing intellects, they understand emotions as well as ideas. They are explorers by nature.
Return to initial shot.	Travel entices them, but they are home-bodies too. In fact, children and family are very important to Planarians. They seek to keep their families together by having lots of *fair* children.
Picture of the First 1K Dynamic RAM Visual changes. Visual changes.	The eighth House of the Semi-Zodiac is the sign of the First 1K Dynamic RAM. The symbol—a dense, symmetrical rectangle—indicates this sign's extreme intelligence. Those lucky enough to be born under the sign of the 1K Dynamic RAM are gifted with prodigious memories. They are also very creative. These movers and shakers often change history. Never *static,* they demand stimulation to refresh their *dynamic* spirits.

Figure 13.3: Excerpt from Interactive Videodisc Program (Cont.)

VIDEO	AUDIO
Picture of the Magnetic Bubble Domain Visual changes.	The seventh House of the Semi-Zodiac is the sign of the Magnetic Bubble Domain. As the name suggests, those born under the sign of the Bubble exhibit an intuitive ability to grasp the Truth behind life's veil of illusion. In fact, Magnetic Bubbles often become spiritual leaders. Spiritually evolved and morally enlightened, they also have a practical side, an uncanny ability to think fast on their feet.
Picture of a Micralign System Visual changes.	The sixth House of the Semi-Zodiac is the sign of the Micralign. Those born under the powerful sign of the Micralign exhibit unusual analytical prowess. They see clearly, without distorting the truth. And they project their force for positive change on all they meet, helping others overcome mistakes. They are forward-looking, yet always in line with the times. If they have any fault, it is that they tend to be perfectionists.
Picture of the DAC-08	The fifth House of the Semi-Zodiac is the sign of the DAC-08. Those born under this influential sign display a unique ability to illuminate and educate others. Possessing special powers of understanding, children of the DAC-08 are very popular. They can communicate with all types of people. Perhaps that is why they often are to be found in the helping professions. As mediators and negotiators, they heal wounds and resolve conflict.
Picture of the S4535 32-Bit High Voltage Driver Visual changes.	The fourth House of the Semi-Zodiac is the sign of the S4535 32-Bit High Voltage Driver. The icon of this sign resembles a densely woven Oriental tapestry. Its geometrical detail suggests a contained energy waiting for the right opportunity—to *transform*. Those born under this sign

Figure 13.3: Excerpt from Interactive Videodisc Program (Cont.)

VIDEO	AUDIO
	are ambitious. Though not necessarily powerful themselves, they aspire to high places by associating with the powerful.
Visual changes.	Like the Oriental tapestry, High Voltage Drivers moderate their intensity with a large measure of sensitivity. This makes them such finely tuned receptors that they become indispensible to those who depend on them.
Picture of a Gallium Arsenide Chip	The third House of the Semi-Zodiac is a relatively new sign in the semi-universe— the sign of Gallium Arsenide. Those born under this young sign are multi-faceted communicators. They are equally skilled at giving and receiving messages.
Visual changes.	Although sensitive, Gallium Arsenides give new meaning to the expression "life in the fast lane." They do everything quickly. They want life to be easy, and they take their pleasures with a sophisticated insulation from danger.
Picture of a Megabit Memory Chip	The second House of the Semi-Zodiac is the amazing sign of the Megabit Memory Chip. This is the sign of illumination. Megabitians are gifted with a special vision which surpasses mere intelligence.
Visual changes.	Geniuses or visionaries, these are the beings who will transform the future. However, they are not ivory-tower intellectuals. They are committed to action—to *high performance* and to service. They understand that "in giving, so shall ye receive."
Picture of a Gate Array	The first House of the Semi-Zodiac is the sign of the Gate Array. The symbol for the sign of the Gate Array is depicted by what appears to be a densely circuited

Figure 13.3: Excerpt from Interactive Videodisc Program (Cont.)

VIDEO	AUDIO
Visual changes.	mask. The mask hides the Arrayan's true nature. Although they appear rigid, those born under this sign are actually very *flexible*. Their flexibility allows Arrayans to put forth great thrusts of energy. This energy is often directed to the good of others. Known for their selflessness, those born under the sign of the Gate Array make up in action for what they may lack in creativity.

Source: From "Perkin-Elmer Game 3," written by Alice N. Stitleman, Ph.D., produced by Joan Cianci, and directed by Marc Schwartz of CAVRI Systems, Inc., for Perkin Elmer. Used by permission.

anatomy of the heart by calling out specific valves and chambers. Joysticks are usually associated with video games. Keyboards are needed when the subject matter involves more complex interactions than simple multiple-choice Q&A.

Another important element characterizing both excerpts is a critical component of good interactive program design: they are fun! They invite viewers to become involved with the content and have a good time. The most successful *training* applications also manage to play up the novel aspects of man-machine interface.

Interactive Videodisc Training Applications

From the beginning, astute trainers recognized the potential synergy which resulted from combining a powerful teaching machine (CAI—computer-assisted instruction) with a more personal, highly visual and very familiar "instructor" (the videodisc).

As a rule, training applications generally require more complex branching than pure informational applications, because the subject matter is usually dense and difficult. For similar reasons, videodisc training applications usually involve more factual rather than conceptual material involving value judgments. Excellent interactive training programs have, however, been designed to illustrate the fine points of buyer-seller relations in sales situations. So a skilled interactive program design team will find ways to use the technology for subjects which involve value judgments and conceptual thinking.

The branching required in training programs can become quite complex, because a single response may lead to a variety of follow-up interactions to confirm the

Figure 13.4: Design Overview, Storyboards and Script Excerpts from "Play Away, Please"

A. DESIGN OVERVIEW

The purpose of this document is to provide a detailed account of *Play Away, Please,* and suggest the experience a typical viewer might have. It is to be read in conjunction with other design documents, namely:

Storyboard
Structure Chart
Video Treatment

General Characteristics

The exhibit is designed for viewing by a general public (golfers and non-golfers) of all ages. There are five principal topics:

- SWING STYLES
- COURSE ARCHITECTURE—Design Your Own Hole
- MATCH PLAY—Test Your Knowledge
- USGA NEWS
- CLASSIC ERAS

Each topic has a brief audio (or audio and video) introduction played from the videodisc. The topics are described below.

Visual and audible feedback are used to indicate which of several choices has been made and to indicate the "current" state of the program. This is generally achieved by changes in color for words and other symbols.

If a viewer does not touch the screen, a prompt is given to encourage interaction. Generally, two prompts are given. Then, the program changes to its "cover screen." The time interval of prompts and "timeouts" varies from section to section, but will generally be relatively brief, in consideration of the museum environment and "traffic flow."

Cover Screen

A video "loop" plays continuously on the screen. The title *Play Away, Please,* "Narrated by Steve Melnyk," and the instruction "Touch the screen to begin" appear throughout. A touch anywhere on the screen causes display of the "main menu" and an audio.

Introduction

During the introduction, graphics and text for the main menu (Tee Off!) appear. The "Tee Off!" symbol appears in the lower, left corner during the narration. It is not touch-sensitive in this case.

Figure 13.4: Design Overview, Storyboards and Script Excerpts from "Play Away, Please" (Cont.)

When the main menu is called from the cover screen, touch-sensitive "targets" are not active until the audio introduction is complete.

Tee Off! (Main Menu)

This graphics screen is displayed as rapidly as possible whenever the Tee Off! symbol in the lower, left corner is touched. Targets are active for each topic as soon as possible.

Principal Topics

Swing Styles

A video introduction shows slow-motion swings and places Palmer and Nicklaus side-by-side at the top of the screen and black below. Their names are added below their pictures. Audio continues as the "speed control" is displayed and explained. The wood-grain background and brass nameplates are added. Finally, the two simultaneously take their swing.

Touching any nameplate causes the previous nameplate to be "un-highlighted," and the new nameplate is highlighted. The golfers fade to black, and the names below the pictures are replaced by the new names. Fading up from black, then freezing for one second, the appropriate new pair of golfers is displayed, and they take their swing. The point of synchronization between the two golfers is always the moment of the club striking the ball. At the end of the swing they freeze. Touching the same nameplate again, causes the swing to be repeated, with no change to the names.

The speed control allows the viewer to see the swing at normal speed or various slow speeds. Speed is changed by touching a point along the "speed bar." "Repeat Swing" causes the swing to be repeated.

"Solo Shots" shows a still frame of a golfer at the end of a swing. The golfer's name is highlighted on the left side of the screen. Any of the names can be touched, causing display of that player taking a swing.

Names are arranged alphabetically, from top to bottom. "Other Players" displays a new set of names, continuing the alphabetical order. When the last "page" of names is listed, "Other Players" causes the name display to "wrap" to the first set of names.

Course Architecture

A video introduction shows scenes of several golf courses around the world. Graphics cover the video and show a set of "icons" that can be used to design a fanciful hole. Instruction on use of the symbols is heard. When an icon is touched,

Figure 13.4: Design Overview, Storyboards and Script Excerpts from "Play Away, Please" (Cont.)

it is redrawn with an outline designating it as the "current symbol." This symbol is then placed on the landscape by touching the screen. The icon area cannot be drawn over. "Start New Hole" causes the landscape to be cleared. "Instructions" causes the introductory explanation about the use of the symbols to be repeated.

The "skip ahead" button shown during the video introduction causes audio to be muted as graphics for "design-a-hole" are displayed.

Match Play

A video introduction shows scenes of various awards ceremonies. Graphics (the scorecard, etc.) appear at the bottom of the screen. At the end of the introduction a graphic appears, to allow indication of "one player" or "two players." When this is answered, the first of nine quiz questions is presented.

The questions consist of approximately 9 silent motion video segments and 27 still photos. They are presented sequentially, so that viewers playing multiple games are unlikely to encounter the same question twice.

Questions, and choices for answers, are displayed in either a multiple-choice or true/false format. There are four answers for each multiple-choice question. Questions appear as text overlaid on video.

When a question is asked, each player must touch an answer, in turn, as indicated by illumination of a name on the scorecard. After the second player answers, score is registered for both players (in the case of a single player, only "player 1" is illuminated).

If both players are correct, polite applause is heard. If both are incorrect a crowd "sigh" is heard (for a single player no sounds are heard). At the end of the game (except for a tie?), video fades to black and robust applause is heard.

The option is then presented to:

1. Print the questions and answers
2. Play another game
3. Explore other parts of the program

If the print option is chosen, the questions and answers, with the correct answer identified, are printed out. The printout also includes the USGA name and address and an invitation to visit the museum store.

"Play another game" removes the above buttons. Sound is heard, asking the number of players, and a graphic allows indication of the answer. When the answer is given, the game procedes as before.

"Explore other parts of the program" causes display of the "Tee Off!" menu. This third choice might simply be offered implicitly through the "Tee Off!" button in the lower left corner.

Figure 13.4: Design Overview, Storyboards and Script Excerpts from "Play Away, Please" (Cont.)

USGA News

A royal blue background is displayed, featuring the USGA seal in a low-contrast, "watermark" fashion. Text is written over the background, describing championship results, current news, upcoming events, etc. The text display consists of a single font (typeface) in one color.

The text is drawn from a file prepared by USGA personnel using an IBM PC-XT or PC-AT. The TOUCHCOM screen displays the text in a manner that mimics, as closely as technically possible, the PC screen.

Classic Eras

A timeline is displayed, portraying five groups of famous players. Touching any group causes the timeline to fade to black, followed by a fade up on a video clip of that era. The viewer may return to the timeline by touching "Other Eras," or waiting for the end of the clip. At the end of the clip, video fades to black, then fades up on the timeline.

Figure 13.4: B. "Play Away, Please" Structure Chart

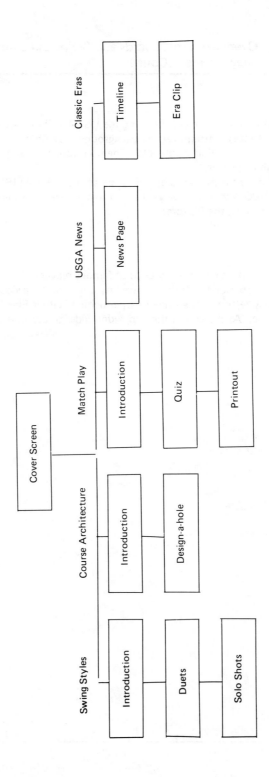

Figure 13.4: C. "Play Away, Please" Storyboards

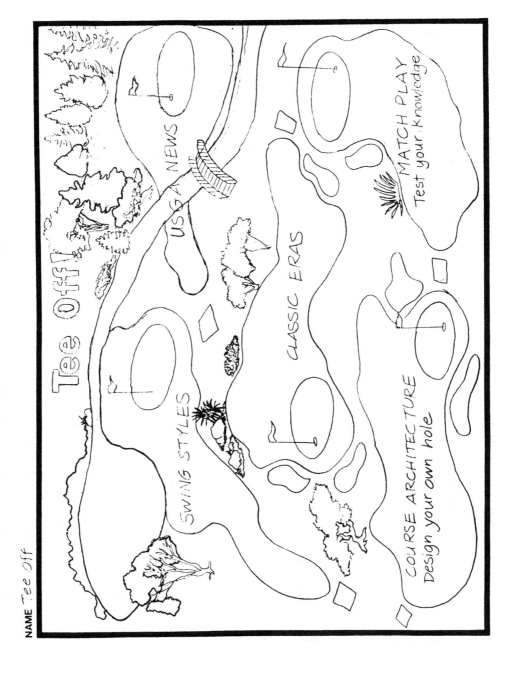

Figure 13.4: C. "Play Away, Please" Storyboards (Cont.)

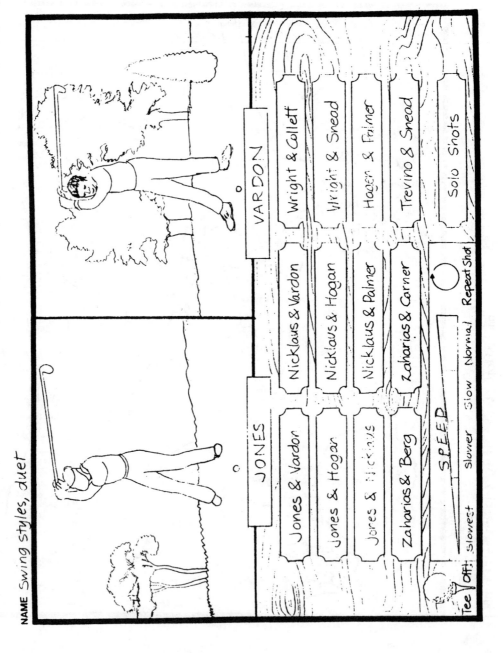

NAME Swing styles, duet

Figure 13.4: C. "Play Away, Please" Storyboards (Cont.)

NAME swing styles, solo

Figure 13.4: C. "Play Away, Please" Storyboards (Cont.)

NAME Design-a-hole

Figure 13.4: Design Overview, Storyboards and Script Excerpts from "Play Away, Please" (Cont.)

NARRATION: PLAY AWAY, PLEASE

Intro to Main Menu

Welcome to "Play Away, Please."

This exhibit features games, news, photographs, and historic motion pictures, all under your control. Explore them by touching one of these fairways. You'll see the topic and a new display. Touch words and other symbols to guide the presentation.

Feel free to interrupt; touch the screen at any time. Return to these fairways by touching the ball in the lower, left corner.

So go ahead.

As we say at all USGA championships, "Play away, please."

Narration for "Classic Eras"

Each of golf's major eras is remembered for a famous group of players. See them at their best.

Narration for "Swing Styles"

(Bobby Jones traced slow-mo)
Swing styles have changed over the years,
with the introduction of new equipment and balls,
and today's manicured golf courses.

(full frames shrink and squeeze side-by-side, 4 sec)
Here you can compare the great players of this century.

(speed control appears, 5 sec)
Use the speed control for a closer look, or to repeat a swing.

(wood-grain, plaques, and names fill in, 6 sec)
Watch for placement of feet relative to the ball, turning of the hips, and
    height of the backswing.

(they swing together, 2 sec)
Give it a try.

Alright.

Play away, please.

Figure 13.4: Design Overview, Storyboards and Script Excerpts from "Play Away, Please" (Cont.)

Narration for "Course Architecture"

Just as the Industrial Revolution changed the characteristics of golf equipment, the 20th century brought changes in golf course design and construction techniques. As land became more precious, designers had to alter the terrain rather than rely on the natural features. But whatever the landscape, certain elements appear in all courses. One of golf's great pleasures is the variation in design among thousands of courses in the world today.

These elements are derived from characteristics of the Scottish seacoast. St. Andrews shows off the natural landscape—exposed land and bunkers. Golfers playing the nine holes "out," share double greens with other golfers playing back "in."

Dramatic cliffs and foggy weather mark Pebble Beach in California. The short 7th hole with its isolated green is merely warmup for the chasm one encounters on the 8th.

Bobby Jones was co-designer, with Scottish architect Alister Mackenzie, of Augusta National. There is no real rough, only trees and shrubbery along wide fairways leading to large, undulating greens. Perennial site of the Masters tournament, the course boasts beautiful foliage and immaculate grounds.

Shinnecock Hills, Long Island, is reminiscent of St. Andrews. Both are "links" courses, having been reclaimed from dunes and near the ocean. Shinnecock Hills is one of the few such courses in the United States.

Narration for "Design a Hole"

You are the architect now. Join Alister Mackenzie, Donald Ross, and A.W. Tillinghast. Try your hand at designing a golf hole.

Everything you need is at the bottom of the screen.

Touch one of these symbols
and place it on the landscape above.
You only need to touch the symbol once, but you can use it many times.
Slide your finger to fill in large areas.
You can always clear the screen by touching "Start New Hole."

Play away, please.

Prompts

Go ahead. Make a selection.

Just touch the screen to indicate your choice.

Figure 13.4: Design Overview, Storyboards and Script Excerpts from "Play Away, Please" (Cont.)

Touch the screen to operate this exhibit.

Remember, you can also slide your finger across the screen.

Take a swing at it.

Take a shot at it.

Git it a shot.

Stop putting around. Touch the screen.

Please make a choice, or let other people play through.

Can't you make up your mind?

Congratulations.

Thank you.

Nice work.

Play away, please.

Alright.

Source: From "Play Away, Please," written by Carol Strohecker, produced by Brian Raila and Gabriel Savage Dockterman of Digital Techniques, Inc., for the United States Golf Association. Used by permission.

learner's understanding or to correct mistaken answers. Furthermore, design components often include several linear segments to present new information, then use interactive techniques to test the learner's comprehension.

Learners work their way through the material individually in non-linear fashion, at their own pace based on their specific learning needs. The computer does not allow learners to proceed to new material until they successfully master the previous block of instruction. This is done through "competency gates"—tests, quizzes, identification of on-screen material, simulations or any type of interaction to demonstrate the learner is ready to receive new instructional content.[2]

Figure 13.5 is an example from a highly technical training application used to teach refrigeration concepts as well as the operation and maintenance of commercial refrigeration units. The excerpt is not from the script, but from the writer's design

**Figure 13.5:   Design Documents for Interactive
Technical Training Application**

DESIGN OVERVIEW

All interactions on the "Refrigeration Videodisc" will be TOUCH SCREEN DRIVEN using IBM's InfoWindow videodisc system. KEYBOARD or MOUSE-driven features can also be incorporated, if desired.

Choices will be made from ON-SCREEN MENUS. These menus will feature GRAPHIC ICONS, as well as text, to guide the user to the correct touch area.

Wherever we can, we will record LIVE VIDEO of the equipment to illustrate our lessons. This refers primarily to the Refrigeration hardware itself. This will assist the student in becoming familiar with the devices before they ever come in contact with them. Every attempt will be made to help the Student keep his or her spatial orientation as they investigate the machine.

There are times, however, when PC GRAPHICS will be used as principal illustrations. These occur when the subject matter is abstract and lacks a physical model—the description of Boiling and Condensing, for example. Or it occurs when the subject is a difficult one to videotape, like the internal workings of a Compressor. In these cases, we will create a graphic model and use it to illustrate portions of our lesson.

These graphics will often be accompanied by VOICE-OVER NARRATION, so that the narrator will still clarify, explain or focus attention to details of the image on the screen. Elements of the graphic may change color, position or size as well, often synchronized with the narration to emphasize a point.

We will regularly mix video with TEXT and GRAPHIC OVERLAY to add detail.

During all lessons, the program will display CONTROL COMMANDS on the screen. These touch areas will appear on a pop-up menu when the student touches a PAUSE or STOP icon. The student will then be able to RESUME, REPLAY, SKIP AHEAD to the next point or lesson, and return to the MAIN MENU.

The TECHNICAL DETAIL icon will reveal another SUBMENU with optional choices available. These options could include definitions, specifications or other details that will provide a better technical understanding of that specific part of the program. The options in this SUBMENU will change throughout the program to follow the content.

One more icon on the screen will provide an INDEX to the information. Users may use this feature to look up specific information directly. Index items will be listed alphabetically and will refer to the portions of the training program where the item was introduced. These portions may be motion or still frame, PC Graphics or Live Video. Students will be able to access the Index from any point in the program. And the system will mark their place, allowing them to return to where they left off.

If necessary, a GLOSSARY of terms may also be made available. This alphabetical listing of the terminology used throughout the lesson would be presented as PC graphics text-screens. These definitions could serve as additional information or reviews for the students using the program.

**Figure 13.5:　Design Documents for Interactive
　　　　　　　Technical Training Application (Cont.)**

The program will also provide TESTING. It will begin with a Pre-Test, which will determine the Student's level of expertise. In addition, throughout the training, lessons will end with tests that review the major points of information. These tests will feature multiple-choice questions. The student will simply touch the screen to choose the correct answer.

Much of the testing will take the form of SIMULATIONS. Students will adjust controls and see the results of their actions in real time. If they add heat to a system, the temperature gauge will rise. If they increase the turbine speed, the Freon® flow will increase.

And the videodisc program will provide FEEDBACK. Students will be told when their answers are correct, either directly or by watching the results of their actions. They will also be able to go back into the presentation from the question screen and review the material if they do not know the answer to a question.

Student Management

A student management system will be built into the program. It will keep track of who has used the system, what material they have been through, and how they have performed on the tests and simulations. This information will be formatted into a text file that can be read by word processors or database management systems. Here the information can be analyzed and printed out. We will also allow opportunities for individual Du Pont locations or departments to tailor certain elements of the program to meet their local needs.

The Narrator

The Narrator is a man in his late thirties or early forties. A "regular guy," he looks like he could be a plant supervisor. He sounds like one as well. He is comfortable with the jargon of the industry and his specialty, but he will not explain his lessons with a slew of buzzwords.

Our Narrator should be good-looking, but not a "pretty boy." He should be dressed in a work shirt and slacks, or coveralls, whichever is most appropriate to the job. Care should be taken that nothing about his dress will later date this program.

During the progression of the segments, he can change from his full dress "presentation outfit", which he would wear for the Introduction Segment, to a rolled-up shirtsleeves appearance for the later Operations and Maintenance segments. He will wear the appropriate safety equipment as required by the situation.

The Technician

The Technician is the person who actually operates and maintains the Refrigeration Unit, while the Narrator explains what is going on. He should be distinguishable from the Narrator, and will not need to speak. Nor will he interact with the Narrator. An actual DuPont Operator would make a good Technician.

**Figure 13.5:   Design Documents for Interactive
           Technical Training Application (Cont.)**

The Set

The program visuals will be shot on the plant floor, in front of a Centrifugal Compressor Refrigeration System. This will provide a realistic setting and a rich environment for the "hands-on" training that will follow. The area will also feature a pedestal-type table (or a turntable top), and whatever equipment is on top of the pedestal.

From segment to segment that space will feature various pieces of Refrigeration equipment, or tools, or an IBM InfoWindow. The Narrator will work with whatever is on the pedestal, as well as speak directly to the audience.

Tone of the Script

The narration will be clear and straight forward. The spoken word will be used for giving overviews and explaining frameworks and important theories. These overviews will be broken into a series of short pieces of information. The student can then watch the program piece by piece, pausing, repeating or going forward only as they feel they need to.

The details, which are important but often distracting to the overall framework, will be kept in text, available through pop-up menus. For example, the Narrator may speak of the Brine "being heavier or lighter than water," but the specific gravity and specific heat curves of Brine will be made available in text form only, available through the "TECHNICAL DETAIL" menu option.

This will provide students the opportunity to interrupt the narration only when they wish to interrupt the flow of the explanations for greater technical information. The part of the audience that needs the specific technical information can get it as it becomes appropriate to the lesson. And those viewers who seek a more general understanding of the technology or the machine will not get lost in a sea of data.

OUTLINE
0000 PROGRAM INTRODUCTION AND OVERVIEW

Visual Treatment

0100 Segment One will begin with a shot of the Earth, as seen from space. Narration will describe the threat to the atmosphere produced by chemicals in the ozone layer. As the images "zoom in" on the surface of the planet, Freon® will be identified as one of the hazardous chemicals.

The images will continue to narrow their focus to an aerial view of an industrial plant. Narration will promote the role of careful operation of air conditioning and refrigeration units as important to the control of Freon® in the atmosphere, as the

**Figure 13.5:   Design Documents for Interactive
                 Technical Training Application (Cont.)**

camera comes to rest at the Centrifugal Compressor Refrigeration Unit which will become our set.

The segment to this point can stand alone as an Attract Loop, playing over and over until interrupted, or it can lead directly into the program by touching the screen.

Next, the user is asked to indicate whether this is the first time they have used an interactive system. If the person is a first time user he will be routed to the course introduction (0200), otherwise he will go right to the main menu (0400).

In the Course Introduction, the user or student will be introduced to the Narrator. He will be on site, in front of a Refrigeration Unit.

0200 The Narrator will welcome the viewer to this interactive program. He will describe briefly the nature and intent of the videodisc. He may have an InfoWindow system on the set to refer to.

The Narrator will then introduce the Refrigeration system. He will briefly explain the theory and operations of the system. He will indicate that more information will be presented in the rest of this training.

Throughout the presentation the student will be told that he will have the option of repeating points, skipping forward, or proceeding to the next piece of the lesson. In addition, the student can seek greater detail by accessing the TECHNICAL DETAIL icon. The narrator will explain all these functions.

After the Introduction Segment ends, the user will be asked if he is a Student taking the refrigeration course or someome who wants to "Browse," or use the system as a job aid to look up some information.

0300 If the user is a Student he will log his name and ID number so the system can keep track of his performance.

After the Log On, the Student will take a test to verify his understanding of basic refrigeration. If he passes he will be introduced to the course. If he does not pass he will be branched automatically to the segment on Fundamentals (1000).

The Narrator will then introduce the Main Menu, describing the course and giving the students a rough idea of what is where on the disc. He will describe the types of features available and invite the students to use them throughout the lessons to follow.

INSTRUCTIONAL OBJECTIVES

1. Students will be able to describe the threat that Freon® poses to the Earth's atmosphere.
2. Students will relate the importance of proper equipment operation to the minimizing of refrigerant leakage into the atmosphere.
3. Students will be able to describe the function of each of the touchscreen icons in the InfoWindow presentation. They will also be able to operate the videodisc system and access all of the features of the system.

**Figure 13.5:   Design Documents for Interactive
Technical Training Application (Cont.)**

4. Students will also be able to describe the contents of the videodisc course and how it is organized. They will also be able to proceed with the training on a path appropriate to their background.

CONTENT

1. Effects of pollution on Earth Atmosphere
   Freon® vs. ozone
   need for careful operations of refrigeration

2. Log on
   first time user?

3. Introduction
   course description
   VD introduction
       How to operate videodisc
   course structure
       explain Technical Information
       explain Other Systems,
           e.g., reciprocal or screw

4. Register
   browse versus take course
   student sign on
       name, ID number

5. Pre-test
   accurately reflect entry level knowledge
   unlocks "browse program" feature
   Pass; gives access to main menu
   Fail; forced through Fundamentals

KEY MENUS

0400
MAIN MENU
(touch one)

OVERVIEW

1000.   REFRIGERATION FUNDAMENTALS
2000.   THE REFRIGERATION CYCLE

**Figure 13.5:   Design Documents for Interactive
Technical Training Application (Cont.)**

3000.	SYSTEM CONTROLS
4000.	START-UP PROCEDURES
5000.	OPERATIONS OVERVIEW
6000.	ROUTINE MAINTENANCE
7000.	TROUBLESHOOTING/DIAGNOSTICS

Source: From "DuPont Refrigeration Video Disc—Design and
Treatment," written by Kevin Padden, produced by Jack Noon,
president MIDI, Inc., directed by Tom Barnett; interactive
programmers Greg Feliz, Steve Saporta, and Ken Rosenblad, for the
DuPont Co. Used by permission.

document, which functions in the same manner as the content outlines and treatments described in Part I of this book.

As you can see, the training experience is enhanced by a combination of live action video and PC graphics. A touch screen facilitates interactions as well as on-screen menus and graphic icons.

Testing takes the form of simulations allowing students to add heat or increase turbine speed and see the effect on temperature and Freon® flow.

The videodisc is programmed to provide feedback as well as the option to go back into the instructional presentation from a question screen to review material.

Next, Figure 13.6 provides an excerpt from the shooting script leading to a simulation.

This example is clearly more complex than the two previous script excerpts because of the highly technical content. In order to communicate the branching possibilities in each segment, the author includes a flowchart (see Figure 13.7) with each unit. (Figure 13.8 provides a key to symbols used in flowcharting.)

Monitoring and Measuring Capabilities

With the computer's ability to monitor and record, it's possible to give both participant and designer feedback on each participant's performance. Participants receive immediate feedback; designers and trainers can analyze comprehensive stored data for an individual student or a group of participants. As described in the design document in Figure 13.5, this data can also be printed out for record keeping or detailed analysis.

In this respect, interactive videodisc lends itself to highly measurable, quantifiable training applications. Interactive videodisc presentations are consistent—each learner works through the same content at his/her own pace. Little wonder the U.S. Army, for one, has been a major player in adopting IVD for consistent training of large numbers of people with varying educational levels and/or deficiences.

Figure 13.6: Excerpt from Shooting Script for Interactive Technical Training Application

VIDEO	AUDIO
REFRIGERATION FUNDAMENTALS	
EVENT #1000	A—:28 B—:00
HOST IN CORNER OF SCREEN, WITH MENU ITEMS FULL	HOST: This topic covers the fundamentals of refrigeration—what heat is and how it flows. . .how temperature affects liquids, causing them to boil and condense. . .how pressure and temperature affect refrigeration. . .some basic information on refrigerants. . .and how to describe the amount of refrigeration taking place, the system "load."
	Touch the item you want to see. . .we suggest you start with "basic heat flow" and go through each part of the topic in order.
EVENT #1050	
STILL:	
GRAPHIC:	
TEXT: REFRIGERATION FUNDAMENTALS	
(touch one)	
• BASIC HEAT FLOW 1100	
• BOILING/CONDENSING 1200	
• PRESSURE/TEMPERATURE 1300	
• INTRODUCTION TO REFRIGERANTS 1400	
• REFRIGERATION "LOAD" 1500	
EVENT #1100	A—:68 B—:00
SUPER: BASIC HEAT FLOW HOST ON SET, IN FRONT OF TABLE WITH HOTPLATE, TEAKETTLE	

Figure 13.6: Excerpt from Shooting Script for Interactive Technical Training Application (Cont.)

VIDEO	AUDIO
COFFEE CUP, MAKES CUP OF INSTANT COFFEE, PUTS THERM. AND SPOON IN COFFEE	HOST: To understand refrigeration, we have to understand heat. . .what it is, how it moves. We can't measure heat, but we can measure temperature. We call this coffee hot because we can measure its temperature at about 200 degrees Fahrenheit. . .
GRAPHIC OF MOVING MOLECULES AT VARIOUS TEMPS SHOW VAPOR/GAS EVAPORATION GO BACK TO HOST W/CUP	What do we mean when we call something "hot"? We're talking about how fast the atoms and molecules that make up something are moving. . .the faster they move, the hotter something is. If the molecules move fast enough, they'll overcome the forces that hold them together and turn into a vapor—gas. . .like the steam coming off this coffee. . . .
CUT TO GRAPHIC OF CONDUCTION	Heat flows to whatever a hot substance touches, unless there is "insulation" in the way. . .the spoon handle, for example, is becoming as hot as the end in the coffee. This flow of heat directly to something it touches or through a solid object is called "conduction."
CUT TO CU, HAND OVER CUP CUT TO GRAPHIC OF CONVECTION	The heat is also flowing to the air above the coffee. . .and this warmed air rises, flowing past and warming my hand. This process is called "convection." Try changing the heat under the water and see how convection and conduction work. . .

**Figure 13.6:   Excerpt from Shooting Script for
                 Interactive Technical Training
                 Application (Cont.)**

VIDEO	AUDIO
EVENT #1110 STILL: GRAPHIC: TEXT: SIMULATION—[SIMULATION OF FLAMES UNDER CYLINDER OF WATER, COOLING FAN, SHOW WATER TEMPERATURE, RAISE AND LOWER FLAMES FUNCTION, SHOW CONDUCTION OF HEAT AND TEMPERATURE TO MASS OF CYLINDER, LABEL CONDUCTION, SHOW CONVECTION TO AIR ABOVE, TEMPERATURE, LABEL CONVECTION. RAISE AND LOWER HEAT PROMPTS]	

Source: From "DuPont Refrigeration Video Disc-Script," written
by Glen Grabenstetter, produced by Jack Noon, president MIDI,
Inc., directed by Tom Barnett, interactive programmers Greg Feliz,
Steve Saporta and Ken Rosenblad, for The DuPont Co. Used by
permission.

IMPLICATIONS FOR THE WRITER

Clearly, writing scripts for an interactive training program using a videodisc, computer and software package requires conceptual and organizational skills quite distinct from those needed for straightforward linear presentations. In addition to writing a script, the writer performs the role of a program designer (or works with an instructional designer) to assess the training task, set instructional objectives and format the array of interactions and reinforcements necessary to impart new information and assess the learner's comprehension.

Collaboration

Although the writer will not actually program computer software or translate film/video frames into videodisc index numbers, he or she will certainly need to understand how these processes interrelate and what capabilities and limitations are inherent in the hardware/software package in use.

As one experienced group of videodisc producers wrote, "Probably more than any other discipline in Training and Development, IVD production requires a team of individuals with varied backgrounds, experiences and skills. Among these are video producers, instructional designers, writers, software engineers, audio and video technicians, quality control specialists and graphics designers."[3]

**Figure 13.7: Flow Chart for Technical
Training Videodisc (Cont.)**

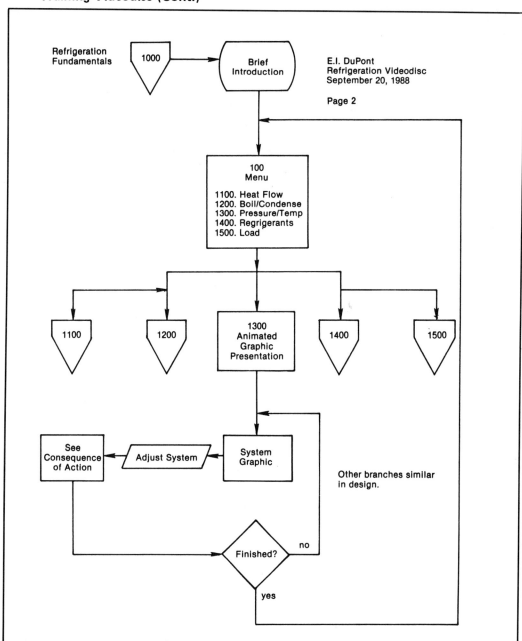

Source: Flowchart used for E.I. DuPont Refrigeration videodisc.

Figure 13.8: Interactive Flowchart Symbols

Symbol	Indicates
	Video motion
	Video still
	Go to or come from
	Tag: used to name a certain sequence that is frequently accessed
	Subroutine: a self-contained unit that is accessed and then returns the viewer to the main body of the program

Figure 13.8: Interactive Flowchart Symbols (Cont.)

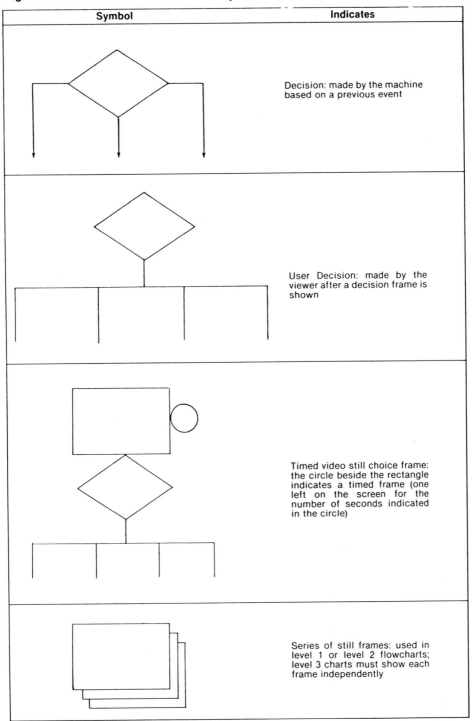

Symbol	Indicates
	Decision: made by the machine based on a previous event
	User Decision: made by the viewer after a decision frame is shown
	Timed video still choice frame: the circle beside the rectangle indicates a timed frame (one left on the screen for the number of seconds indicated in the circle)
	Series of still frames: used in level 1 or level 2 flowcharts; level 3 charts must show each frame independently

Figure 13.8: Interactive Flowchart Symbols (Cont.)

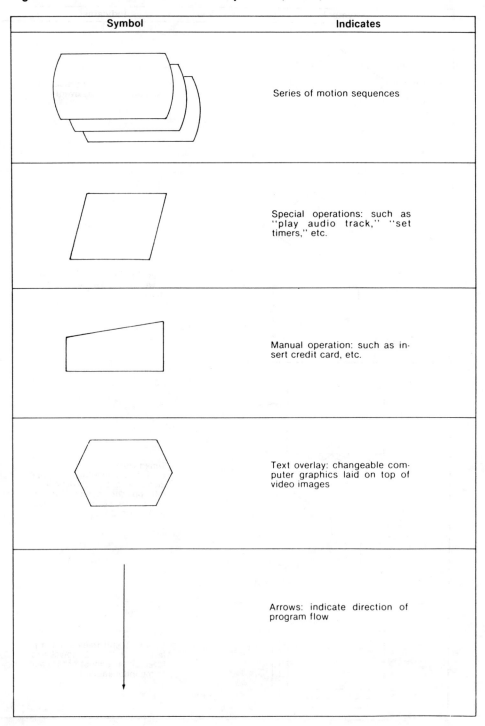

Symbol	Indicates
	Series of motion sequences
	Special operations: such as "play audio track," "set timers," etc.
	Manual operation: such as insert credit card, etc.
	Text overlay: changeable computer graphics laid on top of video images
	Arrows: indicate direction of program flow

Figure 13.8: Interactive Flowchart Symbols (Cont.)

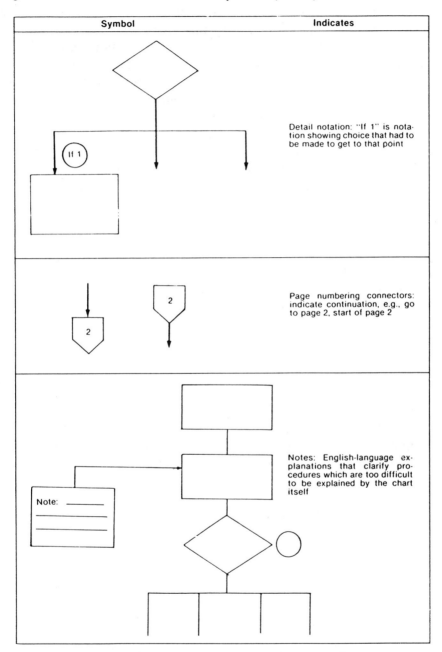

Source: *A Practical Guide to Interactive Video Design,* by Nicholas
V. Iuppa. White Plains, NY: Knowledge Industry Publications, Inc.,
1984. Used by permission.

But whether the initial assessment of training problems, skills to be taught, etc., is done by the instructional designer, the writer or both, the process begins with the same vigorous, up-front effort discussed in the Assimilation section. And the program designer's products should also include an analytical audience profile, instructional objectives (relating to the skills to be taught and stated in behavioral terms), content outline and creative treatment. In addition, interactive program design documents generally include a design worksheet (see Figure 13.9).

The design worksheet is used to organize the content into structural sequences and strategies. Such worksheets are useful in communicating the overall structure and instructional strategies you're recommending. It's an important "checkpoint" document since the more detailed flowchart used by writers, graphic artists, TV director and software programmers evolves from the design worksheet.

Differences in Scripting Interactively

I once heard Jack Noon, President of MIDI, an interactive video production firm in Princeton, NJ, organize a presentation by describing what he considered the main differences facing producers of an interactive videodisc project. He listed the following topics on a flip chart:

1. Continuity
2. Flowcharting
3. Dual Audio Tracks
4. Production Graphics vs. Computer Graphics
5. Single Frame Capabilities
6. MAP (Determining what and where information is placed on the videodisc master, since the program has no natural linear order or sequence.)
7. Discipline

Of these seven items, all but one have direct implications for the scriptwriter.

Continuity

The problem of continuity results from interactive video's most significant strength—branching. The ability to vary content based on the learner's responses makes this teaching machine highly flexible and individualized while ensuring a level of consistency. For the writer, however, each branching point involves scripting several different transitions. Return to the flowchart sample in Figure 13.7. In order to move from the user's decision point to each of the 5 possible branches, the writer must successfully negotiate 5 different transitions.

Figure 13.9: Major Segments of the Design Worksheet

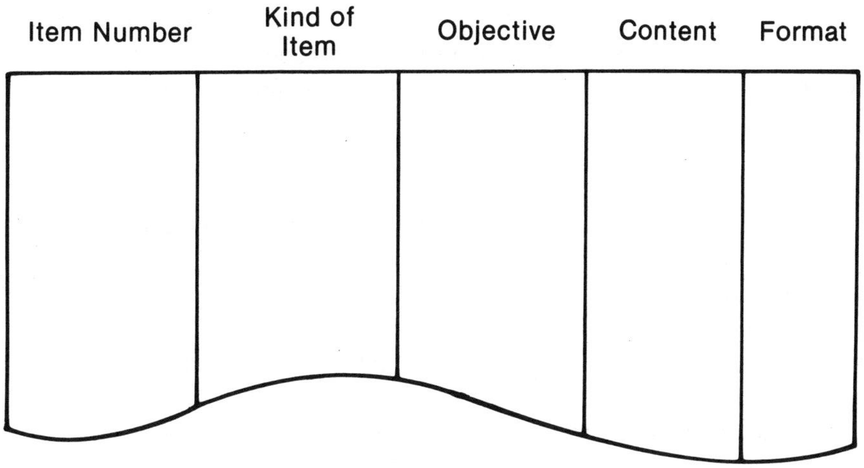

Item number: A breakdown of the instructional sequences—usually a number followed by a letter followed by a number, etc.   The letter-number "combo" allows you to identify parts of the same item, such as different feedback sequences relating to the same exercise.

Kind of item: The major kinds of items include demonstration, exercise question, correct feedback, incorrect feedback, etc.

Objective: Tells the purpose of each item. Usually the objective only applies to each full item, e.g., Item 1, rather than the parts of the item; 1.A., 1.B., etc.

Content: A complete statement of the content presented in each part of an item. It can be an outline of the kind of activity taking place, or suggested words for the item itself. For example, "Customer: 'These bills are kind of wrinkled.' Teller: 'You mean you want all new money.' "

Format: The way the content is presented, for example, still frame, motion sequence, motion followed by still frame, etc.

Source: *A Practical Guide to Interactive Video Design,* by Nicholas V. Iuppa, White Plains, NY: Knowledge Industry Publications, Inc., 1984. Used by permission.

Equally important, and often tougher, are the transitions necessary to go forward from each individual branch to the *next* viewing segment or transition the viewer back to the previous instructional block for review.

Such transitions must be transparent to the videodisc user. (Ironically, the user should actually enjoy a *linear* viewing experience of his/her own creation.) Transitions should appear seamless so that the user focuses solely on content, never aware of the designer's machinations which would only intrude on the learning process.

Flowcharting

Flowcharting is also a natural outgrowth of branching and a key step in ensuring "global" continuity. The flowchart provides the structural spine for everything that happens within a videodisc presentation. As such, every possible video/computer happening and the various training activities must be included in the flowchart. Flowcharts communicate decision points, branching and the flow of information.

Interactive production specialists agree that "designing flowcharts requires three basic characteristics: a logical mind, tremendous patience and strict attention to detail."[4] Sounds like the requirements for any type of writing.!

Specific interactive video flowchart symbols are shown in Figure 13.8. It's my belief the flowcharting process is facilitated by making the floor your work area and using index cards as a tool to develop the organic growth of the program's interactions, decision points and competency gates. (One symbol, and one symbol only, per card.)

Dual Audio Tracks

With IVD you can use different words and music to describe the same picture or video scene—that's the essence of dual audio tracks in interactive video. (Obviously, this does not work with on-camera talent.) It's one way of providing more detail, or a different explanation for a review of identical video information. It's a new tool in the writer's kit.

Production Graphics versus Computer Graphics

Everyone who owns a personal computer knows what computer-generated graphics look like. Unless you're using a high-end PC with a sophisticated graphics program, PC generated graphics are limited in style and detail.

By contrast, large dedicated computer-generated video production graphics came into their own in the late 1980s. Today even modest video production companies are offering state-of-the-art computer graphics capabilities. These generally permit simple animation techniques and/or three-dimensional modeling, which give graphic artists a tool to build and manipulate images in a variety of useful, revealing ways. (See examples in Chapter 7.)

Other sophisticated graphics programs, known as "paint-boxes," provide video artists the capability to create video images in more realistic styles, using "electronic air brush" techniques to mold soft contours as opposed to the hard edges of simpler computer graphics.

Furthermore, these computer graphics devices can take input from other video sources, giving designers and artists the opportunity to use still graphics, live video still frames and other sources of input limited only by one's imagination.

This does not mean personal computer graphics or on-screen type would never appear in an IVD production. Iuppa offers this rule-of-thumb: Rely on computer graphics. . .

> "Whenever the information is subject to change. . .
>
> "Whenever the system is displaying words or numbers entered by the user. . .
>
> "Whenever a teaching exercise requires simulation of typing or word-entering behavior that cannot be simulated by multiple-choice or other limited keypad exercises.
>
> "For games or behavior simulations that require lightning-quick response time. The trick is to lay the computer image over the video image in such a way that it appears to be part of the video image."[5]

Discipline

Writers are notorious for the pitiful state of their manuscripts. Clearly, interactive video requires greater discipline than many writers are accustomed to.

Granted, word processors make our final drafts immaculate in today's electronic writing world. And in most tasks, word processing encourages a certain freedom. Most writers have known the flight of fancy that occurs when inspiration takes hold—we are airborne. Before we know it, the writing takes on a life all its own. We become pleasantly surprised by the unpredictable results. And the end is never really in sight until we arrive.

Such spontaneous "free writing" is often encouraged as a way to generate first-draft material. Later, after this "passion hot" period, we turn to "critic cold" and trim back the excesses.

With interactive video scripting, however, there is no room for "flights of fancy" and the luxury of "free writing." One is confined to the strictures of the flow chart. The freedom afforded by branching and its possibilities places a new "yoke" on the writer—new boundaries in the name of non-linear continuity. (Of course, as students of creativity know, boundaries and limitations are essential elements in crafting any creative product.) Jack Noon considers discipline a quality he looks for in interactive video writers—"you must script to precise time limitations. Many industrial writers are not very disciplined when it comes to the length of a program. If it's 22 minutes instead of 20, that's no problem in a linear program. But on an interactive disc, we can't use those extra two minutes."

Magic

Here's a final requirement not listed previously. The user's experience with interactive videodisc must always retain a magical quality. As Cohen, L'Allier and Stewart write: "the program has to be more than the obvious, more than the mundane, more than totally transparent. In other words, as in any creative work, there has to be at least some element that's beyond the audience's immediate grasp."[6]

In other words, simply walking viewers through a programmed instruction format with its array of multiple-choice answers, and then returning viewers to the identical content if they fail to proceed through a competency gate, is neither an imaginative nor instructionally sound use of IVD.

Assume for a moment that after presenting some original material on disc, we have a short quiz to test the learner's comprehension: a competency gate. If the learners fail to achieve a satisfactory score, they should not be sent back over the identical original material. After all, if they failed to grasp the concept originally, what's to say they'll understand any better the second time through?

Ideally, the content should be explained a second time, either in more detail or by using new analogies or metaphors, new audiovisual combinations—something to make the concept come to life in a more vivid way. It's also less patronizing to the viewer.

Training Benefits of Interactive Video

To summarize, interactive video offers the following benefits to trainers:

1. Increased achievement by learners through hands-on involvement.
2. The potential for interesting, motivational instructional materials.
3. Efficient, immediate means of testing the learner's comprehension.
4. Consistent presentation of materials to all learners.
5. Self-paced instruction to aid advanced or entry level learners.

6.   Remote location access to professional training.
7.   Cost effective when travel expenses, instructor time and classroom time are considered.

PUTTING IT ALL TOGETHER

Of all possible forms of audiovisual writing, IVD offers writers one of the most challenging and demanding experiences. Throughout our educational and business lives we've been rewarded for thinking and composing in linear sequences: beginnings, middles and ends. IVD offers the freedom of many different middles and beginnings and ends based not on *our* decision but upon the viewer's preferences. With IVD, we have the possibilities of non-linear structures combined with all the creative challenges inherent in maximizing those capabilities to meet client needs.

FOOTNOTES

1.   Nicholas V. Iuppa, *A Practical Guide to Interactive Video Design* (White Plains, NY: Knowledge Industry Publications, Inc., 1984), p. 3.
2.   Stephen L. Cohen, James J. L'Allier, and Douglas Stewart, "Interactive Videodisc—Then, Now, and Minutes from Now," *Training & Development Journal,* October, 1987.
3.   *Ibid.,* p. 33.
4.   Iuppa, op. cit., p. 25.
5.   Iuppa, op. cit., p. 11.
6.   Cohen, L'Allier, and Stewart, op. cit., p. 32.

14 Writing for Live Media

I remember an ITVA chapter meeting not long ago on comedy in corporate video. There were three presenters. First, a producer and writer showed some very funny corporate presentations. Second, a producer from Prudential Insurance Co. showed a video example from one of my scripts. (I have a hard time viewing my work with a group of peers. It's the problem of "claiming your writing," which I'll talk about more in Chapter 15.)

Then came the third presenter. A trio approached the podium. Their very entrance was highly theatrical. Within moments, it became clear they were doing a prepared skit, comedic, of course. Well, at first, the audience seemed to cringe collectively. "Oh, no—they're going to do something foolish," we all seemed to be thinking. Or, perhaps it was something more along the lines of "Let's hope this doesn't evolve into an audience participation thing. I'm not up to that."

Then a rather wonderful thing happened. Within minutes, we all relaxed and genuinely began to enjoy the experience. Here were people performing *live,* laying it all on the line—just for *us.* Their material was clever and relevant to the topic. At the conclusion, they drew a big round of applause, the biggest of the evening. And as a short group discussion took place, one younger member of the audience said, "You know, it's really amazing. Sometimes there's an impact to a live performance you just can't get from that little box over there," pointing to the monitor.

"What an electronic world kids grow up in today," I thought to myself. "They see thousands of hours of television before graduating from college, but how many live performances of theater or dance or even rock concerts do they get to experience?"

Clearly our youthful observer was on to something: the magic of *live* performance. The Greeks knew it as the theater of Dionysius. It held the same imaginative potential as American Indian storytellers spinning webs of wonder around moonlit campfires.

There's something compelling about living, breathing human beings performing just for other humans sharing the same space. No camera to get in the way. No editing. No special effects and glitz. (Well, yes, the Broadway musical does go overboard on the side of spectacle.)

That same magic is available to the media writer when developing material that will be delivered live. Generally, these presentations involve one of three events: live speeches, teleconferences and industrial stage shows.

SPEECHWRITING

Executive speechwriting is a craft in itself. Some writers even specialize in this field which probably is more closely aligned with public relations or corporate communications than media writing. However, suggestions for writing for the ear in Chapter 8 certainly apply to speech writing.

The audiovisual writer usually enters the scene when speakers use slides or other graphic materials as speech support. This may range from the most rudimentary, inexpensive aids, such as flip chart materials (popular in Pentagon and other governmental agency briefings) and overhead transparencies, to sophisticated computer-generated slides or other electronically produced visual aids using combinations of computer and television projection technology. In many instances, speech support consists of rather mundane but utilitarian visual content: charts, graphs, trend lines and, of course, text which uses key words and phrases in bulleted form. This is the only media writing assignment where it is sometimes appropriate to focus on narrative content first, then develop illustrative material to support that content. After all, in a speech, what the speaker wants to say must come first. Presentation graphics provide *support.*

Of course, if you have a highly visual creative concept which can enhance communication of content and help make the speech more memorable and effective, then by all means propose it and get the speaker's reaction. If positive, you can script text and speaker support graphics just as you might write a visuals and voice narration.

Role Models

If you're new to this kind of writing, look at famous speeches of statesmen, politicians, generals and others for a sense of the rhetoric required. Students interested in media writing should certainly take public speaking courses to learn the unique requirements speaking imposes on treatment and organization of content as well as the dramatic opportunities available to speakers in front of live audiences. (Audience size and the speaking occasion have a big impact on selection of appropriate tone and voice.)

A major difficulty in speech writing involves access to the speaker for input on content and, often just as important, a sense of the speaker's attitude, vocabulary, presence and verbal style. The acid test for a speech manuscript, as with any other writing for the ear, is to read copy aloud. If possible, sit in on the speaker's rehearsal of an early draft to look for ways of making the material his or her own.

THE INDUSTRIAL "SHOW"

Throughout this book, we've asked what role entertainment and show business can and should play in industrial, medical and educational media writing. Now we come to the most theatrical media writing of all: scripting material for live stage revues given to a specific audience—frequently on a one-time basis. These revues are generally featured at large motivational sales meetings, conventions or similar celebratory events.

People who do this type of writing are truly a rare breed. Imagine writing clever, catchy lyrics and tunes—about the latest model car, this year's blockbuster break-through cholesterol-reducing drug, or sales projections based on consumer demographics—and making them meaningful to the target audience.

Figure 14.1 is a sample of the type of material written for these shows.

Role Models

Advertising copywriters must craft clever lyrics about a product's features and benefits, or a bank's free checking plan, so you have role models available right on the car radio. Although lyric writing is beyond the scope of this book, you'll find a few "how to" titles listed in the bibliography. In addition to radio jingles, look to the theater itself, look to Gilbert and Sullivan, Stephen Sondheim (who wrote interesting, compelling lyrics about the creative process for *Sunday in the Park with George*), Andrew Lloyd Webber, Marvin Hamlisch, Mozart's inventive, ground-breaking operas, and all the great poets and playwrights. Grow "bigger ears" and listen critically for the narrative techniques, rhymes or "voice" in top-40 songs, jazz vocals, rhythm and blues, country and folk singers. They all tell stories (sometimes complex and philosophical ones) in two to three minutes through lyrics set to music.

Lyric writing is a highly disciplined form in which theme, content, rhythm, rhyme, word play and pizzaz must all come together. When it works, it all seems so simple, honest and direct—"heart to heart as the crow flies," as a country and western singer, Tom Russell, wrote.

Furthermore, there *are* opportunities for this kind of writing (book or lyrics) and the pay is probably significantly above the average for the media writing field. Most of the work, however, comes from talent pools in New York, Chicago and Los Angeles. As with instructional drama, it's probably tough to break into unless you have a strong theater background, know somebody's cousin or have a portfolio of successful advertising tunes and jingles. But if you're compulsively attracted to writ-

Figure 14.1: Example of Industrial Show Material

MUSICAL COMEDY FORMAT

Meeting Design and Show Elements

a. **The Speakers**

Company Executives and selected Guest Speakers will carry the major thrust of this meeting through educational, informative, and motivational presentations.

b. **A Professional Cast**

A Cast of 6 performers will be on hand to provide all the entertainment, bridging and connecting sequences throughout the entire course of the meeting and any special events.

c. **Music and Orchestra**

The music will consist of six pre-recorded songs with original music and lyrics. A live 6–10 piece orchestra will also be on hand to play the show and to provide musical support for any other events during the meeting. (Note: Parodies would also be used instead of original music.)

d. **Audiovisual Support**

For an audience of this size, we recommend a large 10-foot by 30-foot rear projection screen, which would provide most of the scenic background for the skits and songs, as well as the use of multi-image projections for modules and speech support.

We will, of course, use a totally computerized, fail-safe state-of-the-art projection system.

e. **Stage Setting**

One of the best ways to let your audience know that something exciting is about to happen the moment they enter the meeting room is with a high-impact and spectacular stage setting and design. Such a set will capture the expectations and style of this meeting.

A meeting that shows the company is once again

"A STEP BEYOND"

Figure 14.1: Example of Industrial Show Material (Cont.)

as this Theme is reflected in the handsome mylar set and emblazoned on the large AV screen.

f. **Show Flow for Musical Comedy Format**

1. **Opener**

   A rousing opening number. . .entitled "A STEP BEYOND" or. . ."A NEW BEGINNING" would set the stage for this landmark meeting. This upbeat song, sung by our cast of 6 and backed up by appropriate visuals, would provide a strong multi-media kickoff of the theme and meeting.

   > WE'RE MOVING OUT
   > WE'RE MOVING ON
   > GOT A GREAT NEW OPPORTUNITY
   >   AND WE'RE GONNA RESPOND
   > WE'RE IN THE RACE
   > AND WE'RE GONNA SET THE PACE
   > 'CAUSE NOW THAT WE'VE GOT THE PRODUCT
   >   WE ARE A STEP BEYOND.
   > A STEP BEYOND
   > A STEP BEYOND.

   At the conclusion of this number, one of the cast, a mature, personable male in his early thirties, who can readily be associated with the Sales Force, and who will serve as the Spokesman throughout the show, will then bridge and introduce the Meeting Host who will welcome the audience and then introduce the first speaker.

   #4. Bridge #1 "SALES REP HEAVEN"

   Here our cast would find themselves in a wonderful, out of this world, celestial place. Finally they recognize that they are in:

   > HEAVEN, HEAVEN
   > PHARMACEUTICAL SALES HEAVEN
   > WHERE EVERYTHING'S A. O. K.
   >
   > HEAVEN, HEAVEN
   > PHARMACEUTICAL HEAVEN
   > WHERE EVERYTHING'S DONE OUR WAY.
   >
   > DELIVERIES AND SHIPMENTS ARE A JOY TO BEHOLD
   > AND WE'RE PRICED SO COMPETITIVELY WE'RE

Figure 14.1: Example of Industrial Show Material (Cont.)

```
        NEVER UNDERSOLD
A BONUS EVERY MONTH IS SIMPLY PAR FOR THE COURSE
AND RETAIL WORK IS HANDLED BY A MERCHANDISE
        FORCE.

PROMOTIONS ARE CREATIVE AND THEY'RE THERE ON
        DUE DATE.
WHEN WE ASK FOR UNIT DOSAGES THEY NEVER ARE
        LATE
YOU NEVER HEAR A SINGLE WORD 'BOUT CUTTING
        EXPENSE,
AND OUR CLINICAL PEOPLE NEVER EVER SIT ON THE
        FENCE.

HERE IN PHARMACEUTICAL SALES HEAVEN
WE JUST GO WITH THE FLOW.
HERE IN OUR SALES FORCE HEAVEN
MANAGEMENT NEVER SAYS NO.
        HO HO HO HO
        HO HO HO HO
        NO NO NO NO
        NO NO NO NO
```

This song would then be developed to capture all those daily problems that would be eliminated in a Sales Force Heaven—unnecessary paperwork, no minimum amounts to sell, etc. . . .and other "inside" frustrations, which we would get from researching with the company.

The number would then build to a climax by pointing out that one of the great things in Sales Rep Heaven would be to have a breakthrough new Beta Blocker that would get us into that big $900 million market.

The Host would then introduce *Speaker #3*.

#6. Bridge #2 "BREAKING THROUGH THE CLUTTER"

This song/multi-media segment will perhaps start out as an AV Module showing how various winners throughout history—such as Sinatra in music, Picasso in art, O.J. Simpson in football, Campbell in soups plus several "drugs of choice" have managed to break through the clutter of existing competition to become the recognized leader and #1 choice.

Once this is established, our cast will then come out to sing

Figure 14.1: Example of Industrial Show Material (Cont.)

WE'RE MAKING OUR MOVE
WE'RE GOT THE KIND OF DATA
THAT'S GONNA BREAK THROUGH IT ALL
AND MAKE COMPETITION SCATTER.

'CAUSE NOW THAT THE PRODUCTS' HERE
COMPETITION'S GONNA SHUDDER
'CAUSE WE'VE GOT THE PRODUCT
TO BREAK THROUGH ALL THE CLUTTER.

This number will then continue to set-up the competitive marketplace and lead to the Host introducing *Speaker #4.*

#8. Bridge #3   Into Coffee Break

A skit into a song into the Coffee Break

#10 Bridge #4   "CREDIBILITY"
                    WE ARE THE FORMULARY COMMITTEE

In this skit and song, we will capture the humor, the problems and the difficulties encountered in selling the Formulary Committees—and/or various doctors—in a humorous way.

For example, after establishing the various members of a Formulary Com-Committee, they all come together and sing:

THE FORMULARY COMMITTEE ARE WE
IT'S A SIMPLE NAME
BUT SELLING US IS A BRAND NEW GAME
LET'S HEAR IT FROM THE HEAD OF CARDIOLOGY.

FIRST THERE'S [competing company names]
I GET SO MANY PITCHES, MY RIGHT EAR'S GONE
    DEAF.
SO IF YOU WANT A CARDIOLOGIST LIKE ME TO TRY
    YOUR DRUG FOR HYPERTENSION
YOU GOTTA *PROVE* TO ME THAT YOUR DRUG OFFERS
    A WHOLE NEW DIMENSION

We would then hear from other members of the formulary committee who all voice their particular points of view and then sing—

Figure 14.1: Example of Industrial Show Material (Cont.)

THE MORAL TO THIS STORY
IS VERY PLAIN TO SEE
THOUGH WE'RE COMING FROM A DIFFERENT SENSIBILITY,
THE BOTTOM LINE IS ONE ON WHICH
WE ALL CAN AGREE
WE ARE SIMPLY ASKING YOU
FOR CREDIBILITY.

YOU SAY YOU GOT A BRAND NEW PRODUCT
THAT IS REALLY GREAT
WELL, BE SURE YOU'VE GOT THE RESEARCH
THAT IS FAR BEYOND DEBATE
WE WANNA KNOW FOR CERTAIN
THAT WHAT YOU'RE SAYING'S TRUE
JUST AS WE WANT TO KNOW
THAT WE CAN COUNT ON YOU.

At the end of this number the Host introduces the Clinical/Medical
Segment.

Source: From a sales meeting proposal by Ed Nayor for The O'Hara
Company. Used by permission.

ing for the musical theater, developing a commercial bent is a good way to support
your "habit" while peddling your pure music works.

TELECONFERENCING

Here's an interesting "hybrid" medium. On the one hand, two-way videoconferencing and business television can be thought of simply as television. The only
distinguishing characteristic is it's distribution form—the use of satellites for multi-
point distribution to several cities or locations simultaneously.[1]

The live quality of a teleconference, as well as the potential for two-way interaction between receiving and sending locations, provides unique opportunities for
communication.

Teleguide, A Handbook on Video-Teleconferencing offers the following
description:

1. A video teleconference is a television program produced using conventional
    television technologies and techniques.
2. The program originates live.

3. The program is transmitted to one or more places where it is viewed, usually, but not always, by groups gathered just for the occasion.
4. Viewers have opportunities to place telephone calls to the originating location to ask questions or make statements "on-air," or to have their question or statement noted and addressed later in the program.[2]

Typically, a teleconference is the medium chosen when a geographically dispersed organization needs to communicate a consistent message to several locations as quickly as possible. The cost of teleconferencing is sometimes offset by savings in travel as well as the capability to deliver a memorable message with a single presentation. A teleconference, for example, is often chosen as the optimum way to introduce a new product to a sales force. Regional or district meetings can be scheduled across the country and the corporate or organizational headquarters personnel can make their presentations from a central studio location in or near the home office.

Ad Hoc and Private Satellite Networks

A video teleconference can be produced on a one-time, "ad hoc" basis by any company or organization. Since the elements required for production and distribution are not in place as a ready-made system, all elements (personnel, satellites, receiving stations, etc.) have to be contracted for and coordinated for the one event.

Dedicated networks, by contrast, are owned by companies and organizations in-house or have been formed as for-profit networks offering daily programming aimed at specific industry segments. A recent *Business Week* article counted "61 satellite-based business TV networks, up from four in 1983. . . .Industry observers expect that by 1992 there will be 141 (dedicated teleconferencing) networks."[3] ComputerLand Corp., for example, trains repairers at 106 sites instead of sending them to class. The Automotive Satellite Network (ASTN) is among the largest and broadcasts to 3000 subscribing dealerships.

At first, the use of a teleconference may be novel enough to hold employee audience attention. But as with every other media application, once the novelty wears off, audiences demand a higher level of quality in production design and execution.

What's Different about Teleconferencing?

Aside from the mode of distribution, two qualities make a teleconference different from other types of media programming:

1. It is *live* television, with all the pluses and minuses of live, studio switched productions, and. . .

2.   Generally, it is *interactive* television in that audiences have an opportunity to respond through one-way video and two-way audio systems.

How do these traits affect scriptwriters? First, the writer's role is not limited to scriptwriting. Usually, the writer must become involved in all the up-front analysis and planning essential to coordinate live teleconferences and produce the voluminous proposals, show-flow run-downs and other conceptual or planning documents. (Typically, these documents include the same writing products described in the Assimilation and Rehearsal periods: objectives, audience analysis, content outline and treatment.) As the teleconference draws closer to production and air date, the writer obviously scripts some, but not all, of the material.

Implications for Writers

The key to a successful teleconference, from a creative point of view, is to achieve a proper balance between scripted, pre-produced material and the spontaneous live segments. Obviously, some teleconference program segments can be fully scripted and involve either professional or non-professional talent, based on message, audience and objectives. By contrast, the program structure must also allow for the heightened and shared interest, give-and-take and interactive qualities of a live teleconference unfolding in real time on air date.

Generally, elements such as the program opening, major transitions, speaker introductions and closing segments can be fully scripted and, many times, pre-produced as roll-ins on air date. Speaker support may or may not be pre-recorded depending on the nature of the visual material. Frequently, visual and voice clips showing action outside the studio (say a product being manufactured at the plant or installed on location) can be a pre-produced, free-standing module.

However, pre-produced video segments can sometimes be more subtle, seamlessly integrated into live video action. For instance, I once worked on a teleconference which involved physician interviews. Unfortunately, not all of the physicians were available to appear live on the air date. By pre-taping on-location interviews with an off-camera interviewer, the director edited roll-ins of physicians' answers which then appeared in a screen area as though the physicians were being interviewed by someone live in the studio. (The visual and psychological effect is the same as watching Ted Koppel's "Nightline" interviews. The live feel is simulated through a seamless integration of studio interviewer and location interviewees.) This effect is probably best left in the hands of a professional studio narrator with the acting ability and sense of timing to give the interview a sense that it is happening live.

Another example: the same teleconference used pre-produced dramatic vignettes which, because of the product and theme, revolved around a "Star Trek" parody. At one point in these sequences, look-alike actors for Dr. Spock were "beamed down" to appear magically and in-person at *each* one of the receiving sites. A period followed in which each "Dr. Spock" had a brief interaction with the local audience.

From a production standpoint, pre-produced segments should be shot on video-tape rather than film to maintain a live presence. Electronic video pictures signify a present tense while the photographic film image signifies past tense. If motion picture material is incorporated into a teleconference, it will be more clearly perceived as a "canned" element.

In addition to pre-produced material, however, teleconferences will have un-scripted, free-flowing segments in which content points are covered extemporaneously through panels, interviews or question and answer periods.

Two-way Audio

Two-way audio is a practical way to make audience members at diverse locations participate in the live experience. Each location is wired for taking questions or com-ments from audience members over telephone hook-ups, the same technique that is used in broadcast talk shows by Donahue and Oprah Winfrey.

This interactive technique is often employed through question and answer periods after key content has been communicated by content experts and/or pre-produced roll-ins. In the case of a new product introduction, for example, the field sales force audience might be given the opportunity to direct questions to a panel of content experts who have delivered their prepared material. The panel might consist of the inventor, the product manager, the marketing manager, sales promotion manager, and vice president of sales.

The teleconference can be a powerful way to use the medium of television to reach a geographically dispersed audience, so all receive a consistent message on a single day, while retaining some benefits of a larger meeting at a single location (e.g., the ability to ask questions through two-way audio).

The documents in Figure 14.2 illustrate the type of writing products script-writers generate in the planning and conceptual phase of conceiving a teleconference.

As more companies and organizations discover ways in which video telecon-ferencing can serve their individual communication or training needs, media writers will need to understand the special features and benefits of this form of distribution and be prepared to employ the medium to reach specific goals and objectives.

Figure 14.2:   Sample Teleconference Launch Action Plan

TELECONFERENCE RATIONALE

In all likelihood the company will be launching three major products in the remainder of the year. Two are planned as live national meetings while (product) will be a one-of-a-kind live satellite teleconference.

Precedents have been established on speakers (internal and external), various topics and the use of audiovisual modules to add interest, drama and creativity to the production. These established formats, however, could become repetitive. This repetition tends to be accentuated when launch meetings are carried out within a few months of one another.

As a satellite teleconference, we believe the company has a unique opportunity to use video in a way which is more integrated and powerful than more traditional multi-image modules. (For specifics on the approach, see the Videotape Teleplay Treatment.)

Teleconferencing Background

Closed-circuit telecasts have been a part of the television communications scene for more than thirty years. The evolution has run from electronic distribution and exhibition of boxing matches to other sporting events, theater, opera, concerts and the like. In the past decade, satellite videoconferencing has played an increasingly important role in business, industry and medicine for both sales and corporate communications as well as a way to reach customers. As the uses of the medium have multiplied, so have production complexities.

Success in videoconference production is based on the effective combination of many elements, customized specifically to each project. This includes knowledge of when and how to employ redundant systems, the strengths and weaknesses of equipment and personnel, an understanding of the needs of the client and the viewers, an ability to communicate effectively, and unequaled attention to detail.

To integrate these elements professionally, within budget and on schedule, The O'Hara Company will contract with JOCOM International on your behalf for technical/logistical teleconferencing support.

TELECONFERENCING LOGISTICS

Technically, the live teleconference network will consist of one originating region (Chicago or Cincinnati) transmitting video and audio to the remaining seven regional headquarters. . .

Figure 14.2:   Sample Teleconference Launch Action Plan (Cont.)

Originating Region: **Receiving Regions**

Cincinnati   Chicago
                                           Atlanta
                                           Baltimore
                                           Dallas
                                           Denver
                                           Los Angeles
                                           New York

Meeting Site Facility Criteria

1. Sleeping rooms for 75 people for two nights (preferably in one hotel rather than being scattered throughout the city).
2. A large 6000-foot ballroom for three days in Cincinnati which will accommodate 100 people and the TV equipment.
3. Four conference rooms for one day.
4. Large room for dinner for 100 people for two nights.
5. Large room for lunch for 100 people for one day.

Two-way audio will be used to link the receiving regions to the originating city, allowing the conference to be genuinely interactive and provide the entire sales force with a sense of local participation. This high-tech communication medium reflects state-of-the-art technology. It will be unlike any other company launch meeting which may take place during 1987 or early 1988. That in itself serves as an affirmation that the product is *One Step Beyond* in every conceivable aspect.

Technical Aspects

Success in videoconference production results from the effective coordination of many elements, customized specifically for the product launch. This includes the knowledge of when and how to employ redundant systems, the strengths and weaknesses of equipment and personnel, an understanding of the needs of the client and the viewers, the ability to communicate effectively and unequaled attention to detail.

The O'Hara Company will assemble the video production and teleconferencing team with the combined expertise to assure an exciting, well-planned and technically competent coordination of events—from initial planning to execution. The O'Hara Company will work closely with to integrate all these elements professionally, within budget and on schedule.

The following provides an overview of the elements which will be developed and produced in a time frame which assumes a late summer/early fall launch date.

Figure 14.2:   Sample Teleconference Launch Action Plan (Cont.)

Pre-production Planning and Scripting

Up-front editorial planning is essential to develop the content and audiovisual support necessary to maximize the communication opportunity. Live versus taped program segments will be identified and scripted accordingly.

In addition to executive presentations, exciting, videotaped modules will be created to kick off the meeting with plenty of punch and sustain such excitement throughout the launch meeting. Pre-taped modules require production prior to the meeting date, so these elements must be planned, scripted and produced well in advance of the launch date.

Equipment

We suggest three color cameras, a digital effects generator, a character generator, a random-access still store and other videotape equipment as required for visual inserts and recording.

JOCOM will provide two broadcast-quality 1-in. videotape recorders to make a continuous high-quality recording of the entire program. In addition, we will make a simultaneous 3/4-in. U-matic recording and a 1/4-in. audio recording for future transcription services.

Production of Pre-taped Segments

As video modules and executive presentations are developed, those intended for pre-taped transmission will be produced as high-quality video modules prepared for transmission over the network on launch day.

Prompting/Coaching and Rehearsal

JOCOM will use one entire day for studio preparation, set, lighting and camera positioning. Production meetings with the studio staff will be held to coordinate the various technical requirements and schedule.

The "shoot day" will begin with camera blocking and includes a full dress rehearsal, with visual materials and pre-recorded tapes or films. A mock Q & A period will give the participants an opportunity to practice fielding questions and help develop a pace for the telecast to follow.

With the exception of the Q & A period, live and pre-taped segments will be fully scripted. Dry runs will be integrated into the schedule to insure all participants are comfortable with the content of the teleconference as well as their individual participation.

Figure 14.2:   Sample Teleconference Launch Action Plan (Cont.)

Site Selection/Engineering Field Coordination

As discussed, we will give Regional Managers the option of selecting the hotel in their area they believe most suitable for hosting the event. As soon as the date and host hotels are designated, we will initiate site surveys to personally visit each proposed location, meeting with the site account representatives and other technical or service representatives as may be needed. The field engineer will assess each site in terms of size, ceiling height, accessibility, sound, lights and other elements which affect local reception/participation.

Exhibition: The GEMINI Concept

As a way of dramatizing the transition between the Starship [See Videotape Teleplay Treatment] and executive presentations, we propose use of two large-screen color television projectors at each receiving location. One screen could be used to display the science fiction "entertaining" portion of the meeting, the second used to deliver executive material.

Variations on this could include having an executive or physician appear on one screen—speaker support slides and graphics on the second screen. Or, perhaps one screen shows the Starship, while the second displays the competition's alien control center. At key moments, people could walk from one screen to the second, or be electronically "beamed" from one screen to the other.

Technically, this would be done by providing two separate television pictures from the Cincinnati site. Transmission would require an additional uplink aimed at the same satellite as the first uplink. Two different transponders on the same satellite would carry the two signals. Downlinking involves the addition of another receiver at the same dish. The dishes are redundant, so one more receiver provides two-channel reception with a backup.

We normally recommend one 6 ft. by 8 ft. screen with a backup, so we normally have two. A third screen would function as backup. The two screens side by side will give an overall display of 6 x 16 feet.

We will have each projector/screen delivered, checked out and placed in each location as early as feasible. We will evaluate and recommend those projectors which will be best for each individual viewing application, based on audience size, room dimensions, lighting conditions, etc.

Graphic Design/Sets and Room Decoration

As part of the pre-planning process, we will develop a graphic "signature" for the product and the meeting theme of *One Step Beyond.* These graphics will function as room decor not only from the original site, but as an integral part of the communication at each regional facility.

Figure 14.2:   Sample Teleconference Launch Action Plan (Cont.)

Transmission

The television signal will be transmitted, audio and video, via satellite from the originating hotel to each of the viewing sites. We will provide a separate communications and network control center at the originating location for immediate status assessment of all telecast elements. This will include a network status board and provide a means of communication to each city moderator.

In as many instances as possible, we will use satellite receiving dishes to receive the signal. In congested areas, we will use a microwave system. JOCOM will make all transmission arrangements.

JOCOM System of Q & A

Both the logistical technique and technical quality of two-way communications have been the subject of JOCOM's innovative leadership. Through a formulated method of question submission, we will be able to make random city assignments and control the thrust of the subject matter to ensure equal representation from each network location.

REGIONAL MANAGERS' PREVIEW

Approximately two to three weeks before the launch date, Regional Managers will meet for an overview briefing. At this overview, all meeting elements will be previewed to generate excitement and enthusiasm for the upcoming telecast.

This overview will take the form of a "train-the-trainer" workshop so Regional Managers are fully briefed on the logistics of the teleconference and overall content and flow of the meeting, as well as their role working with District Managers in workshop break-out sessions.

At this meeting, they will receive master copies of the executive talks and videotaped modules. They will also receive a briefing on the technical logistics of the teleconference and procedures to follow to sign on to the teleconference network.

ROOM DECOR AND LOCAL PARTICIPATION

The local environment is a key factor in creating the sense of participation which is possible with a live teleconference. Through this local environment, each of the receiving cities will have a sense of participating in a larger event. Here are some of the ideas we have for generating this sense of excitement at the local level. . . .

Figure 14.2:   Sample Teleconference Launch Action Plan (Cont.)

Entrance Tunnel

This special entrance to each regional meeting room is designed to help create excitement and a sense of local involvement. The entrance tunnels are part room decor, part audiovisual display areas. As participants file into the room, they physically traverse a special passageway.

Each passageway consists of strategically placed video monitors which are used to preview upcoming events. For example, here are some of the visual "mood setters" which could appear on the video monitors:

A three-dimensional starfield to simulate the sense of space travel.
A revolving, rotating, pulsating product monolith—a three-
   dimensional rendering of the product presentation visualization.
A view of Planet O-B-G-Y-N.
A shot of the Starship traveling through space.
A digital countdown clock displaying the minutes and seconds until the
   next satellite transmission.

In addition, the tunnel would consist of special audio messages, coming either from the video monitors or from speakers built into the passageway. Audio messages would be brief mood-setters, teasing the Sales Reps about what is to come. . .

"Escape—go to another dimension. Experience the existence of life on another planet."

"Journey—come with us on a voyage beyond the outer limits of the pharmaceutical universe."

"Travel—take one step beyond and move ahead of the competitive clutter."

Throughout the main show day, the entrance passageway video and audio environment will be changed prior to each major assembly and satellite transmission, updating the local participants on the progress of the meeting.

Handling of Local Q&A—The Beam Down!

This exciting moment climaxes the day's live satelite television transmission. It is a take-off on an old magic trick intended to break the artificial barrier between transmitting location and all receiving locations. Here's how it works:

Just prior to the local Q & A session, the dramatic vignette will be written so that Mr. Crock is to beam down to a special location for a secret mission. Since he

Figure 14.2:   Sample Teleconference Launch Action Plan (Cont.)

must journey to several locations at once, the final video effect is a "cloning" of Crock, a video special effect which allows him to appear as nine individual Crocks. Then, these nine Mr. Crocks prepare to beam down for the secret mission.

At this moment, the local sets featuring a beam down area are activated. Lights and smoke appear—and presto! Mr. Crock now appears live at each location. He takes a microphone and leaps into the audience. Mr. Crock now becomes the local "Phil Donahue" at each location, working the audience for questions and becoming the interface between mission control and the local regional sites.

The "piece de resistance" comes at the conclusion of the question and answer session. At that time, each Mr. Crock prepares to beam back up to the Starship. But before leaving, each selects one Sales Representative from the audience to beam up with him. (These people will be pre-chosen, based on the fact that they will have appeared in a pre-taping of the final dramatic vignette.)

At the appropriate moment, Mr. Crock and the local Sales Representative enter the beaming device and with the appropriate special effects soon appear all together on the Starship. With representatives from each region joined together, they participate in the final battle scenes against the competition—dramatizing that the real battles will be waged and won by the company sales force.

Source: From a sales meeting proposal by William Van Nostran for the O'Hara Company. Used by permission.

FOOTNOTES

1. The International Teleconferencing Association (ITCA) Program Committee suggests the following teleconferencing industry definitions:

    Teleconferencing—an industry term that has become generic to incorporate three major forms—**audio, audiographic and video**—all have several factors in common.

    - they use a telecommunications channel and station equipment
    - they link individuals or groups at multiple locations
    - they are interactive, providing two-way communications
    - they are dynamic, involving the active participation of users
        - **Audioconferencing**—voice-only communication linking people in remote locations using ordinary telephone lines. Audio systems include telephone conference calls as well as more sophisticated systems that connect many locations via a central bridge that ties all lines together.
        - **Audiographics**—systems that transmit visual information (e.g., graphics, alphanumerics, documents, still video pictures) as an adjunct to voice communications. These devices can include electronic tablets and boards, freeze-frame video terminals, integrated graphic systems as part of personal computers and voice/data terminals.

— **Videoconferencing**–combines audio and video mediums to provide both voice communications and motion video images.

Two-way videoconferencing–a fully interactive audio and motion video medium creating a social presence between two locations that resembles face-to-face meetings.

Business Television–one-way broadcast via satellite to multiple locations with two-way interactive audio.

Teletraining/Distance Learning–the use of teleconferencing to convey educational and training information to participants geographically dispersed.

2. Doug Widner. *Teleguide, A Handbook on Teleconferencing.* (Washington, DC: Public Service Satellite Consortium, 1986), p. vii. An excellent source of newer information about all forms of teleconferencing is *The Teleconferencing Manager's Guide,* edited by Kathleen J. Hansell (White Plains, NY: Knowledge Industry Publications, Inc., 1989).
3. Kevin Kelly. "Why Business Is Glued to the Tube," *Business Week,* March 20, 1989, p. 160.

15 The Business of Writing for the New Media

Not long ago, I attended a local International Television Association (ITVA) session on the topic "Working with a Professional Writer." It was billed as an educational exchange between independent producers and freelance scriptwriters. One would expect the discussion to focus on the secrets of successful collaboration, ideas on how to increase rapport, to improve client service and produce more creative results.

There was some discussion of these topics. But not nearly so much as down-to-earth exchanges on more mundane issues. Like—why is it when writers ask for a third of their fee *in advance* to generate cash flow while doing research, conducting interviews and other start-up activities, payment rarely comes until weeks or months *after* submitting the initial invoice?

Or, why do some producers and clients expect writers to develop lengthy proposals on a speculative basis? "Writers are like any other persons providing a service—they deserve to be paid for their work!" was the view expressed by several writers. And, as a veteran scriptwriter stated, "Why should writers be asked to share in the producer's risks without also sharing in the eventual profits?"

I also attended another meeting—at the Writer's Guild of America's New York offices—to discuss the pros and cons of establishing minimum fees for nonbroadcast television writing. (In the 1970s, nonbroadcast writers were all but totally ignored by the Guild and its members, helping to foster a feeling we were outsiders.) Ironically, at the very time when opportunities and demand for imaginative, talented, disciplined scriptwriters is mushrooming, the relative youth and maverick nature of writing for the new media poses unique business considerations.

In this chapter, I'll comment on a variety of practical writing topics—from the creativity conundrum to writer's block, word processing, and staying sane. I'll begin by exploring how the growth of new media has spawned an industry which seems to teeter between profession and prostitution.

367

FEES FOR SERVICES

Case in point: the Writer's Guild (which has offices in Los Angeles and New York) currently includes writers of feature films, network dramas, sitcoms, broadcast journalists and news writers. When, in the late 1980s, network TV schedules were disrupted by several Writer's Guild strikes, one of the primary issues involved the writer's claim to revenues collected from rental and sale of home video releases. The home video market didn't even exist as early as 1979! So as new media earthquakes rumble, management/labor fault lines slowly shift to issues never considered before, causing disruptions in the marketplace and the incongruous picture of bearded writers in sneakers hefting picket signs as though they belonged to the Local Brotherhood of Electricians.

Although it's idealistic and romantic to think of writers, artists and other creative individuals as above the din of marketplace barter, the reality is quite the opposite. If you're writing for the new media, you've got to face these issues.

Fees versus Royalties

There are two types of programming produced for the new media:

1. Programs intended for internal audiences (employees or members of organizations) in which the message furthers corporate or organizational goals. The medium is a management tool.
2. Media programming which has value in the marketplace. In this case, the media product is itself a commercial commodity. Most of these media products fall into the category of training, informational and motivational films, videotapes and interactive videodiscs.

Typically, in the first category programs are written by staff scriptwriters or freelancers specializing in new media writing. Salaried staff writers should join the International Television Association (ITVA) and become members of its Scriptwriter's Special Interest Group. ITVA conducts annual salary surveys among the membership which provide a benchmark of where scriptwriters stand in relation to those doing similar work.

For freelance scriptwriters, determining fees, billing and collection procedures is part art and part luck. Writers charge clients based on hourly or daily rates or take assignments for a fixed fee which is not dependent on time devoted to the project.

I prefer to negotiate a fixed fee per project because I believe variables other than time affect my rate. Organizations vary in their capacity to pay for media production services. I expect Fortune 500 companies to pay more handsomely than local hospitals, non-profit organizations and most universities. Other considerations include:

1. Program use: If you develop a sales promotion program for a customer audience to support launch of a new product, the fee should be more than for similar work on a project for an internal employee audience on employee benefits. There is more at stake.

2. Program shelf life: Generally, programs with long shelf lives (a major training program, for instance) should pay more than a similar project with a one-time application (a quarterly video report on the state of the business).

Other factors influencing fees include the difficulty of the subject and its impact on the research and assimilation process, lead time and potential for overtime, visibility of the finished program within the organization (a major sales meeting versus a divisional orientation for example), and previous relationship with client.

When the media project results in a product with market value, then we enter the realm of fee versus royalty or profit-sharing participation. This area, I believe, is one which could best be subject to Writer's Guild contracts and guidelines. Of course, there is no reason why a scriptwriter could not negotiate a fixed fee or time-based participation for this work as well. However, when the writer creates the framework, creative concept and detailed shooting script for a training program which may make money through rental and licensing fees for years to come, it is often in the writer's best interest to negotiate for a percentage of sales.

Presently, there are no guidelines for such participation. For example, does the writer receive an advance against royalties? What about a reduced up-front fee in return for a percentage? Is the scriptwriter's percentage related to gross or net sales? Is there a bonus clause for a product which exceeds projections? Is the writing done on a work-made-for-hire basis or does the writer own the copyright? In most cases, scriptwriters provide services on a work-made-for-hire basis and the copyright is owned by the content experts or producer. What happens to the writer's financial participation when, at some later date, a portion of the program is re-used as part of another media product, known as a derivative work?

This is where the Writer's Guild could be extremely useful to writers for the new media. In addition, the Writer's Guild provides services which accrue from writers acting as a unified collective bargaining group, compared to individuals negotiating, billing, collecting, and purchasing medical insurance and pension plans.

All professional writers should become involved in these issues and develop an appreciation for the pros and cons of such business matters. As we move toward the 21st century, these issues will grow more, not less, complex.

ONE WRITER'S WELLNESS

Writing is a solitary and except for occasional research forays, sedentary life. But good writing has a sense of energy. Writing scripts that come to life on screen or stage requires a sense of pacing and forward movement when writing.

The writer's ability to focus, concentrate and devote full energy and attention to the task at hand is a critical skill. So, too, is the ability to tap a rich vein of human and emotional experience. To quote Zinsser again: "For ultimately the product that any writer has to sell is not his subject, but who he is."[1]

Scriptwriters are expected to "be creative on demand" and are challenged to be innovative and original in a business, educational or organizational context, often with meager resources and on short notice.

After doing this work month after month, year after year, stress, writer's block, burn-out, and other mental malaise may settle in. As a professional, you need strategies to keep your life in balance.

There's more to life than writing. And life experience is a great source of material. I've learned this from the "school of hard knocks." Earlier in my career, I sneered at so-called "writer's block," even challenged the validity of the syndrome. Sure, there are projects and days when it seemed harder to get started. Or, the amount of usable copy produced seemed paltry. "But," I reasoned, "I'm a pro. A man's gotta do what a man's gotta do. The show must go on."

Little did I know how devastating a condition such as manic-depression can be. Suddenly, for no apparent reason, your emotional gas tank is on "empty." There's nothing to draw on. Willpower doesn't help either. I now know how frustrating it is to *want* to write and be unable. Dr. Nancy Andreason, a psychiatrist, has done clinical studies on the incidence of manic-depression among writers at the University of Iowa's famed Writing Workshop. Her results show a higher incidence of clinical depression among the writers compared to a control group.[2]

For whatever the reason, being blocked comes with the territory. Maybe it's due to a physical condition such as the small chemical imbalance in the brain which causes severe mood swings. Maybe it's plain, old-fashioned burn-out and time for a good, long vacation. Sometimes, the block is your subconscious mind telling you something is amiss in your plan of attack. You're overlooking a serious conceptual flaw. Or, the highly distinctive voice you've assumed may not be appropriate, given your audience and objectives.

When you're blocked, something is out of whack. Your mind or body is sending a message. Listen and let up. Often you're just trying too hard.

Athletics and Hobbies

Corporations today appreciate that healthy employees are more productive than overweight, burned out, stressed out employees. Physical fitness centers show that major corporations see the need for aerobic exercise. Corporations have also developed major communication campaigns to encourage employees to develop healthy lifestyles.

In *The New Freelancer's Handbook,* Marietta Whittlesey devotes an entire section to "Your Mind and Body." (Even if you're a staff writer, check this book out of the library and browse. You'll find lots that pertains to managing your life and work.) Whittlesey offers several reasons for writer's block—fear of rejection, fear of success, perfectionism, etc.[3] She describes the beneficial effects of exercise: reduced muscular tension, improved sleep, better body chemistry and a general feeling of fitness.

Creative people need a balanced, healthy lifestyle as much, if not more, than their counterparts in accounting, marketing, or manufacturing. Writers need to engage in activities which "clear the brain," wipe the mental slate clean and result in renewed enthusiasm, energy and fresh viewpoints.

Over the years, I've found two activities that fulfill that function: one is athletics, the other, dog training. (That's right. Dog training.) Both are useful outlets for the negative energy and frustration induced by stress, overwork, unreasoning clients, financial and family worry and just plain burn-out. Each brings a little balance and perspective into my life.

Jogging, tennis, playing in a softball league, they all offer the benefits of physical exercise. Team sports provide the additional advantage of getting out with people from different walks of life and relating to folks for pure enjoyment.

Jogging, by contrast, offers solitude and freedom from telephones, kids, cars and blaring electronic appliances. Dr. George Sheehan, writer of *Running and Being, The Total Experience,* expresses it well when he says, "There are times when I am not sure whether I am a runner who writes or a writer who runs. Mostly, it appears that the two are inseparable."[4]

"What running does," he describes, "is allow it to happen. . .there are times when I take a column on the road and it is like pulling the handle of a slot machine. Bang comes down the first sentence. Bang comes down the second, and the paragraphs unfold. And then Bang, jackpot, the piece is finished, whole and true and good!"[5] (Sheehan finds the idea of "suffering" so natural to "both writers and runners, it seems to be a common bond.")

Dog training, while not so physically demanding, still provides some exercise. But more than that, it puts me in touch with the instinctive, live-for-the-moment joie devivre of animal behavior. Belonging to a dog training club and showing in obedience trials is another way I found a whole world of most unusual folks outside the "business."

And I even learned things about training people from dog training. With dogs—you can't teach 'em a damn thing until you get their attention. Same holds true for people. In dog training, you learn to read an animal to determine the root cause for Fido having difficulty with an exercise. In the same way, instructional designers need to identify the root cause for job performance problems.

Of course, there's also battling wits with children. That'll get your mind off your writing in a hurry.

To sum it up: seek a fulfilling, creative life *outside* your creative writing life. As Joseph Campbell puts it in *The Power of Myth*:

> "If you follow your bliss, you put yourself on a kind of track that has been there all the while, waiting for you. And the life that you ought to be living is the one you are living. Wherever you are—if you are following your bliss, you are enjoying that refreshment, that life within you, all the time."[6]

THE CREATIVITY CONUNDRUM

Almost all clients *think* they want creativity. A few clients even *ask* for creativity. Rarely do clients *demand* creativity.

Occasionally, projects come along which have "award-winning" potential. Subject matter, client attitudes, budget, production team and other factors all seem favorable to developing a distinctive, memorable media presentation. Such windows of opportunity don't come along often, however. I feel fortunate if I get more than one of those "juicy" assignments a year.

Of course, experienced, technically skilled and imaginative scriptwriters consciously strive to produce creative scripts each and every time out. Sometimes the magic works, sometimes it doesn't.

But the harsh reality of writing scripts for organizations, corporations and even educational institutions is that we seem to fail at being creative to a far greater extent than we actually succeed. For all the lip service, very few media scripts—still fewer finished productions—result in genuinely creative works. Of this small body of original work, fewer still become award winners while a small percentage are shunned by clients and award committees alike. Why?

Creative Paradoxes

Since the ancient Greeks and their nine muses, creativity and the creative process have been shrouded by a dark veil of mystery, as though we aren't supposed to understand the ways of the creative mind. After all, isn't creativity the business of the unconscious, residing in that affective "right brain" that's garnered so much recent publicity? Perhaps that's one reason there are so many perplexing questions and paradoxes when discussing the creative process.

What does a client *really* mean when she says she wants a creative approach? What should the client *expect* to get in return? Do clients *know* a creative script from one riddled with cliches? Will producers and managers be supportive of the most creative solutions to writing problems? Whose *responsibility* is it to make a program creative? The writer's? The director's? Can it be made creative "in post," through digital electronic effects?

Such questions seem to support the contention that we have little conscious control of the creative process. We appreciate why the Greeks put creativity into the hands of nine muses of music, song, poetry, corporate video, and so on. To create, one courted favor from one of these muses, hoping for an inspirational "gift" from the goddess.

How does this relate to writing corporate and instructional scripts that contain the magic to entrance, entertain and capture viewer's hearts and minds? And what do our clients *really* mean when they say "We're really looking for something creative on this project"?

Creativity: a Working Definition

To get more objective and analytical, let's turn to Webster for definitions:

Creativity:
1.   the quality of being creative
2.   the ability to create

Create:
1.   to bring into existence
2a. to invest with a new form
2b. to produce or bring about by a course of action (Producer/Director)
3.   to produce through imaginative skill (Actors/Musicians)

Creative:
1.   marked by the ability or power to create
2.   having the quality of something created rather than imitated

From the definition of "create" we get the sense that creativity involves making a *product*. That product may be a painting, a poem, an invention, a novel, a film, a piano sonata, a TV program. Clearly we are in the realm of the creative, not the interpretive, arts such as acting or playing Ravel's Sonatina on the piano.

Another glimmer of insight comes from the second definition of creative: "having the quality of something created rather than *imitated*." That tells us genuinely creative products are *originals* in some manner. It is not enough to be simply productive. We can bang out script after script, but if each is imitative and cliche-ridden, the results cannot be praised for creativity.

Rollo May, in his wonderful short book, *The Courage to Create,* defines creativity as "the process of bringing something *new* into being."[7] It's that simple.

Help in identifying the qualities of a creative product comes from D. N. Perkins, one of the psychologists heading Harvard's Project Zero, an interdisciplinary research group in the Graduate School of Education investigating creation and comprehension in the arts.

Perkins sets up these parameters for describing creative activities;

> "(1) A creative result is a result both original and appropriate.
> (2) A creative person—a person with creativity—is a person who
> fairly routinely produces creative results."[8]

Perkins argues that "we do not call something creative unless we classify it as both original and appropriate. If we do not see it as original, it may count as fine craftsmanship but not as creative. If we do not see it as appropriate, its originality simply makes it off the wall."[9] (Note that Perkins' criteria correspond to many of the criteria for evaluating media concepts using the concept evaluation matrix in Chapter 5.)

In *The Mind's Best Work,* Perkins modifies his definition to include the element of quality. "Creative means original and of high *quality*. Thus a stereotyped product does not count as creative, however fine it may be. Likewise, a product with nothing else to recommend it does not count as creative, however original it may be. Such products are just superficially novel. With these definitions in mind," concludes Perkins, "explaining creating means explaining how the originality and the quality 'get put into' the developing creative outcome during the making process."[10]

Creativity in Art

If we look at creative products from the arts or sciences, we can identify many examples of quality products which happen to be *imitative*. Beethoven's early works, for example, are imitative of Haydn and Mozart (Haydn was Beethoven's teacher) and the classical tradition. Beethoven wrote his first two symphonies in this classical mode. Once he "mastered" the mechanics of symphonic writing, he moved on to Symphony #3, *The Eroica.* From the very first punctuated chords to the high drama of the melodic and haromic invention, the compelling rhythms and extended form, the listener senses the excitement, originality and daring of Beethoven. He breaks from the classical tradition propelling listeners headlong into the Romantic period.

When Stravinsky's ballet *The Rite of Spring* premiered in Paris in 1913, it was so original (and therefore *in*appropriate to novice ears) that his primitive, brutal use of orchestra and dancers incited a riot. The history of music, art and literature is filled with examples of the public scorning originals because these works break so boldly from tradition.

This is what Picasso was driving at when he said: 'Every act of creation is first of all an act of destruction.'[11] The original, creative product destroys, in some manner, its antecedents.

Creativity in Business

We can begin to appreciate why the word "creativity" is bandied about with such blatant misunderstanding in the hallowed halls of commerce. When clients say they want creativity, I believe most mean they want something "clever." Cleverness is a superficial quality, an aspect of technique which makes a work appear to possess more originality than it does. Advertising strives for cleverness far more than for genuine originality. Many ads are clever. Few are creative.

This is also why Hollywood sequels have mushroomed to the point of absurdity. Even so commercial a publication as *The Wall Street Journal* ran a front page feature titled: "Sequels and Stars Help Movie Studios Avoid Major Risks" (June 6, 1989). There is always safety in a proven product. Corporations and institutions are run by business people or bureaucrats who don't like making decisions which can easily be second-guessed.

The Risk Factor

Meanings are in people, not in words. So when clients say they want creativity, they probably don't have a full appreciation of what the word means to a writer or director and what the consequences of creative acts mean to an organization. The more original a media presentation, the greater the element of risk that the audience may respond negatively, just as Parisians spurned Stravinsky. The more a media script departs from standard corporate fare, the higher the risk involved in executing the concept and pulling it off. At the same time, the potential rewards are far greater. An original product is usually more compelling and memorable and has a greater impact on viewers than one which takes the safe but predictable route.

This element of risk is illustrated in Figure 15.1. The vertical axis plots creativity on a scale of one to ten—ten being the most creative. If you correlate that to the

Figure 15.1: Ratio of Creativity to Risk

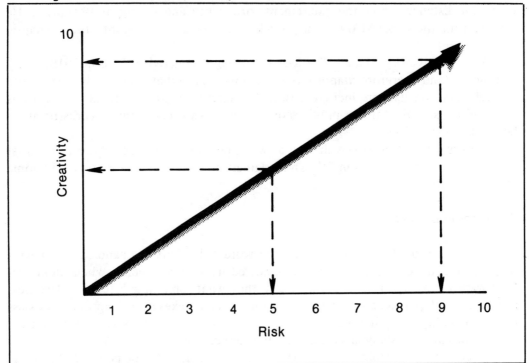

degree of risk involved as plotted on the horizontal axis, an interesting relationship emerges. The more daring, bold and original a creative concept, the higher the risk involved in executing the concept.

And what is the chief role of management, whether in Hollywood, Madison Avenue or Akron, Ohio? Sure. It's to eliminate risk as much as possible. . .to constantly look at the "down side" and consider what happens if the "creative types" fail to pull it off.

Figure 15.2 shows the result of such thinking. Here, creativity and originality are displayed in terms of a continuum—one being the most imitative, ten the most creative. The tug-of-war between management and the creative team often causes the compromises which tend to dilute the originality of a concept, script or production. The resulting bell curve illustrates how the vast majority of our programming falls somewhere in the middle. It is not devoid of creativity, but neither does it display the originality marked by daring, risk taking and working at the outer limits of one's technical capacity.

Of course, the management-creative team "tug-of-war" is not the *only* reason for a glut of mediocre media presentations. Sometimes a writer's wonderful concept gets destroyed in the journey from script to screen. Sometimes, writers fail to invent an original, appropriate concept and fall back, instead, on tried, true and imitative products. Some writers consciously recycle the same few ideas from client to client instead of doing the hard work of solving the unique problems inherent in each assignment.

Sometimes formulas are embraced by producers because they simplify production. Creativity is traded off for productivity. Others systematically shoot down creative ideas because "that would never go over with our audience."

Worst of all is the client who gives lip service to creativity yet slowly, inexorably chips away at each succeeding draft, eventually wringing the script dry of the surprises and human interest elements which made the concept creative.

So the creative process always involves a daring, high-wire balancing act between originality and risk. Paradoxically, the more often a writer, producer or director

Figure 15.2: Programming and Creativity

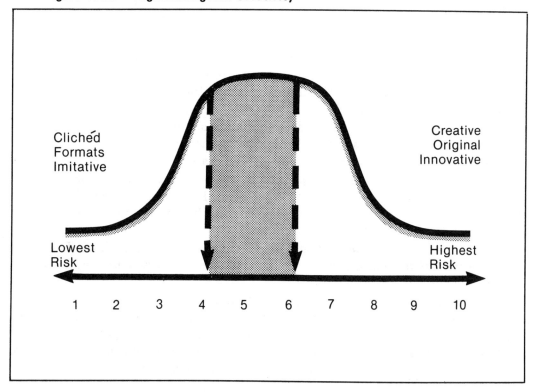

strives for genuine creativity, the more likely they will encounter failure. Yet this tension between safety and risk, success and failure is precisely what fuels the creative mind. Two of my favorite quotes embody this paradox:

"Writing that is written to avoid failure guarantees mediocrity."[12]

Donald Murray
A Writer Teaches Writing

"The game is not avoiding failure at all costs—the game is giving triumph a chance, isn't it."[13]

Huw Weldon
Former BBC Managing Director

WORD PROCESSORS FOR SCRIPTWRITERS

I have a dim recollection of how I used to write. I vaguely remember scratching out tentative, rough first drafts on yellow legal pads in the felt-tip pen color I favored at the time. Scratch outs and arrows showed evidence of the difficulty of getting "black on white."

On completing the rough initial draft, I proceeded to the next step—typing *another rough* draft, using the legal pad copy as a guide. Invariably, I revised as I typed. But now I could see the script as a script for the first time, even though there were beaucoup typos.

This version would be read (ideally, out loud) and revised, once again using the felt-tip pen. Finally, I did a serious typing job on the script. This time, I focused on preparing a pristine manuscript—the client's first-draft script. Generally, I use a two-column format and so I had to keep switching between single- and double-spacing. I typed slowly, methodically, striving to avoid typos. I consumed gallons of correction fluid. As I neared the bottom of what appeared to be a well-typed script page, I'd sense a certain pressure: "Don't blow it now!"

And so it went. Burning midnight oil. Or rising at the crack of dawn. Feverishly finishing the last few pages just before the appointed delivery hour. All that simply to generate a clean first-draft script!

Revisions were another nightmare. What pages to salvage by cutting and pasting? Would surgery show on photocopies? Would the client notice page 12 was short if I used correction tape to make the deletion at the bottom of the page? Did I really feel like retyping a page if I wanted to change only a few words? And so it would go, often through a third, even fourth draft, an unrewarding, labor intensive aspect of my business. And none of it had anything to do with the quality of my solutions to writing problems.

I tried alternatives. I'd send my typing out to a pro. This absolved me from much of the drudgery. But it added new problems. I had to schedule my work so it meshed with another person's. I lost the flexibility to make those spontaneous changes that would come during typing.

When I got the script back, although squeaky clean, it was like reading someone else's term paper. I'd notice a long copy block which really should be broken and edited. But was I prepared to send it back and lose another day? Tough choices.

Enter, stage left, the word processor. . . .

The Dedicated Word Processor

My introduction to word processing resulted from researching a video project. In the early 1980s, I was working with John Sheehan at Johnson & Johnson on a series of programs about productivity. One program focused on productivity in the office. The topic? Word processing.

This was in the days of dedicated word processors, before personal computers with word processing software became popular. Back then, the word processor was a substitute for the secretarys' or typing pool's typewriters. Believe it or not, there was a stigma attached to managers and professionals improving their productivity by using such technology.

But the benefits of word processing captured my imagination.

1. There was something inviting about the electronic touch of the keyboard. Letters and words and sentences appeared on the screen instantaneously, almost magically. You didn't worry about typos or paragraphs out of sequence. It was all so easily changed or rearranged. You kept the good stuff and, with the touch of a key, the unwanted material melted into nowhere.
2. Word processing gave writers the ability to facilitate the major revision functions: adding, deleting, moving or changing.
3. Word processors offered new possibilities for managing the business side of writing—functions such as mail merge, document storage on disk and the ability to recycle paragraphs or key phrases into customized memos or promotional materials.
4. And, of course, there was that wonderful sound of a high-speed daisy-wheel printer flawlessly obeying each and every command to produce impeccable-looking, pristine copy.

Well, I was hooked. At the time personal computers did not offer features I sought: powerful word processing capabilities combined with easy to use dual column formatting and daisy-wheel printing. (Back then, personal computers featured dot matrix printers. Fine for most personal applications, but not for producing professional-looking manuscripts.)

So I went to my banker, floated a loan and the bank and I soon became joint owners of a Micom 2001 dedicated word processor from Philips Information Systems. This book was composed on the identical equipment—about six years later.

The PC and Word Processing

Once the PC provided an "electronic window" to the company's mainframe databank, the clerical stigma associated with word processors slowly lifted. Once managers found their way around the PC keyboard, it was easy enough to learn the new word processing software.

Writing Scripts with a Word Processor

Today, many software programs are designed specifically for scriptwriters to facilitate formatting. Some even offer electronic storyboarding. As PCs were integrated into the audiovisual production process—providing budgeting spreadsheets and production schedules—resistance to change among scriptwriters broke down. Today, I cannot imagine writing well or productively without word processing.

A word processor facilitates each stage of the writing process outlined in this book. During Assimilation, I "throw" a lot of interview quotes, print references and other useful material onto the disk, building a research database.

When it comes to getting "day-glow green down on black," the electronic touch of the personal computer keyboard facilitates "free writing." You don't fret over typos. You don't stop when you go blank on a word—just leave a space and come back later. Content outlines and treatments fall in place quickly with a spontaneity resulting from knowledge of how easy it is to make changes.

In the section on drafting, I suggested pulling sentences and paragraphs from the treatment and content outline into appropriate "Visual" or "Audio" columns to begin generating a first-draft script.

We've spoken of the ongoing dialog writers have with the emerging text: "passion hot" to "critic cold." Word processing facilitates that dialog. Not only can paragraphs, sentences and words be manipulated on-screen, material can be quickly printed out at any stage of the scripting process. Sometimes it helps to see type on paper and the relationship between ideas on widely separated pages.

The word processor makes revision much less intimidating. Material can easily be added or deleted. Content and structure can be rearranged pages or paragraphs at a time. Narrative copy can be polished time and again. Visual descriptions can be altered while narrative copy remains the same or vice versa.

What to Use

When selecting a PC word processor combination begin by listing the "specifications" you seek in hardware and software. Dual column formatting has always been the major "bug" for scriptwriters. If you or your clients prefer this format, then your specs start with dual column capabilities.

See these capabilities demonstrated. Are you able to work with the two columns independently while seeing each on the screen in relative position? What kind of hardware is needed to run the program?

Make a list of other kinds of word processing, graphics or computing tasks you will do routinely. Will you be writing lots of workbook or brochure text? How about mass mailings? What other software capabilities will you want? A spelling checker? Production management functions such as scheduling and budgeting programs? What graphics capabilities do you desire? Will your PC also be used in a production mode, say for doing off-line rough-cut editing? What kind of documentation, support and service capabilities do you get with the hardware and software?

When I first explored word processing, one of my specs was a printer offering typewriter quality, a daisy wheel versus dot matrix. Today the laser printer offers even greater quality, speed and a variety of features that translate into user benefits.

Will you be doing desktop publishing? Will you be the only one using the system or will others in an A/V department or production company also need these capabilities? Compatibility may be a prime consideration.

In drawing up a list of specs, make two columns: "Need to Have" and "Nice to Have." Somewhere along the line, of course, you'll also consider price.

Recently, a scriptwriting member of ITVA, Andrea Boardman, conducted a survey of writers to gather data on software in use and how well it met scriptwriters' special needs. It might be a useful tool to have when shopping around.

A Word of Warning

After this "commercial" for word processing, consider this. You're on vacation at the beach. Suddenly, in typical "Eureka!" fashion, the concept for a script comes to you in a flash as an unexpected gift. Do you still have the ability to use that old felt-tip pen and legal pad?

Or, suppose you're flying coast to coast. This often provides a good time for writing. Or, you're early for a client meeting and waiting in a coffee shop. You should be able to make productive use of that time by putting pencil to paper.

The *quality* of your thinking and writing should never be dependent on bits and bytes. The first two thousand-plus centuries of the world's greatest literature was produced without the aid of a word processing program and spelling checker.

The ability to write anywhere anytime is equally powerful for achieving personal writing productivity and quality. Never let go of this powerful capability.

ON MY SOAPBOX

In writing workshops, with a captive audience, I like to designate an area in the room as my "soapbox." It's where I go when I want to pontificate. I'm venting my emotions by discussing pet peeves. This way, students know I may not be totally rational. In closing, here are some subjects which send me to my soap box. . .

Writer/Producer/Director/Editor/Coffee Maker

I don't know how many times I sit in ITVA chapter meetings and hear young people in the business introduce themselves as "writer/producer/director." (I usually counter by saying "I'm *just* a writer.") There are a couple of problems inherent in this triple-hyphenate syndrome.

First, when do you have time to learn *one* of those jobs well enough to be truly proficient and thoroughly professional at it? In the motion picture industry, there are only a few triple-hyphenates I can think of: Alan Alda and Woody Allen come to mind. But they didn't start out as triple threats. They have grown into playing each role exceedingly well.

Another question: if you're writing, producing and directing a program, who do you have to argue with? Who are you relying on for honest feedback? This is a collaborative business.

Finally, some are born to be triple hyphenates, some achieve the status—and a few poor souls have it thrust upon them. We've all read trade journal ads for one-person video or A/V shops. Employers need to be educated. It amazes me that executives assume a one-man shop should be able to turn out programming as routinely as the evening news. Such executives should be forced to count the list of credits that roll at the end of each day's newscast.

Boring Subjects

One question invariably sends me to the soapbox: "What do you do with a boring subject?"

My response: "There's no such thing as a boring subject—only boring writing. It's *your* job to make it interesting."

A Writer Is a Writer

Novice and apprentice writers don't always get the "plum" assignments. If you're just beginning a writing career, you may find it easier to land an entry-level job as a print writer or journalist. You may find yourself doing routine news releases. Copy for brochures. Training manuals. Or editing an employee publication. But don't underestimate the significance of this work. You will be learning discipline, facility. The ability to write on demand—even when you're not inspired.

No, these may not be the media projects and assignments you *want* to do. But in the hurly-burly of writing for a living, this work is as important as anything you might do later. If you're stuck doing print (as I was for several years) when your heart's really in scriptwriting, remember that it takes as much imagination and skill to craft solid, interesting print copy as it does to write narration or script videowall and multi-image shows.

Even when you begin to specialize in media, you're likely still to be called on for expertise as a print writer. Most media productions are not stand-alone presentations. They require collateral print in the form of leave-behinds. or instructional manuals and leader's guides. Or promotional materials.

A writer is a writer is a writer. If you want to work in media badly enough, you'll find your way. And there are many more "ground floor" opportunities in private television and instructional media writing than there are in broadcast and network television these days. So hang in there and remember, "you learn something from each and every writing assignment, no matter how mundane." When you start thinking otherwise, you're on the road to becoming a hack.

Production Experience

Eventually a writer must devote full time to putting "black on white." I don't think it's possible, however, to write imaginatively or pragmatically for an audiovisual medium without some "hands-on" production experience. Few will have the talent and inclination to develop craftsmanship in more than one phase of media production. A media writer, however, needs an intuitive sense of what is both possible and impossible, given the realities of time, money, resources, equipment and logistics for a project.

"Someday I'll Be a Real Writer"

When I teach seminars for advanced scriptwriters, I have them begin by filling out a short profile on themselves as writers and how they feel about their present stage of development. In one section, I ask if they've ever said to themselves, "Someday, I'll be a real writer."

It's surprising how many people share this feeling of inadequacy, even after writing professionally on an award-winning level for many years. Of course, I pose the question because I often have such thoughts.

Even though I've made a living writing in some form or another for more than twenty years, it's difficult to feel effervescent about your own work when there are so many wonderful writers to admire. Novelists and poets and screenwriters. Wonderful essayists and commentators such as Russell Baker and Stephen Jay Gould. And, of course, those writers who found a permanent place in the annals of western civilization because of their originality and relevance.

It's easy to denigrate writing about employee benefits or how to operate a centrifugal gas compressor. But if you can do that well—you're among a handful of people in this day and age who possess the vision and craft to create a functional script which works with its intended audience. And the longer you stick with it, the more confident you'll become. As David Lyman likes to point out in his creativity sessions at the Maine Photographic Workshops, the road from student to apprentice to craftsperson is a long one. Typically, it takes at least ten years. So. . . .

CLAIM YOUR WRITING

I remember a screening in which the president of the company I worked for was watching the final cut of a video report to employees. There were animated segments he'd never seen before. They were of my own creation. My writing. My children. They'd been shot by a husband and wife film team. But I was present as every frame was shot and I called the post-production edit on videotape.

At one point he turned to me in the darkened room and said quite bluntly, "Who did this?"

"Uh-oh," I thought, "He hates it."

"We used an outside production company," I said.

He shot back, "It's quite good."

I'd fallen prey to a common malady: failure to claim my writing, to celebrate my creation. In her inspirational book, *Writing Down the Bones,* Natalie Goldberg writes: "Time and again, I have experienced a peculiar phenomenon in writing groups. Someone will write something extraordinary and then have no idea about its quality. It doesn't matter how much I may rave about it or the other people in the group give positive feedback; the writer cannot connect with the fact that it is good writing. He doesn't deny it; he just sits there bewildered and later, through the grapevine, I hear that he never believed a word of what was said. . .

"I do not mean for us all to become braggarts. I mean we should recognize that we are good inside and emanate our goodness and create something good outside us. . . .It is not as important for the world to claim it as it is to claim it for ourselves. That is the essential step. That will make us content. We are good, and when our work is good, it is good. We should acknowledge it and stand behind it."[14]

With that said, I'm sure my editor, Ellen Lazer, would say I've been on my soap box long enough. So I'll step down.

FOOTNOTES

1. William Zinsser, *On Writing Well* (New York, NY: Harper & Row, Publishers, 1980), p. 5.
2. Nancy C. Andreasen, M.D., Ph.D., "Creativity and Mental Illness: Prevalence Rates in Writers and Their First-Degree Relatives," *American Journal of Psychiatry,* October 1987, p. 1289.
3. Marietta Whittlesey, *The New Freelancer's Handbook* (New York, NY: Simon & Schuster, Inc., 1982, 1988), p. 116.
4. George A. Sheehan, M.D., *Running and Being, the Total Experience* (New York, NY: Warner Books, 1978), p. 13.
5. *Ibid.,* p. 15.
6. Joseph Campbell with Bill Moyers, *The Power of Myth* (New York, NY: Doubleday, 1988) p. 91.
7. Rollo May, *The Courage to Create* (New York, NY: Bantam Books, 1975), p. 37.
8. D. N. Perkins, "Creativity & the Quest for Mechanism," (from manuscript to appear in R. S. Sternberg & E. Smith, Eds., *The Psychology of Human Thought* (Cambridge, England: Cambridge University Press), p. 3.
9. *Ibid.,* p. 3.
10. D. N. Perkins, *The Mind's Best Work,* p. 6.
11. Rollo May, *The Courage of Create,* p. 63.
12. Donald M. Murray, *A Writer Teaches Writing* (Boston, MA: Houghton Mifflin Company, 1985), p. 86.
13. Huw Weldon.
14. Natalie Goldberg, *Writing Down the Bones* (Boston, MA: Shambhala, 1986), pp. 154 and 156.

Glossary

Actuality audio: Audio recorded on location to capture the sounds and ambiance of an environment. Generally, this is unscripted audio, used more as a sound effect than to convey content. Examples: sounds of an airport terminal, hospital lobby or playground.

Assimilation: The first phase of the writing process. It includes research but also involves the snythesizing necessary to make a subject one's own. The writing products which result from Assimilation are objectives, audience profile and content outline.

Audience profile: Description of the intended audience and relevant information regarding the communication environment and viewing situation.

Branching: Interactive videodisc term describing the decision tree created by the program designer to give the viewer the sense of controlling the outcome of the material. Produced on videodisc and combined with the random access features of computer control, programs can incorporate a number of nonlinear paths or branches through the material.

Camera directions: These terms, originated in motion picture production, were adopted by the fledgling television industry. Some are also used conceptually to describe special effects in multi-image production or in computer animation.

The video/film writer uses the following terms to describe the *distance* between camera and subject:

> LONG SHOT (LS)
> MEDIUM SHOT (MS)
> CLOSE UP (CU)
> EXTREME CLOSE UP (ECU)

To describe *movement* of the camera in relation to the subject, the writer uses such terms as:

> PAN RIGHT/LEFT—A horizontal rotation of the camera along a fixed
> axis parallel to the ground.

387

TILT UP/DOWN—Vertical movement of the camera on a fixed axis perpendicular to the ground.

DOLLY—Physically moving the camera closer to or farther from the subject.

TRUCK—Physically moving the camera left or right on a horizontal plane, parallel to the subject.

ZOOM IN/OUT—Changing the focal length of the lens to make the subject appear larger or smaller.

Caricature: A portrayal which seizes upon certain individual qualities of a person through exaggeration or distortion. Related to Comedy of Humours—a type of realistic comedy developed in the late 16th century by Ben Jonson and George Chapman—which depicted persons whose behavior is dominated by a single characteristic, whim or humour.

Character generator: An electronic titling system to superimpose text or numbers over a video picture. Text is created on a keyboard, then electronically superimposed over another video image.

Characterization: The creation of imaginary persons so credible they exist for the viewer as real within the context of the program.

Character narrations: Narrative information conveyed as a monologue in which the narrator assumes the identity of a character.

Client: The person who "commissions" a media presentation. Generally, the client has a business "problem" or organizational need which can best be met by a media presentation or combination of media working in consort. Usually, the client also holds the "purse strings" and approves the overall budget.

Computer animation: Generating and manipulating frames of animation by computer and transferring the output to videotape.

Concept: A single idea or premise which shapes style, format, content and structure into a unified, interesting, and aesthetically pleasing whole. Once a concept is set, parameters for aesthetic and production considerations are established. Also:

The creative vehicle for conveying content.

A unique, involving method of delivering content to the target audience.

A storytelling theme used to provide a warm, human touch to the cold facts which constitute the content.

Often, the scriptwriter's most important contribution to a project is a strong, viable concept.

Content outline: Description of the points that will be covered in a media presentation with no reference to visualization, format or style.

Creative product: A creative result that is original, appropriate, and of high quality. We cannot call something creative unless we classify it as both original and appropriate. If we do not see it as original, it may count as fine craftsmanship but not as creative. If we do not see it as appropriate, its originality simply makes it off the wall. In addition, an original, appropriate creative concept must be executed in a craftsmanlike manner so as to result in a product of high quality.

Creativity: The process of bringing something new into being; having the quality of something created rather than imitated.

Cyclorama (cyc): A curved curtain or wall, usually white, used as a studio background to suggest unlimited space. Lights with colored gels can vary the intensity and shade of the cyc.

Dialog: Conversation of two or more people as reproduced through a script. Gives the impression of naturalness without being a verbatim record (a semblance of reality, not reality itself). Good dialog varies in diction, rhythm, phrasing, sentence length, etc., according to the character of the speakers.

Drafting: Third stage in the writing process following Assimilation and Rehearsal. In drafting, the scriptwriter's primary goal is to generate a rough, first-draft script. In the drafting phase it is often helpful to suspend critical thinking and use "free writing" techniques to get scenes fleshed out. The writer's product is a first-draft shooting script.

Dramatization: Any situation in which there is conflict between two or more characters. Dramatization usually means communicating all content through dialog and action. Dramatic vignettes, however, can also be freely intermixed and combined with other narrative formats.

Digital effects: Electronic manipulation of video images, graphics or animation using computer hardware and software designed specifically for television production. Some simple, standard digital effects include "page turns," "flips," "wipes," etc.

Docudrama: Strictly speaking, a docudrama is a dramatization of an actual event which combines elements of documentary film production and style with dramatic re-stagings using actors/actresses to capitalize on the entertainment value of characters in dramatic situations. The term is also used more loosely to suggest any dramatization done in a documentary style.

Film chain: Projection equipment and video camera configuration used for transferring motion picture footage or 35mm slides to videotape.

Flow chart: A chart used in interactive videodisc program development to map and illustrate the branching possibilities as the user would interact with the finished program. There are standard symbols used industry-wide for this purpose.

Format: A generic method of presenting information through audiovisual media. These include:

Talking Head	Interview
Talking Head with Props	Drama
Visuals and Voice	"Apples and Oranges"

The scriptwriter must select one or more of these formats for any audiovisual presentation.

Freeze frame: Technique of taking a single video or film frame and "freezing" the action to create a still-picture image on video or film.

Fully developed character: A realistic portrayal of an individual which reveals a variety of complex, sometimes contradictory, motivations. Usually the individual's reaction to a situation cannot be easily predicted.

HDTV (High Definition Television): A new video production/display system with pictures composed of 1125 scan lines compared to the traditional 525 scan line picture. This produces an electronic image with the resolution and definition of 35mm motion pictures. With HDTV, the familiar three-by-four video aspect ratio gives way to something new: large-screen projection of a picture which stretches the horizontal aspect ratio to something approximating 35mm motion picture projection.

HDTV is ideally suited for high impact presentations needed for sales meetings, conventions and trade shows. Since broadcast and cable applications are bogged down in standardization issues, meetings and other special viewing situations may prove HDTV's most useful point of entry into the media field during the decade of the 90s.

Interactive video/interactive videodisc (IVD): Involves use of random access capabilities of the videodisc in combination with computer software in which the viewer appears to control what happens next. The interactive television viewer affects the outcome by selecting a specific sequence of events, using a keypad, touch-screen, mouse, or other interface mechanism.

Non-training applications include video catalogs, informational kiosks and exhibitions. When used as a teaching machine, IVD instruction is nonlinear and individualized, allowing a learner to repeat material that proves difficult or skip information already mastered. Trainers can also receive print-outs of each user's scores for analysis or to demonstrate subject matter mastery.

Interruptive video: A videotape presentation with pre-determined stopping points built in. Although similar to interactive video, the interruptive program remains a linear presentation. The stopping points are often used in training situations to allow participants to discuss or test their knowledge of material presented so far.

M.O.S.: An abbreviation for footage shot without audio. Tradition has it the term comes from early motion picture days when a German director working in America would call for shots "mit out sound!" Also known as "wild footage" or "B-roll footage."

Multi-image: This involves display of two or more images *simultaneously*. The viewing audience responds to several presentational symbols often presented in rapid succession. Technically, a multi-image presentation is usually produced using still photograpy (35mm slides), multiple projectors and a computer controlled cueing device to synchronize projectors with audio events.

Multi-media: The audience watches two or more media in the same audiovisual presentation. For example, a multi-image module which includes a motion picture clip in combination with 35mm slides as part of the viewing experience is a muiti-media presentation.

Objectives: Expressions of the client's expectations for a media presentation. Objectives should be expressed in terms of communication/training outcomes.

P.O.V.: Abbreviation for "point of view"; used to indicate that the camera is positioned to represent the viewpoint of a character or individual in the program. (It's analogous to writing in the first person.) The technique is also used to create a sense of viewer involvement when screen action is shot as though the viewer is on-scene seeing what the camera sees.

Presentational style: Dramatic writing in which the writer intentionally shatters the illusion of reality through dialog in which actors "break character" to address the audience or through striking use of stylized scenery, acting, costumes or music.

Random access: The capability to access any frame of program material in a matter of seconds using the videodisc.

Rehearsal: The stage of the writing process when the scriptwriter focuses on how best to use media to present content as a chronological sequence of events unfolding on screen in time. (Brainstorming and incubation are often used to stimulate concept development.) The Rehearsal phase results in a single writing product: the media treatment.

Revision: Literally, it means to "see again." This phase generally incorporates feedback from client, content experts, producer, director and others involved in script development. The scriptwriter's ability to revise is often enhanced by setting the first-draft script aside for a period of days or more.

Script: A chronological sequence of events describing sounds, pictures and ideas in media production terminology. Can also be thought of as the scriptwriter's instructions to the production team on how to make this media presentation.

Segue: (Pronounced seg-way.) Originally a smooth transition between musical numbers, this generally involves an overlap or cross-fade audio. Today, the term is used more loosely to describe transitions that involve overlapping audio and visual cues.

Storyboard: A series of simplified drawings, sketches or computer graphics assembled to illustrate what happens visually on screen as synchronized to audio cues.

Style: The writer's (or client's or character's) viewpoint toward the content expressed through tone, word choice, music and sound effects, visualization, special effects and use of on- and off-camera participants.

Structure: A planned framework for revealing the chronological sequence of events on screen.

Subject matter expert: (Also, content expert.) The individual or group providing the technical input for script development and reviewing draft scripts for technical accuracy.

Subtext: Usually used in dramatization to suggest the character traits or relationships which are implied or known to the writer but do not play a major storytelling or instructional role. Subtext gives drama a sense of reality, as well as rich, full, character development.

Super: Term used to indicate the superimposition of text or graphics over another picture, often live video. Most frequently used to indicate titles or text to be superimposed over another video image.

Teleconference: A television program produced using conventional television technologies and techniques during which elements of the program originate live. The program is transmitted to one or more places, via satellite, where it is usually viewed by groups gathered specifically for the occasion. Sometimes viewers have opportunities to place telephone calls to the originating location to ask questions or make statements "on-air" or have their question or statement noted and addressed later in the program.

Time code: The signal encoded on videotape to provide a readout of elapsed time on the reel expressed in minutes, seconds and frame numbers. The Society of Motion Picture and Television Engineers (SMPTE) has set a standard for recording such signals on videotape. Time codes are useful to the scriptwriter for identifying content from production footage to incorporate into a script.

Transitional effects: Media production terms used to describe the way in which one scene is joined to another. Scriptwriters frequently use the following terms to describe a transitional effect in a shooting script:

> FADE UP/FADE TO BLACK—All film and television programs begin and end in black. The very first image FADES UP from a black screen. The final image FADES TO BLACK. A momentary FADE TO BLACK can be used as a transition between major program segments.
>
> CUT—An instantaneous change between two shots or scenes.

DISSOLVE—A momentary overlapping of two scenes or images. The tail end of Scene 1 fades out as the first image of the next scene fades up. The two images overlap for a moment, creating a fluid transition which signals shifts in locale, time or content. (Dissolves can be used in slide presentations through two projectors and a dissolve unit.)

WIPE—A visual effect as though Scene 1 is being wiped off the screen by the appearance of Scene 2. Wipes can take a variety of formats: horizontal, vertical, diagonal, etc.

Treatment: The writer's verbal description of sights and sounds imagined as a result of rehearsal and concept development. The treatment expresses the concept *chronologically,* describing how action will unfold on the screen from beginning to end. The treatment is written as a result of the rehearsal stage of the writing process.

Videowall: Use of several video monitors (typically 16 in rows or four) ganged together to create one large video "billboard" for which videotape can be programmed to appear on monitors in various configurations.

Voice: As defined by Donald Murray, voice is the "illusion of individual writer speaking to individual reader" (viewer). It is the element of narration that gives a program its emotional force. A scriptwriter may choose from a range of human emotions when using voice: sad, detached, angry, amused, bewildered, etc. Voice is similar to tone or style.

Bibliography

Brady, John Joseph, *The Craft of the Screenwriter* (New York, NY: Simon & Schuster, Publishers, 1981).

Brooks, Paul, *Rachel Carson at Work—The House of Life* (Boston, MA: G.K. Hall & Company, 1985).

Campbell, Joseph, with Moyers, Bill, *The Power of Myth* (New York, NY: Doubleday, 1988).

Cartwright, Steve R., *Training with Video* (White Plains, NY: Knowledge Industry Publications, Inc., 1986).

Davis, Sheila, *The Craft of Lyric Writing* (Cincinnati, OH: Writer's Digest Books, 1985).

Dreyfuss, Henry, *Symbol Sourcebook* (New York NY: McGraw-Hill Book Company, 1972).

Edison, Thomas A., *The Diary and Sundry Observations of Thomas Alva Edison* (New York, NY: Philosophical Library, 1948).

Elbow, Peter, *Writing With Power, Techniques for Mastering the Writing Process* (New York, NY: Oxford University Press, 1981).

Gardner, Howard, *Art, Mind and Brain* (New York, NY: Basic Books Inc., 1982).

Gardner, John, *On Becoming a Novelist* (New York, NY: Harper & Row, Publishers, 1983).

Goldberg, Natalie, *Writing Down the Bones* (Boston, MA: Shambhala, 1986).

Goldman, William, *Adventures in the Screen Trade* (New York, NY: Warner Books, Inc., 1983).

Hilliar, Robert L., *Writing for Television and Radio* (New York, NY: Hastings House, Publishers, third edition, 1976).

Iuppa, Nicholas, V., *A Practical Guide to Interactive Video Design* (White Plains, NY: Knowledge Industry Publications, Inc., 1984).

John-Steiner, Vera, *Notebooks of the Mind* (New York, NY: Harper & Row, Publishers, 1985).

Langer, Susanne K., *Philosophy in a New Key* (Cambridge, MA: Harvard University Press, 1956).

Mager, Robert, *Preparing Instructional Objectives,* second edition (Belmont, CA: Pitman Learning, Inc., 1975).

May, Rollo, *The Courage to Create* (New York, NY: Bantam Books, 1975).

Matrazzo, Donna, *The Corporate Scriptwriting Book* (Philadelphia, PA: Media Concepts Press, 1980).

McLuhan, Marshall, *Understanding Media: The Extensions of Man* (New York, NY: McGraw-Hill Book Company, 1964).

Murray, Donald, *A Writer Teaches Writing,* second edition (Boston, MA: Houghton Mifflin Company, 1985).

Murray, Donald, *Writing for Your Readers* (Chester, CT: The Globe Pequot Press, 1983).

Noble, William, *"Shut Up!" He Explained!* (Middlebury, VT: Paul S. Eriksson, Publisher, 1987).

Peck, Robert Newton, *Fiction Is Folks* (Cincinnati, OH: Writer's Digest Books, 1983).

Perkins, D. N., *The Mind's Best Work* (Cambridge, MA: Harvard University Press, 1981).

Rico, Gabriele Lusser, *Writing the Natural Way* (Los Angeles, CA: J. P. Tarcher, Inc., 1983).

Sheehan, George A., M.D., *Running and Being, the Total Experience* (New York, NY: Warner Books, 1978).

Swann, Brian, ed., *Smoothing the Ground, Essays on Native American Oral Literature* (Berkeley, CA: University of California Press, 1983).

Van Nostran, William, *The Nonbroadcast Television Writer's Handbook* (White Plains, NY: Knowledge Industry Publications, Inc., 1983).

Von Oech, Roger, *A Kick in the Seat of the Pants* (New York, NY: Harper & Row Publishers, 1986).

Von Oech, Roger, *A Whack on the Side of the Head* (New York, NY: Warner Books, 1988).

Whittlesey, Marietta, *The New Freelancer's Handbook* (New York, NY: Simon & Schuster, Inc., 1982, 1988).

Widner, Doug, *Teleguide, A Handbook on Teleconferencing* (Washington, DC: Public Service Satellite Consortium, 1986).

Zinsser, William, *On Writing Well, An Informal Guide to Writing Nonfiction* (New York, NY: Harper & Row, Publishers, second edition, 1980).

Appendix:
Professional Organizations

The following associations provide useful contacts and services for their membership. Most of these organizations have local chapters that meet on a regular basis. In addition, the national organizations typically hold annual conferences, sponsor contests, publish newsletters and, in some cases, serve as a source of job leads. For more information, write the national office or contact a local chapter of the organization.

Don't overlook other industry trade groups as research sources for writing projects. All these groups serve as advocates for their industry.

AMERICAN FILM INSTITUTE
John F. Kennedy Center
Washington, DC 20566

Although the organization centers on the feature film industry, there are good reasons for becoming a member (such as *American Film* magazine), especially if you have an interest in using dramatic techniques in nonbroadcast programming.

AMERICAN SOCIETY FOR TRAINING AND DEVELOPMENT INC. (ASTD)
1630 Duke Street, Box 1443
Alexandria, VA 22313

This group consists of organizational and industrial trainers who may use video, film and other audio-visual media to achieve training objectives.

ASSOCIATION FOR MULTI-IMAGE INTERNATIONAL, INC. (AMI)
8019 N. Himes Avenue
Tampa, FL 33614

Especially useful for writers specializing in multi-image and multi-media productions for sales meetings, conferences and other theatrical, large audience events.

ASSOCIATION OF VISUAL COMMUNICATORS (AVC)
900 Palm Avenue
South Pasadena, CA 91030

Media producers, managers, creative and technical people in film, video, slides and multi-image audio and videodisc production.

AUDIO VISUAL MANAGEMENT ASSOCIATION
PO Box 165887
Irving, TX 75016

Managers of corporate AV departments.

INDEPENDENT MEDIA PRODUCERS COUNCIL (IMPC)
3150 Spring Street
Fairfax, VA 22031

Individuals and firms who produce films, videotapes, slide shows and audio programs for outside clients.

INTERNATIONAL ASSOCIATION OF BUSINESS COMMUNICATORS (IABC)
870 Market Street
San Francisco, CA 94102

This organization centers on business and organizational communication, regardless of the medium. Although traditionally the membership consisted of print-oriented people, recent years have seen more emphasis on audio-visual media used to achieve business communication objectives.

INTERNATIONAL COMMUNICATIONS INDUSTRIES ASSOCIATION (formerly the National Audio-Visual Association)
3150 Spring Street
Fairfax, VA 22031

Although equipment supplier/dealer oriented, the group is quite active in the total audio-visual arena.

INTERNATIONAL INTERACTIVE COMMUNICATIONS SOCIETY (IICS)
2120 Steiner Street
San Francisco, CA 94115

For those interested in interactive video in education, point-of-purchase, and archival storage.

INTERNATIONAL TELEVISION ASSOCIATION (ITVA)
Three Dallas Communications Complex
6311 N. O'Connor Road
Irving, TX 75039

This is an association of video professionals working primarily in nonbroadcast television. There are local chapters throughout the United States, Canada and overseas.

THE MUSEUM OF BROADCASTING
1 East 53rd Street
New York, NY 10022

Although not a trade association, the Museum of Broadcasting houses and catalogues thousands of hours of broadcast television programming—from documentaries to sitcoms and dramas dating back to the 1950's. Viewing facilities are available on site in this comprehensive collection.

NATIONAL ASSOCIATION OF BROADCASTERS
1771 N Street, NW
Washington, DC 20036

Radio and TV stations, equipment manufacturers and program producers.

PUBLIC RELATIONS SOCIETY OF AMERICA (PRSA)
845 Third Avenue
New York, NY 10022

For communicators involved in public relations and employee communications.

WOMEN IN COMMUNICATIONS, INC.
PO Box 9561
Austin, TX 78766

Women in journalism and public relations.

WRITERS GUILD OF AMERICA, WEST
8955 Beverly Blvd.
Los Angeles, CA 90048

WRITERS GUILD OF AMERICA, EAST
555 W. 57th Street
New York, NY 10019

Labor union for writers in film, TV and radio.

ABOUT THE AUTHOR

William Van Nostran is an award-winning writer specializing in industrial, medical and other nonbroadcast television markets. He has written many scripts for clients such as AT&T, General Foods, Prudential, DuPont, Bellcore and Warner-Lambert. He has been an innovator in using dramatizations for training and informational programs and has been involved in several video publishing projects.

Prior to devoting his time completely to writing, Mr. Van Nostran developed programming in the communications departments of Owens-Corning Fiberglas and Crum & Forster Insurance. Mr. Van Nostran lectures frequently on informational scriptwriting and the creative process, conducting workshops in the U.S. and Canada. His previous book on scriptwriting, **The Nonbroadcast Television Writer's Handbook,** was also published by Knowledge Industry Publications, Inc.